AN EXPLORER'S GUIDE

Kansas

Lisa Waterman Gray

with photographs by the author

The Countryman Press ✳ Woodstock, Vermont

FIRST EDITION

Explorer's Guide Kansas
978-0-88150-897-0

Interior photographs by the author unless otherwise specified
Maps by Erin Greb Cartography, © The Countryman Press
Book design by Bodenweber Design
Composition by PerfecType, Nashville, TN

Published by The Countryman Press, P.O. Box 748, Woodstock, VT 05091

Distributed by W. W. Norton & Company, Inc., 500 Fifth Avenue, New York, NY 10110

Printed in the United States of America

10 9 8 7 6 5 4 3 2 1

I couldn't have created this book
without my loving and wonderfully supportive family and friends;
delightful and professional colleagues at
Countryman Press, Kruzic Communications and area visitors bureaus;
and every Kansan who graciously shared
their thoughts on this amazing state with me.

Many, many thanks, to all of you.

EXPLORE WITH US!

Welcome to the first edition of *Kansas: An Explorer's Guide.* As with every book in this series, all attractions, inns, and restaurants are chosen based on personal experience rather than paid advertising.

WHAT'S WHERE

At the front of this book you'll find an alphabetical listing of items from throughout the state that fit into different categories, such as wineries or military forts.

LODGING

Unless otherwise noted, assume that all lodging is generally available year-round; however, making a reservation is always recommended. It's also a good idea to ask about smoking, children, and pet policies, and whether an establishment takes credit cards. If Wi-Fi, television, or a private telephone is important, ask about these as well, particularly for bed & breakfasts or rural inns. In most cases, lodging rates listed reflect double occupancy, but be sure that you clarify this when you book a room.

Prices. Room rates listed were current as of 2010, but please don't hold us, or individual property owners, responsible for these rates. In addition, our prices do not include tax, which can vary from one city to the next.

RESTAURANTS

Restaurants listed in *Dining Out* sections are generally pricier and more upscale, while those in the *Eating Out* category are generally less expensive and typically most appropriate for families. Price codes for entrées include inexpensive: up to $15; moderate: $15–40; and expensive: $40–65.

KEY TO SYMBOLS

- ✎ **Child-friendly.** The child-friendly symbol appears beside lodging, restaurants, activities, and shops that will especially appeal to youngsters.
- ♿ **Wheelchair-accessible.** The wheelchair symbol appears beside lodging, restaurants, and attractions that are primarily disabled accessible, although the wheelchair entrance may not be at the main entrance. In the case of lodging, at least one guest room is Americans with Disabilities Act (ADA) compatible.
- ♈ **Bar/nightspot.**
- ((ɣ)) **Wi-Fi access.**

I appreciate your comments and corrections regarding places that you visit, and, if you find a true gem that I didn't include, please let me know for future editions. Address correspondence to Explorer's Guide Editor, The Countryman Press, P.O. Box 748, Woodstock, VT 05091; or e-mail us at countrymanpress@wwnorton.com. Contact me directly through my website: www.thestorytellerkc.net.

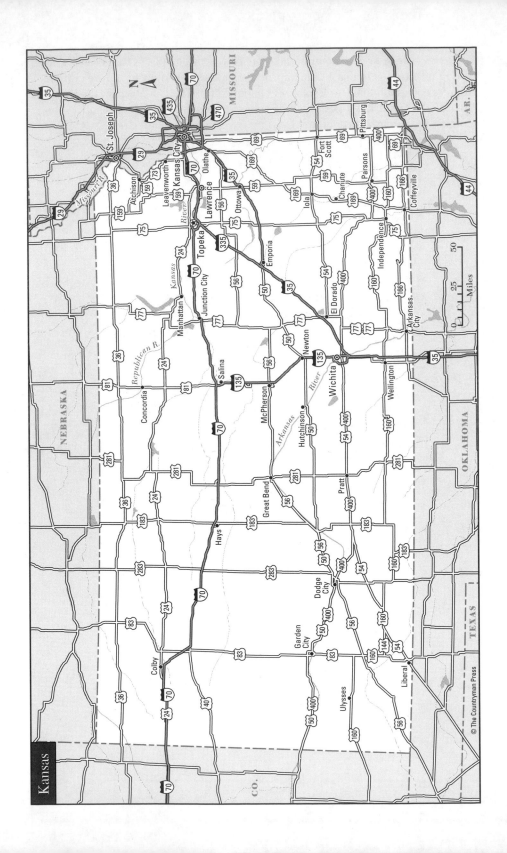

CONTENTS

8 Southwest Kansas: The Old West / 353

"Kansas is the most quintessential of American states.
It is, after all, where Superman and Dorothy from the Wizard of Oz grew up, and
all the towns I went through had a cozy, leafy, timeless air to them"
—from *The Lost Continent* by Bill Bryson.

INTRODUCTION

I t's been 25 years since I moved to the state of Kansas after marrying a native Kansan. I'll never forget when my uncle, a longtime New Yorker, called this area "the sane part of the country" at our wedding. Maybe the fact that the geographical center for the 48 contiguous states lies in Kansas helps to keep us grounded.

Kansas became the nation's 34th state in 1861. It was named after the American Indian tribe, the Kansa, which already lived here when fur trappers arrived in the 1830s. It later became known as the Sunflower State (after the state flower) and the Wheat State because both crops are so abundant and Kansas still produces 20 percent of the nation's annual wheat supply. It's also known as the Jayhawk State, which refers to people from Kansas who were opposed to slavery, went to Missouri, freed slaves, and brought them here. Kansas was the first state west of the Mississippi to set up oil operations, in 1892, and the state still produces 30 million barrels annually, putting Kansas among the nation's top 10 oil-producing states. Kansas also extrudes up to 560 billion cubic feet of natural gas per year. It's the nation's largest producer of helium and also produces petroleum, propane, cement, salt, and natural gas. Known as the Aviation Capital of the World, Wichita companies manufacture half of the world's general aviation aircraft.

Kansas is a huge state with a relatively sparse population. Less than 3 million people call Kansas home, despite the fact that it covers nearly 83,000 square miles. More than 400 towns have a population of less than 1,000, and 330 of them have less than 500 residents. That leaves a lot of undeveloped land.

It also leaves a lot of land for farming and grazing. Agriculture still occupies an enormous amount of the state's landmass. Kansas leads the United States in wheat production, producing 20 percent of the nation's annual supply. Other principal crops include sorghum, hay, and corn. Kansas is one of the nation's top three beef producers and first in the number of commercial cattle processed. In addition, more than six thousand head of buffalo graze on the state's ranches and refuges.

In 1955 the Kansas legislature designated the American buffalo as the state animal because there were so many in the area during territorial days and early statehood. Today there are two cows for every human in this state, and more than five hundred bald eagles winter in Kansas, too, from October through February.

For many Kansans, spending time outdoors is sheer joy. Visitors can experience the magic while hunting pheasant in western Kansas or quail in eastern Kansas or catching fish in a reservoir or farm pond. With rich traditions of hunting, fishing, camping, and most other outdoors activities you can think of, Kansas hosts five river systems, more than 50,000 streams with names, 24 state parks, 45 fishing lakes, and nearly 100 wildlife areas. Visit the last 16,000 square miles of the nation's tallgrass prairie or watch buffalo roam in many places throughout the state.

Kansans are proud of where they live, and family and heritage mean a great deal to them. American Indian culture is evident in dozens of powwows and historic sites across the state. You'll see this pride in Lindsborg, known as Little Sweden USA, the thriving Amish settlement in Yoder, and Wilson's Czech culture, just to name a few.

Kansas is more than the birthplace of the Wizard of Oz. There is a yellow brick road in Sedan and one in Liberal, but this state has long been the home of trailblazers and explorers, too, from Taos Indians, who briefly migrated to the southwestern part of the current state in the 1500s, to Spanish explorer Francisco Vázquez de Coronado. It was ground zero for violent conflicts over slavery—a state torn apart by pro- and antislavery sentiments—and site of the last stop on the Underground Railroad. Catch another glimpse of African American history at Nicodemus National Historic Site—the only remaining all-black town established along the western frontier after the war.

SEE MEMORABILIA RELATED TO *THE WIZARD OF OZ* AT THE OZ MUSEUM IN WAMEGO.

Prohibitionist Carry Nation promoted her cause here, and native daughter Amelia Earhart became a legendary aviator. Kansan Fred Harvey opened eateries along railway lines, which later became part of a restaurant chain staffed by Harvey Girls. Chrysler's founder grew up in Kansas, as did renowned photographer Gordon Parks. Other famous Kansans include President Dwight D. Eisenhower, Clyde Cessna, George

THERE IS PLENTY OF GREAT HORSEMANSHIP ON DISPLAY AT THE KANSAS STATE FAIR.

Washington Carver, Buster Keaton, Vivian Vance, as well as Senator Bob Dole, Barry Sanders, Dennis Hopper, and Erin Brockovich. And Kansas was the first state to have females serving simultaneously in the roles of governor, senator, and U.S. representative—Joan Finney, Nancy Landon Kassebaum, and Jan Meyers.

Kansans know how to have a good time. From rodeos to pancake races and the state fair or cultural, music, and food festivals, you'll find plenty of opportunities to celebrate. Visit the largest Christmas display between Kansas City and Denver or a two- day Oz Fest, or check out one of the more than three hundred agritourism businesses across the state.

Urban energy is particularly evident near Kansas's eastern border, where Kansas City, Overland Park, Lawrence, and a host of smaller cities offer a plethora of shopping, restaurants, and dozens of bed & breakfasts, boutique hotels, inns, and resorts. Other big cities surrounded by wide-open spaces include the state's largest, Wichita, as well as Dodge City, Manhattan, Goodland, and Salina.

But small towns still compose much of the state. Be prepared to pay with cash—though some people take credit cards or checks—and realize that you won't find museums and shops open for as many hours as in large cities. There may not be a gas station in town when you want to fill up or a large grocery store like those found in many suburbs.

Particularly when exploring rural areas, you may run into plenty of gravel or dirt roads, and, sometimes, signage is sadly lacking. You could end up in Nebraska after driving through Arikaree Breaks for a while, or drive miles past your desired destination because you missed a tiny sign beside the highway.

WINFIELD'S WALNUT VALLEY FESTIVAL IS ONE OF THE STATE'S LARGEST MUSICAL EVENTS.

When you're lost or want a recommendation for a place to eat, you'll find Kansans extremely willing to help out. Sit and chat with the locals at their favorite soda fountain or watering hole and you'll hear all kinds of interesting tidbits about the community. Or stay in a bed & breakfast, where the owners are often unofficial ambassadors for their town and state. And, while you're at it, enjoy freshly prepared food, including plenty of beef and game, pies, and cinnamon rolls.

Kansas is full of diversity, whether you're exploring the outdoors and attending festivals or learning about American Indians, immigrants, and Western pioneers who settled here. You're bound to make some delightful discoveries. Enjoy the ride.

CROSSING THE BORDER

Many people who hear the name Kansas City automatically assume that this large city is in Kansas. However, the larger of two cities with this name actually lies just across the state line, in Missouri. In fact, you'll drive through Missouri while in the east lane of State Line Road and through Kansas when driving in the west lane. Kansas City, Missouri, and suburban Missouri cities in this metropolitan area have a lot to offer, too, from the renowned Country Club Plaza shopping district and the Kansas City Power and Light District to professional sports events and wonderful museums. We've concentrated on the Kansas side of the metropolitan area in this book, but you can learn about Kansas City, Missouri restaurants, entertainment, and attractions through the Kansas City Convention and Visitors Association (1-800-767-7700; visitkc.com).

THIS AND THAT

As of July 2010, smoking is banned from restaurants, bars, work places, and within 10 feet of building entrances; the only exception is on casino floors.

Children under 18 who are driving may not use cell phones, and texting while driving is prohibited. Police can also pull over cars and ticket every person who is not wearing a seat belt.

You will see many museum and historical listings that say *free*. Although this is true, many greatly appreciate and often suggest a cash donation.

We have published golf yardage for the farthest tees.

WHAT'S WHERE IN KANSAS

AGRICULTURAL FAIRS In a state with such a diverse and prominent agricultural background, it's no wonder that more than one hundred county fairs take place across the state, primarily in July and August. Some also feature rodeo events, including the **Chautauqua County Fair and Rodeo** in Sedan and the **Inter-State Fair and Rodeo** in Coffeyville (fairandrodeo.com). But the largest agricultural event is the **Kansas State Fair,** held in Hutchinson for 10 days each September. More than three hundred thousand people attend this popular annual event full of livestock competitions, farm equipment, and crop displays, plus food, old-fashioned carnival games, and more. For a complete listing of county fairs, visit kansasfairsassociation.com and click on Fairs and Festivals.

AIR SERVICE **Wichita Mid-Continent Airport** (316-946-4700; flywichita.com), Kansas's largest, offers nonstop service to 10 major U.S. cities with flights on these airlines: AirTran, Allegiant, American, Continental, Delta, Frontier, and United. The closest large airport for the eastern part of the state is **Kansas City**

International Airport in Kansas City, Missouri (816-243-5237; flykci .com). Other close major airports may be **Denver International Airport** (303-342-2200; flydenver.com) or Will Rogers World Airport in Oklahoma City (405-680-3200; flyokc.com). Regional airports also include **Garden City Regional Airport** (620-276-1190; flytogkc.com), **Manhattan Regional Airport** (785-587-4560; fly mhk.com), and **Dodge City Regional Airport/**Great Lakes Airlines (620-225-5065). Others include **Hays Regional Airport** (785-628-7370; haysusa.com/html/airport.html) and **Liberal Mid-America Regional Airport** (620-626-0103).

AMUSEMENT PARKS Kansas City offers two chain water park experiences. Play on indoor tube slides, a toboggan-style ride, and an enormous tipping bucket at **Great Wolf Lodge** (1-800-608-WOLF) or at the enormous indoor/outdoor **Schlitterbahn Vacation Village** (913-312-3110), a Texas-based entertainment venue. Or visit **Kansas Splashdown** (1-800-362-5018) in Hutchinson, with a space theme.

ANTIQUES There are antiques shops located throughout the state. Known as Kansas's antiques capital, tiny Paxico offers many individually owned stores within several blocks. Visit **Paramount Antique Mall** (316-722-0500; paramountantique mall.com)—recognized by the website Discover Mid-America as one of the top antique mall destinations in the Midwest—or **Flying Moose Antique Mall** (316-721-3197; flying-moose .com) in Wichita. Specialty antiques stores include **Northglen Antiques** (785-623-4005; northglenantiques .com), a Hays store that focuses on Scottish antiques; **Southwind Antiques** (785-460-6483; southwind antiques.com) in Colby, with many items from old homesteads and farms; or **Happy Trails Antiques** (785-793-2777) in Scranton, with many Santa Fe Trail items.

AREA CODES Kansas has four area codes, so check this before making a call. You'll dial 913 throughout much of the Kansas City metropolitan area, on the Kansas side, but sometimes you'll also need to dial 1. Much of the central part of the state uses the 316 area code and much of northern Kansas has a 785 area code. Many locales farther south carry a 620 area code.

ART MUSEUMS AND CENTERS Art museums throughout the state range from the small **5.4.7 Arts Center** (620-723-2600), Greensburg's LEED Platinum "green" building and community arts center, to the state's largest, **Wichita Art Museum** (316-268-4921). Others include the seven-gallery **Helen Foresman Spencer Museum of Art** (785-864-4710) at the University of Kansas/Lawrence; **Lincoln Art Center** (785-524-3241) in Lincoln, in a beautiful modern setting; **The Grassroots Art Center** (785-525-6118) in Lucas; **Marianna Kistler Beach Museum of Art** (785-532-7718), with its primary focus on art by Kansas artist John Stuart Curry, at Kansas State University/Manhattan; the largest contemporary art museum in the four-state area, **Nerman Museum of Contemporary Art** (913-469-3000) in Overland Park; **Mulvane Art Museum** (785-670-1124) in Topeka; and **Ulrich Museum of Art** (316-978-3664), with more than 70 outdoor art pieces, at Wichita State University/Wichita.

BED & BREAKFASTS Hundreds of bed & breakfasts and inns operate across the state, from modern log cabins to 1800s limestone cottages. Many provide full hot breakfasts amid loads of antiques. Although not all bed & breakfasts are members, many are registered with and listed by the **Kansas Bed & Breakfast Association.** Learn more at 888-572-2632; kbba.com.

BICYCLING For a comprehensive listing of bicycling trails, including mountain bike trails, rails-to-trails, paved paths, and more, visit **Kansas Bike Trails** (kansasbiketrails.com).

BIRDING With more than 450 bird species in Kansas, this is a prime spot for bird watching; in fact, birding opportunities here are greater than in Oklahoma, Colorado, Nebraska, Missouri, or Iowa. Favorite bird-watching areas include the central flyway wetlands of **Cheyenne Bottoms** (620-793-3066) and **Quivira National Wildlife Refuge** (620-486-2393) and the 108,175-acre **Cimarron National Grasslands** (620-697-4621), near the state's southwest corner. You'll also see many bird varieties at **Chaplin Nature Center** (wichitaaudobon.org /cnc.html), run by the Wichita Audubon Society. The Nature Conservancy of Kansas staffs the **Konza Prairie/Konza Environmental Education Program** (785-587-0381), outside of Manhattan, and birding is also popular at **Tallgrass Prairie National Preserve** (620-273-6034), near Cottonwood Falls/Strong City.

BOATING Eighteen large lakes and reservoirs available across the state include the highly popular **Lake Cheney** (316-542-3664), near Wichita;

Clinton Lake (785-843-7665), a favorite of Lawrence residents and Kansas University (KU) students; the 8,000-acre **El Dorado Lake** (316 321-7180); **Milford Lake** (785-238-3014), outside of Junction City; **Pomona Lake** (785-828-4933) in Vassar/near Topeka; and the state's clearest lake, **Wilson Lake** (785-658-2465), in Sylvan Grove/west of Salina. There are also many smaller lakes available.

BUS AND TRAIN SERVICE Greyhound (greyhound.com) serves 10 Kansas cities, including Chanute (620-431-9540; at Pumping Petes); Coffeyville (620-251-9600; at Muffler City); Emporia (no tickets sold here; at Short Stop Phillips 66); Hays (785-628-8321; at Golden Ox Truck Stop); Iola (no tickets sold here; at Pumping Petes); Junction City (785-238-3161); Lawrence (785-843-5622; at Stop 2 Shop); Salina (785-827-9754; at AMOCO Travel Plaza); Topeka (785-233-2301; at Barnwell Service Inc.); and Wichita (316-265-7711; at Wichita Greyhound Station). **AMTRAK's Southwest Chief** train stops in Lawrence, Topeka, Newton, Hutchinson, Dodge City, and Garden City. If you're traveling across the state, be sure you know when to change from central standard to mountain standard time, which only four Kansas counties observe.

CAMPING Each of Kansas's 24 state parks offers camping options that are generally close to water. The 1,600-acre park at Kanopolis is quite popular, with two-dozen miles of trails and hundreds of campsites. Learn more about state park camping and cabin rental at kdwp.state.ks.us/news/state -parks. The **Kansas Association of**

RV Parks and Campgrounds (no phone listed; ksrvparks.com) offers park listings and access to the Kansas Camping Guide online or by mail. **Kansas RV Parks and Travel Inc.** offers another link for RV parks, campgrounds, and cabins throughout the state (kansasrvparks.org).

CASINOS Six casinos operate in Kansas, with **Boot Hill Casino** (620-225-0374; boothillcasino.com) as Kansas's first state-owned casino. American Indian tribes operate the others, which include **Golden Eagle Casino** (785-486-6601; goldeneagle casino.com) in Horton; Wyandotte **7th Street Casino** (913-371-3500; 7th-streetcasino.com), open around the clock in Kansas City; **Prairie Band Casino** (785-966-7777; pbpgaming.com) in Mayetta; and **Casino White Cloud** (785-595-3430; casinowhitecloud.org) in White Cloud, near the Nebraska border.

CHILDREN, ESPECIALLY FOR Throughout this book ✵ indicates child-friendly attractions, lodging, and dining. Several highlights include Wichita's **Sedgwick County Zoo** (316-942-2213; scz.org), **Museum of World Treasures** (316-263-1311; worldtreasures.org), and **Exploration Place** (877-904-1444; exploration .org), which offers learning experiences that focus on flight, Renaissance life, Kansas, and national traveling exhibits. Other kid-friendly sites include Overland Park's **Deanna Rose Children's Farmstead** (913-897-2360); Kansas City's **Schlitterbahn** and **Great Wolf Lodge** (see Amusement Parks); the **KU Natural History Museum** (785-864-4540) in Lawrence; **Rolling Hills Refuge Wildlife Center** (785-827-9488) in

Salina; **Sternberg Museum of Natural History** (785-628-4286) in Hays; and **Wonder Workshop** (785-766-1234) in Manhattan. Many nature centers and wildlife areas also offer tours and guided nature walks.

CLIMATE Kansas has four seasons and weather can change dramatically, particularly during springtime, when the temperature may hit 70 degrees before plummeting 30 or 40 degrees within minutes or hours. The average annual temperature is 56 degrees with annual rainfall of about 45 inches in southeastern Kansas and about 15 inches per year in the west. We receive the fourth largest number of tornadoes among other states and weather can become particularly unstable during tornado season, which is strongest from April through June. But twisters may occur any time the weather turns ugly, and winter can have plenty of ice and snow. High winds often blow through Kansas, too. In fact, Dodge City is considered the windiest city in the United States, with average wind speeds of 14 miles per hour.

EDUCATIONAL INSTITUTIONS

Kansas has two major state universities, the **University of Kansas** in Lawrence and **Kansas State University** in Manhattan. More than two-dozen private universities also operate throughout the state, from **Wichita State University, Newman University, ITT Technical Institute,** and **Friends University**, in Wichita, to faith-based schools that include **Benedictine College** in Atchison, **Kansas Wesleyan University** in Salina, and **MidAmerica Nazarene University** in Olathe.

EMERGENCIES Try 911 first. For state police phone 785-827-4437.

EVENTS This guidebook lists many annual events at the end of each chapter. To obtain more information, contact **Kansas Travel and Tourism Division/Kansas Department of Commerce** (785-296-6988; travelks .com). Another great resource is the **Kansas Sampler Foundation** (620-585-2374; kansassampler.org), which works to "preserve and sustain rural culture by educating Kansans about Kansas and by networking and supporting rural communities." They also sponsor **8 Wonders of Kansas,** a competition designed to inform people about and encourage them to explore the state.

FARMERS' MARKETS Dozens of farmers' markets offer fresh produce, homemade food items, crafts, and more, throughout the state, particu-

larly during spring and summer months. Several Johnson County cities host markets, with **Overland Park Farmers' Market** (913-642-2222) among the largest. **Lawrence Farmers' Market** (785-331-4445) is the state's oldest and a "producer only" market. **Kansas Grown Farmers' Market** (kansasgrownfarmers market.com) offers four locations in the Wichita area. You'll also find farmers' markets in Dodge City (620-227-3936); Fort Scott (620-547-2158); Topeka (785-234-9336; topekafarmers market.com); and Emporia (620-343-6555; emporiafm.com), to name a few. Learn more at travelks.com/farmersmarket or contact local visitors bureaus and chambers of commerce.

FISHING AND LAKES Twenty-four large built reservoirs offer enormous fishing opportunities. There are also 40 state fishing lakes and 200 community lakes available, plus privately owned streams and rivers. Common species include bass, trout, black crappie, blue and channel catfish, walleye, striped or small mouth bass, and bluegill and palmetto bass, and stocking occurs in multiple locations throughout the state, often by the **Kansas Department of Wildlife and Parks (KDWP).** There are also four fish hatcheries in Kansas. Purchase 24-hour fishing permits for $5.50, or $12.50 for trout/paddlefish (15 and younger $7.50 for paddlefish). Bass passes are $12.50, and hand-fishing permits cost $27.50. Lifetime fishing licenses are also available. For complete information contact **KDWP** (620-672-5911; kdwp.state.ks.us).

FORTS Once located near this country's western frontier, this territory and state housed eight major forts.

What began in 1859 as a series of dugouts and tents became **Fort Larned National Historic Site** (316-285-6911). During the 1860s it was an agency of the federal government's Indian Bureau. Located near Larned, it offers nine original and restored buildings. **Fort Leavenworth** (913-684-5604) served as the state governor's territorial capital, a site for Union training during the Civil War and home of the Black Dog 10th Cavalry Regiment, whose soldiers included Lt. Col. George Custer, Dwight D. Eisenhower, and Gen. Colin Powell. The still-active fort houses the U.S. Army Command and General Staff College. **Fort Scott** (316-223-0310) operated from 1842 to 1853, assisting in relations with American Indians and non-Indians, participating in the Mexican War, and providing military escorts to the west. The restored fort lies only steps away from downtown Fort Scott. Located near Junction City, **Fort Riley** (785-239-2737) opened in 1853 and is current home to the Army's 1st Infantry Division, the 1st Armored Division. The fort housed the 7th Cavalry Regiment, overseen by Lt. Col. George Custer, and helped to protect the western frontier. Four original structures remain at **Fort Hays State Historic Site** (785-625-6812), which operated from 1865 to 1889. Soldiers protected military roads, mail delivery, and Union Pacific construction workers, and provided depot services for other posts in western and southern parts of the state. Information kiosks inform visitors about other buildings that existed. **Fort Dodge** (316-227-2121) operates as the Kansas Soldiers Home, outside of Dodge City. Established in 1865, it once hosted four infantry companies

but was abandoned in 1882. It became a soldiers' home in the 1890s. **Fort Harker** (785-472-4071) began as Fort Ellsworth, and was built near current-day Kanopolis. The fort protected the Butterfield Overland Despatch, on its way to Denver, and Bill Cody was once a scout here. Fort Harker was a supply and distribution site for southern and western forts in the country until it closed in 1872. Most land is now private property, but a museum is available. Opened in 1865 near Wallace and Sharon Springs, **Fort Wallace** (785-891-3538) protected travelers to the Denver gold fields. The fort closed in 1882 and building access is quite limited, but there's a wonderful museum.

GARDENS Numerous botanical and other public gardens that operate in the state introduce visitors to native plantings and lush manicured planted areas. The 300-acre **Overland Park Arboretum and Botanical Gardens** (913-685-3604) is one of the largest. Others include **Botanica, The Wichita Gardens** (316-264-0448; botanica.org); **Dyck Arboretum of the Plains** (620-327-8127; dyckarboretum.org) in Hesston College/ Hesston; **The International Forest**

of Friendship (913-367-1419; ifof
.org) in Atchison; **Kansas Landscape
Arboretum** (785-461-5760) in Wakefield; **Kansas State University Gardens** (785-532-3271; ksre.ksu
.edu/ksugardens); **Parsons City
Arboretum** (620-421-7088) in Parsons; and **Reinisch Rose Garden
and Doran Rock Garden** (785-272-
5821) at Gage Park or **Ward-Meade
Park Botanic Gardens** (785-368-
3888) in Topeka.

GEOGRAPHY Although the sheer
flatness in a wide swath of western
Kansas surprises many visitors, the
state is full of rolling terrain, with
some landscape near Oklahoma that
resembles the Southwest, and areas of
southeastern Kansas seem like an
extension of Missouri's famed Ozark
Mountains.

Kansas slants from east to west,
with towns in the Kansas City area at
approximately 700 feet above sea
level, and an altitude around 4,000
feet at the state's highest point near
the Colorado border. Kansas has nine
scenic byways, two of which are
National Scenic Byways.

GOLF Visit GolfLink (golflink.com
/golf-courses/state.aspx?state=KS) for

a listing of courses throughout the
state. Their list of top 10 Kansas golf-
ing destinations includes Wichita,
Topeka, Overland Park, Hutchinson,
Lawrence, Lenexa, Manhattan, Newton, Olathe, and Salina.

HIKING Whether you prefer relatively flat and open trails or trails with
rugged terrain, you'll find it in
Kansas. **Lake Scott,** near Scott City,
offers a multiuse 7-mile trail surrounded by High Plains buttes,
mesas, cacti, and sage, with rugged
side paths and beautiful views. A 3-
mile trail in the Rocktown Natural
Area at **Wilson Lake** (west of Salina)
has some steep slopes, rocky terrain,
and scenic overlooks of the lake. Red
sandy trails, with stone cliffs and outcroppings, characterize the 5.5-mile
Horsethief Trail at **Kanapolis Lake.**
Another great trail through the **Tallgrass Prairie** begins at Emporia,
with bison and endless horizon views.
You'll also find hiking trails throughout 24 state parks.

HISTORIC HOMES AND SITES
Once part of this country's western
frontier, Kansas is full of gorgeous historic homes, many of which are open
to the public. The Victorian **Evah C.
Cray Historical Home Museum** in
Atchison is full of period furnishings,
while the nearby **Muchnic Art
Gallery** is part Victorian living quarters and part gallery. Eastlake and
Queen Anne–style structures characterize many homes in historic
McPherson. Visit the stunningly gorgeous Victorian **Warkentin House**
museum in Newton or the **Brown
Mansion** in Coffeyville. See more
historic homes in Fort Scott, Dodge
City, Garnett, Leavenworth, and
Wichita—which has seven historic

neighborhoods of homes and other structures—and many additional cities.

HOTELS AND MOTELS We have rarely listed chain hotels and motels since you can generally contact them with ease by phone or the Internet. There may be a few when other lodging choices are limited, but we have generally concentrated on individually owned and operated hotels, motels, inns, and B&Bs instead.

HUNTING The **Kansas Department of Wildlife and Parks** regulates hunting areas throughout the state. You can reach them at 620-672-5911; kdwp.state.ks.us. Locate many outfitters through the **Kansas Outfitters Association** (866-294-1947; kansasoutfittersassociation.com) and through individual listings in each chapter.

INFORMATION Two travel information centers operate in the state, at Belle Plaine/milepost 26 on I-35 and Goodland/east milepost 7 on I-70. Community-owned information centers also operate in Abilene, Atchison, Colby, Concordia, Dodge City, Garden City, Great Bend, Hays, Lawrence, Liberal, Ottawa, Paxico, and Wilson.

For information and park passes, contact **Kansas State Parks: Kansas Department of Wildlife and Parks** (620-296-2281; kdwp.state.ks.us) or **Kansas Department of Commerce/Travel and Tourism Division** (785-296-2009; travelks.com).

After-hours highway emergencies can be reported to the **Kansas Highway Patrol** (785-827-4437), and Kansas road condition reports are provided by the **Kansas Department of Transportation** (511; ksdot.org/#).

INTERSTATES Kansas is served by I-35/135, whose route extends from the Kansas City metropolitan area to Wichita and the Oklahoma border, and I-70, which crosses the state from east to west, beginning in Kansas City and reaching the Colorado border.

MUSEUMS Most of the 105 counties in Kansas have museums that primarily reflect the history of their area, and several are terrific. Some of our favorite museums of any size include: **Eisenhower Library and Museum** (785-263-4751; eisenhower.archives .gov) in Abilene, with five buildings that introduce visitors to Ike's life from boyhood through his military service and presidential years; **Amelia Earhart Birthplace Museum** (913-367-4217; ameliaearhartmuseum.org) in Atchison, where visitors tour her

with reservations recommended at least three to six months in advance; each June, **Country Stampede Music and Camping Festival** (1-800-795-8091), the Midwest's largest four-day country music festival; and one of the state's largest annual musical events, the bluegrass and acoustic festival called **Walnut Valley Festival** (620-221-3250; wvfest.com).

NATIONAL HISTORIC SITES
Three national historic sites in the state include the restored and reconstructed **Fort Scott National Historic Site** in Fort Scott and **Fort Larned National Historic Site** near Larned (see *Forts* above). **Nicodemus National Historic Site** (785-839-4233; nps.gov.nico) in Nicodemus is the nation's only remaining town located at the western frontier that African Americans established following the Civil War.

NATURE CENTERS The natural world is an important aspect of life in Kansas, from hunting and fishing to bird watching and hiking. Nature cen-

birthplace home with period furnishings and museum exhibits; **The Martin and Osa Johnson Safari Museum** (620-431-2730; safarimuseum.com), ranked the state's number one museum, is Chanute's memorial to hometown boy Martin and his wife, Osa, who traveled extensively and documented their tours; **Mennonite Heritage Museum** (620-367-8200), a complete Mennonite village in Goessel; **Grant County Museum** (620-356-3009), with wonderful displays in a historic Ulysses adobe building; and Hutchinson's **Kansas Cosmosphere and Space Center** (620-662-2305; cosmo.org) and **Kansas Underground Salt Museum** (620-662-1184; undergroundmuseum.org/index.php).

MUSIC FESTIVALS Major music festivals throughout the state include the springtime **Messiah Festival of Music and Art** (75-227-3311) at Bethany College in Lindsborg; **Symphony in the Flint Hills** (785-449-2621; symphonyintheflinthills.com) each summer, on private property,

ters operating throughout the state allow visitors to get up close and personal with wildlife and native plants. They include **SouthEast Kansas Nature Center** (620-783-5207; seks naturecenter.com) in Galena; **Dillon Nature Center** (620-663-7411; hutchrec.com/dnc) in Hutchinson; **Milford Nature Center** (785-238-5323) near beautiful Milford Reservoir in Junction City; and **Great Plains Nature Center** and adjacent trails (316-683-5499; gpnc.org) in Wichita.

PARKS AND FORESTS, STATE
Kansas has 24 state parks that provide ample opportunities for boating, fishing, picnicking, swimming, hunting, mountain biking, and hiking; many surround built reservoirs and resulting lakes. Camping options include RV sites, primitive camping, and cabins for rent in all parks. Whether you prefer the High Plains environment of **Lake Scott State Park** or the rolling hills, dense forests, and enor-

mous variety of camping locales of **Cheney State Park,** there's a park for every taste. To find detailed information on state parks, contact the **Kansas Department of Wildlife and Parks** (620-672-5911; kdwp .state.ks.us/news/state-parks).

SCENIC BYWAYS Nine scenic byways cross the state (ksbyways.org), including **Flint Hills:** covering 48 miles through the flint hills from Council Grove to Cassoday; **Frontier Military:** a 167-mile route that travels along the eastern border from Leavenworth to Oklahoma, including Fort Scott National Historic Site and multiple Civil War sites; **Glacial Hills:** a 63-mile byway that traces the travels of Lewis and Clark, from White Cloud and Troy through Atchison and Leavenworth; **Gypsum Hills:** traveling through southwestern Kansas along 42 miles full of rock landscape like the Southwest; **Native Stone:** this 42-mile route through the eastern Flint Hills is full of local limestone;

Post Rock: You'll see plenty of limestone fence posts along this 18-mile byway from Wilson to Lucas; **Prairie Trail:** This 56-mile trail travels by Maxwell Wildlife Refuge and Kansas's Little Sweden USA in Lindsborg; **Smoky Valley:** Coneflowers, yucca, and sage mark this High Plains area along a 60-mile route that begins at I-70, near WaKeeney; and **Wetlands and Wildlife:** Take this 76-mile route through Quivira National Wildlife Refuge and Cheyenne Bottoms Wildlife Area.

THEATER Vintage theaters and some newer facilities offer theater opportunities across the state. More than 40 years old, **Music Theatre of Wichita Inc.** (316-265-3107; musictheatre-ofwichita) offers five major shows each summer, from *The Music Man* to *The Little Mermaid,* and has served as a starting point for many Broadway performers, including Kristin Chenoweth. Wichita also offers **Wichita Community Theatre** (316-686-1282), one of the oldest community theaters in the United States, and **Mosley Street Melodrama** (316-263-0222; mosleystreet.com). **Salina's Stiefel Theatre** (785-827-1998; stiefeltheatre.org) occupies a fully restored 1931 theater, with plays and musical performances that run the gamut from Merle Haggard to the Salina Symphony; or enjoy dinner theater at **New Theatre Restaurant** (913-649-7469; theatre.com) in Overland Park, ranked the nation's best dinner theater by the *Wall Street Journal.*

TRAIN AND TROLLEY RIDES, RECREATIONAL The volunteer-run, nonprofit **Midland Railway** (913-236-9305; midland-ry.org) offers 20-mile tours on 1867 excursion trains from Baldwin City to Ottawa Junction, through farmland and woodland areas. Ride in a one-hundred-year-old train pulled by a 1945 ALCO S-1 engine from early May through Labor Day on a Train Excursion (888-750-3419), or request a Steam Engine Excursion.

Historical trolley rides are available in several places, including the extremely popular **Haunted Atchison Trolley Tours** (913-367-2427), which offer visitors a look at Atchison, the "most haunted town in Kansas." Contact the Atchison chamber of commerce (913-367-2427) about other tours throughout the year. Narrated tours through historic **Dodge City** (620-225-8186) operate from Memorial Day through Labor Day. **River City Trolley and Charters** (316-773-1931) in Wichita offers 1.5-hour historic tours April–July, plus a Frank Lloyd Wright Tour/Allen Lambe Interior Tour to a local home designed by Wright, and holiday or chartered tours. Hitch a ride on **Dolly the Trolley** (620-223-3566; fortscott.com/trolley.php) in Fort Scott, which includes visits to Fort Scott National Historic Site, the

National Cemetery, historical mansions and homes, and other historic sites.

WINERIES Fourteen wineries operate across the state, with the majority located in northeastern Kansas. They include **BlueJacket Crossing Vineyard and Winery** (785-542-1764) in Eudora; **Campbell Vineyard and Winery** (785-872-3176) in Holton; **Davenport Orchards and Winery** (785-542-2278) in Eudora; **Dozier Vineyard and Winery** (620-564-0195) in Ellinwood; **Grace Hill Winery** (316-799-2511) in Whitewater; **Holy-Field Vineyard and Winery** (913-724-9463) in Basehor; **Kugler's Vineyard** (785-843-8516) in Lawrence; **Oz Winery** (785-456-7417) in Wamego; **Slough Creek Vineyard and Winery** (785-863-3439) in Oskaloosa; **Smoky Hill Vineyards and Winery** (785-825-2515) in Salina; **Somerset Ridge Vineyard and Winery** (913-491-0038) in Paola; **Vin Vivante** (785-458-2930) in Wamego; **Windswept Winery** (620-782-3952) in Udall; and **Wyldewood Cellars Winery** (316-554-WINE) in Mulvane.

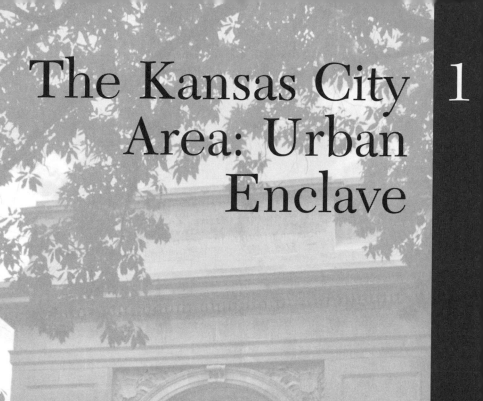

The Kansas City Area: Urban Enclave

1

INTRODUCTION

Although much of Kansas is known for its wide-open spaces, communities on the Kansas side of the greater Kansas City metropolitan area include the state's second and third largest cities—Overland Park and Kansas City. Major interstates that lead to the metropolitan area through Kansas include I-70, I-35, and I-635. US 169, US 69, US 40/24, US 73/KS 7, KS 10, KS 32, and US 56 are other major highways.

Whether you explore the many amenities in Kansas City, where new commercial development has exploded in recent years, or in suburban Johnson County, the Kansas City area is a different animal from much of the state.

Kansas City composes much of Wyandotte County, named for the Wyandot Indians who lived here beginning in the 1800s. Twenty years ago most people did not think of Kansas City as a growing and thriving metropolis. But all that has changed in recent years, largely through development in the county's western area.

The Kansas Speedway draws top NASCAR and other racing activities. Massive chain stores, Cabela's and Nebraska Furniture Mart, were at the beginning of a retail boom in Kansas City. Today, Legends Outlets at Village West offers 1.2 million square feet of open-air shopping, dining, and entertainment options with a mix of chains such as Gap Outlet, Forever 21, Tommy Hilfiger, and Banana Republic. Dine at Dave & Buster's, T-REX Café, or Wild Bill's Legendary Steakhouse and Saloon. Dozens of statues and portraits are just a few ways that Legends Outlets honors legendary Kansans, from musicians such as Charlie Parker to athletes such as Tom Watson and Jim Ryun and pioneers like Amelia Earhart and Walter P. Chrysler.

Kansas City has a great deal of history, from immigration by Lithuanian, Polish, and neighboring people to the antislavery settlement of Quindaro Township and its involvement with the Underground Railroad. Lewis and Clark camped in this area during 1804. The city also features the Rosedale Memorial Arch, a miniature version of Paris's Arc de Triomphe that honored World War I veterans from the town of Rosedale, which Kansas City later absorbed.

Johnson County hosts the last working stagecoach stop on the National Historic Santa Fe Trail, and Shawnee recognizes its pioneering heritage at the historic site of Old Shawnee Town. The state's 7th largest city has a population of

31

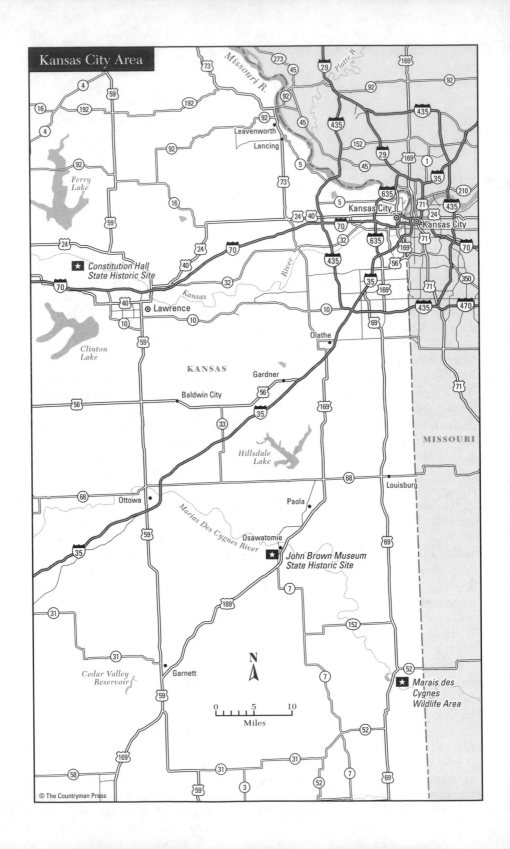

Kansas City Area

around sixty thousand. Shawnee was ranked by *Money* magazine as the 39th best place to live in this country, among cities with a population between fifty and three hundred thousand. Despite its size, there's a small-town feel here, from Old Shawnee Town to a small downtown area. But Shawnee also continues to grow, particularly westward.

With more than one hundred sixty-five thousand residents, Overland Park is Johnson County's largest city. It was incorporated in 1960 and has grown to include more than 75 square miles. In 2003 *Money* magazine ranked Overland Park number three among its "hottest towns" with populations of at least one hundred thousand people, in the central part of the country. In addition, *Employment Review* magazine called it one of the 20 best places to live and work. The 20-building Sprint World Headquarters campus was also built here. Overland Park is known for excellent schools, a family-friendly environment, and a huge variety of shopping venues, including the area's largest and most success-ful indoor mall, Oak Park Mall, plus Hawthorne Plaza and Town Center Plaza. Additional popular Johnson County malls include Merriam Town Center, Shawnee Station, Fountains Luxury Retail Center, One Nineteen and Roe Lifestyle, and Overland Pointe Marketplace.

Olathe is another Johnson County city, whose name means *beautiful* in the Shawnee Indian language. Olathe includes a juncture point between the Santa Fe, Oregon, and California trails and has become the country's 24th fastest-growing city. With the county's fourth largest population, Lenexa was platted by Wild Bill Hickok. The suburban city hosts several major festivals created to cele-brate its spinach, heritage, BBQ, and chili heritages. There are also multiple shopping venues and restaurants.

The city of Leawood has grown by leaps and bounds in recent years, with a population of more than thirty thousand residents and constant commercial growth that only expands its dining and entertainment options. It's a pretty town with plenty of green space and broad streets.

Johnson County cities that lie north of Overland Park include Fairway, Roe-land Park, Mission, and Prairie Village, with older and often smaller homes built along tree-lined streets. Prairie Village is the largest of these cities, with several long-term and highly successful shopping "neighborhoods." Approximately twen-ty-two thousand residents call this town home and have a median household income near $60,000.

Fairway is home to the 12-acre Shawnee Indian Mission, which was estab-lished as a manual training school for children from various Indian nations who lived in this area. Known as the City of Trees, it was incorporated in 1949. Today this suburb has approximately four thousand residents who live in older, well-maintained homes. Bordered by Overland Park, Shawnee, and Kansas City, Mer-riam has approximately ten thousand residents and was incorporated in 1950. Interesting shops include I Love a Mystery bookstore and KC Strings, a nation-ally renowned maker of handcrafted violins, violas, cellos, and basses.

Hugging the state line with Missouri, Mission Hills is a residential city full of gorgeous old mansions, private country clubs, the state's largest per capita income, and a population of under four thousand. Enormous homes on large lots characterize old Mission Hills, while newer areas attract upper-middle-class

A BEEF TRADITION THAT CROSSES THE STATE LINE

The Kansas City strip steak is a cut from the short loin, also known as a New York strip steak, or shell steak, depending on the region where it is served. A tradition of great beef in the Kansas City metropolitan area began with the Kansas City Stock Yards in Kansas City, Missouri, which opened in 1871 and closed in October 1991. They played an important role in the metropolitan area's early development, growing from 13 to 55 acres and handling cattle, hogs, sheep, horses, and mules.

In 1899 the **American Royal Livestock and Horse Show** took place for the first time, in cooperation with Hereford cattle breeders, and it was the nation's second busiest stockyard (after Chicago) by 1900. By the 1940s activity reached its highest level, but the massive 1951 flood caused severe damage to the area, with many businesses closing.

The local beef tradition lives on, and the legendary **Golden Ox Restaurant** (816-842-2866; goldenox.com) still operates in the Kansas City, Missouri, Livestock Exchange Building. Other popular restaurants for great beef include **Hereford House** (herefordhouse.com), begun in Kansas City, Missouri, and now with multiple locations throughout the metropolitan area; **Jack Stack Barbecue** (913-385-7427; jackstackbbq.com; multiple locations); **Pierpont's at Union Station** (816-221-5111; pierponts.com; in Missouri); **Plaza III-The Steakhouse** (816-753-0000; plazaiiikcsteakhouse.com; in Missouri); and **LongHorn Steakhouse** (longhornsteakhouse.com; multiple locations).

BBQ BONANZA

Early BBQ favorites in this bistate metropolitan area included Arthur Bryant's BBQ, opened in the 1930s, and Gates Bar-B-Q, which followed in 1946. The classic sauce in this area is thick, tomato-y, and reddish-brown and is often used on pork ribs with some variations in sweetness. Several Kansas City, Missouri, BBQ spots now have outposts on the Kansas side, and plenty other BBQ destinations operate here, too. They include:

In Kansas City (KS)

Oklahoma Joe's BBQ (913-722-3366; oklahomajoesbbq.com), Kansas City. When the American Royal International Sauce Contest dubs your BBQ the best on the planet, it's no wonder crowds flock in. Customers devour pulled pork and beef brisket sandwiches, and rib dinners and prices can't be beat. Inexpensive.

Woodyard Bar-B-Que (913-362-8000; woodyardbbq.com), Kansas City. Guy Fieri, with *Diners, Drive-ins and Dives,* recently discovered what locals already knew—that a one-time firewood seller has turned fruit, pecan, oak, and hickory woods into a dynamite smoking source. Pecan smoked salmon sandwich, burnt end chili, and ribs galore are just a few choices.

Gates Bar-B-Q (1-800-662-7427; gatesbbq.com), Kansas City. After more than 60 years of making sauce, this spot is a true legend. Buy a slab of ribs, burnt ends, or sliced turkey by the pound. Then take some sauce home with you.

Arthur Bryant's Barbeque (913-788-7500; arthurbryantsbbq.com), Kansas City. President Jimmy Carter and Tom Watson have eaten where BBQ got a jumpstart in the 1930s. Enjoy upscale surroundings with legendary taste.

Rosedale Barbecue (913-262-0343), Kansas City. Opened more than 65 years ago, this spot is known for great ribs and sauce that people may or may not love. Dinners come with coleslaw, smoky beans, and toast. Nothing fancy, but it tastes good.

In Overland Park

Hayward's Pit Bar-B-Que (913-499-7836; haywardsbbq.com), Overland Park. This legendary BBQ restaurant opened in 1972 in Kansas City, Missouri, and now has additional locations. Smell the parking lot smoker and then enjoy ribs or smoked sausage with onion rings, coleslaw, or even fried okra.

Jack Stack Barbecue (913-385-7427; jackstackbbq.com), Overland Park. Dark wood, comfortable booths, and 50 years of barbecuing experience add up to great dining, from meaty pork spare ribs to grilled jumbo shrimp or painted chicken kabob cheese and southwestern sauce.

Elsewhere

Hillsdale Bank Bar B-Q (913-783-4333; barbqthesauce.com), Hillsboro. Open for lunch and dinner Fri.–Sun., 11–9. Closed Christmas to early March. Known for burnt ends and ribs and especially their sauce, this popular restaurant head-quartered in an antique bank also offers wood-fired pizzas after 5. Eat in the bank, the restored caboose, or the garden.

Gates Bar-B-Q (913-383-1752; gatesbbq.com), Leawood. See *In Kansas City* above.

Smokin' Joe's BBQ (913-780-5511; smokingjosebbqolathe.com), Olathe. A BBQ landmark since 1989, they're especially known for their BBQ sauce and rub.

families. Notable residents have included George Brett, and Russell Stover.

Once a rest stop along the Santa Fe Trail, Mission has a small-town feel, with older homes and several unique shops. A large development project that recently razed an existing shopping center will feature private residences, shopping and dining options, and office space.

During 1829 approximately one hundred Shawnee Indians were settled on a reservation, in what is present-day Roeland Park; 35 years later they were relocated to Oklahoma. By 1906 the Missouri–Kansas Railroad, also known as the Strang Line, began operations here. The small suburb has approximately seven thousand residents.

Once the world headquarters of Sprint Corporation, affluent Westwood shares borders with Roeland Park, Fairway, Mission Hills, Mission Woods, Westwood Hills, Kansas City, Kansas, and Kansas City, Missouri. Approximately 1,500 people live in the city. Tiny Westwood Hills is nearby.

It's no wonder that much of this bustling metropolitan area's "landscape" is urban, with great restaurants and shopping for every taste and budget. Entertainment options abound, from world-class auto racing and casino gaming to live theater and musical performances. Historical outposts educate and entertain visitors while festivals celebrate the area's diverse history and culture.

Lovers of the outdoors will find plenty to like here, too. Rolling hills, old-growth trees, and loads of park space characterize this urban area. Golfers can enjoy more than a dozen public courses while many lakes offer multiple opportunities for fishing and/or boating. The choices are endless for visitors to this thriving, energetic urban area.

JOHNSON COUNTY CITIES

AREA CODE 913

GUIDANCE Convention and visitors' bureaus that serve this area include:

Lenexa Chamber of Commerce (913-888-1414), 11180 Lackman Rd., Lenexa. Open 8:30–5 weekdays.

Merriam Visitors Bureau (913-403-8999; exploremerriam.com), 6304 E. Frontage Rd., Merriam.

Mission Convention and Visitors Bureau (913-671-8564; missioncvb.org), 6090 Woodson/city hall, Mission. Building open 8–5.

Olathe Chamber of Commerce (913-764-1050; olathe.org/cvb), 18001 W. 106 St., Ste. 160, Olathe. Open 8:30–5 weekdays.

Overland Park Convention Bureau (913-491-0123; opcvb.com), 9001 W. 110th St., Overland Park. Open 8:30–5 weekdays.

Shawnee Convention and Visitor's Bureau (888-550-7282; shawneekscvb .com), 15100 W. 67th St., Shawnee. Open 8:30–5 weekdays.

GETTING THERE *By car:* See above. *By air:* Because the metropolitan area encompasses cities in both Kansas and Missouri, major airlines fly to **Kansas City International Airport** (816-243-5237), 601 Brasilia Ave., Kansas City, MO. *By train:* **AMTRAK** (1-800-872-7245) brings passengers on the Missouri River Runner to Kansas City, Missouri, daily on the **Southwest Chief** as a stop between Chicago and Los Angeles. The Station Building is beside Union Station at 30 West Pershing Road, Kansas City, Missouri. There is a Hertz rental car desk across the street. *By bus:* **Greyhound** stops in Kansas City, Missouri, but the distance from this stop to destinations on the Kansas side is impractical without easy access to rental cars.

GETTING AROUND Driving is the best way to get around this area. However, **The JO** (913-782-2210; thejo.com) offers bus service through much of Johnson County, Kansas, with occasional stops in De Soto and Gardner. Check the web for additional information.

MEDICAL EMERGENCY (arranged alphabetically by city name)

Providence Medical Center (913-596-4180), 8929 Parallel Pkwy., Kansas City.

Shawnee Mission Medical Center (913-676-2000), 9100 W. 74th St., Mission.

Menorah Medical Center (913-498-6000), 5721 W. 119th St., Overland Park.

Overland Park Regional Medical Center (913-541-5000), 10500 Quivira Rd., Overland Park.

✳ To See

HISTORIC PLACES, LANDMARKS, AND SITES 1950s All-Electric House (913-715-2550; jocomuseum.org), 6305 Lackman Rd., Johnson County Museum/Shawnee. Tours on the half hour, 1–4 Tues.–Sun. This ranch-style house was built by Kansas City Power and Light to showcase its latest home electronics innovations—from an electric switch above the couch that adjusts the curtains to a television that hides behind a remote-controlled painting. (The Museum holds 15,500 donated items and more than 558,000 photographs and negatives that reflect life in Johnson County.) Adults $2; children under 12 $1.

✎ **Mahaffie Stagecoach Stop and Farm** (913-971-5111; olatheks.org/mahaffie /about), 1100 E. Kansas City Rd., Olathe. Open 10–4 Wed.–Sat., noon–4 Sun.; closed most major holidays. Grounds for the last working stagecoach stop on the National Historic Santa Fe Trail feature an 1865 farmhouse with 1.5- to 2-foot-thick walls. Additional buildings include an icehouse, barn, and other reconstructed structures. The spacious heritage center features displays that include farm implements, antique buttons, and a jaw harp. During the annual Bull-whacker Days, authentic children's games and reenactments are just a few activities offered. Admission varies with season/day of the week.

✎ **Shawnee Indian Mission** (913-262-0867; kshs.org), 3403 W. 53rd St., Fairway. Open March–Nov., 9:30–5:30 Wed.–Sat.; Dec.–Feb., 9:30–5 Thurs.–Sat. Once a manual training school for children from the Shawnee, Delaware, and other Indian nations, it is now a national historic landmark. Several restored mission buildings occupy 12 tree-rich acres, with exhibits that focus on Thomas Johnson, a missionary to the Shawnee Indians, plus Indian agents and missionaries, Kansas settlement, Bleeding Kansas, and the Civil War. Adults $3; seniors/students/members/current military $2; children under six free.

✎ **Lanesfield School** (913-893-6645), 18745 S. Dillie Rd., Olathe. Open 1–5 Tues.–Sun. Built in 1869, this one-time mail stop on the Santa Fe Trail is the only building remaining from the old town of Lanesfield. Free.

The Ensor Farm Site Museum and Park (ensorparkandmuseum.org), 18995 W. 183rd St., Olathe. This is a national historic site. Marshall Ensor, his wife, Ida, and his sister were avid amateur ham radio enthusiasts. The Ensors also owned a dairy farm; visitors can visit their spacious 1892 farmhouse with broad front porch full of handcrafted furniture, Ida's handmade quilts, and antique household utensils.

✎ **Historic Oxford School** (913-339-6700; leawood.org/parks/oxforschool.asp), 14601 Mission Rd., Ironwoods Park/Leawood. Open March–July and Sept.–Nov., 11–2; tours available by appointment. Costumed docents educate

visitors about the area surrounding one of the state's oldest schools, which opened in 1877 and continued operation until 1955. Free.

Lone Elm Park Historic Campsite (913-971-6263), 167th and Lone Elm, Olathe. This is the only spot in the nation where the Santa Fe, Oregon, and California trails met and designated a historic site on all three trails. There's a picnic shelter, or hike as you read about the trails where people camped and prepared to travel westward. Free.

Chief Charles Bluejacket Fountain and Plaza (913-631-5200), 11600 Johnson Dr., Shawnee. See an unusual piece of history cast in life-size bronze. Two adoring children sit with this Shawnee Indian war chief who also was a minister, a farmer, and a Union Civil War captain. Free.

MUSEUMS & **Deaf Cultural Center and William J. Marra Museum** (913-782-5808; kefdcc.org), 455 E. Park St., Olathe. Open 10–4 Tues.–Fri., 10–3 Sat. Located across the street from the Kansas School for the Deaf, this cultural center and museum educates visitors about the use of sign language, with displays of a TTY/Teletype writer machine and items made by KSD students—including a desk used in the state capitol. Free.

THE NERMAN MUSEUM OF CONTEMPORARY ART AT JOHNSON COUNTY COMMUNITY COLLEGE IS THE LARGEST CONTEMPORARY ART MUSEUM IN A FOUR-STATE REGION.

& **Nerman Museum of Contemporary Art** (913-469-3000; nerman museum.org), at Johnson County Community College, 12345 College Blvd., Overland Park. Open 10–5 Tues.–Thurs. and Sat., 10–9 Fri., 12–5 Sun. The largest contemporary art museum in a four-state region, the Nerman features a Kansas-limestone-clad exterior and nine galleries with permanent pieces and temporary exhibitions. Enjoy breakfast or lunch at Café Tempo and find handmade Indian pottery or an art book in the museum store. Free.

Shawnee Town and Museum (913-248-2360; shawneetown.org), 11501 W. 57th St. (visitors center), Shawnee. Self-guided tours March–Oct., 10–4:30 Tues.–Sat. Established in 1966, Shawnee Town encompasses 19 historical buildings that inform visitors about farming life during the 1920s. Special events include a garden party with dolls, Straw Hat Saturdays, and the annual arts and crafts fair where more than one hundred crafters display homemade food items, pottery, candles, and more. Admission $1.

✳ To Do

DAY SPAS **Natural Body Spa and Shop** (previously Serenity, The Rejuvenating Day Spa; 913-341-0025), 119th St. and Roe Ave., Leawood. Check for hours. Serenity merged with another business to become Natural Body Spa and Shop at One Nineteen in November 2010. The Kansas City area's only accredited spa offers a calm, soothing environment with services from massage to body wraps and scrubs, facials, and foot treatments. Serenity received a 2009 Distinguished Day Spa Award from the Day Spa Association.

Salon Bliss (913-451-7780; salonbliss.com), 11904 W. 119th St., Overland Park. Open 9–9 Mon.–Thurs., 9–5 Fri., 8–4 Sat. Readers of a Johnson County newspaper have voted Salon Bliss their favorite spa for 10 consecutive years. Try the Bliss signature massage with hot point foot massage treatment, anti-aging facial, or La Licious body sugar scrub, plus hair, nail, and waxing services, and more. Anti-aging facial, $110.

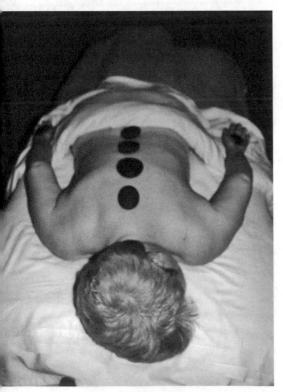

HOT-STONE MASSAGE IS A FAVORITE TREATMENT AT NATURAL BODY SPA AND SHOP.

Par Exsalonce, an AVEDA Lifestyle Salon/Spa (913-469-9532; parexsalonce.com), 11849 College Blvd., Overland Park. Open 9–9 Mon.–Fri., 8–6 Sat., noon–6 Sun. One of this area's oldest continuously operating salons and spas, Par Exsalonce offers massage, facial, nail, and hair services and retail AVEDA products. 60-minute massage, $85; Elemental Nature facial, $80.

Indulgé Salon and Day Spa (913-953-8700), 7236 W. 121st St., Overland Park. Open 9–8 Mon.–Thurs., 9–7 Fri., 9–4 Sat. One of Johnson County's newest day spas offers massage, body treatments, foot reflexology, and special packages, as well as salon services, in a fresh, modern space. Foot reflexology, $45.

La vita bella day spa (913-441-9090), 5416 Roberts St., Shawnee. Open 10–8 Mon.–Thurs., 9–5 Fri.–Sat., noon–5 Sun. Winners of the 2008–2009 Kansas City A-List award for best day spa, this soothing spot offers private secured lockers, showers/towels, and spa robes and slippers for clients. Try a couple's Swedish massage with reflexology add-on or a whole-body detox seaweed masque. Swedish massages from $75 for 60 minutes.

FARMERS' MARKETS &. **Downtown Overland Park Farmers' Market** (913-642-2222), between 79th and 80th Streets at the Clock Tower Plaza, Overland Park. Open April–Oct., 6:30 Sat./7:30 Wed., until sellout. One of the bistate metropolitan area's largest, this market has vendors who offer produce, herbs, and more.

&. **Olathe Farmers' Market** (913-764-6163), 200 W. Santa Fe, Olathe. Open May–Oct., Sat. 7 AM; June–Sept., 3 PM Wed. to sellout. Customers can buy produce herbs, flowers, and baked goods from producers within a 125-mile radius.

&. **Shawnee Farmers' Market** (913-631-2500), 1110 Johnson Dr., Shawnee. Open May–Oct., 7–4 on first Sat. This is another great place to find fresh produce, baked goods, and even arts and crafts.

THE DOWNTOWN OVERLAND PARK FARMERS' MARKET IS PACKED ON SATURDAY MORNINGS.

GOLF Falcon Ridge Golf Course (913-393-4653), 20200 Prairie Star Pkwy., Lenexa. *Golf Digest* 2008/2009 called this course a Best Places to Play 4.5-Star Rated Golf Course, one of only two in the metropolitan area. It feels like a private country club. Par 72, 18 holes, 6,820 yards.

St. Andrews Golf Club (913-897-3804), 11099 W. 135th St., Overland Park. Voted one of the top courses for women by *Golf for Women* magazine, this public course is built to USGA specifications. Par 71, 18 holes, 6,362 yards.

The Golf Club of Kansas (913-888-4894), 18145 W. 87th St. Pkwy., Lenexa. Challenge yourself with an elevation change of 140 feet, where rock bluffs help to create a spectacular landscape and golf experience. Par 71, 18 holes, 7,000 yards.

Tomahawk Hills Golf Course (913-631-8000), 17501 Midland Dr., Shawnee. Located near Shawnee Mission Park, this is the oldest course in the metropolitan area and one of the most challenging public courses. Par 70, 18 holes, 6,074 yards.

Heritage Park Golf Course (913-829-4653), 16445 Lackman Rd., Olathe. This beautiful and spacious course features three lakes and Coffee Creek so that water comes into play on 11 holes. Par 71, 18 holes, 6,876 yards.

Shawnee Golf and Country Club (913-422-8357; shawneegolfcc.com), 6404 Hedge Ln. Ter., Shawnee. With tree-dotted gentle slopes and water near some holes, this course emphasizes quality and affordability. Par 72, 18 holes/extra 9 holes, 6,754 yards.

Smiley's Golf Complex (913-782-1323), 10195 Monticello Ter., Lenexa. Holes 6, 9, and 18 cross water on this compact course. Practice drives at 180 hitting stations on natural or artificial grass with evening lighting, three putting greens, and a chipping green. Miniature golf is also available. Par 60, 18 holes, 3,400 yards.

Deer Creek Golf Club (913-681-3100; deercreekgc.com), 7000 133rd St., Overland Park. Known for beautiful wooded areas and winding creeks, this is a local favorite. Par 72, 18 holes, 6,811 yards.

HORSEBACK RIDING Heritage Park (913-831-3355), in southern Johnson County. Mid-America Combined Training Association leases 150 acres of open riding area, with approximately 5 miles of trail open to the public. A permit is required for organized rides or activities that involve this area. Free.

✐ **Leawood Stables** (913-642-2288; leawoodstables.com), 2600 W. 135th St., Leawood. Billing themselves as "horse country" in the heart of the city, this stable operation offers horse boarding and cowboy camps as well as horseback riding lessons/training and even Scout merit badges. With hourly horse rentals and monthly horse leases and organized trail rides that include monthly overnight campouts.

LEAWOOD STABLES

✐ **Shawnee Mission Park Equine Trails** (913-894-3350), 79th and Renner Rd., Shawnee. Ride on approximately 8 miles of trails, with parking at North Walnut Grove or the Archery Range. Free.

OUTDOORS ✐ ⅙ **Deanna Rose Children's Farmstead** (913-897-2360), 138th St. and Switzer Rd., Overland Park. Open April 1–Oct. 31, 9–5 daily and until 8 Tues./Thurs. during summer. This popular 12-acre spot was named for a local police officer killed in the line of duty. Children of all ages grin as they interact with cows and goats and explore the pioneer village, Indian encampment, fishing pond, playgrounds, and garden. You'll also learn about life on a 1900s Kansas farm. Free Mon.–Thurs.; $2 Fri.–Sat.; children under two free.

✐ ᕫ **Ernie Miller Nature Center** (913-764-7759; erniemiller.com), 909 N KS 7, Olathe. Trails open dawn–dusk; nature center open 9–noon/1–5 and Sun. afternoons; closed June–Aug. Check for special events and family activities. See owls from this area, as well as numerous reptiles and amphibians in the 500-gallon aquarium. There are live animals on hand and a variety of other nature displays. Enjoy the 0.3-mile Bittersweet Trail that surrounds the Nature Center, have a picnic along the South Trail, or take the Upper Ridge Trail near Little Mill Creek. Free.

Olathe's outdoor sculptures (913-971-8600), throughout downtown Olathe. With names like Rockslide, Metamorphosis, and the controversial Prayer Booth, these eight loaned sculptures decorate the downtown landscape as their predecessors have for five years. Maps available from city hall.

✳ Green Space

In Olathe
Kill Creek Park (913-831-3355), between Olathe and DeSoto. Open May 31 through Aug. 10, Fri.–Sun. This secluded regional park in Johnson County offers 880 acres with a marina and 17 miles of hiking, mountain bike and equestrian trails, plus an asphalt walking, hiking, and bicycling trail. Enjoy boat and canoe rentals, pedal boats, small sailboats, and fishing boats. The park also features a swimming beach and off-leash dog walk area.

Lake Olathe (913-971-6263), 625 Lakeshore Dr., Olathe. Several nearby housing developments carry the word *estate* in their names. Gorgeous summer sunsets reflect upon 170 acres of water at one of the area's older parks, dedicated in 1959. Catch a fish, have a picnic, or enjoy a spin on your boat. There's also an outdoor educational lab nearby.

Heritage Lake (913-894-3341), 169th and Pflumm, Olathe. This beautiful lake in the 1,238-acre Heritage Park offers a marina with pedal boat rentals available and fishing at any time. To learn conditions at any Johnson County Parks and Recreation Department lake, ask about the weekly online fishing report.

In Shawnee
Shawnee Mission Park Lake (913-438-8075), 79th St. and Renner Rd., Shawnee. With 121 surface acres, this urban lake offers trout, bass, crappie, and bluegill, to name a few. Use worms under bobbers, jigs or minnows, and suspending jerkbaits.

Elsewhere
Antioch Lake North/Antioch Lake South (913-894-3341), 6501 Antioch, Merriam. Located in Johnson County's oldest and most popular park, these lakes offer 3 acres of good fishing in the heart of the city. Fishing license required for ages 16–64. The park also offers a Vietnam memorial, basketball and tennis courts, and an enormous play area.

SHAWNEE MISSION PARK LAKE

Overland Park Arboretum and Botanical Gardens (913-685-3604), 8908 W. 179th St., Overland Park. Open daily except Christmas; 8–5 or 8–7:30, Oct. 1–early April. Rushing waterfalls, native Kansas plants, and a garden reminiscent of Monet's impressionist paintings are only a few of the natural beauties awaiting visitors to this 300-acre site. See eight different ecosystems and hundreds of bird species, too. It's a little off the beaten path but well worth a trip. Free.

SAR-KO-PAR TRAILS PARK

Sar-Ko-Par Trails Park (913-477-7500), 87th St., Lenexa. Fish in the 2-acre lake, have a picnic, use a walking trail, or visit the Legler Barn Historical Museum, which includes a restored railroad museum and waiting station and a vintage caboose. Basketball, baseball, tennis, and volleyball facilities, and a popular skateboard park are also here.

Mill Creek Streamway (913-438-7275), 19405 Midland Dr., Shawnee. Enjoy more than 17 miles of biking/hiking trails, plus 4 miles of riding trails. Picnic facilities are also available. The mostly flat trail follows the course of historic Mill Creek, with occasional steep inclines. There are nine trail access points in Shawnee, Lenexa, and Olathe.

Overland Park South Lake, at 87th St. and Valley View, Overland Park. Fish for channel catfish, green sunfish, and largemouth bass in this 5.5-acre community lake set amid a pretty city park.

Turkey Creek Streamway Park (913-322-5550), 75th St. to Werner Park, Merriam. Visit nature amid a 37-acre suburban park along a 4-mile trail. It's a great route for hiking or biking.

South Johnson County Trail System, one trailhead at Tomahawk Creek Parkway near 119th Street. The system includes three trails, the Indian Creek/Overland Park Bike and Hike Trail in Overland Park, Tomahawk Creek Greenway in Leawood, and Indian Creek Greenway in Olathe, for a combined length of about 30 miles. There are some hills, but also plenty of flat land.

✳ Lodging

CABINS AND CAMPING Walnut Grove RV Park (913-262-3023; walnutgroverv.com), 10218 Johnson Dr., Merriam. When this park opened in 1958 there was a freshwater spring for swimming and very few houses nearby. Today there are 56-, 30-, and 50-amp RV slots in the tree-ringed park with laundry facilities, a tornado shelter, Wi-Fi, and a notary public. Rigs over 32 feet are $32 for two people, under 32 feet $30, $2 for additional people.

✳ Where to Eat

DINING OUT ⅃ Hereford House (913-327-0800; herefordhouse.com), 5001 Town Center Dr., Leawood. Open 11–10 Mon.–Fri., 3–10 Sat., 3–9 Sun. Hereford House is known for great beef, from rib eye to prime rib. But they also prepare dynamite cedar plank salmon with garlic herb butter, and decadent chicken piccata with artichokes, capers, tomatoes, and béchamel. Enjoy a full bar and great desserts, too. Moderate.

⅃ **Bo Ling's** (913-888-6618; bolings .com), 9576 Quivira Rd., Lenexa. Open 11–9:30 Sun.–Thurs., 11–10:30

Fri.–Sat. This nationally recognized, family-owned Chinese restaurant does everything right, from food to service and decor. Sizzling black pepper beef has just the right amount of pepper and tender-crisp vegetables, steamed salmon with scallions and ginger is perfectly prepared, and there are enough dim sum choices for a week of meals. Inexpensive–moderate.

⅃ **Yia Yia's Eurobistro** (913-345-1111; yiayiaskc.com), 4701 W. 119th St., Overland Park. Open daily. This whimsical upscale restaurant is a Kansas City favorite with a mix of American, French, Italian, and Greek cuisines. Natural stone and dark wood create a soothing atmosphere for dining on fresh bruschetta with tomatoes, roasted garlic and warm goat cheese, fluffy risotto paired with succulent black tiger shrimp, or prosciutto asparagus pizza with perfectly caramelized yellow onions. Inexpensive–moderate.

⅃ **J Gilbert's Wood Fired Steaks and Seafood** (913-642-8070; jgilberts .com), 8901 Metcalf Ave., Overland Park. Open 5–10 Mon.–Thurs., 5–10:30 Fri.–Sat., 5–9 Sun. Great tasting upscale dining options include chipotle cheddar mashed potatoes, which are great with the city's only USDA Prime Certified Angus Beef, or George's bank scallops. Or try vegetable ravioli with sautéed lobster. Moderate.

& **Tatsu's** (913-383-9801; tatsus.com), 4603 W. 90th St., Prairie Village. Open 11:30–2 Mon.–Fri., 5:30–9:30 Mon.–Thurs., 5:30–10 Fri.–Sat., 5–9 Sun. The French food at Tatsu's is so good that it's among this area's highest-rated restaurants. Try beef bourguignon made with boneless short ribs, succulent lamb inside light-as-air puff pastry, and *veau au citron,* veal in a tangy, smooth lemon butter sauce served with fresh vegetables. Moderate.

& Y **WestChase Grille** (913-663-5400; westchasegrille.com), 11942 Roe Ave., Overland Park. Open for lunch weekdays, seven nights a week. Natural stonewalls, large windows, and wide-open spaces characterize this pretty restaurant that serves "contemporary American cuisine." Try seasonal dishes such as succulent New Zealand rack of lamb, jumbo sea scallops with cremini mushroom risotto, or salt and pepper pork with a twice-baked potato cake, and brussels sprouts with bacon and apples. Moderate.

EATING OUT

In Fairway

✨ & **Stroud's South** (913-262-8500; stroudsrestaurant.com), 4200 Shawnee Mission Pkwy., Fairway. Open 4–9:30 Mon.–Thurs., 11–10 Fri.–Sat., 11–9:30 Sun. The second location of the James Beard award-winning restaurant in nearby Kansas City, Missouri, is renowned for its pan-fried chicken,

broiled pork chops, and decadent cinnamon rolls. Moderate.

In Mission

& Y **Lucky Brewgrille** (913-403-8571; luckybrewgrille.com), 5401 Johnson Dr., Mission. Open 11–10 Mon.–Thurs., 10–12 Sat., 9–10 Sun. This popular cozy eatery offers daily food and drink specials and $3 Bloody Marys during Sunday football games. Try their Frisco burger with bacon, melted cheddar, and Thousand Island dressing or the High Plains steak salad. Inexpensive.

In Lenexa

& Y **Carlo's Copa Room** (913-825-5200), 14944 W. 87th St., Lenexa. Open 11–10 Mon.–Thurs., 11–11 Fri.–Sat., 10–2 Sun. Sinatra is ever-present at this popular family-owned Italian bistro. Try a sands martini (gin or vodka with dry Vermouth) with steak *modiga* or luscious grilled shrimp *spiedini.* Or order a little comfort food; ravioli Sinatra is a combo of cheese-filled pasta with tomato cream sauce, fresh peas, prosciutto, and mushrooms. But save room for homemade cannoli. Moderate.

& **Holy Land Café** (913-310-9911), 12275 W. 87th St. Pkwy., Lenexa. Open 11–9 Mon.–Thurs., 11–10 Fri.–Sat., noon–6 Sun. There's lamb roasting on a spit and fresh pistachio baklava in the bakery case at this tidy little Middle Eastern restaurant. Try the falafel or chicken breast with creamy artichoke sauce. Inexpensive.

& **Café Augusta** (913-859-9556; cafeaugusta.com), 12122 W. 87th St., Lenexa. Open 9–8 Mon.–Thurs., 9–9 weekends. This eclectic menu uses fresh ingredients amid art deco decor. Try signature fries with rosemary, blue cheese, and garlic, plus chipotle mayonnaise. Curried squash soup or the turkey and Brie sandwich are other favorites. Breakfast and live music are also available. Inexpensive.

In Leawood

&. Y **Blue Koi** (913-383-3330; bluekoi.net), 10581 Mission Rd., Leawood. Open 11–9:30 Mon.–Thurs., 11–10:30 Fri.–Sat. Dine on wraps like basil chicken in lettuce, à la carte dumplings, and shrimp asparagus or ginger basil chicken amid soothing earth and sky colors. There's a modern vibe, plus nearly two-dozen flavors of bubble tea and cheesecake wontons for dessert. Enjoy a blue koi martini with your meal. Inexpensive.

&. Y **Blanc Burgers + Bottles** (913-381-4500; blancburgers.com), 10583 Mission Rd., Leawood. Modern and bright are good ways to describe this popular burger restaurant and its menu. If you love lobster, try the decadent surf and turf burger with a grilled lobster tail atop a juicy Kobe beef burger. The Inside Out burger pairs beef with blue cheese stuffing and smoked bacon on an onion brioche bun. Or try an appetizer with a twist—fried Peppadew peppers full of goat cheese mousse. Inexpensive–moderate.

In Olathe

&. &. **Jumpin' Catfish** (913-829-3474; jumpincatfish.com), 1861 S. Ridgeview Rd., Olathe. Open 11–9 Tues.–Thurs., 11–10 Fri.–Sat., 11–8 Sun. Offering freshwater, farm-raised and grain-fed catfish, this suburban favorite serves Southern-style hush puppies/wedge-cut fries or mashed potatoes, coleslaw, and white beans and ham with every catfish meal. Try Dave's creamy parmesan catfish with seafood cream sauce. Moderate.

&. **Garozzo's** (913-764-6969; garozzos .com), 13505 S. Mur-Len Rd., Olathe. Open 11–9:30 Mon.–Thurs., 11–10:30 Fri., 4–10:30 Sat., 5–8:30 Sun. Visit this classic Italian restaurant favored by Kid Rock, Ray Liotta, and Jerry Lewis, and enjoy free chicken *spiedini* on your birthday. There are numerous veal dishes, plus plenty of beef, chicken, and pasta dishes to enjoy amid white linen surroundings. Moderate.

&. **Ari's Greek Restaurant** (913-393-3950; arisgreekrestaurant.com), 2049 E. Santa Fe St., Olathe. Open 11–9 Mon.–Sat., 6–9 Fri.–Sat. The city's first Greek restaurant offers classics such as avgolemono, dolmades a la Sophia, and souvlaki made from family recipes. Try the baklava sundae for dessert. Inexpensive.

&. Y **Johnny's Tavern** (913-378-0744; johnnystavern.com), 10384 S. Ridgeview Rd., Olathe. Open 11–2 AM daily. Come for the fun atmosphere and cold beer and enjoy classic tavern fare such as soft pretzels 'n' cheese and Guinness melt burgers. There's even a steak for under $15. Inexpensive.

In Overland Park

&. &. **Santa Fe Café** (913-648-5402; sfcafekc.com), 9946 W. 87th St., Overland Park. Open daily for breakfast and lunch. This place is packed on Sunday morning and full of Southwestern decor. Try crunchy-soft biscuits and gravy or a four-egg south-of-the-border omelet. And don't forget their signature trail taters. Inexpensive.

&. **Dragon Inn** (913-381-7299; dragon inn.us), 7500 W. 80th St., Overland Park. Lunch Mon.–Sat. and dinner daily. This family-owned restaurant has served Peking and spicy Szechuan cuisine since 1975, including such favorites as scallops in garlic sauce, crispy duck, and sizzling hot beef. Inexpensive.

& **Ricco's Italian Bistro** (913-469-8405; riccoskc.com), 11801 College Blvd., Overland Park. Open 11–11 Mon.–Thurs., 11–12 Fri.–Sat., 4–10 Sun. Once you see the rustic pizza oven and low lights, it's easy to forget you're in a strip mall. Try Sonoma torte, veal parmesan, and garbage truck pizza. And save room for their scrumptious cannoli. Inexpensive.

& ⛾ **Johnny Cascone's Italian Restaurant** (913-381-6837), 6863 W. 91st St., Overland Park. Open 11–9 Mon.–Thurs., 11–10 Fri.–Sat., 4–9 Sun. The Cascone's name has been synonymous with classic Italian cuisine in the metropolitan area for more

THE DRAGON INN IN DOWNTOWN OVER-LAND PARK HAS SERVED CUSTOMERS SINCE 1975.

than 50 years. You'll find stuffed artichokes, traditional Caesar salad, baked lasagna, and veal parmesan amid the large menu, served in a dining room with an Old World feel. Ask about chef specials, too. Moderate.

& ⛾ **Coach's Bar and Grill** (913-897-7070; coach-s.com), 14893 Metcalf, Overland Park. Open Mon.–Sun. 11–2 AM. One of the Kansas City area's oldest sports bars also operates in Overland Park, offering an upscale bar menu and fun atmosphere full of enormous high definition plasma screens. Try meaty, savory Coach's chili topped with cheese, tomato, and onions; an enormous chicken pecan salad with warm honey mustard dressing; or a classic pork tenderloin sandwich. Check out daily food specials on the web. Inexpensive.

The Other Place American Sports Grill & Pizzeria (913-652-9494; theotherplace.com; also in Olathe), 7324 W. 80th St., Overland Park. Open 11–midnight Sun.–Thurs., 11–2 a.m. Fri.–Sat. This original Kansas City location opened in 1997, almost 30 years after the business began as a college bar for the University of Northern Iowa. The always-busy downtown Overland Park fixture is also a magnet for UNI fans, who enjoy chicken tenders, quesadillas, and meal-size salads, as well as specialty pizzas, subs and other sandwiches, and half-pound burgers with their brews. Inexpensive.

t•a•s•t•e (913-766-0320; taste-kc .com), 7938 Santa Fe Dr., Overland Park. Open 11–close Mon.–Thurs., 11–11 Fri.–Sat. Located inside a vintage brick building with a massive, glass-faced garage door that opens in nice weather, t•a•s•t•e is well known for its small plates that range from chili-glazed grilled salmon with Asian salad to a crispy calamari tasting. Entrées include seared sea bass or crab cake, bone-in pork chop or rib eye, filet mignon, and more. Save room for a chocolate tasting or visit their adjacent gelato shop, Crave. Inexpensive–moderate.

&. Ⴘ **Sunset Grill** (913-681-1722; sunsetgrillrestaurant.com), 14577 Metcalf, Overland Park. Open 11–10 Mon.–Thurs., 11–11 Fri., 9–11 Sat., 9–9 Sun. Take a vacation with your meal in this island-inspired restaurant. Try shrimp tacos; a sweet and spicy Maui burger with prosciutto, Monterey Jack cheese, grilled pineapple, and pineapple Dijon sauce. Weekend breakfast favorites include flamingo French toast topped with fresh fruit and vanilla sauce or breakfast quesadillas. Inexpensive.

&. Ⴘ **Talk of the Town** (913-661-9922; talkofthetowngrill.com), 11922 W. 119th St., Overland Park. Open 11–2 am Mon.–Sat., 10–10 Sun.; breakfast 9–11 Sat.–Sun. Some locals say this place is a lot like *Cheers*. Eighteen HDTVs broadcast sports as you enjoy burgers, create-your-own pizza, or chicken-fried steak. The bar is the big draw, with dozens of beer selections and eight wines. Try their bombs or shots, too. Inexpensive.

In Prairie Village

&. **Kokopelli Mexican Cantina** (913-385-0300; kokopellimexican cantina.com), 5200 W. 95th St., Prairie Village. Open 11–9 Sun.–Thurs., 11–10 Fri.–Sat. Cozy and full of kokopelli figures, this urban cantina offers favorites such as the Rio Grande burrito and Santa Cruz enchiladas. There's also fried ice cream and plenty of margaritas. Inexpensive.

&. **The Salty Iguana** (913-381-3888; saltyiguana.com), 8228 Mission Rd., Prairie Village. Open 11–10 Mon.–Thurs., 11–10:30 Fri.–Sat., noon–9 Sun. This original location is full of hand-painted murals picturing iguanas in sombreros. Menu favorites include Iggy's spinach enchiladas. Enjoy the Prairie Village burrito or a guiltless quesadilla with a margarita or food/drink specials. Inexpensive.

&. **Café Provence** (913-384-5998; kcconcept.com), 3936 W. 69th Ter., Prairie Village. Open 11–2:30 and 5–9 Mon.–Thurs., 11–2:30 and 5–10 Fri.–Sat. Enjoy French Provençal cuisine in a European bistro setting, from French onion soup to Dover sole and foie gras, served primarily with French wines or bar drinks. Inexpensive–moderate.

In Shawnee

&. Ⴘ **Barley's Brewhaus and Restaurant** (913-268-5160), 16649 Midland Dr., Shawnee. Open 11–midnight Sun., 11–12:30 AM Mon.–Thurs., 11–1 AM Fri.–Sat. You'll find 99 beer taps on the wall and a full bar, plus meats and cheeses smoked in-house. Try smoked sharp cheddar ale soup or a hickory-smoked Kansas City strip. Inexpensive–moderate.

&. **Paolo and Bill** (913-962-9900; pauloandbill.com), 16501 Midland Dr., Shawnee. Open 10–9 Sun., 11–9 Mon., 11–9:30 Tues.–Thurs., 11–10:30 Fri., noon–10 Sat. Enjoy this cozy spot and classy bar where Italian inspiration creates favorites such as chicken piccata and pasta osso bucco—with multiple seafood dishes, too. Moderate.

SNACKS &. **Pie Lady Coffeehouse** (913-438-7200), 13408 Santa Fe Trail

Dr., Lenexa. Open noon–6 Mon., 8–6 Tues.–Fri., 8–3 Sat. Pies made from scratch in this tiny bakery with loads of seasonal varieties. Cream pies have massive meringues and apple pies use Granny Smiths. Order a piece of quiche or a sandwich and a latte, but save room for a slice of pie or a cookie. Inexpensive.

✐ ♿ **Mochi-Yo Yogurt Bar** (913-338-0557; mochi-yo.com) 4535 W. 119th St., Leawood. Open 11–10 Mon.–Thurs., 11–11 Fri.–Sat., noon–10 Sun. Mochi balls are Japanese rice cakes on the outside with plain, green tea, or strawberry ice cream inside, and the unusual treat has many fans. Or enjoy yogurt—tart, green tea, and two rotating flavors—topped with fruit, Captain Crunch cereal, or sliced almonds, all in this cheerful orange and white environment. Inexpensive.

✐ ♿ **Aunt Jean's** (913-268-0550), 11210 Johnson Dr., Shawnee. Daily, noon–10 in summer; shorter winter

hours. With 200 gelato flavors and 18 in the case daily, this cute and fun shop offers inventive tastes such as cappuccino coffee crunch, black raspberry, and dark chocolate sea salt. Inexpensive.

✐ ♿ **Mely's Yogurt and Ice Cream** (913-381-9642), 4051 Somerset Dr., Prairie Village. Open 11–9 Mon.–Sat., 1–9 Sun. With 28 ice cream flavors, 4 yogurt choices, fresh lemonade, and their new Hawaiian shaved ice, Mely's continues a 25-year tradition of sweet treats. Buy a gingerbread house during the holidays. Inexpensive.

✐ ♿ **Georgetown Pharmacy** (913-362-0313), 5605 Merriam, Merriam. Open 9–6 Mon.–Fri., 9–1 Sat. or by appointment for group tours. For a bit of nostalgia, enjoy a classic Green River or handmade shake at this recreated soda fountain with antique bar stools, counter equipment, and glasses. Buy a sandwich or pick up a prescription while you're there, too. Inexpensive.

MELY'S YOGURT AND ICE CREAM IS A FAVORITE SPOT FOR COOL SUMMER TREATS.

✳ Entertainment

🎧 ♿ **Martin City Melodrama and Vaudeville** (913-642-7576; martin citymelodrama.org), 9601 Metcalf, Overland Park. Call for schedule. See original adaptations of literature performed as melodramas, plus classic stage musicals such as Marx Brothers comedy. Call for ticket prices.

♿ **Performing Arts at Johnson County Community College** (913-469-2522; jccc.edu/theseries), 12345 College Blvd., Overland Park. This is one of the region's largest performance centers with diverse programs, plus an arts center. Ticket prices depend on program.

EVENING OUT ♿ **New Theatre Restaurant** (913-649-7469; new theatre.com), 9229 Foster, Overland Park. Box office open 9–6 Mon.–Sat., 11–3 Sun. The *Wall Street Journal* has called this "the best dinner theatre operation in the country." Nationally known actors work with talented local performers to create classic shows that have included *The Sunshine Boys* and *Nunsense!* Gourmet meals are part of the entertainment, too, whether brunch, matinee, or dinnertime. Call for ticket prices.

♿ **Carlsen Center** (913-469-4445; jccc.edu/performing-arts-series), 12345 College Blvd., Johnson County Community College/Overland Park. In gorgeous, modern surroundings, the Carlsen Center offers a wide variety of concerts and theatrical and other fine arts performances. Choose from more than 250 performances throughout the year. Admission varies by performance.

FAMILY FAVORITES 🎧 ♿ **The Theatre in the Park** (913-312-8841; theatreinthepark.org), Renner Rd. and Memorial Dr. in Shawnee Mission Park. Amateur theater never looked so terrific. The country's largest outdoor community theater, TTIP has wowed audiences with Broadway musicals and other popular shows each summer for 40 years. Adults $8; children 4–10 $6, and under 4 free.

🎧 ♿ **Incred-A-Bowl** (913-851-1700), 8500 W. 151st, Overland Park. Open noon in summer, 11 AM in winter; closes 11 PM weekdays, midnight weekends. Bright colors and lights and an enormous waterfall at the indoor minigolf area are highlights. Ask about laser tag or Cosmic Bowl with black lights, fog, and glow-in-the-dark pins/balls. Admission $4.75 per game, $4 shoes required. Golf is $6.

🎧 ♿ **Mission Bowl** (913-432-7000; missionbowl.com), 5399 Martway, Mission. Call for lane availability. Enjoy 24 lanes that have operated for five decades and special events such as buck night or rock 'n' bowl Saturdays. Also, check out their Mission bowl 'n one, an 18-hole miniature golf course with multiple water features. Adult bowling $4; junior/senior $3, shoe rental $3.25. Adults $6; children under 13 $5.

KID FAVORITES 🎧 ♿ **Skate City** (913-888-6688; skatecitykansas.com), 103rd and US 69, Overland Park. Open for public skating 12–2 and 2–4 Sun., 7–10 Fri., 10–noon, 12–2, 2–4, and 7–10 Sat. With a disco ball, shiny floor, and personal storage lockers, this longtime entertainment destination has a full-service snack bar and an arcade, too. Skate sessions $4–7, extra session $2.50, skates $1.50–3.50.

∂ よ **Wonderscope Children's Museum** (913-287-8888; wonder scope.org), 5700 King St., Shawnee. Open 10–4 Tues.–Fri., 10–5 Sat., noon–5 Sun. Enjoy the indoor picnic area after visiting Lego Ocean Adventure, Tinker Space, or the Wonder Why Children's Garden full of fresh vegetables and annual flowers. Ages 3–63 $7; 64 and up $6; 1–2 $4.

✴ Selective Shopping

In Merriam
Guitarlamp.com (913-362-5004), 5848 Merriam Dr., Merriam. Call for appointment. It's well worth a visit to see Dan Leap's guitar lamps, owned by celebrities such as Bret Michaels and featured on HGTV. You won't find these anywhere else.

よ **K. C. Strings** (913-677-0400; kcstrings.com), 5842 Merriam Dr., Merriam. Open 10–7 weekdays, 10–6 Sat., 1–5 Sun. Concert masters from across the nation use this company's beautiful stringed instruments. Marvel at hundreds of world-class violins, violas, cellos, and basses handcrafted onsite, as they have been since 1992. Purchase a new bow or even a guitar amplifier.

In Mission
よ **I Love a Mystery** (913-432-2583), 6114 Johnson Dr., Mission. Open 10–6 Mon.–Sat. Murder, mayhem, and international espionage are several topics in the hundreds of books at this unusual store. Grab a cup of coffee beside the hanging skeleton and browse your mystery selections in the comfort of a wingback chair.

TWO SHOPPING NEIGHBORHOODS

THE VILLAGE shopping area in **Prairie Village** features more than 50 shops, restaurants, and service providers, including:

Toon Shop (913-362-6800). They're still going strong after more than 60 years. See dozens of grand pianos, thousands of pieces of sheet music for vocal, band, orchestral instruments, and piano, and much more.

∂ **Mady and Me** (913-648-0200). Previously rated the metropolitan area's best children's store, this brightly decorated shop offers brands such as Flowers by Zoe and Mudpie. For boas and tiaras, visit the nearby The Princess Club and A Fairytale Ballet.

Dolce Baking Company (913-236-4411). Gourmet, made from scratch, and decadent describe this tiny bakery's offerings, especially the 6-inch cinnamon rolls.

The Better Cheddar (913-362-7575). This legendary store offers samples, decor, and products with the flare of a gourmet party shop, including imported and specialty cheeses, chocolate, and more.

Southwest Jewels Gallery (913-432-8555; southwestjewels.com), 6909 Johnson Dr., Mission. Open 10–6 weekdays, 10–5 Sat. In one of the area's largest selections of Native American–made and Southwest gifts, visitors will find flute music, handwoven rugs, and stunning sterling jewelry with natural stones. And there isn't a better place to take broken Southwestern jewelry for repair.

In Overland Park

&. **888 International Market** (913-341-8700), 10118 W. 119th St., Overland Park. Open 10–8 Sun.–Thurs., 9–8 Fri., 9–9 Sat. Browse Chinese, Korean, Japanese, Thai, and Vietnamese products across a 6,000-square-foot store and be transported to another country. Purchase pad thai noodles, boneless chicken feet, or

CONCERT MASTERS FROM ACROSS THE NATION USE HANDMADE STRINGED INSTRUMENTS FROM K. C. STRINGS.

DOWNTOWN OVERLAND PARK

Harper's Fabrics (913-648-2739). This is one of the nation's top quilt stores according to *Better Homes and Gardens.*

The Tasteful Olive (913-649-7900). Sample dozens of extra virgin olive oils and balsamic vinegars. You'll also find spice blends, and other gourmet items.

The Culinary Center of Kansas City (913-341-4455). This culinary education center also sells kitchen gadgets and gourmet food.

&. **Clock Tower Bakery Café** (913-948-9559). Find fresh challah bread and brioche, plus handmade cherry-almond scones and chocolate croissants.

Traditions (913-649-2429). Stickley, Charleston, Forge, and Hancock are only a few furniture brands housed in this historic "carbarn."

&. **Prairiebrooke Galleries** (913-341-0333). Beautiful artwork in a beautiful setting characterizes this original location.

Olive Branch Art Gallery & Studios (913-642-2833). Handcrafted scarves, landscape photography, bold ceramics, and more are available in this bright new gallery.

&. **Ten Thousand Villages** (913-642-8368). Purchase handcrafted, fair trade home decor, accessories, and gifts from 131 artisan groups in nearly 40 countries.

Korean frozen foods. Seafood is competitively priced and there are plenty of rice bowls, teapots, and other household items.

Will Wyatt's Cowboy Couture (913-681-9455; willwyatts.com), 15245 Metcalf Ave., Overland Park. Open 10–6 Mon.–Wed./Fri., 10–5 Sat., noon–4 Sun. Look for the yellow building with red trim, where you'll find adult hats, boots, buckles, Western-inspired clothing, and jewelry. Upstairs, carved wood, tooled leather, and animal hides decorate massive Western furnishings; you'll also find children's boots, hats, and a cowboy pup tent.

In Prairie Village

Victorian Trading Co. (913-381-3995), 4107 W. 83rd St., Prairie Village. Open 10–6 Mon.–Sat., 10–4 Sun. Everything here is new but recreates the Victorian era. With a warehouse in nearby Lenexa, this shop functions as an outlet store and items are priced up to 80 percent off. Purchase an antique doll, delicate lace blouse, or vintage picture frame.

& **Mission Road Antique Mall** (913-341-7577; missionroadantique mall.com), 4101 W. 83rd St., Prairie Village. Open 10–6 daily. This upscale antique mall offers 350 dealers on two floors. Buy Mom an antique necklace or find the perfect foyer mirror. Take a shopping break at Bloomsbury Bistro for made-from-scratch lunch or homemade carrot cake.

& **Lilliane's Fine Jewelry** (913-383-3376), 4101 W. 83rd St., Prairie Village. Open 10–5, Mon.–Sat. A star pin from a Maharaja's turban and an Egyptian jewelry piece signed by the Vatican are among dozens of gently used rings, necklaces, bracelets, and much more. Many items feature unusual antique designs, including art deco filigree.

THIS LEATHER LOUNGE AT WILL WYATT'S COWBOY COUTURE ALSO OFFERS GUN STORAGE.

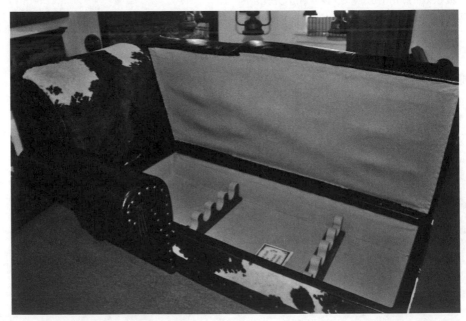

Elsewhere

Rainy Day Books (913-384-3126), 2706 W. 53rd St., Fairway. Open 10–6 Mon.–Wed./Fri., 10–7 Thurs., 10–5 Sat. There aren't many independent booksellers that have operated since 1975 or have a national reputation for the authors they bring in to speak (in cooperation with Unity Temple on the Plaza), from John Gray to Terry McMillan. Purchase new hardcover and paperback books for every age and taste.

Churchill (913-262-5240; shopat churchill.com), 5240 Belinder, Fairway. Open to the public by appointment Mon.–Thurs.; 10–5 Fri.–Sat. Beaded dresses that resemble the 1920s, delicate gold and turquoise necklaces, custom diamond earrings, ornate ladies' hats, antique armoires, and studded leather purses are just a few items you'll find at this gorgeous shop, voted among the top three coolest stores by *INSTORE*, a magazine for American jewelry store owners. There's beauty everywhere you look.

✐ **Doll Cradle** (913-631-1900; doll cradle.com), 10910 Johnson Dr., Shawnee. Open 10–5 Mon.–Sat. The oldest doll hospital in the Midwest also sells hundreds of antique and current dolls and some stuffed creatures. Choose a Victorian beauty, Betty Boop, or an old-fashioned Teddy Bear. They also appraise dolls.

Kansas Sampler (913-390-8090; kansassampler.com), 16485 W. 119th St., Olathe (multiple locations). Open 10–9 Mon.–Fri., 9–9 Sat., 11–6 Sun. This store offers every kind of Kansas-themed item imaginable, from university sports jerseys to statues of Dorothy and Kansas-made gourmet foods. Buy Kansas postcards, books, and other memorabilia.

✳ Special Events

February: **Trout Stocking** (913-888-4713), Heritage Park Boat Ramp, 16050 Pflumm, Olathe. One thousand pounds of trout enter Heritage Park Lake in preparation for fishing season. Call for time of release and season start.

March: **Olathe Marathon, Half Marathon and 5K** (olathemarathon .com), Olathe. This is a Boston marathon qualifier and USA Track & Field–certified course that also includes a children's run.

April: **Civil War on the Border** (913-971-6263), Mahaffie Farmstead/Olathe. Experience life on the Kansas–Missouri Border during the 1860s as more than four hundred reenactors become Union and Confederate forces; with 19th-century music and a Civil War dance.

June: **Jazz in the Woods** (816-225-1538), Corporate Woods/Overland Park. Thousands of people gather in this corporate office park to hear live jazz performances sponsored by the Overland Park South Rotary Club to raise funds for local children's charities. **Old Shawnee Days** (913-248-2360), Old Shawnee Town/Shawnee. This three-day event includes one of the state's largest parades, arts and crafts, and historical reenactments. Enjoy music and entertainment from national and local bands, carnival rides, kids' entertainment, and food galore. **Prairie Village Art Show** (prairievillageshops.com/art.html), Prairie Village. View work from dozens of two- and three-dimensional artists in one of Johnson County's oldest shopping neighborhoods. **Great Lenexa BBQ Battle** (913-477-7100, ci.Lenexa.ks.us/parks/bbq.html), Sar-Ko-Par Trails Park, Lenexa. This event was named the official Kansas State Championship in 1984 has nearly two hundred contestants.

July: **Mahaffie Stagecoach Stop 4th of July** (913-782-6972), Olathe. Enjoy an old-fashioned holiday celebration that features an 1860s-era baseball reenactment, replicating what was a great break from farm work during that time.

September: **Lenexa Spinach Festival** (913-541-8592), Sar-Ko-Par Trails Park, Lenexa. During the 1930s Belgian farmers grew spinach here and shipped it by rail. Taste the world's largest spinach salad, enter youngsters in the Swee'pea Baby Crawling Contest, and enjoy plenty of food, music, and games. **Johnson County Old Settlers Days** (913-782-5551; johnsoncountyoldsettlers.org), downtown Olathe. This event has taken place since 1898 with a huge parade, plus arts and crafts, antique cars, carnival rides, and all kinds of food. **Hidden Glen Arts Festival** (913-961-2787),

Cedar Creek housing development, Olathe. This is a national juried art show that includes music, entertainment, and children's art activities.

October: **Lenexa Chili Cook-off** (913-541-8592), Old Town Lenexa. This event includes the Williams Foods Chili Challenge and is sanctioned by CASI (Chili Appreciation Society International Inc.). Sixty-five teams create their signature chili recipes for judges and the public.

November: **Johnson County Young Matrons' Home for the Holidays Tour** (jcym.net). Tour five homes in south Leawood, plus a shopping boutique, while you support several local charities. Tickets available in advance at Hen House and Hy-Vee grocery stores.

December: **Olathe Historical Homes Tour** (olathehistoricalsociety.com), throughout Olathe. A benefit for the Olathe Historical Society, the tour features historical homes and churches throughout the city.

KANSAS CITY
AND BONNER SPRINGS

AREA CODE 913

GUIDANCE Kansas City Kansas-Wyandotte County Convention and Visitors Bureau (913-321-5800; visitthedot.com), 727 Minnesota Ave., Kansas City. Open 8:30–5 weekdays.

Bonner Springs/Edwardsville Chamber of Commerce (913-422-5044; lifeisbetter.org), 129 N. Nettleton, Bonner Springs. Open 8–4 weekdays.

MEDICAL EMERGENCY Children's Mercy West (913-233-4400), 4313 State Ave., Kansas City.

Providence Medical Center (913-596-4000), 8929 Parallel Pkwy., Kansas City.

University of Kansas Hospital (913-588-1227), 3901 Rainbow Blvd., Kansas City.

GETTING THERE See *Johnson County Cities.*

GETTING AROUND See *Johnson County Cities.*

✳ To See

HISTORIC LANDMARKS AND SITES Grinter Place (913-299-0373; kshs .org/places/gringer/index.htm), 1420 S. 78th St., Kansas City. Open March–Nov., 9:30–5 Wed.–Sat.; Dec.–Feb., 9:30–5 Thurs.–Sat. One of the state's earliest settlers, Moses Grinter, traded here with the Delaware Indians and operated the first ferry that crossed the Kansas River, beginning in 1831. He and his wife, Ann, a Delaware Indian, built this two-story brick house in 1857 after flooding destroyed their first home. The house is now a museum surrounded by native prairie grass and woodlands. Adults $2; seniors/students $1; KSHS Inc. members/military/children under six free.

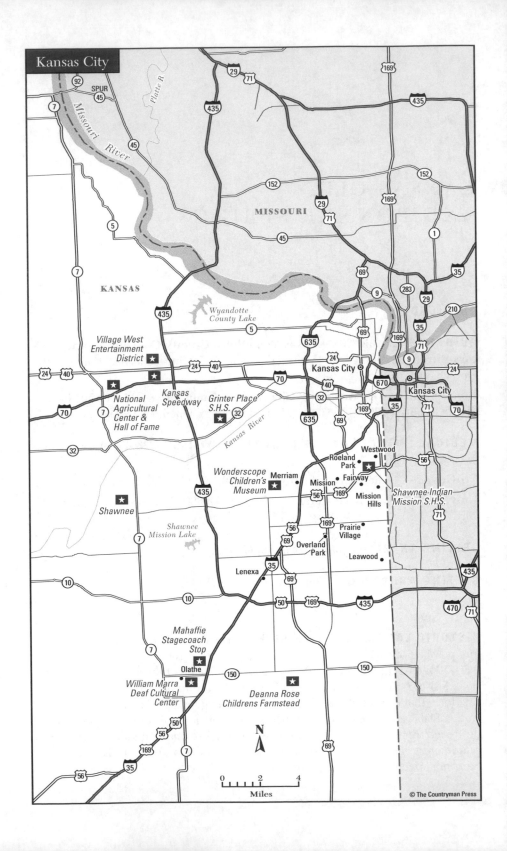

Quindaro Ruins (913-281-1953), 27th St. and Sewell Ave., Kansas City. Open daily. Enormous diversity characterized Quindaro Township, including African and European Americans and partial-blood Wyandot Indians. Located across the Missouri River from proslavery Missouri, the settlement's antislavery sentiment made this a natural stop along the Underground Railroad, but the township was abandoned by 1862 as a result of the Depression and Civil War. An overlook provides easy views of the site, which remains a popular attraction. Free.

Rosedale Memorial Arch (information at Rosedale Development Association [913-677-5097], 35th and Booth Streets, Kansas City. Open daily. This memorial arch based on Paris's Arc de Triomphe was designed by Rosedale resident John LeRoy Marshall to honor local veterans of World War I. In 1993 a second monument was added to honor World War II, Korean, and Vietnam veterans. This secluded, peaceful spot provides gorgeous skyline views of nearby Kansas City, Missouri. Free.

Quindaro Kansas on the Underground Railroad (913-321-8024), 27th St. and Sewell Ave., Kansas City. The site includes the John Brown Statue and Memorial Plaza. Once owned by Wyandot Indians, the town of Quindaro was located on the Missouri River and began to lose population. New settlers, particularly of African descent, and farmers came to the area. Archaeological ruins relate to abolitionist efforts, the Underground Railroad, and the temperance movement. This was also a port-of-entry along the river and site of the African American Quindaro-Western University. Tours include still-existing homes and the brewery ruins, believed to be a stop on the Underground Railroad. Call for price.

Huron Indian Cemetery (913-321-5800), Seventh and Ann Streets, Kansas City. Open daily, daylight hours. This cemetery was established in the 1840s after illness took the lives of more than 50 Wyandot Indians who had moved here from Ohio. The cemetery continued to be used until the early 1900s, when the secretary of the interior said the remains should be moved to Quindaro to allow for development on the cemetery land. After a highly visual protest by the daughters of one man buried there, the potential sale was repealed and the site was placed on the National Register of Historic Places in 1971. Free.

Korean-Vietnam War Memorial (913-573-8327), 91st St. and Leavenworth Rd., Wyandotte County Lake/Kansas City. Open daily. This was the nation's first memorial dedicated to soldiers from both of these conflicts. A bronze eagle with outstretched wings and life-size soldiers decorate the rock wall where name plaques are displayed. Free.

Lewis and Clark Historic Park at Kaw Point (913-573-8327; lewisandclark wyco.org), 1 River City Dr., Kansas City. See where the historic expedition arrived, on June 26, 1804, and then camped near the Kansas River for three days. An open-air pavilion educates visitors about the expedition. Free.

MUSEUMS ♿ **Strawberry Hill Museum and Cultural Center** (913-371-3264; strawberryhillmuseum.org), 720 N. Fourth St., Kansas City. Open noon–5 Sat.–Sun. For more than 20 years the museum has offered a glimpse of this neighborhood's close-knit Croatian population and other ethnic groups such as Lithuanian, Polish, Slovakian, Slovenian, Russian, and Dutch. Enter this gorgeous 1880s house with handcrafted wood banisters, stained-glass windows, turn-of-the-century clothing, and handcrafted musical instruments. Enjoy tea and Slavic desserts and purchase items made by community members and craftspeople from Baltic and Slavic countries. Adults $7; children six and younger $3.

&. **Wyandotte County Historical Museum** (913-573-5002; wycokck.org), 631 N. 126th St., Bonner Springs. Open 10–4 Mon.–Fri., 10–noon Sat. Historical displays include a gallery with information about the Shawnee, Delaware, and Wyandot tribes, and another about life among Wyandotte Countians during the 1800s and 1900s. There's a 1944 B-25, vintage clothing, a fire gnome from a local fire station, and President Truman's 1945 "Message about Food," telling Americans to increase the nation's food supply. Free.

&. **National Agricultural Hall of Fame** (913-721-1075; aghalloffame.com), 630 Hall of Fame Dr., Bonner Springs. Open 10–4 Tues.–Sat., 1–4 Sun.; closed Nov. 30–mid-spring. A gallery at the Ag Hall honors people who have forwarded the cause of agriculture in the United States, including portraits of Squanto, Abraham Lincoln, and Senator Bob Dole. But this is only a small part of many exhibits, from massive farm machinery to dozens of barbed-wire designs and a room that introduces visitors to contemporary chicken breeding and meat-production practices. You'll never look at agriculture the same way again. Adults $7; 62 and older $6; children 5–16 $3.

TOWNS Kansas City. See *The Kansas City Area.*

Bonner Springs. This city is primarily located in Wyandotte County and under the jurisdiction of the County/Kansas City Unified Government. But portions of the city lie in Johnson and Leavenworth counties. With a population of around seven thousand, Bonner Springs is a small town with easy access to big-city amenities and a median household income of around $44,000. Bonner is home to the National Agricultural Center and Hall of Fame, the 30-year-old Renaissance Festival, and Capitol Federal Park at Sandstone—a popular concert site, particularly during the summer months. The town also offers multiple dining and shopping options, including the renowned Moon Marble Company.

Edwardsville. This town of approximately four thousand people lies near the Kansas Speedway and households have a median income of more than $40,000.

✳ To Do

DAY SPAS Elements Spa at Great Wolf Lodge (913-334-3070), 10401 Cabela Dr., Kansas City. Open by appointment Mon.–Thurs., 11–8 Fri., 9–8 Sat., 9–5 Sun. While the kids enjoy Great Wolf Lodge's expansive indoor water park, take a break at this full-service Zen-like spa. Get a Swedish or hot-stone massage, manicure, pedicure, or facial in calm, adult-friendly surroundings. Signature standard massages are $90.

BOATING AND FISHING Wyandotte County Park (913-596-7077), 126th St. and State Ave., Bonner Springs. Open 6–midnight. This is a well-maintained park with much new blacktop, Frisbee golf, and multiple ponds that allow fishing with a state license, but no swimming. Rolling hills create a soothing environment.

Wyandotte County Lake (913-573-8327), 91st St. and Leavenworth Rd., Bonner Springs. Open 6–. Built in 1943, this is a 300-acre lake with 1,500 land acres surrounding it. You'll find everything from channel catfish and bass to crappie, walleye, bluegill, and green sunfish here. With steep hills, sharp turns, deep woods, deer-crossing signs, an archery range, and an expansive marina, the range of activities is endless. There are shelter houses, a playground, and nature or bridle/hiking trails. The Mr. and Mrs. F. L. Schlagle Library environmental learning center offers field guides, binoculars, and age-specific summer children's programs.

GOLF Dub's Dread Golf Club (913-721-1333), 12601 Hollingsworth Rd., Kansas City. *Golf Digest* ranked this as the state's ninth best public course in 1996. Challenge yourself with sand bunkers and several water hazards, but wide fairways. Par 72, 18 holes, 6,993 yards.

Painted Hills Golf Club (913-334-3114), 7101 Parallel Pkwy., Kansas City. Hills and trees can impact shots throughout this bent grass and bluegrass course, which includes three par threes of more than 200 yards. Enjoy a clubhouse bar and grill. Par 70, 18 holes, 5,914 yards.

Sunflower Hills Golf Course (913-721-2727), 122nd St. and Riverview Rd., Bonner Springs. Open sunup to sundown. This public course features wide-open spaces with plenty of shade and manageable crowds. Par 72, 18 holes, 7,032 yards.

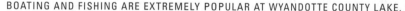

BOATING AND FISHING ARE EXTREMELY POPULAR AT WYANDOTTE COUNTY LAKE.

✳ Lodging

BED & BREAKFASTS Back in Thyme Guest House and Herb Gardens (913-422-5207; backin thyme.com), 1100 S. 130th St., Bonner Springs. Reservations recommended. This bed & breakfast sits amid acres of woods with a pond, an outdoor grill, and stone tables. Enjoy breakfast in the antiques-filled dining room and slumber in a brass bed with ceiling fans, plantation shutters, VCRs, and CD players. Enjoy complementary pop and popcorn, plus gourmet appetizers and wine/beer on weekends. There are also fresh herbs and antiques for sale. Full breakfast. $129–159.

HOTELS, RESORTS, AND LODGES ♿ (((ᵖ))) **Chateau Avalon** (913-596-6000; chateauavalonhotel .com), 701 Village West Pkwy., Kansas City. Take a French château and add a Roman dynasty suite with an enormous mural and sumptuous brocade, plus a pirate cove where skulls and crossbones decorate the bed. No two suites are alike here, but each one features a chromotherapy whirlpool spa with colored lights and water jets. Rose petals strewn across the bed or chocolate strawberries couldn't be more romantic extras. $139–509.

✐ ♿ (((ᵖ))) **Great Wolf Lodge** (913-299-7001; 1-800-608-9653 for reservations), 10405 Cabela Dr., Kansas City. From its rustic log walls to its 38,000-square-foot indoor water park, this is the ultimate family-focused resort. Kids love the multistory totem pole and four-story treehouse/water fort. More than a hundred competitive games in the Northern Lights Arcade and nightly story time keep kids busy for hours, while Mom and Dad enjoy

spa services and hit the treadmill in the Iron Horse Fitness Room. $150–400 (4–8 people).

✳ Where to Eat

EATING OUT

In Kansas City (KS)

♿ ♟ **Amigos Restaurant** (913-766-3300), 1709 Steele Rd., Kansas City. Open 8–2 AM daily. The Food Network featured this spot on its series *Meat & Potatoes,* but local Mexican food lovers already knew about their pleasant atmosphere, great food, and amazing prices. Try the giant burritos or even a burger and tall, cheap margaritas. Inexpensive.

✐ ♿ **Fritz's Union Station Restaurant** (913-281-2777), 250 N. 18th St., Kansas City. Serving breakfast, lunch, and dinner. Since 1954 this legendary restaurant has offered burgers and fries to visitors who place their orders by the phone at each table and then watch as a mechanical arm near the overhead train track delivers their meals. Shakes and chili are favorites, and kids love the atmosphere. Inexpensive.

♿ **Jazz, A Louisiana Kitchen** (913-328-0003; jazzkitchen.com), 1859 Village West Pkwy., Kansas City. Open 11 AM daily until 2 AM Fri.–Sun. Located just north of the Kansas Speedway, this popular spot offers French Quarter cuisine with spiciness for every taste. Try Cajun popcorn crawfish, oysters on the half shell, or shrimp Pierre on grits. Fried okra and po'boy sandwiches are other classics. Inexpensive.

In Bonner Springs

♿ **Freseros Mexican Restaurant** (913-441-4161), 220 Cedar, Bonner Springs. Open 11–9 Mon.–Sat. From the horse trough full of iced beverages to the bright yellow walls, a meal at Freseros will transport you to Mexico. Guacamole is made tableside and you can order sangria with lunch. Try the chimichangas steak fajitas or a lunch special served with rice and beans, and save room for Mexican fried ice cream. Inexpensive.

& Y **Kobi's Bar and Grill** (913-422-5657), 113 Oak St., Bonner Springs. Open 10–2 AM. Mon.–Sat., noon–2 Sun. Known as a bikers' bar, this establishment was originally opened by Czech immigrant Mama Kobialka. The family-owned bar offers favorites such as foot pegs (hand-battered mozzarella sticks), The Monster pork tender (a 12-ounce hand-breaded tenderloin), and Mexican specialties. Look for drink specials, and enjoy live entertainment on the back deck during summer weekends. Inexpensive.

& **Red Fortune Chinese Restaurant** (913-441-1988), 117 Oak St., Bonner Springs. Open 11–9 Mon.–Thurs./Sat., 11–10 Fri. This family-owned restaurant has served customers since 1993 with a brief intermission due to a fire. Try beef

THE FAMILY-OWNED RED FORTUNE CHINESE RESTAURANT OFFERS SPECIAL LUNCH PRICES.

with orange flavor, featuring crispy beef, dry orange peels, and chili peppers, or empress delight—batter-dipped and deep-fried chicken chunks and shrimp with vegetables and sweet sauce. There are bargain lunch combos with fried or plain rice, crunchy egg rolls or crab rangoon, and a delicious egg drop soup. Inexpensive.

✴ Entertainment

In Kansas City (KS)
✎ **Schlitterbahn Vacation Village Waterpark** (913-312-3110; schlitterbahn.com/kc), 9400 State Ave., Kansas City. Call for schedule. The world's largest tidal wave river, loads of slides, a giant hot tub, and even a beach are just a few offerings at this popular new water park. Contact them for current admission prices.

7th Street Casino (913-371-3500; 7th-streetcasino.com), 803 N. Seventh St., Kansas City. Open 24 hours. This sparkling new casino, in a renovated Masonic temple, is the first Native American–owned casino operation in the heart of Kansas City. The Wyandotte nation even offers penny slot machines.

& **Kansas City T-Bones** (816-931-3330; tbonesbaseball.com), 1800 Village West Pkwy., Kansas City. Check website for schedule. Offering minor league baseball with old-fashioned flair, the T-Bones were 2008 Northern League Champion in their independent professional league. There's also an extensive snack menu. Admission $6–16.

& **Kansas Speedway** (913-328-3300; kansasspeedway.com), I-70 and I-435, Kansas City. Contact them for events schedule. Offering the NASCAR

Sprint Cup Series and additional Indy Racing League (IRL) and Automobile Racing Club of America (ARCA) events, the Speedway also features the Sprint FanWalk, where selected guests may hang out between the garages, get driver autographs, and have their picture taken in the victory lane. Free parking, RV camping available, and tailgating is encouraged. Tickets $13–100s.

& **Kansas City Wizards** (913-387-3400; kcwizards.com), 1800 Village West Pkwy., Kansas City. Popular with local fans since they began playing in 1995, this soccer team won the MLS Cup in 2000 and the Lamar Hunt U.S. Open Cup in 2004. They posted their second-best home playing record in 2008. Their new KC Soccer Stadium opens in summer 2011, seating eighteen thousand fans for soccer. It will be the first soccer stadium in the country that includes both European and South American stadium features, plus typical American stadium amenities. Admission $15–125.

Lakeside Speedway (913-299-2040; lakesidespeedway.net), 5615 Wolcott Dr., Kansas City. Gates open at 5, April–Oct., hot laps 6:30, races 7:30; call for event schedule. If you love NASCAR and dirt track racing, this is the spot for you. Lakeside Speedway has hosted the national touring series for more than four decades, sometimes including dozens of custom-painted cars. Since 2000 the track has also crowned many Modified, Grand National, and Factory Stock champions. Adults $10; children 8–14 $6.

& ♈ **Stanford's Comedy Club** (913-400-7500; stanfordcomedyclub.com), 1867 Village West Pkwy., Kansas City. Check for scheduled performances.

Among the longest running, family-owned comedy clubs in the nation, Stanford's has drawn plenty of big names and up-and-coming stars in three decades, including Robin Williams, Roseanne Barr, and Damon Wayans. Enjoy food and beverages with the performance, too. Check for individual ticket prices.

✳ Selective Shopping

A note about shopping in Kansas City, Kansas: The city's largest concentration of retail is at The Legends, where most stores belong to major chains.

In Kansas City

& **Nigro's Western Store** (913-262-7500; nigroswesternstore.com), 3320 Merriam Ln., Kansas City. Open 10–5:30 Mon–Thurs., 10–6 Fri., 10–5 Sat. There must be a thousand pairs of jeans in this 70-year-old family business. Purchase Justin, Old West, and Durango boots or a new saddle and bridle for your horse, plus sterling jewelry and much more.

& **Knotty Rug Company** (913-677-1877; knottyrug.com), 4510 State Line Rd., Kansas City. Open 10–5 Tues.–Sat. or by appointment. Darrel Wingo bought a rug for an interior paint client in the early 2000s and never looked back. Today his shop offers antique and new Persian rugs, plus couches, tables, art, pillows, and home accessories.

✿ & **Palmer's Candies and Ice Cream** (913-788-2101), Village West Pkwy. #C115, Kansas City. Open 1–8 Mon.–Thurs., 10–9 Fri.–Sat., 11–6 Sun. If you love old-fashioned candy then be sure to stop here. This family-owned operation offers hundreds of varieties in bulk bins, from candy cigarettes and wax lips to NECCO

NIGRO'S WESTERN STORE

Wafers and Laffy Taffy. Grab an ice cream cone, too.

In Bonner Springs

Provence on the Prairie (913-441-6491; provenceontheprairie.com), 228 Oak St., Bonner Springs. Open 11–3 Tues.–Sat. Set inside the Madame Hatter Tea Room, the shop offers children's items, plus home decor and gifts with a French country focus, as well as seasonal decor.

✍ ♿ **Pink Zebra** (913-422-1555; pinkzebraboutique.com), 221 Oak St., Bonner Springs. Open 10–6 Tues.–Fri., 10–5 Sat. Jamie Istas says the store is a takeoff on her daughter's room and a store for girls of all ages.

Find leopard print and faux turquoise-encrusted purses, mini and maxi dresses, and loads of jewelry. Istas tries to keep items affordable and makes buys from markets in New York, Chicago, Dallas, and Las Vegas. There's also a room for princess parties.

✍ ♿ **Moon Marble Company** (913-441-1432; moonmarble.com), 600 E. Front St., Bonner Springs. Open 10–5 Tues.–Sat. You'll find every size and color of marble here, from cat's-eyes to confetti. Buy them individually or by the pound. On Tuesday, Friday, or Saturday in the summer watch marble artisan and co-owner, Bruce Breslow, craft a custom marble. This unusual 12-year-old store also offers old-fashioned toys including Big Wheels and die-cast cars, Abe Lincoln paper dolls, and even a Curious George jack-in-the-box. Purchase bulk gems, too.

✳ Special Events

May: **The Great American Barbecue** (847-232-9680; thinkbbq.com), 633 N. 130th St., Bonner Springs. Nearly two hundred BBQ teams compete for $90,000 prize money with brisket, ribs, side dishes, and more. Plenty of carnival rides and live bands provide entertainment.

July: **Wyandotte County Fair** (913-788-7898). Held since 1863, this annual event is the state's largest county fair, with petting zoos, 4-H exhibits, carnival rides, bucking bulls, and musical entertainment. Pets and camping gear are welcome.

September: **The Kansas City Renaissance Festival** (913-721-2110), Bonner Springs. Weekends, Labor Day–early Oct. This annual event recreates a 16th-century English village across 16 acres, with 165 artisans, 13 stages, strolling musicians, and food from enormous turkey legs to handmade pastries. Visitor costumes encouraged.

October: **NASCAR Car Sprint Cup Series** (866-460-RACE; kansasspeed way.com), 400 Speedway Blvd., Kansas Speedway/Kansas City. Opens at 8. Enjoy professional racing at one of NASCAR's newest tracks. Check for other special events.

November: **Olde World Christmas** (913-371-3264; strawberryhillmu seum.com), Strawberry Hill Museum and Cultural Center, Kansas City. Set in a 121-year-old Queen Anne–style mansion, this holiday celebration includes a display of ethnic and Victorian trees.

December: **Olde World Christmas** continues through December 27.

SOUTH AND WEST OF KANSAS CITY

GUIDANCE Baldwin City Chamber of Commerce (785-594-3200; baldwincitychamber.com), 720 High St., Baldwin City. Open Tues.–Fri. 10–2.

Franklin County Convention and Visitors Bureau (785-242-1411; visit ottawakansas.com, Ottawa/Wellsville), 2011 E. Logan, Ottawa. Open 9–5 weekdays, 9–4 Sat., noon–4 Sun.

Gardner Area Chamber of Commerce (913-856-6464; gardnerchamber .com), 109 E. Main, Gardner. Open 9–4 weekdays.

Garnett Area Chamber of Commerce (785-448-6767; garnettchamber.org), 419 S. Oak St., Garnett. Open 9–2 Mon.–Fri.; closed holidays.

Louisburg Chamber of Commerce (913-837-2826; louisburgkansas.com), 5 S. Peoria St., Ste. 103, Louisburg. Open 8–noon weekdays.

City of Osawatomie (913-755-2146; osawatomieks.org), 439 Main St., Osawatomie. Open 8–5 weekdays.

Paola Chamber of Commerce (913-294-4335; paolachamber.org), 202 W. Wea, Ste. 1, Paola.

GETTING THERE See *Johnson County Cities.*

GETTING AROUND See *Johnson County Cities.*

MEDICAL EMERGENCY (arranged alphabetically by city name)
Anderson County Hospital (785-448-3131), 421 Maple, Garnett.
Ransom Memorial Hospital (785-229-8200), 1301 S. Main St., Ottawa.
Miami County Medical Center (913-294-2327), 2100 Baptiste Dr., Paola.

✳ To See

HISTORIC PLACES, LANDMARKS, AND SITES

In Baldwin City

Santa Fe Trail Wagon Ruts and Ivan Boyd Prairie Reserve (785-594-3200), US 56 near Baldwin City. Stop at Black Jack Park, a roadside highway park along US 56, located 3 miles east of Baldwin City. Cross the footbridge and climb the short path into the Ivan Boyd Prairie Reserve. See native grasses and wild flowers growing in this area near the Santa Fe Trail.

Black Jack Cabin Roadside Park (785-883-2106; blackjackbattlefield.org), 163 E. 2000 Rd., near Baldwin City. Open dawn–dusk. Wagon ruts from the Santa Fe Trail are still clearly visible amid 18 acres of virgin prairie, just south of this site beside US 56—named for the black jack oaks that grow profusely in this area. In May 1856 men who supported slavery destroyed buildings and newspaper presses in nearby Lawrence, where the Free State movement had its headquarters. Abolitionist John Brown and his group subsequently killed five proslavery men on nearby Pottawatomie Creek. Many saw this altercation as evidence of civil war. Free.

Black Jack Battlefield and Nature Park (785-883-2106; blackjackbattlefield .org), 163 E. 2000 Rd., east of town. Daily, dawn–dusk, in winter; scheduled tours May 1–Oct. 17, Sat.–Sun. 1 PM. Self-guided tour materials are in the picnic shelter. This is the actual battlefield where John Brown led his militia against a proslavery force on June 2, 1856. This armed clash, the Battle of Black Jack, is considered by many to have been the first battle before the Civil War. Free.

Santa Fe Trail Well. Located along US 56, east of town. A short drive west from Black Jack Park, north on Washington Street, is the hand-dug well used by the inhabitants of Palmyra and travelers along the Santa Fe Trail and the last remnant of the former town. Palmyra's blacksmith shops kept busy repairing harnesses, fixing wagon wheels, and shoeing horses. Artifacts from this town site are stored in Baker University's Old Castle Museum. Free.

Clarice L. Osborne Memorial Chapel (785-594-4553; bakeru.edu/baker-life /spiritual-life/Osborne-chapel), Baker University campus/Baldwin City. Inside group tours available. Built in 1864, this chapel was disassembled in Sproxton, England, and rebuilt on the campus in 1996. Margaret Thatcher, former prime minister of Great Britain whose father had preached from the pulpit, and one surviving congregant, attended the dedication. The chapel is now a place for student worship services and small weddings. Free.

Quayle Rare Bible Collection (785-594-8393; bakeru.edu/baker-life/spiritual -life/quayle-collection), Baker University campus/Baldwin City. Open by appointment. Visit the Collins Library/Spencer Annex to view the collection of rare Bibles gifted to the University from the estate of Bishop William A. Quayle in 1925. Donation.

Midland Historic Railway and Santa Fe Depot (913-721-1211; midland-ry .org), 1515 W. High St. (beside the grain elevator), Baldwin City. Open June–Oct., Thurs.–Sun. runs; check schedule on website. Director Robert Altman featured this beautifully restored depot, on the National Register of Historic Places, in his movie *Kansas City.* An 1898 passenger car has a faithfully reproduced interior with exterior restoration underway. Ride the restored tourist excursion train for 11 miles or explore the Santa Fe depot and gift shop during Midland Railway hours. Thomas the Tank Engine also visits occasionally. Adults $7–10; children 2–11 $5–7.

Women's Bridge, near High and 11th Streets, Baldwin City. In the early 1890s Lucy Sweet Sullivan was mayor here for one year. She and her all-female council commissioned this beautiful arched stone and brick bridge and sidewalks to alleviate dirty skirts as women walked between the downtown area and the railroad depot. Look carefully, as the arch lies below road grade. Free.

In Ottawa

Dietrich Cabin, Fifth and Main Streets, Ottawa City Park/Ottawa. Located within view of the Carnegie Cultural Center, this 1859 log cabin was placed on the National Register of Historic Places in 1972. Free.

Franklin County Courthouse (785-242-6000), 301 S. Main St., Ottawa. This beautiful brick building with multiple towers and an expansive front "porch" celebrated a hundred years of service in 1993. It is considered one of the most outstanding designs of George P. Washburn, one of Kansas's best-known architects from the 19th-century.

Elsewhere

Gardner Junction Park (913-856-7535), 32500 W US 56, Gardner. A pretty little roofed kiosk marks the juncture of the Santa Fe, California, and Oregon trails amid a 1-acre park planted with 1800s-era flowers and native grasses. Information is available about the people who traveled through this area along a 400-foot paved trail.

St. Boniface Church (785-835-6341), 32300 NE Nevada Rd., Scipio/Garnett. Always open. Built in 1881, this simple white sanctuary with stained glass and an ornate altar was built in 1881 but is still in use weekly. Free.

Mine Creek Battlefield (913-352-8890), 20485 KS 52, Pleasanton. Open first Wed. in April through last Sat. in Oct., 10–5 Wed.–Sat. The deadly battle that raged in this now quiet and peaceful spot occurred on October 25, 1864, when 2,800 Union soldiers attacked—and defeated—8,000 Confederates along the Creek banks. The on-site museum offers exhibits related to life in this time period, with clothing, tools, and photographs; a walking trail with signs provide additional education. Adults $3; students $1; children under five free.

1857 Mineral Point Stagecoach House (785-489-2444; no calls on Sun.), 27851 NW Barton Rd., Westphalia. Samuel S. Tipton brought the first purebred shorthorn cattle to the state and later served weary travelers from this spot, too. There are beautiful views of the surrounding countryside from this 1857 three-story limestone building. See original wagon trail ruts and the site of coal digs used to keep the stagecoach stop operating. The original post office window and a copy of a stagecoach ticket, before Kansas statehood, are in the basement. A self-guided tour features 24 historical sites, or hitch a ride with the current owners, who have painstakingly restored the property and now offer bed & breakfast accommodations. Call for pricing.

THIS COPY OF A STAGECOACH TICKET BEFORE KANSAS STATEHOOD IS DISPLAYED AT 1857 MINERAL POINT STAGECOACH HOUSE.

MUSEUMS Baker University and the Old Castle Museum Complex (785-594-8380/2667; bakeru.edu), 618 Eighth St., Baldwin City. Call for an appointment. In the 1840s the Methodist church split over slavery. Founded in 1858 by Northern Methodists and abolitionists, the state's oldest four-year college was named for Methodist Bishop Osmon Baker. The famous Bishop Quayle Bible collection resides here. The Old Castle Museum Complex was the original university building. It includes a museum, the Kibbee log cabin, and the town of Palmyra's post office from 1857 to 1862. It also houses artifacts from early Kansas, Baker University, and the Methodist church, including a Potawatomi children's shirt and a Castle Mills cornmeal sack. Free.

Old Depot Museum (785-242-1250; old.depot.museum), 135 E. Tecumseh St., Ottawa. Open 10–4, Tues.–Sat., 1–4 Sun. Renovated in 1999, this museum is packed with memorabilia on two floors. See a one-room school with potbellied stove, a Victorian parlor with a vase of peacock feathers, and a complete dentist office. Vintage bags sit below a 1903 railroad timetable and the HO model train display fills an entire room. Adults $3; students $1.

John Brown Museum State Historic Site and John Brown Memorial Park (913-755-4384; kshs.org/places/johnbrown/index.htm), 10th and Main Streets, Osawatomie. Open 10–5 Tues.–Sat.; group tours by appointment. The last stop on the Underground Railroad, this museum was built around the 1854 Adair log cabin, where Reverend Samuel and Fiorella Adair (John Brown's half sister) allowed Brown to establish an informal headquarters during his efforts to halt slavery in the Kansas Territory. Spacious for its time, the cabin still showcases period furnishings, including a full kitchen, parlor, and attic bedroom with child's cradle and pallet. Suggested donation: adults $3; students, $1. KSHS Inc. members and children under five free.

Osawatomie History Museum (913-755-6781), 628 Main St., Osawatomie. Open 1–4 Tues.–Sun. There's a straitjacket from the state hospital that once operated here, farm axes, prairie dresses, and a hall of honor for police and veterans. See the last-known metal and wood-walled caboose from the 1930s when one train per hour came through town.

TOWNS Aubry. William Clarke Quantrill, a Confederate fighter, led raids in and around this tiny town, killing many and taking property. Union troops often camped along the military road (now Metcalf Avenue), between Fort Leavenworth and Fort Scott, as they sought the raiders. Seeing their retaliatory actions, Aubry resident Bill Anderson joined Quantrill's Raiders and became known as Bloody Bill.

Baldwin City. From here and 300 miles westward, US 56 roughly follows the Old Santa Fe trail. Kansas became a territory and white settlement began in this area in 1854, and the town of Palmyra was founded the following year. Baker University was established three years later and the town of Baldwin was named for John Baldwin, a fellow from Ohio who hauled a steam sawmill here in 1857. Palmyra and Baldwin merged by 1863.

Edgerton. This town was named for a railroad engineer who helped lay track nearby in 1883. Today Edgerton is returning to its railroad past with an upcoming "inland port" that will create a path from Edgerton and greater Kansas City to the Pacific Rim.

Gardner. This small town was incorporated in 1886 and named for Governor Gardner of Massachusetts because most settlers favored Kansas being an antislavery state.

Garnett. This is the largest city in Anderson County and, some people say, the best kept secret in Kansas. There's plenty of outdoor activity, from lakes to thousands of acres of parkland, a trailhead for a 51-mile hiking trail, and a bustling downtown. Restaurants and shops offer Italian, diner, and Mexican food, plus coffee, antiques, and gifts. There's a thriving community theater, too.

La Cygne. The town was founded in 1869 after it became certain that the St. Louis and San Francisco Railroad would come through. Flour manufacturing took hold in the 1870s and a coal mine opened in 1881. Today the Burlington Northern Santa Fe Railroad passes through the town, which has a population of around a thousand people.

Louisburg. With less than three thousand residents, this small town served as home for a number of American Indian tribes in the 1800s, with traders, missionaries and settlers following by the mid-1850s. After the Civil War it was called New St. Louis until 1870. A railroad depot and school soon followed. The present town was incorporated in 1882. Beautiful wooded areas, plentiful streams, and native prairie land characterize the area, from which many residents commute to larger cities.

Osawatomie. The "Cradle of the Civil War" combines names of Osage and Potawatomie tribes and was incorporated in October 1854. The Missouri Pacific Railroad came through in 1879 and continues to influence the town's development. Five Osawatomie sites are listed on the National Register of Historic Places, including John Brown Memorial Park, John Brown Museum State Historic Site, the Queen Anne–style Mills House, and the Creamery Bridge and Asylum Bridge. Other historic sights include a monument to men killed in the Battle of Osawatomie, the Old Stone Church—one of the first built in Kansas—and a memorial honoring John Brown's son who died on the day of the battle.

Ottawa. Eight interactive kiosks located along Ottawa's main street tell the story of each block on which they were placed, including black-and-white photos. The 200 block, in Ottawa's central business district, is listed on the National Register of Historic Places, including the Franklin County Courthouse.

ONE BLOCK OF OTTAWA'S DOWNTOWN AREA IS LISTED ON THE NATIONAL REGISTER OF HISTORIC PLACES.

THE DOWN TOWN OTTAWA HISTORIC DISTRICT

Is a block of commercial structures built between 1872 and 1900 of late Victorian styling with Renaissance, Eclectic and some Classical features. The buildings are individualistic but have the same underlying style and character. Their uniqueness lies in almost unaltered facades and great aesthetic compatibility. This block was placed on The National Register of Historic Places, June 29, 1972.

FRANKLIN COUNTY HISTORICAL SOCIETY MARKER

Paola. Previously settled by Indian tribes and called Peoria Village, Paola was named for an Italian town by an Italian missionary in the 1850s and incorporated in 1855. Approximately five thousand residents currently live here. A beautiful Victorian gazebo anchors the town square park with fountains, mature trees, and plenty of park benches. A nearby circus program mural from 1924 commemorates Paola as a regular circus performance location.

Wellsville. Located just off I-35, the county's second largest town was founded in 1884. Senior artist Grandma Layton is one of Wellsville's most famous residents. She escaped years of depression through art, and a display of her work is at the Wellsville Library.

✳ To Do

DAY SPAS ♿ **Capelli Salon and Day Spa** (785-242-4477; capelli-dayspa.com), 129 S. Main St., Ottawa. Open in summer 9–noon Tues., 9–6 Wed.–Fri., 9–3 Sat.; check for winter hours. Francine Leone has created an

PAOLA'S TOWN SQUARE

upscale, urban environment in her full-service salon and spa, with marble floors, Grecian columns, and her grandmother's dazzling crystal chandelier. $50 for 60-minute massage; $45 and up for a facial.

GOLF Garnett Country Club and Golf Course (785-448-7709), N. Lake Rd., Garnett. Open sunrise–sunset in peak season; 9–dark in winter. Check out this course for a challenging game. There's also a 10-tee driving range and semiprivate club with large grass greens. Par 35, 9 holes, 5,600 yards.

Falcon Lakes (913-724-4653), 4605 Clubhouse Dr., Basehor. Enjoy a links-style layout with zoysia fairways, undulating hills, and multiple tee decks for every hole. Par 72, 18 holes, 7,098 yards.

Osawatomie Golf Course (913-755-4769), 327 Bethel Church Rd., Osawatomie. Play on bent grass and bluegrass with wide fairways and fast greens as you enjoy this scenic course. Par 71, 18 holes, 6,147 yards.

HORSEBACK RIDING Hillsdale State Park and Wildlife Area (913-783-4366), 26000 W. 255th St., Paola. Horseback riding enthusiasts enjoy the Saddle Ridge equestrian area with 32 miles of marked trails and camping available.

HUNTING Madl Outfitters (785-594-3900), 502 Ames St., Baldwin City. Ted Madl arranges individual hunting trips, particularly for white tail and turkey and black powder bow or rifle. A five-day white tail hunt, including lodging, costs $2,000–3,000. The nearby Santa Fe Market sells hunting licenses.

Hillsdale State Park and Wildlife Area (913-783-4366), 26000 W. 255th St.,

Paola. During hunting season hunters may bag waterfowl and game big and small across 7,000 designated acres.

✳ Green Space

Marais des Cygnes National Wildlife Refuge (1-800-344-WILD), 24141 KS 52, Pleasanton. This area, with the Marais des Cygnes River as its primary water feature, was once Osage Indian hunting ground. The name of the refuge, previously known for its abundance of swans, is French for "marsh of swans." Huge pelican flocks, brilliant hued wood ducks, and mallards are only a few species in this enormously diverse wildlife and marsh area. Hunt for deer during archery season and turkey during spring hunting season, although primary hunting is for waterfowl. Fish for sunfish, bass, crappie, and catfish, or hike up to 1.5 miles while photographing wildlife. Primitive camping allowed.

Hillsdale Lake (913-783-4366), 26000 W. 255th St., Paola. This Army Corps of Engineers lake area offers 51 miles of shoreline with plenty of fish, including walleye, catfish, largemouth bass, crappie, and bluegill. Thirty-two miles of marked trails that wind through hardwood forests, occasional cliffs, and meadows are available for hiking, backpacking, and mountain biking.

Hillsdale State Park and Wildlife Area/Jayhawk Marina (913-783-4366), 26000 W. 255th St., Paola. The 4,500-acre reservoir was completed in 1982. This busy facility offers boat and personal watercraft rentals, fuel, and a convenience store. There are also 163 boat slips and 35 hydroports for personal watercraft and seven boat ramp areas.

Douglas State Fishing Lake (785-842-8562; baldwin-city.com/rec/douglas lake), 1 mile north and 3 miles east of Baldwin City. Travel on gentle hills near this 180-acre lake full of bluegill, channel catfish, and many other fish. There are two boat docks, fish cleaning stations, and primitive camping with pit restrooms. Hunting and trapping are also allowed.

Miami State Fishing Lake (913-783-4507), 359th St., west of Somerset Road. This lake offers 101 acres of water bordered by 150 acres of tree-filled hills and the Marais des Cygnes River. You'll find a boat ramp, a courtesy dock, and multiple piers. Permits required.

Louisburg Middle Creek State Fishing Lake (913-783-4507), south of 335th St. on Metcalf Rd., Louisburg. The 220-acre land area surrounding this lake offers gravel pullouts for camping, plus picnic tables, fire rings, and toilets.

Lake Garnett, off N. Lake Rd., North Park/Garnett. This park offers plenty of options, including swimming, trap shooting, and rifle ranges, plus horseshoe pitching, sand volleyball, basketball and tennis courts, and a municipal swimming pool.

Cedar Valley Reservoir, CR 1500, near Garnett. Water sports are big business at Garnett's largest lake, from water skiing, jet skiing, and boating to fishing and RV or wilderness camping in designated areas. There's also an ATV trail for use with a permit from Garnett city hall.

Lewis-Young Park/Lake (913-837-5371), 271st and Jingo Rd., Louisburg. This 2-acre community lake in a pretty park offers decent populations of channel catfish, crappie, and largemouth bass.

✳ Lodging

BED & BREAKFASTS ♿ Canaan Oaks
(913-557-5378; canaanoaks.com), 21125 W. 303rd St., Paola. This lovely, modern bed & breakfast with expansive deck and wooded surroundings offers seven rooms (two have kitchenettes) and one suite with a full kitchen and sleeper couch. Individual rooms feature beautiful quilts, antique furnishings, and soothing colors, many with private baths. Full breakfast. $125–145.

Victorian Lady (913-294-4652/888-VICLADY; viclady.net), 402 S. Pearl St., Paola. Located near Paola's quaint town square, this B&B has been called "one of the top 50 romantic getaways in the country" by *Kansas City Magazine*. This family-owned Victorian colonial revival home offers three rooms full of period antiques, hardwood floors, florals, and lace. Make a reservation for afternoon or Victorian high teas and schedule a massage or candlelight dinner. Full breakfast. $125–135.

((ȹ)) **Three Sisters Inn Bed & Breakfast** (785-594-3244; 3sistersinn.com), 1035 Ames St., Baldwin City. Enter a world of jewel-tone floral carpet and wallpaper, hand-carved wood banisters, and lovely antiques. The treetop attic suite offers privacy, loads of space, and multiple skylights. The gazebo and surrounding gardens provide a gorgeous spot for outdoor events. Continental breakfast weekdays; full breakfast weekends. $99–149.

CAMPING ((ȹ)) Homewood RV Park and Campground
(785-242-5601, homewoodrvpark.com), I-35 Exit 176 and one block north, between Ottawa/Williamsburg. Office opens at 3; self-check-in available. This small but tidy park offers plenty of shade at the perimeter and great bird watching. The owners live next door. Pull-throughs and back-ins for 1–2 people are $20; $3 per extra person. Tent camping for 1–2 $14; $3.50 for more than 8 people; dump station $7.50.

♿ ((ȹ)) **Garnett Inn Suites/RV Park** (877-448-4200), 109 Prairie Plaza Rd., Garnett. A favorite in Garnett, this inn offers refrigerators and microwaves, plus continental breakfast, on-site laundry facilities, and a full-service

THREE SISTERS INN BED & BREAKFAST OFFERS TURN-OF-THE-CENTURY-INSPIRED ACCOMMODATIONS.

bar (no food). Two suites have king beds and whirlpool tubs. Five pull-through RV slots with full hookups and six others are around a circle drive. $63–80; $15 RV slots.

Garnett Campground/Cedar Valley Reservoir (785-448-5496), Kentucky and 1500 Roads, 7 miles west of Garnett. This is a great spot for boating, with three boat ramps and three floating docks. Twelve RV spots are near the park entrance, and primitive camping is also available. Camping/RV rates $5–16.

Hillsdale Lake (913-783-4366), 26000 W. 255th St., Paola. The massive Army Corps of Engineers lake area also offers camping. With 200 designated sites; 157 with electric/water hookups and nightly utility fee; three bath/shower houses available April 15–Oct. 15.

LODGES AND INNS

((ᵞ)) **Kirk House** (785-448-7514; thekirkhouse.net), 145 W. Fourth Ave., Garnett. Spacious rooms with gorgeous antique and reproduction furnishings, original woodwork, and sumptuous linens characterize this recently restored 1913 mansion. Massive sunrooms, a tile fireplace face that was perhaps crafted by Tiffany's, and a dining room so large that it's called a hall are only a few other features. Six bedrooms are available for groups only. House rental/10 adults $600; $25 per additional guest.

Grand Suites (913-731-3344), 509 Main, Osawatomie. Nan Bewley transformed several previous apartments into inviting multibedroom guest suites up the stairs from her hand-painted garden mural. Skylights and live plants decorate the hallway.

One suite features two dedicated bedrooms with a third bed in the main room, a fully equipped kitchen, a bath, and a small sunporch. $75.

& ((ᵞ)) **The Lodge at Baldwin City** (785-594-3900; baldwincitylodge .com), 502 Ames St., Baldwin City. Award-winning wildlife mounts line lobby and lounge walls in this pretty log-faced property beside US 56, and co-owner Ted Madl handles their Madl Outfitters business. The lounge once served as the office of Modle Implement, owned by the current owner's father. Twenty rooms offer coffeepots, refrigerators, and microwaves; two suites have full kitchen, fireplace, and Jacuzzi tub. Enjoy mini-golf, a full-service bar/lounge, and a banquet room. Mini-golf rates: adults $3.50; children 5–12 $3; children 4 and under $2; check for specials. $69–99.

✱ Where to Eat

EATING OUT

In Baldwin City

& **The Melange Apron** (785-594-0519; melangeapron.com), 519 Ames, Baldwin City. Open 11–9 Mon.–Thurs., 11–10 Fri.–Sat., 11–8 Sun. This fun little place offers a coffee/alcohol bar and a children's playroom. Customers can also buy most furnishings in the restaurant. Try savory black bean vegetable soup, custom burgers, or apple smoked grilled salmon with a salad and grilled vegetables. Choose from 40 bottled beers, wine, or cocktails and save room for chocolate bread pudding. Inexpensive.

& **Cordoba's Family Restaurant** (785-594-3123), 516 Ames, Baldwin

City. Open 6–3 Mon., 6–9 Tues.–Fri.,
7–9 Sat., 7–3 Sun. Metal folk art turtles and fish decorate brilliant-hued
walls throughout this cheerful place,
with a large menu. A floor-to-ceiling
mural with massive Mayan pyramids,
painted by Japanese and German foreign exchange high school students,
reflects the co-owner's heritage as a
Mayan Indian. Try breakfast eggs and
chorizo with creamy refried black
beans and rice or home fries and
toast. Inexpensive.

In Garnett
& **The Coffee Loft** (785-448-2253),
130 E. Fifth Ave., Garnett. Open 7–8
Mon./Tues./Thurs., 7–9 Fri., 9–9 Sat.
Two-story stone walls, hardwood
floors, and a display case full of goodies characterize this spacious and cozy
café. But there's more than espresso
and homemade cookies here. Breakfast, sandwiches, soups, salads, and
Kansas wine round out the menu.
Stop in for live music, book signings,
or even a live talk show. Inexpensive.

Y **Trade Winds Bar and Grill** (785-
448-5856), 110 W. Fifth St., Garnett.
Open 11–midnight Tues.–Thurs.,
11–2 Fri.–Sat. A popular local hangout since 1991, this is a great spot to
play pool, find an inexpensive cheeseburger, enjoy a bottle of beer, or try
homemade peanut butter pie. Inexpensive.

& **Bellini's Italian Café** (785-448-
6896), 604 N. Maple/Economy Inn,
Garnett. Open 11–9 Tues.–Sat., 11–3
Sun. This motel café is known for its
lasagna and fettuccine sauce, plus
pizza and fried calamari. Check out
their new place next door, too—The
Five Spot Mexican Grill and Bar.
Inexpensive.

In Louisburg
& **La Mesa Mexican Restaurant**
(913-837-3455; la-mesa.com), 2 W.
Amity St., Louisburg. Open 11–10
weekdays, 11–10:30 weekends. This
family-owned restaurant has 10 locations through Kansas, Nebraska, Iowa,
and Missouri, but the bright decor
will take you straight to Mexico. Try
the cheese dip, *chilaquiles,* or steak
charro—a 12-ounce rib eye with
charro beans, rice, and potatoes. They
also make great margaritas. Inexpensive.

& **Phoenix Chinese Restaurant**
(913-837-2088), 108 S. Broadway St.,
Louisburg. Open 11–9 daily. Delicious General Tso's chicken and house
fried rice are highlights at this popular restaurant, which serves large portions. Inexpensive.

Louisburg Hometown Pizza (913-
837-2211), 19 N. Broadway, Louisburg. Open 11–2, 4–9 weekdays,
11–11 Fri., 7–11, Sat., 8–9 Sun. This
no frills spot serves great pizza. Crispy
thin crusts and good sauce are highlights. Specialty pizzas include the Big
Kahuna, Caveman (all meat), and
Everything But the Pizza. No credit
cards. Inexpensive.

In Paola
Beethoven's #9 The Restaurant
(913-294-3000; beethovens-paola
.com), 110 W. Peoria St., Paola. Open
11–9 Thurs.–Sat. This popular restaurant is best known for its German
dishes, from sauerbraten to Wiener
schnitzel, but you'll also find steak,
seafood, sandwiches, and salads amid
rustic decor. Inexpensive–moderate.

Emery Steakhouse (913-294-4148),
119 W. Peoria St., Paola. Open 11–9

Wed.–Sat. Customers say that Emery serves the best tenderloins in the state. Other favorites include sirloin tips, all-you-can-eat boiled shrimp or crab, and prime rib dinners. Inexpensive–moderate.

Elsewhere

&. **Sandbar Sub Shop** (785-242-5555), 127 S. Main, Ottawa. Open 11–8 Mon.–Sat. Step into this tropical environment and order a luscious smoothie or The Cyclone, a combination of grilled chicken, cheddar cheese, lettuce, tomato, and Patty's Killer Dip. Everyone agrees it's what makes this sandwich dynamite. Inexpensive.

GARNETT'S CHAMBER PLAYERS COMMUNITY THEATRE OFFERS PRODUCTIONS IN A RENOVATED CHURCH.

&. **Brandi's Grill and Bakery** (913-757-3663), 110 S. Fourth St., La Cygne. Open 11–8:30 Tues.–Sun. Inside this bright yellow building, the Pattersons are known for homemade pies, cakes, and other baked goods. More goodies include caramel malts; the Sunrise Sandwich, with fried egg, bacon, tomato, and melted cheese; or hand-tenderized and breaded pork medallion sandwiches. Inexpensive.

Whistle Stop Café (913-256-4110), 901 S. Sixth St., Osawatomie. Open 5:30–8 Mon.–Sat., 6:30–8 Sun. A pebbled train track leads from the front desk to the buffet area of this popular restaurant, known for breakfast all day, excellent broasted chicken, 8-ounce pork tenderloins, and a daily buffet with food like you're at grandma's house. Inexpensive.

The Taste of China (913-592-2636), 22382 S. Harrison, Spring Hill. Open 11–10 Mon.–Sat., 11–9 Sun. This is a favorite spot for Chinese food. Try their pineapple chicken, Thai curry, Peking duck, or fried mushrooms. Inexpensive.

✳ Entertainment

In Garnett

&. **Walker Art Collection** (785-448-3388/library), 125 W. Fourth Ave., Garnett Library/Garnett. Open 10–8 Mon./Tues./Thurs. 10–5:30, Wed./Fri., 10–4 Sat. Maynard Walker was a local art enthusiast. Whenever the library is open, visitors may enter the gallery. It's one of the most impressive small collections west of the Mississippi, with dozens of pieces from artists such as Dale Chihuly, Walter Kuhn, Mary Ronin, and Louis Wain. Free.

Valley View Elk Farm (785-448-6788/3085), 19324 NW KS 31/27640 NW Jewel Rd., Garnett. Get within a fence away from more than 120 head of elk, which are most active in early morning and evening. Tours available; call ahead (no Sundays). $2.50 per person.

&. **Chamber Players Community Theatre** (785-304-1683; thechamberplayers.org), 140 W. Fifth Ave., Thelma Moore Community Playhouse/Garnett. Check for schedule. This dinner theater in a renovated church is a delightful activity. Enjoy a multicourse meal prepared and served by folks involved with the theater, and then watch a stage production such as *Rumpelstiltskin* or *Steel Magnolias* in this intimate setting. Look for the turquoise doors and prepare for fun. Adults $22; high school and under $17.

Elsewhere

Baldwin City Community Theater (785-594-7440; baldwintheater.com), 816 High St., Baldwin City. There's always a summer musical, a spring dinner theater, and a fall melodrama offered by this nonprofit company. Toddlers to seniors participate together in all aspects of production, from acting to stagehand. Recent shows have included *Seussical*, *Music Man*, and, of course, *The Wizard of Oz*. Adults $8; children $6.

&. **Louisburg Cider Mill** (913-837-5202; louisburgcidermill.com), 14730 KS 68, Louisburg. Ranked by MSNBC among the nation's top 10 cider mills, Louisburg Cider Mill presses millions of pounds of Jonathan and Red Delicious apples each year to create their all-natural cider. Purchase a wide range of beverages, foods, cookware, and food-related gifts, including cider and cider donuts, in the gift shop.

&. **Cedar Cove Feline Conservation** (913-837-5515; saveoursiberians), 3783 KS 68, Louisburg. Open in summer 10–3, Sat.–Sun., and 10–dusk on first Sat.; tours also available year-round. You'll be blown away by this feline conservatory located in the midst of Miami County countryside. Marvel at the size and power of these magnificent tigers, and see mountain lions and African spotted leopards up close. Folks who work here speak passionately about these animals and their preservation. Adults/children 4 years and up $5.

&. **Barnhart's Honey-Berry Farm** (785-489-2565), 25571 NW Barton Rd., Westphalia. Open most days except Sunday. Pick your own blueberries, in season, and enjoy pancakes with fresh blueberry compote on Saturday mornings. Buy fresh honey and honeycomb, 10 different flavors of lip balm, neck pillows, frozen blueberries, and other goodies at their on-site store, anytime. Group tours $3 per person.

&. **Lumberyard Arts Center** (lumberyardartscenter.org), 718 High St., Baldwin City. Open 3–6 Tues.–Fri., noon–6 Sat. Call for a tour. Volunteers are converting an old lumberyard into a home for the arts in downtown Baldwin City. Phase I includes a one-room gallery with rotating displays by various artists. There's space awaiting a theater, art sales, and private events.

&. **Powell Observatory** (913-837-5305; askonline.org), 10297 W. 263rd St., Lewis/Young Park/Louisburg. The Astronomical Society of Kansas City built this observatory in 1984 with one of the nation's largest telescopes that is regularly open to the public and the largest in a five-state area. Public programs take place every weekend, from May through October, and ASKC members frequently bring personal telescopes to the courtyard so visitors may view and learn about the night sky. Ask about StarBright programs, with talks on astronomy and personal viewing. Free.

WINERIES Holy-Field Vineyard and Winery (913-724-9463; holy fieldwinery.com), 1807 158th St., Basehor. Open 11–6 Mon.–Fri., 9:30–6 Sat., noon–6 Sun. This 14-acre vineyard includes Native American and French hybrid grapes with original vines planted in 1986. Taste more than a dozen vintages, featuring some that have received international wine-making awards and medals, including the Jefferson Cup, a top wine industry award.

Somerset Ridge Vineyard and Winery (913-491-0038; somerset ridge.com), 29725 Somerset Rd., Somerset. Open Wed.–Sun. Located near Louisburg Cider Mill, this is a family-run operation where you can see grape vines from the tasting room doorway. If you're lucky, proprietors Dennis or Cindy Reynolds will pour their wines for you. Several won 2009 Jefferson Cup Awards.

✴ Selective Shopping

In Baldwin City
Kiss Me Kate's: A Celtic Conspiracy (785-979-5887; trubrit.com), 813 Eighth St., Baldwin City. Retail open 10–5 Tues–Sat.; lunch served 11:30–2; treats and refreshments available any time; call about dinner. Groups should make reservations. This little store is full of Irish T-shirts, Connemara marble, jewelry, and sou-

venirs. Soups and salads, meatloaf, and chicken panini sandwiches are a few offerings you may find, with desserts from Scottish shortbread to coconut cream pie. As you wait for your order, a small slice of blueberry bread with a sweet glaze arrives on a tiny silver tray. The owner often sits down with solo diners.

The Pink Lady Consignment Clothing Boutique, Charlotte's Daughters Antiques and Gifts, Gathering Grounds Coffee Bar and Bistro and Design Specialties (785-594-7465), 715–721 Eighth St., Baldwin City. Open daily 11 AM; closes 5 PM Mon.–Tues/Fri.–Sat., 6 Wed., 7 Thurs. There's a lot happening under this roof! Grab a latte as you enter and stop by Mike Langrehr's jewelry design business, established in 1976, before you pass Francelle's original art and portraits booth and a case full of Summit's Steps Minerals. Purchase upscale consignment clothing and antiques at the back of the building.

Vesecky Farms (785-594-2493), 1814 N. 600 Rd., Baldwin City. Open weekdays 8–12, 5–dark; all day Sat. Sharon and John Vesecky sell pasture-raised heritage and broad-breasted turkeys at Thanksgiving and typically welcome strawberry pickers from late May to early June. Pick them yourself, and John will charge by the pound. No credit cards.

& **Quilter's Paradise** (785-594-3477; quiltingfabricsupply.com), 713 Eighth St., Baldwin City. Open 10–5 Mon.–Sat. Quilters will appreciate three thousand bolts of fabric in this packed store. Gorgeous hanging quilts, plus patterns and kits provide added inspiration.

♿ **Mitch's Custom Motorcycles** (785-594-3822), 713 High St., Baldwin City. Open 9–5 Mon.–Fri. Mitch Donovan usually has a dozen Harleys and custom bikes on hand and repairs include full engine rebuilds. He's always hard at work on the retail floor. No credit cards.

Antiques on the Prairie (785-594-7555), 520 High St., Baldwin City. Open 10–6 Mon./Tues./Fri., 10–7 Wed.–Thurs., 9–7 Sat. About 35 vendors offer everything from antique wall telephones and bicycles to handmade lace doilies, Pfaltzgraff tableware, baby doll clothes, and weather-beaten license plates.

In Garnett
Passing Thru Clocks (913-448-6724), 305 N. Spruce, Garnett. Open when the door's open; the owner lives on site. Myron Harsch creates enormous handcrafted oak, walnut, or cherry clock cabinets with amazing mechanized designs that include a little girl brushing her dog's teeth and a locomotive engineer who rings the bell. He also restores clocks using a parts inventory that spans three rooms of his barn workshop.

♿ **Country Fabrics** (785-448-0003), 108 E. Fifth Ave., Garnett. Open 10–5 Tues.–Fri., 9–2 Sat. Ninety percent of customers come from outside of Garnett because they know they can find more than two thousand bolts of quilt-shop-quality cottons for under $5 a yard. The shop is jam-packed and also sells 108-inch backing material at under $8 per yard. No credit cards.

Schmucker's (785-448-6728), 19777 NW 1700 Rd., Garnett. Open 9–12 and 1–5 weekdays, 8–noon Sat. Customers from Yates Center, Wichita,

and Colorado travel gravel roads to this tiny shop, renowned for its health supplements plus horseshoes and Amish hats. Elmer and Katie Schmucker started their business after she became seriously ill and believes supplements cured her.

♿ **Cedar Creek Outfitters** (785-448-3781), 317 S. Maple, Garnett. Open 7–6 Tues./Fri., 1–5:30 Wed.–Thurs., 8:30–4 Sat. An official gun dealer of the National Wild Turkey Foundation (NWTF), this is a spot where stuffed bobcat and wild turkeys watch you, a telescope beckons, and dozens of minnows await hooks.

In Ottawa
Ottawa Music (785-242-4800; ottawamusicstore.net), 120 E. 19th St., Ottawa (this is a one-way street, going north, which runs parallel to US 59). Open 10–7 Mon.–Thurs., 10–5 Fri.–Sat. This shop has offered everything from electric and acoustic guitars to clavinovas, recorders, banjos, trumpets, and mandolins for more than 30 years. Check their enormous selection of Broadway, rock, country, wedding, and guitar sheet music and all sizes of amplifiers. These fellows also teach music lessons and rent and repair instruments.

♿ **Aunt Jenny's Stitch 'n' Stuff** (785-242-2440), 204 S. Main St., Ottawa. Open 10–6 Mon.–Sat. This is an interesting combination of quilt fabric store and display space for members of the Ottawa Art Guild—approximately two dozen craftspeople—most of whom create quilts and other fabric items. You'll also find Paper Haven—once a freestanding business—offering vellum, card stock, mini stamps, stickers, and ribbons.

& **Country Living** (785-242-1465; atouchofcountryliving.com), 123 Main St., Ottawa. Open 10–5 Tues.–Sat. Country gifts and decor fill floor to ceiling of what was Blum's Meat Market in the 1920s. Amid country-inspired decor, candles, and furniture lies a big—and very popular—surprise—the "bling room." Purchase sparkling T-shirts, purses, scarves, jewelry, and more, located in this country haven.

Elsewhere
Rutlader Outpost (866-888-6779; rutladeroutpost.com), 335th St./KS 69, Louisburg. Behind old-fashioned storefronts this multifaceted operation begins with Rutlader Antique and Trading Co., a cavernous space packed with antiques, collectibles, and crafts. You'll also find the Middle Creek Opry show here, performances by the seven-member Middle Creek Band, a gift shop, and even an RV park. Check for show schedule and pricing.

✳ Special Events

February: **Chocolate Auction** (785-594-3200; baldwinarts.org), Stony Point Hall, Baldwin City. This event features hundreds of chocolate cookies, cream puffs, pies, and more, plus art by local and regional artists. It's a major fundraiser for the Baldwin Community Arts Council.

April: **Midland Railway's Easter Egg Hunt Trains** (1-800-651-0388; midland-ry.org), Santa Fe Depot/Baldwin City. The historic train takes children to Easter egg hunts in the former town site of Norwood.

May: **John Brown's Battle of Black Jack Celebration** (785-594-2100; blackjackbattlefield.org), park 2 miles east of Baldwin City on 2000 Rd., Baldwin City. This event includes battlefield tours, cabin tours, a campfire supper, and trips down the Black Jack Nature Trail. **Kansas City Hot Air Balloon Invitational** (913-338-2628; kchabi.com), Gardner. Mass ascensions, competitive flights, and 45-minute individual balloon rides are part of this three-year-old event. **Miami County Farm Tour** (913-294-4045), Louisburg. See modern and unique farms throughout the county raising emus and blackberries and much more during this popular weekend event.

June: **John Brown Jamboree** (913-755-4114), Osawatomie. Enjoy a carnival, food and craft booths, plus an ice cream social car show and talent shows. Enter a fishing or tennis tournament, too. **Edgerton Frontier Days** (913-893-6682; frontier-days .com), downtown Edgerton. This three-day event has something for everyone, from an auction and truck pull to a canoe race, vendor booths, and ice cream social. **Garnett "Hydroplane Thunderfest"** (913-515-3237; RACENRA.com), 100 Park Rd., Lake Garnett. This festival showcases hydroplane drivers from 12 states, with contests and action for three days.

July: **Heartland Car Show** (913-294-4335; paolachamber.org), downtown Park Square, Paola. If you love vintage cars and trucks you'll enjoy this afternoon–evening event that fills the square. **Miami County Fair and Rodeo, ATV/Motorcycle Flat Track Race and Demolition Derby** (913-294-4306; miamicounty

APPLES ARE PROCESSED AT LOUISBURG CIDER MILL.

fair.com), Miami County Fairgrounds. Rodeo action and vehicle events add excitement to this county fair that offers classic carnival rides, loads of food, and much more.

August: **Roots Festival** (913-557-3893; rootsfestival.org), Historic Downtown Square, Paola. Enjoy two days of music, a BBQ cook-off that is part of the Kansas City Barbecue Society circuit, and loads of vendors.

September: **Louisburg Cider Mill Ciderfest and Craft Fair** (913-837-2143), Louisburg. Sample freshly

brewed cider and cider donuts and purchase food/beverage items made by the mill and other Kansas purveyors. Enjoy live country music, visit dozens of craft and food booths, or navigate the corn maze. Kids will love the inflatable carnival games and pumpkin patch, too. **Cornstock/ Anderson County Corn Festival** (cornstock.net; Garnett, experience-garnettks.net). Music, food, a 5K run/walk, a regatta, and a pageant characterize this annual event.

October: **Louisburg Cider Mill Ciderfest and Craft Fair** continues. **Maple Leaf Festival** (785-594-3200). Third full weekend in Baldwin City. Join twenty-five thousand visitors and enjoy food, crafts, and entertainment.

November: **Baldwin City Holiday Light Parade** (785-594-3200), downtown Baldwin City. Santa arrives on an antique fire engine to light the community Christmas tree, dancers perform, and an evening parade features lighted floats and horses.

December: **Holiday carriage rides** in Paola take visitors by 1800s homes located throughout the town.

Northeast Kansas: Cozy Corner

2

INTRODUCTION

Lewis and Clark passed through Kansas in summer 1804, declaring the area "one of the most butifull Plains, I ever Saw." Today the state's two largest universities, a university for American Indian students and a small, highly respected Catholic college, operate in this area.

Benedictine College has been a part of Atchison since its incorporation in 1868. Accredited as a four-year liberal arts college in 1927, and with less than two thousand students, Benedictine has its roots in the Benedictine Order of the American Catholic Church.

The seat of Atchison County, the railroad town of Atchison grew up along the Missouri River, and many early residents were wealthy. It was incorporated in 1855 and became one of the earliest Kansas towns to offer telegraph service connecting to the eastern part of the country. Amelia Earhart is one of the town's most famous residents. Visitors can tour the home where she was born and see more of her personal items at this local museum.

Several grand Victorian homes have become successful bed & breakfast properties, while others star on haunted tours, as does Molly's Hollow in Jackson Park. After all, Atchison has been called one of the nation's most haunted places. This small town brimming with history offers plenty of restaurants, shopping, and performing arts options.

There are treasures in nearby small towns, too. You'll find a bust of Abraham Lincoln in Troy, a wonderful doll museum in the town of Holton, and a fort given by Luxembourg, France, to the town of Elwood following a tornado.

Abolitionists founded Lawrence in 1854, putting it near a major center of slavery conflict in the state. Today, the town is easily accessed from KS 10, has approximately ninety thousand residents, and is home to the University of Kansas.

With academic programs for more than 170 fields of study, KU is an integral part of Lawrence. Dr. James Naismith invented the game of basketball here in 1891 and became the school's first basketball coach. The campus is also widely known for its gorgeous rolling hills and legendary campanile bell tower, with a 53-bell carillon, plus its natural history and art museums.

Formed in 1884, Haskell Indian Nations University lies near the eastern edge of Lawrence. It offers four-year college degrees to members of federally

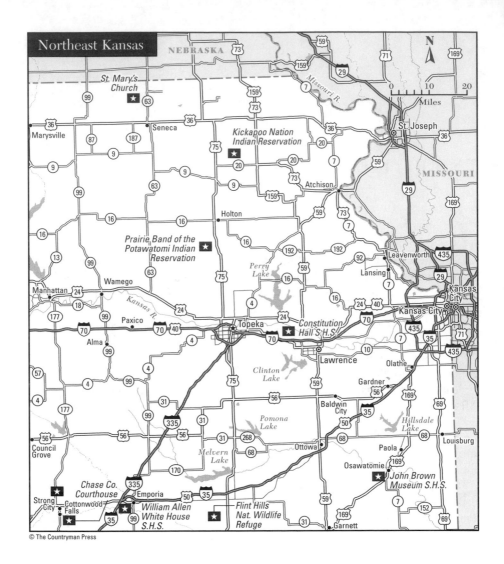

Northeast Kansas

NEBRASKA

St. Mary's Church

Marysville

Seneca

Kickapoo Nation Indian Reservation

St. Joseph

MISSOURI

Atchison

Holton

Prairie Band of the Potawatomi Indian Reservation

Leavenworth

Lansing

Wamego

Perry Lake

Manhattan

Kansas R.

Paxico

Topeka

Constitution Hall S.H.S.

Kansas City

Alma

Lawrence

Olathe

Clinton Lake

Gardner

Baldwin City

Pomona Lake

Hillsdale Lake

Louisburg

Council Grove

Melvern Lake

Ottawa

Paola

Osawatomie

John Brown Museum S.H.S.

Chase Co. Courthouse

Strong City

Cottonwood Falls

Emporia

William Allen White House S.H.S.

Flint Hills Nat. Wildlife Refuge

Garnett

© The Countryman Press

recognized American Indian tribes in the United States. Students come from 150 tribes and every state.

The town of Lawrence is vibrant and progressive, with an enormous variety of shopping, dining, and entertainment options, particularly along and near Massachusetts Street. Have a beer at the state's first brewery created since Prohibition, visit a bakery with a national reputation, or enjoy world cuisine with a top Zagat rating. There are plenty of outdoor activities here, too, particularly at Clinton Lake and State Park. Small towns near Lawrence produce Kansas wine, and the seat of state government was briefly located in nearby Lecompton during the height of pro- and antislavery sentiments.

Manhattan calls itself the Little Apple. Begun in 1858, Kansas State University offers more than a hundred advanced degrees and graduate certificates in addition to its baccalaureate degree program, and no other state university has had more Rhodes, Marshall, Truman, Goldwater, and Udall scholars since 1986. Agriculture is a big focus for many K-State students. Consequently, you'll find an insect museum here and university gardens full of greenhouses and specialty planting beds.

Manhattan's Aggieville "neighborhood" largely caters to students, with such eating and drinking spots as KatHouse Lounge, Purple Pig, and Tubby's Sports Bar. Many downtown shops are closed on Mondays, but the mall at Second Street is open daily. Throughout the town, restaurants range from New York chic to 1920s high style and the ultimate sports bar. Manhattan also offers a wealth of bed & breakfasts, or you can stay in the converted home of natural foods pioneer Grandma Hoerner.

Wide-open spaces surround Manhattan, including the edge of the Tallgrass Prairie, Tuttle Creek Lake and State Park, and the Konza Prairie Biological Station, where hiking trails offer beautiful surroundings and educational markers. Wamego lies east of Manhattan and offers a pleasing mix of Wizard-of-Oz focus combined with locally made wines and even several people who raise buffalo.

Northeast Kansas offers sights and activities for many tastes, from historical and geographical highlights to great dining and entertainment. Go find your favorites.

UNIVERSITY TOWNS

AREA CODE Lawrence and Manhattan are 785 and Atchison is 913.

GUIDANCE Atchison Chamber of Commerce (913-367-2427; atchisonkansas.net), 200 S. 10th St., Atchison. Open noon–5 Mon.–Fri.; check for weekend hours.

Lawrence Convention and Visitors Bureau (785-865-4499; visitlawrence .com), 402 N. Second St., Lawrence. Open 8:30–5:30 Mon.–Sat., 1–5 Sun.

Manhattan Convention and Visitors Bureau (785-776-8829; manhattancvb .org), 501 Poyntz Ave., Manhattan. Open 8–5 weekdays.

GETTING THERE *By car:* Take KS 10 to Lawrence from the Kansas City area. US 59 is the major north–south route through the city. I-70 borders Lawrence on the north. Reach Manhattan via I-70 or US 24. US 59 and US 73, plus KS 7, serve Atchison. *By rail:* **AMTRAK's** (1-800-272-7245; AMTRAK.com) **Southwest Chief** serves Lawrence at 413 E. Seventh St. The route begins in Chicago and ends in Los Angeles. There is no train service to Manhattan or Atchison. *By bus:* **Greyhound** stops in Lawrence and the station is at Sixth St./Stop 2 Shop. The bus line does not serve Manhattan or Atchison. *By air:* The nearest full-service commercial airport in this area is **Kansas City International Airport** (816-243-3100; flykci.com), 601 Brasilia Ave., Kansas City, MO.

GETTING AROUND Plan on driving throughout northeast Kansas.

MEDICAL EMERGENCY (arranged alphabetically by city name)

Atchison Hospital (913-367-2131; atchisonhospital.org), 800 Raven Hill Dr., Atchison.

Lawrence Memorial Hospital (785-505-5000; lmh.org), 325 Maine St., Lawrence.

Mercy Regional Health Center (785-776-3322), 1823 College Ave., Manhattan.

HISTORIC PLACES, LANDMARKS, AND SITES

In Atchison

Amelia Earhart Birthplace (913-367-4217; ameliaearhartmuseum.org), 223 N. Terrace St., Atchison. Open 9–4 Mon.–Fri., 10–4 Sat., 1–4 Sun. Stunning stained-glass windows, a quilt that features airplanes, and memorabilia from the recent movie about her life are displayed amid family furnishings in this lovely 1860 home located on a high bluff and owned by her grandparents. Adults $4; children 12 and under $1.

St. Benedict's Abbey (913-367-7853), campus of Benedictine College, Atchison. Tours by appointment; vigils and masses take place throughout the week. Marvel at the spectacular 610-square-foot fresco at the altar of the modern main sanctuary drenched in natural light. Artist Jean Charlot created this hand-painted plaster piece titled *Trinity and Episodes of Benedictine Life* in 1959, and the colors remain amazingly vibrant. Other key views include the Abbey Crypt, St. Scholastica Chapel, and an art gallery full of donated pieces from Europe and the motherhouse in Latrobe, Pennsylvania, as well as photographs taken of the community in the 1950s by Kansas photographer Gordon Parks. Free.

In Lawrence

& **Robert J. Dole Institute of Politics** (785-864-4900; doleinstitute.org), 2350 Petefish Dr., Lawrence. Open Mon.–Sat. 9–5, Sun. noon–5. Kansas Senator Bob Dole wanted to showcase the role and functions of Congress and depict politics as an honorable profession. This research-based institute features Dole's archives from his political and postpolitical career, with Kansas history interspersed. See video kiosks voiced by Dole, four thousand black-and-white photographs of Kansas World War II veterans, and the largest stained-glass flag in the nation. Two World Trade Center pieces were gifts to Dole from Mayor Rudolph Giuliani. Archive tours available with a reservation on the second and third Saturday of the month. Free.

& **Haskell Indian Nations University and Cultural Center** (785-832-6686; Haskell.edu/cultural_center/index.html), 143 Indian Ave., Lawrence. This center offers a chronological history of Haskell, plus general historical information such as the fact that forty-two thousand American Indians served in Vietnam as advisers or combat soldiers in the 1960s and '70s, and that Navajo code talkers eventually created approximately four hundred military terms in their language. See photographic and other art from current students while listening to recorded Native American chanting and drumming. Free.

Elsewhere

& **Goodnow House State Historic Site** (785-565-6490), 2309 Claflin Rd., Manhattan. Open 9–5 Tues.–Fri., depending on staff, 2–5 weekends. Visit this expansive two-story stone house that was once owned by Isaac and Ellen Goodnow. These "freestaters" were passionate about providing equal education for all children in Kansas. Isaac founded the Kansas State Teachers Association and the current Kansas State University. Filled with original antiques including tufted parlor chairs and elegant chandeliers, it's also a spot to view catalogued native rocks and an original stone barn. Adults $3; students $1; children under five free.

MUSEUMS

In Atchison
Evah C. Cray Historical Home Museum (913-367-1948), 805 N. Fifth St., Atchison. Call for hours. Built in 1882, atop Atchison's first graveyard, this lovely mansion features a guest parlor and a family parlor, an ornate dining room chandelier decorated with carved faces, and a tower room decorated from floor to ceiling with wood paneling and window blinds. Five fireplaces were imported from Europe, a wooden high chair converts to a stroller, and an antique gramophone still plays. See trophies won by the Crays at Kansas City's annual American Royal event, too. A resident ghost has broken the video machine in the carriage house gift shop, turned audiotapes pink, and dropped a speaker off the wall. Admission $3.

& **Atchison County Historical Society** (913-367-6238; atchisonhistory.org), 200 S. 10th St., Atchison. Open winter 9–5 Mon.–Fri., 10–4 Sat., noon–4 Sun.; longer summer hours begin May 1. Located in the old Santa Fe Depot, you'll find arrowheads and other American Indian artifacts, plus Amelia Earhart's graduation hood. Another display honors this rail center of Kansas—home of the Atchison Topeka and Santa Fe Railroad—including a tall stack of antique steamer trunks. Another display documents eight days that Abraham Lincoln spent in Kansas, putting him the farthest west of any time in his life. Free.

In Lawrence
✦ & **Natural History Museum** (785-864-4450; nhm.ku.edu), 1345 Jayhawk Blvd., University of Kansas campus, Lawrence. Open 9–5 Tues.–Sat., noon–5 Sun. The museum honors KU professor and Kansan Lewis Lindsay Dyche, whose enormous dioramas of animals in natural settings appeared at the Kansas Pavilion during the 1893 Chicago World's Fair. Polar bears joust, the reconstructed skeleton of a mosasaur—the T. rex of the sea—menaces, and a fox sleeps in the snow. Visitors learn about changes in our forests and the importance of honeybees. Free.

& **Spencer Museum of Art** (785-864-4710; ku.edu/~sma), 1301 Mississippi St., University of Kansas/Lawrence. Open 10–4 Tues.–Sat., 10–8 Thurs., noon–4 Sun. With exhibits of Renaissance, Medieval/Northern Renaissance, and modern and photographic art, university students visit it extensively for art research. In addition to the permanent collection, there are traveling exhibits and loaned pieces on display and an art space dedicated to children. You may see a 14th-century ivory panel, a war poster, or a pristine silver tea set from the Renaissance, plus a temporary exhibit that featured haunting photos of glaciers by Terry Evans, with the university's Center for Remote Sensing of Ice Sheets (CReSIS). Free.

In Manhattan
✦ **KSU Insect Museum** (785-532-BUGS), Denison Ave., K-State Gardens/Kansas State University/Manhattan. Targeting 5–10–year–olds, this

unusual museum tries to present a message that every animal has a purpose. Children learn to never shake or tap on the cage because these are fragile, live creatures. Mostly live and some preserved arthropods/insects occupy 1,100 square feet. There's a working bee colony and a tarantula collection that includes Latisha, whose shed exoskeletons are still on display. There's also a play corner, a microscope with projection screen, and a pin board that features insects found in Kansas. Admission $2; seniors/military $1.50.

KSU INSECT ZOO

✳ To Do

BOATING AND FISHING Clinton Lake and State Park (785-842-8562), 798 N. 1415 Rd., near Lawrence. Covering seven thousand surface acres and spanning 8 miles up the Wakarusa valley, this lake area features more than 9,000 acres of public hunting lands for mourning dove, turkey, Canadian geese, and teal. Use the well-maintained boat ramps in Clinton State Park, bird-watch as you hike and bike near beautiful bluffs and deep woods, and camp near bridle trails in Rockhaven. Fish in several areas with appropriate licensure.

DAY SPAS Rejuvene Day Spa (785-865-4372; rejuvenedayspa.com), 13 E. Eighth St., Lawrence. Open 9–7 Mon.–Thurs., 9–5 Fri.–Sat. The owner of this popular spa is a licensed esthetician, a nationally board certified massage therapist, and a health educator—and it shows. Clients love their spa packages with massage, reflexology, nail treatments, facials and wraps in the mix, and couples massage. Hour massage $75, day spa packages $100–415.

Shear Dynamics Salon and Day Spa (785-776-9100; sheardynamics.net), A1125 Laramie, Manhattan; also in K-State union. Shear Dynamics is a full-service salon with loads of services, including six different facials, shellac manicures, and hot-stone massage and reflexology. Hot-stone full body massage $65.

GOLF Alvamar Public Golf Course (785-842-1907; alvamar.com), 1800 Crossgate Dr., Lawrence. Open 8 AM until dark. Long considered one of Lawrence's premier golf clubs, Alvamar offers public golf holes with long fairways, plenty of trees and water, plus a beautiful clubhouse. Par 72, 18 holes, 7,092 yards.

Colbert Hills Golf Course (785-776-6475), 5200 Colbert Hills Dr., Manhattan. This expansive, hilly, 18-hole public course offers some of the area's most spectacular views, particularly from the seventh hole. With two par 5s of more than 600 yards, a golf cart is a must. Grab lunch or dinner in the clubhouse amid limestone columns with sleek wood accents. Par 72, 18 holes, 7525 yards.

In Atchison

Warnock Lake, Amelia Earhart Earthworks, International Forest of Friendship (913-367-2427), 17862 274th Rd., Warnock Lake/Atchison. Open 7–11. Surrounded by tree-dotted rolling hills, shelters, and RV/camping, this area hosts a perpetual portrait of Earhart, created through plantings by artist Stan Herd. The forest includes nearly a hundred tree varieties. Park and walk to this unusual garden, with commemorative bricks for President George Bush, J. Willard Marriott Sr., and many others. Profiles of the space shuttle *Columbia* crew are etched into stone. Free; call for camping rates.

Independence Creek Trail, Atchison. This 10-mile hiking and biking trail links Atchison's Riverfront Park with the Independence Creek area, the site where the Lewis and Clark expedition camped on Independence Day of 1804. It's great for walkers or cyclists with views of this historic site, plus interpretive signs and a replica of a Kanza Indian earth lodge home. You'll also travel beside the Benedictine Bottoms Wildlife Area.

Independence Park. River Rd. and Atchison St., Atchison. Travel down a steep hill that would rival San Francisco's tallest to reach this pretty little park beside the Missouri River. There are a dozen life trail kiosks, a small playground, restrooms, picnic tables, and a small telescope.

& **Riverfront Park** (913-367-5500), downtown Atchison. This lovely park along the Missouri River features the Lewis and Clark Pavilion, which tells the history of the explorers' travels through this area. There's a children's play area, a paved hiking/biking trail, and enclosed bathrooms. The Veterans Memorial Plaza is particularly pretty after dark.

In Lawrence

Baker Wetlands Research and Natural Area (785-594-3172), 31st and Louisiana Streets, Lawrence. Park and walk in from the north gate, halfway between Haskell and Louisiana, or from the east gate at 35th and Haskell. Open during daylight hours. Five hundred and seventy-three acres featuring 6 miles of trails expose visitors to dozens of birds, flowers/plants, and insects.

In Manhattan

Tuttle Creek Lake and Tuttle Creek State Park (785-539-7941), 5800 River Pond Rd., Manhattan. When crossing the dam, look north to see miles of water that stretch to the horizon or travel up Observation Point Drive for an unobstructed view. American Indians once crossed the Rocky Ford Fishing Area in this park under normal conditions because of its flat rock bottom. Pioneers also used the ford and operated a gristmill here. Today a rushing waterfall marks the border of this popular fishing spot. At the Spillway there is an ADA (Americans with Disabilities Act)-accessible trail available. Look for fish cleaning stations, trailer parking, and picnic areas. Includes Tuttle Creek Shooting Park.

Manhattan Linear Trail (785-587-2757), multiple access points, Manhattan. This city bike path lies near Wildcat Creek as well as the Kansas and Big Blue Rivers. Walkers, joggers, and cyclists use the trail, which has multiple trailheads that include South Manhattan Avenue, Richards Drive, Kimball Avenue, and Hudson Avenue.

Konza Prairie Biological Station (konza.ksu.edu), outside of town. Hiking trails available dawn–dusk. In April acres of caramel, tan, and deep brown grasses spread before you, some already as tall as 6 feet. Beyond lie brilliant green hills dotted with vibrant purple redbuds.

Kansas State University Gardens (785-532-3271), 2021 Throckmorton Plant Science Ctr., KSU campus/Manhattan. Multiple greenhouse structures surround large planted areas such as adaptive/native plants, a butterfly garden, and a recently redeveloped rose garden. Four enormous rows of irises supply beautiful views for the annual Iris Days display held in May, and inventory for the annual iris sale held in July and sponsored by the Flint Hills Iris Society. Free.

A LIFE-SIZE SCULPTURE SITS IN THE BUTTERFLY GARDEN AT KANSAS STATE UNIVERSITY GARDENS.

✳ Lodging

BED & BREAKFASTS

In Atchison

((ᵛ)) **St. Martin's B&B** (913-367-4964; stmartinsbandb.com), 324 Santa Fe St., Atchison. In 1948 radio inventor Frederick W. Stein Sr. built this American Classic Revival-style home. Calm and peaceful aptly describe this hilltop home listed on the National Register of Historic Places. Warm and inviting describes innkeepers Janet and John Settich. Enjoy a full breakfast and outdoor hot tub. Full breakfast. $95–125.

((ᵛ)) **Tuck U Inn at Glick Mansion** (913-367-9110; glickmansion.com), 503 N. Second St., Atchison. When a guest has stayed here since 1988, there must be something special about it. This grand old mansion is full of antiques, a grand piano—which the owner occasionally plays—and big breakfasts with homemade pastries. Full breakfast. $100–129.

In Lawrence

Circle S Guest Ranch and Country Inn (785-843-4124; circlesranch.com), 3325 Circle S Ln., Lawrence. Circle S has offered guests rustic charm and luxury accommodations for more than a decade. The owners recently added

GUESTS CHOOSE FROM SEVERAL BED-ROOMS IN THE AMERICAN CLASSIC REVIVAL-STYLE AT ST. MARTIN'S B&B.

a bar to their renovated living room, a new entry courtyard, plus a conference and media center that seats up to 35 people. They also renovated the party barn to accommodate up to 200. Use the silo hot tub with views of the sky, catch a fish, visit with cattle or buffalo, or cozy up with a good book. Gourmet dinners are often available for an additional charge. Full breakfast. $150–250.

(•̣•) **Halcyon House Bed & Breakfast** (785-841-0314; halcyonhouse .com), 1000 Ohio St., Lawrence. This bed & breakfast is located within walking distance of downtown Lawrence and the KU campus. Co-owners Constance Wolfe and her daughter Karen Doue stayed at many European bed & breakfasts before they opened Halcyon House. The 1880s home includes two upstairs and two downstairs rooms with shared baths, several rooms with their own bath, and a carriage house. Enjoy breakfast in a sun-filled open kitchen and dining room. Full breakfast. $55–149.

(•̣•) **The Strong Inn Guest House** (785-313-5167; stronginn.com), 1916 Beck St., Manhattan. Henry Strong handcrafted the home for he and his wife, Elenora, in 1867, after a fire. His granddaughter, Mabel Baxter Hoerner—later known as Grandma Hoerner—grew up here. She eventually became famous for her natural and organic foods, which are still produced today. Sleep under the eaves or near the kitchen. Antiques decorate the home, which also offers a fully equipped kitchen and laundry facilities. Full house $175.

HOTELS AND RESORTS

In Lawrence

♿ (•̣•) **Eldridge Hotel** (785-749-5011; eldridgehotel.com), 701 Massachusetts St., Lawrence. Dark wood and upholsteries, black-and-white photographs, high ceilings, and deep crown moldings characterize this legendary hotel, refurbished to reflect its mid-1800s grandeur. And there's no need to leave your cozy accommodations for food

THE STRONG INN

MANHATTAN BED & BREAKFASTS

((y)) **Bed and Buggy Inn** (785-494-8232; bedandbuggyinn.com), 11555 Myers Valley Rd., near Manhattan. Stay in a stunning log home with broad front porch and massive fireplace in the Flint Hills. Dog kennel and full breakfast.

Guest Haus Bed & Breakfast (785-776-6543; guesthaus.com), 1724 Sheffield Cir., Manhattan. Sleep amid rolling hills and wooded terrain at this 1993 Manhattan Garden Tour property. Catch a fish or sit on the deck. Continental breakfast.

& ((y)) **The Morning Star Bed & Breakfast LLC** (785-587-9703; morningstaron thepark), 617 Houston St., Manhattan. This lovely 1902 home features five TV-free guest rooms with Jacuzzi baths, hardwood floors, and all-cotton linens.

Scenic Valley Inn Bed & Breakfast (785-776-6831; scenicvalleyinn.com), 610 S. Scenic Dr., Manhattan. This spacious, modern log home offers three guest rooms with private baths amid 20 wooded acres. Featured in *Manhattan* magazine, the B&B focuses on special events lodging.

and fun. Just inside the front door, TEN Restaurant and The Jayhawker Bar offer plenty of options. $159–175.

& ((y)) **Oread Hotel** (785-843-1200; theoread.com), 1200 Oread Ave., Lawrence. Opened in January 2010, this hotel represents the last of the Big 12 cities to have a hotel attached or adjacent to campus (although it is privately owned). Located on an impossibly tall hill near the north gate of the KU campus with spectacular views, the Oread is built from native limestone and features nearly one hundred sleek modern rooms and suites. Four in-house restaurants offer pizza, full service bars, casual bistro meals, and elegant dining. Visit The Cave, a 21-and-over nightclub with DJ, laser lights, and more, and buy ice cream in the lobby or visit the bookstore and spa. $119–179.

For groups
((y)) **Prairiewood Retreat Center** (785-537-9999; prairiewood.com),

1408 Wildcat Creek Rd., Manhattan. Experience luxury amid the Tallgrass Prairie, from marble and hardwood floors to lush upholstery and linens. Enjoy a massive TV and game tables, a small swimming pool, an indoor grill, and a player piano that plays calming music. There's also a conference room with ergonomic chairs and a TV for electronic presentations. Take a hike or sip some wine as the sun drops behind tall hills. One guest group rents at a time; $845–1,095 daily rate; 4–5 bedroom/bath suites available.

✳ Where to Eat

DINING OUT

In Lawrence
& **Pachamama's** (785-841-0990; pachamamas.com), 800 New Hampshire, Lawrence. Open Tues.–Sat. 11–2, 5–9:30; Fri.–Sat. 5–10. The chef at Pachamama's wants to make sure that every flavor of a dish is evident in

every bite. Such attention to detail has led this stylish, modern restaurant to receive recognition in *Zagat World's Top Restaurants 2009/10.* Most items are made in-house and the menu changes every month. Enjoy unusual cocktails such as the refreshing cucumber lemon tonic or lavender champagne cocktail. In the bar, house-made simple syrups and frequent drink specials accompany a separate menu. Inexpensive–moderate.

&. **Teller's Restaurant and Bar** (785-843-4111; 746mass.com), 746 Massachusetts St., Lawrence. Open 11:30–2 Mon.–Sat. ($5 lunch specials Mon.–Thurs), 5–9 Sun.–Thurs, 5–11 Fri.–Sat., 10–2 Sun. brunch. A bank for over 50 years, this antique building has housed Teller's for nearly two decades. *Wine Spectator* granted the restaurant a 2005 award of excellence and *Santé* magazine gave them a 2006 certificate of achievement. The decor honors its banking past, from an original vault door that opens toward restrooms to mock teller windows beside the bar. Inexpensive–moderate.

In Manhattan
&. **della Voce** (785-532-9000; della voce.com), 405 Poyntz Ave., Manhattan. Sleek, sexy, and modern, this Italian restaurant transports diners to the big city. Black-and-white photos and abstract triptychs depict martinis and women who drink them. Track lighting illuminates the room, subdivided by a chain metal floor-to-ceiling screen and decorated in vibrant hues. Even minestrone soup is served with panache, from the square bowl full of large sausage chunks, fresh vegetables, and basil to a small rectangular plate topped with folded napkin, rosemary focaccia, and garlic herb butter. Moderate–expensive.

&. **Harry's Restaurant** (785-537-1300; harrysmanhattan.com), 418 Poyntz Ave., Manhattan. Named after Harry Pratt Wareham, a lifelong and highly visible Manhattan resident, this restaurant exudes 1920s charm, while half-walls in the lobby mark the height of water here during Manhattan's massive 1951 flood. Upholstered wingback chairs, crystal chandeliers, deep crown moldings, dark wood, and white linens create an atmosphere of understated elegance. Try smoked portobello and goat cheese pizza on a cracker crust and cream of tomato basil soup. Unusual appetizers include andouille sausage and pepperoni pizza; entrées range from pinot noir blackberry duck to filet mignon royale. Inexpensive–moderate.

EATING OUT

In Atchison
Y **Flyers Bar and Grill** (913-367-4837; flyersonriver.com), 102 E. Atchison St., Atchison. Open 11–10 daily. This is a fun spot to find great burgers, wings, and pork tenderloins, and there's a dynamite view of the river. Inexpensive.

&. **Marigold Bakery and Café** (913-367-3858, marigoldbakery.com), 715 Commercial St., Atchison. Open 7:30–4 Mon.–Sat. Savor wonderful baked goods, from a huge wedge of signature pecan praline bread pudding with caramel sauce to enormous apple turnovers. Try a Southwest salad with black beans, corn, tomatoes, chicken, and cheese or a hefty sandwich. Dozens of retail aprons and dishtowels decorate the space. Inexpensive.

Riverhouse (913-367-1010), 101 Commercial St., Atchison. Open 10–9 Mon.–Thurs., 10–10 Fri.–Sat., 10–9

Sun. Try the chicken club, with a half-inch thick chicken breast, thick cut bacon, and a grilled bun, served with creamy coleslaw. Inexpensive.

& **Snow Ball** (913-367-7632), 111 N. Eighth St., Atchison. Open 7–9 weekdays, 8–9 Sat., 1–9 Sun. Located just off the main street, this is a fun little place decorated with corrugated metal walls, vintage signs, and a tin ceiling. Ice cream is their specialty, from the 2-pound banana split to the B.C. shake, with chocolate, caramel, and a shot of espresso. Try a caramel macchiato with your chicken salad sandwich, served on a croissant, also available with curry and cranberries. Breakfast sandwiches and homemade soups are other offerings. Inexpensive.

In Lawrence

& Y **Free State Brewing Company** (785-843-4555; freestatebrewing .com), 636 Massachusetts St., Lawrence. Open Mon.–Sat. 11–midnight, Sun. noon–11. Free State's Ad Astra Ale was the first ale brewed in Kansas since the pioneer days. Today the company produces twenty thousand barrels of beer annually and has a bottling facility. Try Lemon Grass Rye or Copperhead brews with black bean quesadillas or a turkey bacon focaccia sandwich. Watch brewers work and view the original ceiling of this former trolley and bus station. Check for special events like March Mustard Madness. Inexpensive.

& **WheatFields Bakery** (785-841-5553; wheatfieldsbakery.com), 904 Vermont St., Lawrence. Open 6:30–8 Mon.–Fri., 6:30–6:30 Sat., 7:30–4 Sun. This award-winning bakery at the edge of downtown is known for its golden multigrain, wheat/walnut/raisin, sourdough, and other artisan breads. Enjoy French toast, biscuits and gravy, or sandwiches, too, in the large dining room. Inexpensive.

&° & **Sylas and Maddy's Homemade Ice Cream** (785-832-8323), 1014 Massachusetts St., Lawrence. Open noon–10:30 Mon.–Thurs., 11:30–11 Sat., 12:30–10:30 Sun. This original Sylas and Maddy's opened in the early 1990s. Customers choose from 24 flavors made fresh daily, including Gold Dust and Rock Chocolate Jayhawk—vanilla ice cream with a chocolate swirl and brownie chunks. Order thick malts and shakes, fresh-squeezed limeade, or a quarter-pound scoop of coffee cheesecake, green tea, or margarita sherbet flavor in a waffle cone. Inexpensive.

& **Local Burger** (785-856-7827; localburger.com), 714 Vermont St., Lawrence. Open 11–9 Mon.–Sat., 11–8 Sun. Locally produced meats served on organic, whole wheat buns, and the world's best veggie burgers are two things that Local Burger is known for. Savor an elk burger and then purchase beef tenderloin fillets, grass-fed-only buffalo hot dogs, or even bones for your dog. Inexpensive.

In Manhattan

& **The Chef—A Breakfast Café** (785-537-4100; thechefcafe.com), 111 S. Fourth St., Manhattan. Open 6–3 Mon.–Fri., 7:30–3 Sat.–Sun. Featured in *Food Network* magazine, this place has been a Manhattan favorite since 2008. Salmon Benedict combines skin-on, spicy potato chips, poached eggs, and salmon with fresh dill atop toasted rye bread with creamy hollandaise. Biscuits and gravy feature pale brown gravy chock full of sausage bits. It's a bright, fun environment, from the blue ceiling to yellow walls and white window frames full of blue

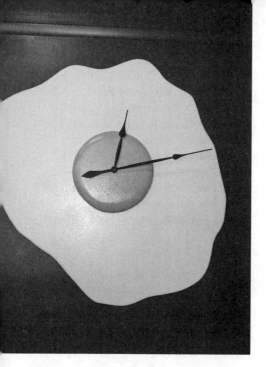

THERE'S A TOUCH OF WHIMSY IN THE DECOR AT THE CHEF—A BREAKFAST CAFÉ.

sky and white clouds. Inexpensive.

🍴 & **KSU Dairy Bar** (785-532-1292), 144 Call Hall, KSU campus/Manhattan. Open 7–6 Mon.–Fri., 11–4 Sat. This cheerful little place, awash in KSU purple and white and open since 1923, offers fresh dairy products from the university's own dairy herd. Try a malt or one of the biggest single scoops ever, such as Chocolate Razz with vanilla ice cream, chocolate chunks, and raspberry. Breakfast sandwiches or pastries are available from 7–10, and there's a nice variety of sandwiches. Purchase packaged pork, beef, lamb, and processed meat from the university's meat lab. Limited, free 30-minute parking is a bonus in a sea of permit-only parking. Inexpensive.

& ⅋ **Kite's Grille and Bar** (785-776-4300; kitesbar.com), 615 12th St., Manhattan. Open 11 AM daily. Keith "Kite" Thomas opened this hotspot

after a professional career playing ball for the Philadelphia Athletics, New York Yankees, and Washington Senators. Kite's was named the nation's #1 sports bar in 2009 by redshirtfiles .com. It's full of K-State sports memorabilia. They're known for 80-percent lean handmade burgers, 48-ounce nightcap well drinks, and dozens of TVs broadcasting sporting events. The huge menu also features a portabella and grilled chicken wrap, *espinaca* dip, and chicken tenderloins. Inexpensive.

✳ Entertainment

In Atchison

Atchison Trolley (1-800-234-1854; atchisonkansas.net/v_trolley.htm), 200 S. 10th St., Santa Fe Depot/Atchison. Call for specific times and reservations; trolleys depart on the hour, April–Oct. The Atchison history tour shows visitors gorgeous antique homes and buildings and scenic views of the mighty Missouri as they travel on comfortable open-air trolleys (windows close in cool weather). Ask about haunted Atchison tours, too. Adults $4; children 4–10 $2.

Muchnic Gallery (913-367-4278; Atchison-art.org/muchnic), 704 N. Fourth St., Atchison. Open 1–5 Sat.–Sun., 10–5 Wed. This mansion built by the prominent Muchnic family still has original furnishings throughout the first floor. Crystal chandeliers glitter, gold-painted wood shines, and the family's faces are carved near the base of the gorgeous staircase. A breathtaking bank of stained-glass windows decorates the stairwell, while fine carvings and ceramic tiles decorate each fireplace. Upstairs, multiple rooms host a rotating art gallery. Free.

In Lawrence

Kugler's Vineyard (785-843-8516; kuglersvineyard.com), 1235 N 1100 Rd., Lawrence. Open by appointment only, mostly on weekday evenings/Sat. afternoons; closed Sun. Visit this small, family-operated vineyard and winery, which creates red and white vintages and won a bronze award in the Norton Wine Competition.

In Manhattan

🐾 **Sunset Zoological Park** (785-587-2737; ci.manhattan.ks.us/index.aspx ?NID=22), 2333 Oak St., Manhattan. Open April–Oct. 9:30–5 daily,; Nov.–March noon–5. Nicely landscaped, with winding paths, limestone walls, and log fences, this little zoo offers close-up views of emu, wallabies, and kookaburras in the Australian walkabout and natural habitat along steep natural hillsides for large African wildlife. On spring weekends and throughout summertime visit the Safari Outpost gift shop or the concession stand. There's playground equipment on a rubber floor and wheelchairs, strollers, and wagons for rent. Adults $4; children 3–12 $2.

Strecker-Nelson Gallery (785-537-2099; strecker-nelsongallery.com), 406 Poyntz Ave., Manhattan. Open 10–6 Mon.–Sat. With five upstairs rooms in their one-hundred-year-old building, this is the oldest art gallery in the state, and the owners live across the hall. Approximately every other exhibit is a group show with up to three-dozen artists, and there's a landscape component in every show. Most art comes from Kansas and Missouri, plus Oklahoma, Nebraska, and Colorado. Ceramics are a big focus in large part because internationally renowned ceramist Yoshiro Ikeda teaches at KSU.

PERFORMING ARTS Theatre Atchison (913-367-1647; theatre atchison.org), 401 Santa Fe, Atchison. Housed in a 1914 building that was once a Christian Science church, Theatre Atchison celebrated its 25th anniversary in 2009. The nonequity theater with volunteer actors produces five main stage shows and five children's shows annually. In 2010 Theatre Atchison was named Kansas's top community theater. Adults $10; students $6.

Lawrence Community Theatre (785-843-7469; theatrelawrence.com), 1501 New Hampshire St., Lawrence. Celebrating its 35th season in 2011, the theater offers six to eight major productions annually, with 25 percent of the audience coming from outside Lawrence. More than four hundred volunteers and actors support professional directors, choreographers, musical directors, and office staff who run the theater. Enjoy free desserts during intermission, rotating art and special exhibits, a full bar, and talkbacks with the cast members. Adults $18–20; children 14 and under $14; student/senior discounts available.

♿ **Lied Center of Kansas** (785-864-2787; lied.ku.edu), 1600 Steward Ave., Lawrence. Check for schedule. Made possible through a private donation from the Lied Foundation Trust. This bright, modern performing arts center offers programs for many tastes, from the KU Symphony Orchestra to professional international folk dance groups and *Fiddler on the Roof*. Ticket prices vary.

✳ Selective Shopping

In Atchison

Nell Hill's (913-367-1086; nellhills .com), 501 Commercial St., Atchison.

Open 10–5 Mon.–Sat. Atchison native Mary Carol Garrity opened this enormous home decor store nearly 30 years ago, and people flock here from miles away. Upstairs rooms have different color schemes reflected in tabletop linens, china, and accessories. Downstairs there are gorgeous lamps, candleholders, silk florals, beautifully upholstered chairs, and much more.

In Lawrence

& **Waxman Candles** (785-843-8593; waxmancandles.com), 609 Massachusetts St., Lawrence. Open 9:30–7 Mon.– Sat., Sun. afternoons. When Bob Werts transferred from Dodge City Community College to KU in 1971, his candle-making enterprise transferred with him. His Lawrence store offers candles in every shape, size, and scent. One looks like a fresh cinnamon roll, another's scent is called Sexy, and there's a 2-foot-tall column candle.

& **Footprints** (785-832-0324; footprints.com), 1339 Massachusetts St., Lawrence. Open Mon.–Sun., 10–6 (phone orders taken from 9–6). Floor-to-ceiling murals and metal dinosaurs inside are just a few unusual decorations at this shop, renowned for its enormous inventory of Birkenstocks. Opened for more than three decades, Footprints also carries Sanita, Dansko, Chaco, Keen, and Tamita brands. Despite the storefront, most of their sales now take place online, where customers receive a guaranteed two-month test walk period. But a trip to Lawrence wouldn't be complete without a stop here, where comfort is key and the selection is exhaustive.

& **The Bayleaf** (785-842-4544; thebayleaf.com), 717 Massachusetts St., Lawrence. Open 9:30–6 Mon.–Wed., Fri.–Sat.; 9:30–8 Thurs.; noon–5 Sun. This very popular store has offered every kind of kitchen gadget, bakeware, and dinnerware available since 1977. You'll also find whole-bean coffees and bulk teas, gourmet oil and vinegar, and much more.

Sunflower Outdoor and Bike Shop (785-843-5000; sunfloweroutdoorand bike.com), 804 Massachusetts St., Lawrence. Open 10–7 Mon.–Wed./ Fri., 10–8 Thurs., 10–6 Sat., 12–5 Sun. Sunflower offers bicycles and equipment for every outdoor activity except snow sports. People visit from 90 minutes away to purchase bicycles, tents, Chaco and Vasque shoes, and even yoga mats. After a 1997 fire the current bicycle room was built with repurposed flooring and ceiling beams.

Pendleton's Country Market (785-843-1409; pendletons.com), 1446 E. 1850 Rd., Lawrence. Open 8–5 Mon.–Sat.; closed Sun. in July–Aug. The Pendleton family started selling asparagus beside the road more than 30 years ago. Today they grow 20

A LINE OF BIKES AWAITS CUSTOMERS AT SUNFLOWER OUTDOOR AND BIKE SHOP.

acres of asparagus and 6 acres of flowers, plus pick-your-own spinach and peas, vine-ripened hydroponic tomatoes, and dig-your-own potatoes. Local products in their shop include lavender, goat's milk cheese, locally roasted pistachios, pickles, and preserves. For $2 mid-Aug. through early Oct., visit the butterfly house with more than 20 indigenous butterflies.

It's about Time (785-842-1500; celestialironworks.com), 816 Massachusetts St., Lawrence. Open 10:30–6 Mon.–Wed., 10:30–8 Thurs.–Sat., noon–5 Sun. Technicolor, waist-high metal flower bouquets, 6-foot-tall anodized metal wheat stalks, and handmade wooden birdhouses are only a few items at this unusual store in the heart of downtown.

& **Signs of Life and Signs of Life Gallery** (785-830-8030; www.signsof lifegallery.com), 722 Massachusetts St., Lawrence. Open 10–11. Part Christian and mainstream bookstore, part art gallery, and part coffee shop, this place really hops in the evening when loads of students stop by for java, a book, or a spin through the gallery, whose exhibits change quarterly. Inexpensive eats.

In Manhattan
(((•))) **Big Poppi** (785-537-3737; big poppibikes.com), 1126 Moro St., Manhattan. Open 10–6/sunset Mon.–Fri., 9–6 Sat., 1–4 Sun. Fast becoming a popular destination for everything related to bicycling, Big Poppi opened in March 2009. Purchase a new ride from the bike tree or buy a cushioned seat, riding sandals, or baby seat. Rent a bicycle or socialize in the back. In fact, Big Poppi has been named one of the top 10 places to meet people in Manhattan; with free coffee and water.

& **Emerald City Market** (785-537-6090; areyouwicked.com), 406 Poyntz Ave., Manhattan. Open 10–6 Mon.–Sat., noon–5 Sun. After three years in Wamego, this classy market moved to town to have a large kitchen area for cooking classes. Gourmet and imported foods—highly favored by many Fort Riley residents—jewel-tone wine glasses, and Nambé silver from New Mexico are just a few of the lovely housewares and home decor items available here.

✳ Special Events

June: **Country Stampede** (785-539-2222; countrystampede.com), Manhattan. This event offers four live stages and nearly two-dozen country music performers/groups, plus dozens of food and shopping vendors. Camping, and single or four-day tickets available.

July: **Amelia Earhart Festival** (913-367-2427), Atchison. This celebration of Atchison's most famous daughter features entertainment, food, children's activities, and carnival rides. There are aerobatic performances and a fireworks display. **LakeFest** (1-800-234-1854), Atchison. Musical artists perform, beginning at 7. **Salute!** (785-840-1605/1604), Lawrence. The three-day event includes the Mass Street Mosey, where visitors stroll through downtown businesses sipping wine and sampling local gourmet food.

September: **Haskell Annual Indian Art Market** (785-749-8404), Haskell Indian Nations University, Lawrence. Lovers of American Indian jewelry, pottery, painting, and carving could spend hours inside the display tents with artisans from throughout the nation. Watch American Indian dances, and then enjoy an Indian taco.

GOVERNMENT TOWNS

Established in 1854, Leavenworth lies about 30 minutes from the Kansas City area near US 73/KS 7, KS 5, and KS 92. The state's first incorporated city is also home to the oldest fort west of the Mississippi that has been used continuously. Buffalo soldiers who came from Fort Leavenworth are immortalized in Fort Statuary and at the Richard Allen Cultural Center, which documents the history of African American residents in this area. Fort Leavenworth still has a major influence on the town, where you'll find the Museum of the Kansas National Guard. Nearby, Lansing hosts the state's oldest prison and is the future home of the Kansas Regional Prisons Museum. It also offers a historical museum located in a renovated 1887 Santa Fe Railroad Depot, one of the town's few original buildings.

Topeka is Kansas's state capital, with easy access to US 75, US 24, I-70, I-335, KS 4, and US 40. Government employs nearly one-quarter of Topeka's workforce. Noting the city's good schools and hospitals, plus Washburn University, friendly people, and low housing costs, Kiplinger's has named Topeka number 10 among the 10 best cities for the next decade. The city's overall unemployment rate also remains below the national average.

Named the Kansas capital in the 1860s, Topeka played major roles in the Underground Railroad and in the Brown v. Board of Education lawsuit, which fought segregation in public schools. Visit the Brown v. Board of Education national historic site for a taste of the times.

Nearby small towns with big reputations include Alma, home of a legendary cheese manufacturer, and Dover, where a coconut cream pie from Sommerset Hall Café was named number one in the nation by *Good Morning America*. Paxico is known as the state's antiques capital and Osage City is a gateway to Eisenhower State Park and Melvern Lake.

AREA CODE Leavenworth is 913 and Topeka is 785.

GUIDANCE Leavenworth Convention and Visitors Bureau (913-682-4113; visitleavenworthks.com), 518 Shawnee St., Leavenworth. Open 8–5 weekdays.

Visit Topeka Inc. (785-234-1030; visittopeka.us), 1275 SW Topeka Blvd., Topeka. Open 7:45–5 weekdays.

GETTING THERE AND GETTING AROUND The best way to reach and tour these cities is by personal car. Topeka is located at the intersection of I-70 and US 75 and on US 24 and 40, and where I-335 begins. Leavenworth is near KS 92 and US 73 and I-29 from the Missouri side of the Kansas City area.

MEDICAL EMERGENCY (arranged alphabetically by city name)

Cushing Memorial Hospital (913-684-1100), 711 Marshall, Leavenworth.

St. John Hospital (913-680-6000), 3500 S. Fourth St., Leavenworth.

St. Francis Health Center (785-295-8000), 1700 SW Seventh St., Topeka.

Stormont-Vail HealthCare (785-354-5225), 1500 SW 10th Ave., Topeka.

GETTING THERE *By car:* Major highways to Leavenworth include US 73 and KS 92. Topeka is located at US 24 and US 40. Other highways include I-70, US 75, and I-335. *By rail:* **AMTRAK's** (1-800-272-7245; AMTRAK.com) **Southwest Chief** serves Topeka at 500 SE Holliday Pl. and Fifth St. The route begins in Chicago and ends in Los Angeles. There is no AMTRAK service to Leavenworth. *By bus:* Take **Greyhound Lines** (785-843-5622) out of Topeka, 600 SE Quincy/Barnwell Service Inc. Greyhound does not serve Leavenworth. *By air:* The nearest full-service commercial airport in this area is **Kansas City International Airport** (816-243-3100; flykci.com), 601 Brasilia Ave., Kansas City, MO.

✳ To See

HISTORIC PLACES, LANDMARKS, AND SITES

In Leavenworth

Riverfront Community and Convention Center (913-651-2132, lvks.org), 123 S. Esplanade, Leavenworth. Open 6–8 weekdays, 9–5 Sat., 1–5 Sun. With numerous pairs of arched windows, a red brick exterior, and limestone accents, this 1888 Union Pacific Depot is listed on the National Register of Historic Places. Indoor recreation is a major focus here, with a pool and gymnasium, track, racquetball courts, weight room, and meeting space. Free.

In Topeka

Cedar Crest (785-296-3636; governor.ks.gov/cedarcrest/index.html), 1 SW Cedar Crest Rd., Topeka. Tours available Mon. afternoons. University of Kansas graduate Frank McClennon and his wife purchased the home—named for cedar trees that grow prolifically in the area—in 1930 after they purchased the *Topeka-Capital Journal* at auction. Willed to the state, it became the smallest governor's mansion in the country, with the most land. Cedar Crest underwent a major renovation in the early 1990s and features a bright, airy sunroom, wood library paneling, and a cabinet filled with a china cup presented to each state governor by the Kansas Federation of China Painters. Free.

Kansas State Capitol (785-296-3966; kshs.org/places/capital), 10th and Jackson, Topeka. Self-guided tours 8–5 daily; free building tours hourly, 9–3 Mon.–Fri.

This gorgeous building took nearly 40 years to build. See original woodwork and gilt banisters, wall-spanning historical murals, and the spectacular multilevel dome with murals, archways, and glass (under renovation until 2012). Free.

Tiffany Windows at First Presbyterian Church (785-233-9601; topeka1st presbyterian.org), 817 SW Harrison, Topeka. Open 9–4 Mon.–Fri. One of only a few churches in the United States with original Tiffany windows, First Presbyterian offers a magnificent collection of Tiffany's work in its main sanctuary, hand-crafted while Tiffany was in his 60s. Free.

Topeka High School (785-295-3150; ths.topekapublicschools.net), 800 SW Tenth St., Topeka. Tours available by appointment and on some first Fridays. Built in 1931 and listed on the National Register of Historic Places, this stunning building features a two-room art gallery with rotating exhibits, a beautifully restored auditorium, and a library that looks like it came straight out of Harry Potter. Free.

Old Prairie Town at Ward-Meade Historic Site (785-368-3888; topeka .org/parksrec), 124 NW Fillmore St., Topeka. Site open 8–dusk; buildings have shorter hours. Order an old-fashioned float in the antique soda fountain, see vintage pharmacy items, and travel the boardwalk beside the 1854 Ward Log Cabin. There's a 1910 Atchison Topeka and Santa Fe Railroad Company Depot on site and a wooden windmill, and you'll always see something blooming. Free.

FIRST PRESBYTERIAN CHURCH TIFFANY WINDOW

MUSEUMS

In Leavenworth
C. W. Parker Carousel Museum (913-682-1331; firstcitymuseums.org), 320 S. Esplanade, Leavenworth. Open 11–5 Thurs.–Sat., 1–5 Sun. Hear the carousel music playing half a block before you arrive at this carnival wonderland. See the oldest operating full-size wooden carousel in the world created by Carnival King C. W. Parker; see carousel horses undergoing restoration (with real horsehair tails), the National Carousel Association Archives, and an old-fashioned band organ donated by Leavenworth native Melissa Etheridge. Free.

Carroll Mansion (913-682-7759; leavenworthhistory.org), 1128 Fifth Ave., Leavenworth. Open 10:30–4:30 Tues.–Sat. This elegant 1890s-era home boasts a living room decorated in deep red, with heavy drapes and a small piano, dining room, kitchen, library, and parlor. There are two bedrooms, another parlor, and a music room upstairs. A small gift shop sells purses, quilts, coloring books, and paper dolls straight from the Victorian era. Adults $5; over 60 $4; children age 5–12 $3.

Frontier Army Museum (913-684-3186), 100 Reynolds Ave., Fort Leavenworth/Leavenworth. Open 9–4 Mon.–Fri., 10–4 Sat. An officer's sword and an 1832 general officer coat worn by Gen. Henry Leavenworth are just a few of more than seven thousand military artifacts on display in the 13,000-square-foot museum. See more than two-dozen horse-drawn vehicles and even a biplane. Free.

THE C. W. PARKER CAROUSEL MUSEUM IS GREAT FUN FOR CHILDREN OF ANY AGE.

National Fred Harvey Museum (913-682-1866), 624 Olive St., Leavenworth. Call for a tour. Fred Harvey was especially known for the Harvey Girls, waitresses who staffed his restaurant chain along the routes of the Atchison, Topeka, and Santa Fe Railroad. His restaurants and hotels also featured Southwest Indian art and crafts. This mansion is undergoing restoration to the time period of the Harvey family's ownership from 1865. Original parquet floors and intact transom windows, large rooms for the period, and maid's and butler's quarters are several features. Free.

In Topeka

Charles Curtis House Museum (785-357-1371; charlescurtismuseum.com), 1101 SW Topeka Blvd., Topeka. Open 11–3 Sat. or by appointment. Curtis was the only Native American vice president of the United States and his home is listed on the National and State Register of Historic Places and the Topeka Landmarks Register. See this beautifully restored home with ceramic fireplace surrounds, hand-carved woodwork, and stunning stained glass. Admission $5.

Museum of the Kansas National Guard (785-862-1020; kansasguard museum.org), 5616 SW Fairlawn Rd., Topeka. Open 10–4 Tues.–Sat. This volunteer-staffed museum added 5,500 square feet to the building during summer 2010, including a research library. See a Vulcan gun pod with rounds of ammunition, mannequins dressed in uniforms from various wars, and a 35th Infantry Division freight wagon that resembles a covered wagon. Display cases house Japanese and German war artifacts, items from Kansas's participation in the Civil War, and a wagon used in Bosnia. Attend special events such as a D-day reenactment in June and a Civil War reenactment in October. Free.

Mulvane Art Museum at Washburn University (785-670-1010, ext. 1324; washburn.edu/Mulvane), 17th and Jewell, Topeka. Open 10–7 Tues., 10–5 Wed.–Fri., 1–4 Sat.–Sun. Kids love the art lab at this metropolitan art museum, with rocks for making hieroglyphics, teaching exhibits such as the art of abstraction, and a large dollhouse. A sculpture by internationally known artist Patrick Dougherty, Stickwork, decorates the lawn with large free-form structures made completely from sticks. There's plenty to look at in the galleries, too. Free.

Combat Air Museum (785-862-3303; combatairmuseum.org), J St., Forbes Field, Topeka. Hours vary by season. This volunteer-operated museum fills two hangers with combat aircraft. It holds all items associated with the USS *Topeka* and a restored Navy plane that was found nose-down and riddled with bullet holes in an Iowa farmer's silo. Most vehicles are inside. Adults 18 and older $6; children/active military $4; 6–17 $4.

  Kansas Museum of History (785-272-8681; kshs.org/places/museum .htm), 6425 SW Sixth Ave., Topeka. Open 9–5 Tues.–Sat., 1–5 Sun.; closed on many holidays. See pictographs about American Indian tribes that have lived in Kansas, including the Wichita, Kansa, and Osage, and information about the state's natural resources, such as sunflowers and prairie chickens. There's also a full-size locomotive with two passenger cars. Adults $6; students with ID $4; children five and under free with family after 4:30.

✷ To Do

BOATING AND FISHING Lake Shawnee Recreational Area (785-267-1156; co.Shawnee.ks.us/parksandrec), 3137 SE 29th St., Topeka. This man-made 411-acre lake hosts the world's only 400-meter dash rowing course and hosts the annual Great Plains Rowing Championships. In addition to the lake, there are tennis courts, trails, gardens, and ball fields.

FARMERS' MARKETS Leavenworth Farmers' Market (leavenworth farmersmarket.com), Haymarket Square, Leavenworth. Open in season 3–6 Wed., 7–11 Sat. All produce is grown or produced by the sellers, who must live within a 40-mile radius.

Topeka Farmers' Market (785-249-4704; topekafarmersmarket.com), SW 12th and SW Harrison Streets, Topeka. Open 7:30–noon Sat. With more than 80 vendors, this market has operated since the 1930s.

GOLF Trails West Golf Course (913-651-7176), Fort Leavenworth, Leavenworth. The public is welcome to play on this course and should enter from Met-

AFRICAN AMERICAN HISTORIC SITES

♿ **Richard Allen Cultural Center** (913-682-8772; richardallenculturalcenter.info), 412 Kiowa St., Leavenworth. This area has a rich history of African American residents, beginning with buffalo soldiers who fought in the Civil War, some of whom were stationed at Fort Leavenworth. See buffalo soldier equipment, Egyptian and African artifacts, a collection of vintage Everhard black-and-white photographs, and a small, reconstructed 1920s house inside.

Buffalo Soldier Cavalry Monument, Fort Leavenworth campus, Leavenworth. Atop a gushing waterfall, this statue depicts a horse rearing up under his buffalo soldier rider. The monument honors these soldiers with the 10th cavalry coming from Fort Leavenworth.

♿ **Brown v. Board of Education National Historic Site** (785-354-4273; nps .gov/brvb), 1515 SE Monroe St., Topeka. Stand in a darkened room between two walls of continuously circulating news footage from that time period, when people held signs that said KEEP OUR WHITE SCHOOLS WHITE as police kept the peace. Hear recorded narratives about the five individual lawsuits that were simultaneously filed across the nation, and watch a powerful film about segregation in this country.

Members of the public wait in line for courtroom seats outside the Supreme Court during hearings for the Brown case, December 1953.

The 1954 Supreme Court decision

On May 17, 1954 the United States Supreme Court issued its unanimous Brown v. Board of Education ruling (called Brown I), declaring segregation in public schools unconstitutional.

The Court held that separate but equal educational facilities were inherently discriminatory. By overturning the legal basis for segregation, the ruling's impact would extend far beyond public schools.

ropolitan Ave. in the far right lane. Enjoy 190 acres of open meadows, a lighted covered driving range, two practice putting greens, and locker rooms, plus a full-service restaurant. Par 71, 18 holes, 6,188 yards.

Lake Shawnee Golf Course (785-267-2295), 4141 SE E. Edge Rd., Topeka. Zoysia fairways and Bentgrass greens characterize this course with water near almost half of all holes. There's a well-stocked pro shop, plus a driving range and chipping and putting greens. Par 70, 18 holes, 6,357 yards.

North Topeka Golf Center (785-357-0026), 350 NE US 24, Topeka. Golfers of all skill levels will enjoy this short course layout. Par 32, 9 holes, 2,309 yards.

Cypress Ridge Golf Center (785-272-0511), 2533 SW Urish Rd., Topeka. Rolling yards and three lakes add challenge to Topeka's oldest and recently renovated municipal golf course. Par 70, 18 holes, 6,188 yards.

HUNTING Ravenwood Lodge (785-256-6444; ravenwoodlodge.com), 10147 SW 61st St., Topeka. Drawing hunting enthusiasts from 15–20 states, Ravenwood Lodge offers guest rooms at Mission Creek Lodge, partially built in 1863 by co-owner Ken Corbett's family when they immigrated from Ireland. A bunkhouse sleeps 10. Pheasant and deer hunts are very popular here. See the Milky Way, owls, and coyotes, or hold group events. At least 80 percent of visitors are repeat customers. Each June Ravenwood hosts a free Kids' Day, when they learn dog-training tips, try hunting and clay shooting, and enjoy outdoor games. Call for rates.

✳ Green Space

In Leavenworth
Leavenworth Landing Park (913-682-9201, lvarea.org), Cherokee and Esplanade Streets, Leavenworth. This lovely park with a walkway that looks like railroad tracks and a long wrought iron fence follows the Missouri River and honors one of the river's major sites for loading or unloading freight and passengers. Multiple sculptures include a steam locomotive and a Conestoga wagon. The new Three-Mile Creek walking and biking trail travels along six blocks and connects to Landing Park.

Riverfront Park (913-682-6398), Metropolitan Ave. and Riverfront Rd., near the Centennial Bridge, Leavenworth. Open April–Oct. 7–10. The park commemorates Lewis and Clark's travels through this area in 1804 and offers the city's only campgrounds. Lots of shade and flat ground flank the bank of the Missouri River. Daily camping $8, with electricity $10; noncamper dump station $1; fees must be paid in advance.

In Topeka
Gage Park (785-368-3700; Topeka.org/parksrec/gage_park.shtml), 635 SW Gage Blvd., Topeka. Open daily. At 160 acres, this multifaceted outdoor entertainment destination, which includes the Topeka Zoological Park and the Topeka Rain Forest—housed in a 30-foot-tall/100-foot diameter geodesic dome—showcases some of the world's most exotic plants and animals. Carousel rides and minitrain rides that flank a playground, an aquatic park with massive slides and

loads of shade umbrellas, and the E. F. A. Reinisch Rose Garden with arbors and a small reflecting pool are other delights. There are also dozens of picnic tables. Zoo admission: adults 13–64 $5.75; children 3–12 $4.25; seniors 65 and over $4.75.

MacLennan Park, near Cedar Crest/Governor's Mansion, Topeka. This 244-acre wildlife refuge and park overlooks the Kansas River and is near the Governor's Mansion. Woodlands and meadows provide wonderful habitat for native birds and animals. Enjoy native prairie and wildflower plantings, fishing ponds, jogging/bike trails, and, in wintertime, a pond for ice skating. Three mountain bike trails range from 0.75 to 1.5 miles through a variety of terrain.

Shunga Trail (785-368-2448), 4801 SW Shunga, Topeka. Approximately 13 miles in length, this paved trail is popular with cyclists. Easy to moderate dirt and mountain bike trails, and a BMX dirt course are also available.

Garfield Park/Garfield Community Center (785-368-3787), 1600 NE Quincy, Topeka. Center open 9–7 Mon.–Thurs., 9–noon Fri., 3–6 Sat., 12–3 Sun. This park has a large accessible gazebo, small gazebos with picnic tables, and an aqua center with a large slide. There's also a large shelter house of gorgeous native limestone. The center offers a gymnasium pool and foosball tables, a kitchen, and a big-screen TV.

✳ Lodging
BED & BREAKFASTS
(ᵞ) **The Woodward Inns on Fillmore** (785-354-7111; thewoodward.com), 1272 SW Fillmore, Topeka. A magnificent 1920s-era Tudor-style home is the centerpiece of a small lodging community located near Topeka's downtown. Step into the luxurious foyer as owner Elizabeth E. Taylor greets you warmly. Cozy dinners and small weddings often take place in the brick-walled library with two stories of stained-glass windows. A Caribbean oasis and pool garden are open to adults, including a nonchlorinated pool and a tree house. Tiny lights decorate the front porch of the Woodward Max, whose interior decor honors artist Peter Max. Other buildings were renovated with business travelers, families, and adult travelers in mind and some stays offer breakfast. Choose which house works best for your needs. Call for rates and ask about the new pet hotel.

✳ Where to Eat
EATING OUT
In Leavenworth
& **Baan Thai** (913-682-6999, baanthaikansas.com), 301 S. Fourth St. and Cherokee, Leavenworth. Open 10:30–9 Mon.–Sat., 11–8 Sun. Dine amid ornately carved wood and imported china. Crunchy, nongreasy spring rolls with shredded cabbage, carrot, and meat, as well as ultra-creamy crab rangoon, are great meal starters. Try tender chicken satay with sweet-spicy peanut sauce and marinated cabbage and cucumbers or comforting pad thai. Inexpensive.

Homer's Drive-In (913-651-3500), 1320 S. Fourth St., Leavenworth. Open 6–9 Mon.–Sat. and 6:30–9 Sun. The first customers here drove Model Ts and male-only carhops wore shirts and ties. This is a favorite among Kansas restaurants, with more than 70 years in operation and a 1962 remodel that honored the old-time decor rec-

ognized by longtime fans. Don't miss
their shakes and custom dressed
burgers. Try the hot beef sandwich
(the Monday special), biscuits and
gravy, or Mac's chili—named after the
founder.

&. **Tampico Authentic Mexican
Restaurant** (913-682-5600; eat
tampico.com), 215B Delaware St.,
Leavenworth. Open 11–9 Mon.–
Thurs., 11–10 Fri.–Sat. This family-
operated spot makes fresh guacamole
with cilantro, tomato, red onion, and
garlic and offers many Mexican
regional favorites. Enjoy a cheap margarita on Mondays, plus creamy
spinach enchiladas, spicy huevos con
chorizo, or sweet Cancun mango fish
with vegetables. Inexpensive.

&. **The Corner Pharmacy Old
Fashioned Soda Fountain** (913-
682-1602), 429 Delaware St., Leavenworth. Open 7:30–6 Mon.–Wed./Fri.,
7:30–7 Thurs., 7:30–5 Sat. Grab a seat
at the counter of this 1871 soda fountain. Try an old-fashioned phosphate
with strawberry, cherry, or vanilla flavor, citric acid and carbonated water,
or the Green River—a combination of
lemon-lime syrup, ice, simple syrup,
and carbonated water. Or enjoy a bot-
tomless cup of coffee for less than a
buck, with breakfast served any time.
Inexpensive.

&. ☿ **The High Noon Saloon** (913-
682-4876; thehighnoon.com), 206
Choctaw St., Leavenworth. Opens 11
AM daily and closing hours vary. You'll
find bright lights, brick walls from the
1800s, and hometown brews at this
spot known best for beer, live entertainment, a giant TV, and fun atmosphere. They also serve food, from
soup, salad, and steaks to stuffed
spuds and mini corn dogs. Inexpensive.

**Harbor Lights Coffeehouse and
Café** (913-682-2303), 316 Shawnee
St., Leavenworth. Open 7:30–5 weekdays, 8:30–3:30 Sat. This family-
owned coffee shop offers great
lunches. Build your own sandwich
with choice of bread, meat, cheese,
vegetables, and condiments, or a cus-
tom-designed salad. There's always a
soup of the day and luscious baked
goods, from gourmet cupcakes to
decadent brownies. Inexpensive.

In Topeka

&. **Hanover Pancake House** (785-
232-1111), 1034 S. Kansas Ave., Topeka. Open 6–3 Sun.–Fri., 6–2:30 Sat.
Step back in time at this homey, 40-
year-old dining favorite of residents
and legislators. Enjoy 1950s and '60s
music while enjoying fluffy biscuits
with perfectly salted, creamy gravy
full of sausage chunks or light butter-
milk pancakes served with whipped
butter and warm syrup. Daily specials
range from breakfast sandwiches and
corned beef hash to French toast and
hot roast beef sandwiches. Inexpensive.

Porubsky's Deli (785-234-5788), 508
NE Sardou, Topeka. Restaurant open
11–2 Mon.–Thurs.; store open 8:30–5
Mon.–Sat. It's well worth a trip to the
top of Sardou Bridge and around the
bend in north Topeka to reach this
eatery. With a cement floor and original wood paneling, this family deli
and restaurant in Topeka's Little Russia district is legendary for spicy chili
served with saltines, ultrahot house-
made pickles, and relish-laced, freshly
ground ham salad. A local favorite
since 1947, it has received kudos from
national restaurant critic Michael
Stern. Just know that they only serve
chili from October through April. Buy
premium meat and cheese or a quart

of pickles at the deli case. No credit cards. Inexpensive.

✍ **Bobo's Drive-In** (785-234-4511), 2300 SW 10th Ave., Topeka. Open 11–8 Mon.–Sat. There are 14 outside bays for cars, with a horseshoe-shaped counter and booths topped in pink vinyl. Try favorites such as the steak burger and the apple pie with its flaky crust and soft apple pieces, served warm beneath a huge swirl of soft-serve ice cream called satin, or crispy onion rings and 24-ounce shakes. *Diners, Drive-ins and Dives* has been here too. Inexpensive.

✳ Entertainment

Trolley Rides (913-682-1331), departing from 320 S. Esplanade, C. W. Parker Carousel Museum/Leavenworth. Available 11 AM Sat., beginning in May. Hitch a ride on Trolley Tyme and enjoy a one-hour tour with recorded history about the development of Leavenworth. Adults $5; children 11 and under $3; children must be accompanied by an adult.

Heartland Park Raceway LLC (785-862-4781; hpt.com), 7530 Topeka Blvd., Topeka. Events are March–Oct. This popular raceway has offered auto drag, road, and dirt racing events for more than 20 years. A Heartland Vintage Racing event took place here for the first time in August 2010. The following month the track hosted the first invitation-only National Hot Rod Diesel Association World Finals, featuring 16 racers from across the nation. On Thursday nights watch NHRA Drags Street Legal Style racing for $10. Check for individual event and ticket information.

✍ ♿ **Topeka Zoo** (785-368-9180; fotz.org), 635 SW Gage Blvd., inside Gage Park, Topeka. Open 9–5 daily. The zoo has been a Topeka favorite since it opened in the 1930s and currently features more than 380 animals. Call for current ticket prices. At press time the zoo also faced possible loss of its accreditation. You might want to check on its status before visiting.

P. T.'s Coffee (785-862-JAVA; pts coffee.com), 929 SW University Dr., Topeka. Make a reservation (one week in advance) for a two-hour tour at P. T.'s, which roasts premium coffee and then distributes it to specialty cafés in more than 20 states. P. T.'s began as a single coffee café in 1993. Today they purchase sustainably grown beans directly from farmers and offer barista training with a focus on helping others open and run cafés. Visit the roasting room, learn about coffee sources and roasting, and taste coffee from different growing regions of the world. This can be a tough place to find amid a large warehouse district. Tours are $10.

♿ **Topeka Civic Theatre and Academy** (785-357-5211; topekacivic theatre.com), 3028 SW Eighth Ave.,

CAPPUCINO AT P.T.'S

Topeka. The nation's oldest community dinner theater celebrates its 75th anniversary in 2011. More than five hundred volunteers perform for and assist this nonprofit organization, which also offers classes for adults and children. Housed in the renovated Gage School, the site features the large Sheffle Theater, offering eight shows per year, a full service bar with desserts for some performances, and improvisational comedy offered on nonshow weekends. A studio theater seats 150. Call for ticket prices.

✳ Selective Shopping

In Leavenworth
The Quilter's Quarters Inc. (913-651-6510, quilterqtrs.com), 200 S. Fifth St., Leavenworth. Open 9:30–5 Mon.–Fri., 9:30–3:30 Sat. Named one of the top 10 quilting stores in the U.S. by *Better Homes and Gardens* (2006), this store is packed with everything quilters need, and gorgeous quilts line the walls. They also offer classes.

The Book Barn (913-682-6518), 410 Delaware St., Leavenworth. Open 10–6 Mon.–Thurs., 10–8 Fri., 10–5 Sat. Twenty-eight years in operation and members of the American Booksellers Association and the Midwest Booksellers Association, this popular store sells mostly new and discounted books with some used. Local authors hold book signings here. There are also poetry readings and dog parties, American Girl events, and even a writer's group.

In Topeka
& **Gallery Classic Inc.** (785-266-5888, galleryclassic.com), 3400 SW Topeka Blvd., Topeka. Open 10–5:30 weekdays, 10–5 Sat., 1–4 Sun. in

Nov.–Dec. Watch for this historic building set back from the street. It's brimming with home decor and European antiques that offer high style and low prices. There's a baby room, tableware, gourmet foods and candles, and leather-bound antique books. Furniture vignettes that resemble entire rooms fill the upstairs. The owner helps design many items and visits Europe at least once a year. She has furnished a client's home in the Bahamas and has customers from Florida. The historic 10,000-square-foot building was previously a dairy barn, the Topeka Golf Club, the White Lakes Golf Course, a USO club, a furniture store, and an office building.

QUILTER'S QUARTERS

&. **Hazel Hill Chocolate Traditions** (785-216-8881; hazelhillchocolate .com), 724 S. Kansas Ave., Topeka. Open 10–7 Mon.–Fri., 10–6 Sat. Most treats are made on site with Guittard chocolate, from dark chocolate hazelnut truffles and trios of chocolate-covered cherries to chocolate-dipped pretzels and melt-in-your-mouth fudge, priced from $11 to $20 per pound. Schedule a free tour by e-mail, and watch employees dipping ganache in chocolate baths or working with soft chocolate on a marble slab. Visitors also receive a free truffle during the month of their birthday.

AN EMPLOYEE COATS CONFECTIONS BY HAND AT HAZEL HILL CHOCOLATE TRADITIONS.

&. **Marion Lane Candles** (785-357-4500; marionlanecandles.com), 713 S. Kansas Ave., Topeka. Open 10–6 Mon.–Fri., 10–4, Sat. A friendly black lab mix named Annie greets customers to this bright downtown shop. Most scented candles are handcrafted on site, with Soyflower wax. They recently introduced soaps and other body products, too. The Absolute Design by Brenda, a florist and home design shop, also operates inside Marion Lane.

&. **Rees Fruit Farm** (785-246-3257; reesfruitfarm.com), 2476 KS 4, Topeka. Open 10–6 Mon.–Fri., 9–6, Sat., 11–5 Sun. Open for 105 years, Rees Fruit Farm is the oldest commercial fruit farm in Kansas and the second oldest business in Jefferson County. The family-operated shop is well known for apples, cider, fresh cider donuts, and soft-serve apple ice cream. The 120-acre farm also grows asparagus, spinach, pumpkins, sweet potatoes, and gourds, as well as gooseberries, elderberries, and tomatoes. Rex and Shannon Rees make cider nine months of the year and then freeze some to bring out each summer.

✳ Special Events

Monthly: **First Friday Art Walk** (785-271-0065; artsconnecttopeka .org), throughout Topeka. Most of the city's 16 art galleries are open late on the first Friday evening of each month.

April: **Tulip Time Festival** (1-800-235-1030), throughout Topeka. Multiple locations throughout the city display tulips, daffodils, and other spring flowers, some with an admission charge or suggested donation.

June: **Sunflower Music Festival** (785-670-1620), Topeka. Celebrating 25 years, this nine-day event offers orchestra concerts, chamber music, and other artistic events on the Washburn University campus.

July: **Fiesta Mexicana** (olg-parish .org/fiesta), Topeka. Sponsored by Our Lady of Guadalupe Church, this is the largest Mexican fiesta in the Midwest and more than 75 years old. Food, entertainment, and even royalty are part of this event.

September: **Inter-Tribal Pow Wow** (785-969-7890), Lake Shawnee/Topeka. Celebrate American Indian culture, including costumed dancers, professional artisans, and food. **Huff 'n' Puff Hot Air Balloon Rally** (huff-n-puff.org.contact.php), Topeka.

Sponsored by the Great Plains Balloon Club, the three-day event features multiple mass launches and evening balloon glows.

October: **Apple Festival** (785-368-3888), Ward-Mead Historic Site, Topeka. See blacksmiths, quilters, culinary artists, and musicians in this highly popular annual event.

December: **Leavenworth's Candlelight Vintage Homes Tour** (913-682-7759; leavenworthhistory.org), throughout Leavenworth. A local church plus seven vintage homes put on their holiday best for this event, which benefits the Leavenworth County Historical Society. Call for more information.

SMALL TOWNS

AREA CODE Most of this area uses 785; some locations use 620 and others use 913.

GUIDANCE **Wamego Convention and Visitors Bureau** (785-456-7849; visitwamego.com), 529 Lincoln Ave., Wamego. Open 9–noon, 1–3 weekdays.

Council Grove Convention and Visitors Bureau (620-767-5413; council grove.com), 207 W. Main St., Council Grove. Open 9–4 weekdays, 10–3 Sat.

Seneca Kansas Chamber of Commerce (785-336-2294; seneca-kansas.us /chamber/index.html), Seneca.

Holton Jackson County Chamber of Commerce (785-364-3963), 416 Pennsylvania Ave., Holton. Open 9–1 weekdays.

City of Horton (785-486-2681), 205 E. Eighth St., Horton. Open 8–5 weekdays.

Lansing Convention and Visitors Bureau (913-727-5488), 730 First Terr., Ste. 2., Lansing. Open 8–5 weekdays.

Osage City, City Hall (785-528-4090), 201 S. Fifth St., Osage City. Open 8–5 weekdays.

GETTING THERE AND GETTING AROUND Plan on driving to these small towns. Major highways include US 24, US 56, US 59, US 73, KS 10, and I-70. See *Getting There* in *University Towns* about buses, trains, and air travel.

MEDICAL EMERGENCY (arranged alphabetically by city name)

Morris County Hospital (620-767-6811; mrcohosp.com), 600 N. Washington, Council Grove.

Hiawatha Community Hospital (785-742-2131), 300 Utah, Hiawatha.

Holton Community Hospital (785-364-2116), 1110 Columbine Dr., Holton.

Community Memorial Healthcare (785-562-2311; cmhcare.org/index_flash .php), 798 N. 18th St., Marysville.

Sabetha Community Hospital (785-284-2121; sabethahospital.com), 14th and Oregon Streets, Sabetha.

Nemaha Valley Community Hospital (785-336-6107; nemvch.com), 1600 Community Dr., Seneca.

Cotton-O'Neil Clinic-Wamego (785-456-2207), 1704 Commercial Cir., Wamego.

Wamego City Hospital and Clinics **(785-456-2295), 711 Glenn Dr., Wamego.**

✳ To See

HISTORIC PLACES, LANDMARKS, AND SITES

In Council Grove

Council Grove Historical Tour (620-767-5413), throughout Council Grove. Council Grove has more than 24 historical sites. Follow this trail, which begins at the Kaw Mission, with stops at the Last Chance Store—"Last Chance for Beans, Bacon and Whiskey"—and at the Custer Elm, with adjacent tiny playground and picnic tables. Stop beside the covered wagon and look at Neosho Crossing, now the site of small waterfalls and lovely footbridges. Then drive a few miles out into the countryside for a look at the Old Stone Barn beside the Morris County Rodeo Arena. The tour includes:

& **Kaw Mission State Historic Site** (620-767-5410), 500 N. Mission, Council Grove. Open March–Nov., 10–5 Wed.–Sat.; Dec.–Feb., 1–5 Sun. This historic stone mission housed and educated 30 Kaw/Kansa Indian boys between 1851 and 1854 before the U.S. government removed them to Oklahoma in 1873. See photos of the Kansa Indians, exhibits regarding the Santa Fe Trail, and early artifacts, including an antique writing desk and spinning wheel moccasins and an eight-minute video called *The Original Kansans*. Adults $3; students $1; children under five free.

In Seneca

& **1922 Stutz Fire Engine,** beside city hall at 531 Main St., Seneca. This gorgeous Model K Stutz engine was built for $6,600 in 1922 and restored for $8,800 in 1976. It's the only one remaining from this year. Get a close look by calling for a tour from phone numbers on the door or checking in at city hall. Free.

Hand-Dug City Water Well, 301 N. 11th St., Seneca. Listed on the National Register of Historic Places in August 2006, this well was the last remaining sign of the town's original water system built in 1895. At 65 by 34 feet, this may be the widest and second largest hand-dug well in the state, with a water depth of about 15 feet. Its use was discontinued in 1937. See the brick structure with red door and cupola behind a fence in a small park area.

Elsewhere

Marshall County Courthouse (785-562-5012), 1207 Broadway, Marysville. Winter hours 1–4 Mon.–Fri., open daily 1–4 Memorial Day–Sept. 15. This beautiful brick Romanesque building-turned-museum has served the county for more than 90 years. See a courtroom with original woodwork, stained-glass windows, and spectator seats, plus displays related to medical and dental offices, a newspaper printing shop, and other items from the time period. Free.

St. Mary's Church (785-336-3174), 9208 Main St., St. Benedict. Always open; services still occur in the sanctuary. Built in the early 1890s, this Roman-style church has an amazing sanctuary reminiscent of small European churches, with gilt-painted altar woodwork; delicate, hand-painted detail along the multiarched ceiling; and a balcony organ with dozens of pipes. The workmanship will take your breath away. Free.

Davis Memorial (785-742-7643), 606 Iowa St., Mt. Hope Cemetery/Hiawatha. Open during daylight hours. This highly unusual family memorial began when Sarah Davis died and her husband, John, started to erect the massive marble structure at the cemetery in her honor. By the time he finished, John had created a marble canopy with many additional human and other figures under or near it. A marble and granite wall followed in the 1940s and John was eventually buried beside Sarah. Free.

& **Abraham Lincoln Monument,** 138 E. Walnut, lawn of Tennent-Baker House/Troy. Always open. Abraham Lincoln spent eight days in Kansas before he received the Republican presidential nomination in 1860. On December 1, 1859, he spoke at the Court House in Troy, and some say the speech was a trial run of his speech at Cooper Union in New York that led to his nomination. This largely brick monument, topped with a bust of Lincoln, was erected in 2002 by the Troy and Community Garden Club and the Doniphan County Historical Society. Free.

& **Peter Toth American Indian Sculpture.** 120 E. Chestnut, grounds of Doniphan County Courthouse/Troy. Always open. Dedicated on September 29, 1979, by Kansas Governor John Carlin, Tall Oak was carved by sculptor Peter Toth from a tree found in Rushville, Missouri. Toth had a goal to create an American Indian sculpture in every state and this magnificent 35-foot tall woodcarving is visible from several blocks away. Free.

Constitution Hall State Historic Site (785-877-6520), 319 Elmore, Lecompton. Open 9–5 Wed.–Sat., 1–5 Sun. Bleeding Kansas historical programs often take place during guided tours. Feel the weight of history at this national historic landmark as you briefly tour one of the state's oldest original wood-frame buildings. This was the capital of the Kansas Territory in the mid-1850s. It was also a U.S. Land Office (see a replica in the museum), a location for the district court, and home of Kansas's proslavery legislature in 1857. A constitution was drafted that would have admitted Kansas as a slave state, but was then rejected after intense debate. James Henry Lane, who later founded Lane University, was part of the antislavery movement. The new legislature met in Constitution Hall. Adults $3; students/seniors $1; children under five free.

MUSEUMS Oz Museum (785-458-8686; ozmuseum.com), 511 Lincoln Ave., Wamego. Open 10–5 Mon.–Sat., noon–5, Sun. (call for winter hours). This museum houses the largest collection of Oz memorabilia on record. See the Wicked Witch's legs under Dorothy's house, and an 8-foot-tall Tin Man, plus dozens of Oz-inspired dolls, movie posters, and photos signed by Judy Garland. The legendary movie runs continuously in a small screening room. Adults 13 and up $7; children 4–12 $4; children 3 and under free; college students with ID $4.

Expressions of Dolls and Other Caricatures (1-800-795-5337), 406 Pennsylvania, Holton. Open 8:30–5:30 Mon.–Thurs., 8–5 Fri., and 9–4 Sat. when the Expressions shop isn't too busy; call ahead. The shop offers gifts, fresh flowers, collectibles, and more. See Asian, John Wayne, or classic baby dolls in this delightful basement museum with multiple rooms. Free.

Pony Express Barn Museum (785-562-3825; 785-562-3101 for Marysville chamber of commerce in off-season), 106 S. Eighth St., Marysville. Open April–Oct., 10–5 Mon.–Sat., noon–4 Sun. Adults $4, children 6–12 $2; children under 6 free. The only original stable used by the pony express that remains in its original site now houses a museum. See blacksmithing equipment, a mint-condition stagecoach, dozens of period firearms and other memorabilia as you learn about behavioral guidelines for pony express riders. Adults $4; children 6–12 $2; children under 6 free.

ASIAN DOLLS ARE IN EXPRESSIONS OF DOLLS AND OTHER CARICATURES, HOLTON.

Wabaunsee County Museum (785-765-2200), 227 Missouri, Alma. Open 10–noon Tues.–Sat., 1–4 Sun. The year 2010 was the 150th anniversary of Wabaunsee County, named after a Potawatomie Indian chief. People from the county donated every item and the real treasures lie on the unheated side of the museum. Individual storefronts depict a general store, a barbershop, a dressmaking/millinery shop, a harness and shoe shop, and a post office. You'll also see farm wagons, carriages, an antique fire engine, and a 1926 Model T. $2 donation suggested.

Territorial Capital Museum (785-887-6285/6148, for guided tours), 609 E. Woodson Ave., Lecompton. Open 11–4 Wed.–Sat., 1–5 Sun. Construction on this building began with $50,000 from the U.S. Congress when Kansas seemed poised to enter the Union as a slave state with the town as its capital. Kansas entered as a free state and the building was finally completed in 1882. It later became Lane University. The building now showcases three floors of historical artifacts, including a rare $3 bill printed by the state bank of Lecompton and a replica of Mamie Eisenhower's wedding dress. See the chapel where President Eisenhower's parents married and an antique melodeon in the music room. Adults $2 with guided tour; students through high school $1.

Roebke House Memorial Museum (785-364-4991), 216 New York Ave., Holton. Open May–Oct., 10–4 Fri. or by appointment, through the Jackson County Historical Society. See vintage clothing and furniture, including beautifully handcrafted high school graduation dresses. Free.

Nemaha County Museum (785-336-6366), Sixth and Nemaha Streets, Seneca. Open Wednesdays in the winter and 9–4, May–Aug. A three-cell jail during the late 1800s through the early 1900s, the building houses dozens of law books dating back to 1874. The jail connected to the sheriff's home, including a pass through from the jail to the home kitchen where the sheriff's wife prepared prisoners' meals. The five-bedroom home and other buildings display memorabilia from three hospitals, physicians, and a pharmacy, plus a military display with 50 uniforms. See railroad and dairy farm items, old electronics, and a 1950s beauty shop. Free.

& **Osage County Railroad and Mining Museum** (785-828-3242), 508 Market St., Osage City. Mining operations and railroad traffic were major forces in the growth and development of this area. See a period chalkboard timetable inside this brick and stucco depot, plus a conductor's uniform and women's suit of the period, as well as original depot benches, railroad china, and a model train. A fully restored caboose from the Atchison, Topeka, and Santa Fe Railway (AT&SF) sits beside the building.

Lansing Historical Museum (913-250-0203), A115 E. Kansas Ave., Lansing. Open 10–5 Tues.–Sat. Visit this historically accurate restored 1887 AT&SF depot and one of Lansing's few remaining historic buildings. See railroad artifacts and memorabilia from the Kansas State Penitentiary, local schools, and businesses, such as a telegraph operator's desk, and permanent plus rotating exhibits. Free.

TOWNS Alma. Rich in German heritage, this town located west of Topeka is part of the Scenic Skyline Byway and is sometimes called the City of Native Stone. Settled in 1858, it has a current population of approximately eight hundred people and is also in close proximity to Junction City, and Manhattan. A self-guided historical tour includes 26 sites.

Burlingame. Located outside of Topeka, Burlingame served as an important stop on the Santa Fe Trail, and Santa Fe Ave. could accommodate U-turns by teams of oxen. The current town name was adopted in 1858. Eight historical sites from the Santa Fe Trail remain in the Burlingame area.

Dover. Once a much larger community, founded in 1860, Dover is located south of Topeka and has only a few commercial buildings. Stop by Sommerset Hall Café for a slice of the coconut cream pie that *Good Morning America* declared winner of their best slice challenge.

Holton. Several buildings in this small town's square are listed on the National Register of Historic Places, where you'll find many shops. The town also has two parks, one with a public swimming pool.

Horton. Located on the original pony express route, this is a town of about two thousand people. It was founded in 1886, is home of the first Rural Electrification Administration project in the state of Kansas, and is dubbed The Electric City. The *Horton Headlight* weekly newspaper has been published since 1896.

Lecompton. Known as the spot where the Civil War began, this town along the Kaw River began with the name of Bald Eagle. Because that didn't seem dignified enough for a territorial capital, it was renamed in honor of Samuel D. Lecompte, chief justice of the territorial supreme court. Civilians settled here beginning in 1854 after decades of military and clerical presence. The original border of the Kansas Territory extended to the Continental Divide, and as far as Boulder, Colorado. The territory had 10 governors, seven capitals, and four constitutions in its first 7 years of existence. A group of Lecompton men platted the town of Denver and named it after James W. Denver, acting governor and governor of the Kansas Territory from 1857 to 1858. In a prelude to the Civil War, the first white man to die over slavery died in this county. The situation in the Kansas Territory was a primary topic of discussion during Lincoln-Douglas presidential debates.

Lyndon. Two dozen historical buildings and homes tell the story of this small town located near Melvern Lake. The first section of McDaniel Hardware Store has operated since 1871. Rev. John Rankin organized the Presbyterian church here and was heavily involved in the antislavery movement. Completed in 1910, the Lyndon Carnegie Library is the smallest one ever built.

Melvern. Located near Melvern Lake, this resort town began as a Scotch settlement. Visitors can enjoy Pride Park, with a large play apparatus, shelter, and BBQ grill, or stop by the Carnegie Library. Enthusiasts of the outdoors who visit the area are a great boost to the local economy.

Osage City. This is the county's largest city, with two original soda fountains downtown. Reproduction antique globe streetlights mark intersections for several blocks. Heading south and starting at Sixth Street and Ellinwood, there are many gracious old two-story homes with gingerbread exterior woodwork. Some are under restoration.

Paxico. Located west of Topeka, just off I-70, Paxico is known as the antiques capital of Kansas, and the big shopping days are Friday through Sunday. See *Antiques Paradise* sidebar for more information.

Seneca. Immigrant farmers and merchants traveling the Oregon Trail established the town in 1858, and wagons that served area army forts frequently stopped here. The town was a pony express stop, and railroads arrived by 1870, with new hotels, shops, and schools arising as the population grew. As automobiles became more affordable, rail travel declined and the town's population shrank. Today, Seneca is creating a Main Street Historic District full of restored and renovated historical buildings.

Tonganoxie. When you visit this town you'll find a historic main street with plenty of small-town pride and chainsaw sculptures throughout. Beautiful countryside surrounds the town.

BOATING AND FISHING Melvern Lake (785-549-3318), KS 31, exit off US 75. This placid and peaceful lake and expansive recreation area includes 7,000 acres of water and 18,000 acres of surrounding land. It offers roped-off swimming, sand volleyball, bathhouses, sheltered individual picnic tables, and much more. Amid the Coeur D'Alene Park, Arrow Rock, Sundance, Turkey Point, and Eisenhower State Park and Outlet areas you'll also find well-maintained playground facilities, boat ramps, and walking/hiking trails. Primitive and RV camping with full hookups are available. Call for current fees.

Perry Lake (785-597-5144), 10419 Perry Park Dr., Perry. Eleven recreation areas surround the lake offering a swimming area, boat ramps, and marina, plus trails, playground facilities and picnic spots.

Perry State Park (785-246-2449), 5441 Westlake Rd., Ozawkie. Located in the southwest portion of Perry Reservoir, the park has a great campsite beside Perry Lake with a sand beach and picnic areas. Ride horseback or find a mountain bike trail.

Pomona Lake State Park (785-828-4933), 22900 S KS 368, Vassar. With quiet hours from 11–6 and secondary roads slightly wider than a single lane, this 4,000-acre lake and surrounding recreation area offers disc golf and a full-service marina. Two log cabins opened in June 2010 with full kitchens, gorgeous lake views, and lots of trees. Enjoy more than 200 primitive and 142 utility campsites. Hike or fish or take in a game of hoops. Campsites are $8.50 plus $9 for two utilities or $10 with three utilities. Includes: **Lighthouse Bay Marina** (785-828-4777; lighthousebaymarina), Pomona Lake. Open April 15–Oct. 15, Sun. 9–6, Fri. 7, Sat. 8, or by appointment in the off-season. This full-service marina offers bait and tackle, skis, and wakeboards. Seasonal, monthly, and daily slip and winter storage rental and boat repair are available and it's a great place to socialize.

Council Grove Lake (620-767-5195), 945 Lake Rd., US Army Corps Office/Council Grove. With areas that include Custer Park, Kit Carson Cove, and Richey Cove Park, this is a lovely lake with plenty of room for boats and swimmers, plus picnic shelters with grills. Many tree-studded campsites overlook the water. Camping $12–23; boat launch $3; swimming $1 per person.

Chase State Fishing Lake (620-767-5900), 1130 Lake Rd., Council Grove. This is a great outdoor spot with boat ramps, picnic tables, campsites, a dock for disabled visitors, and a gorgeous drive deep into the lake valley. The lake offers crappie, bluegill, white bass, and other species. The game population for hunting is limited, but quail, rabbit, white-tail deer, turkey, and prairie chickens are available.

Banner Creek Reservoir (785-364-4236; bannercreekreservoir@yahoo.com), 10975 KS 16, Holton. Open 5:30–10:30 daily. This 535-acre reservoir area is relatively flat with some rolling hills and well maintained. Boating, waterskiing, and Jet Skiing are allowed. Swim from the sandy beach, fish for largemouth bass, crappie, and more, or hike 12 miles of nature trails. This is a great place to see more than 25 bird species or ride your horse along a 6.3-mile trail. Or rent volleyball, horseshoe, or Frisbee equipment during your camping stay. There are 34 RV sites with full hookups and a bathhouse.

Lake Wabaunsee. Near KS 99 and KS 4. Permit office open April–Oct. A sign says WELCOME TO THE NORTH SHORE near a tiny evangelical Lutheran chapel and small homes. You'll also see *USA* spelled out on a hill above the lake. Permits are required for camping, fishing, boating, and shelter use. This 255-acre lake is spring fed, offering fishing, boating, and camping near the perimeter. There's also a swimming beach, boat ramp, and a bait shop. Camping permit $6; RV campsite $10; electric hookup $5.

Osage State Fishing Lake (785-828-3242; Osage County Economic Development), Carbondale. Fish in wading-to-deep water for crappie, bluegill, walleye, and more. Cruise the lake and house your horse at equestrian campgrounds with individual enclosures.

GOLF Oak Country Golf Course (913-583-3503; oakcountrygolfcourse.com), 8800 Scott Dr., DeSoto. This public course promotes their great rates, especially the twilight special. Play an island green on the 18th hole and navigate creeks and ponds. Par 66, 18 holes, 3,937 yards.

Spring Creek Golf Course and Estates (785-336-3568), 1800 Spring Creek Dr., Seneca. This is a course of wide-open spaces with dozens of beautiful new homes nearby. Three dams and three ponds, with occasional trees and narrow fairways add challenge. Par 71, 18 holes, 6,488 yards.

Wamego Country Club Golf Course (785-456-2649), 1900 E. Country Club Dr., Wamego. Brilliant green and plenty of mature trees mark what is among the state's top golf venues. Par 70, 18 holes, 5,707 yards.

HUNTING AND FISHING Eisenhower State Park (formerly Melvern State Park; 785-528-4102), 29810 S. Fairlawn Rd., Osage City. Office open 8–4 Mon.–Fri. Sailboats and catamarans often glide across Melvern Lake, which was a man-made flood control project for the Marais des Cygnes River basin. Motorboats are welcome, as are campers, who can choose from one of eight camping areas. Bow and shotgun hunters may hunt here, and there is camping with horses in Cowboy Camp. Play a game of volleyball, reserve a picnic shelter, or throw horseshoes, too. Contact the office for rates.

Perry Wildlife Area (785-945-6615), Valley Falls. Deer are common and hunting is big business on more than 10,000 acres, plus nearly 1,000 acres of wetlands leased from the Perry Reservoir Project.

OUTDOORS Vermillion Valley Equine Center (785-456-4442), 10705 Camp Creek Rd., Belvue. Call for appointment. Enjoy English and Western riding lessons and guided trail rides. Owner Ann White also teaches jumping, dressage, and event riding. $35 per hour.

Nemaha Wildlife Area (785-363-7316), 4 miles south of US 36 and KS 63, Seneca. This wildlife area offers 705 acres open to hunters, who will find plenty of waterfowl and shorebirds, plus turkey, deer, and other small mammals. There's also an 18-acre fish pond available.

Kickapoo Veterans Memorial Park and Kickapoo Pow Wow Park (877-864-2746), 1107 Goldfinch Rd., Kickapoo township/Horton. Always open. Stop here to see the beautiful memorial dedicated to Kickapoo war veterans.

Skyline Mill Creek Scenic Byway. A 10-mile section runs between Paxico and Alma over dirt/gravel-topped roads where rolling hills and wide-open spaces mean that you can see for miles in every direction. At KS 9, head left toward Alma or right toward Eskridge; no sign points to either town.

Wamego City Park, Wamego Museum Complex, and The Old Dutch Mill (785-456-2040), Wamego City Park on E. Fourth St., Wamego. Open 10–4 daily, 1–4 Sun. (shorter in winter). This park offers loads of green space and gardens, the Wamego Historical Museum, Old Dutch Mill, and Old Prairie Town. Inside the museum, see a parlor with two antique pianos and turn-of-the-century tools. There's also a fully restored miniature train that travels throughout the park. Old Prairie Town features a tiny home, an early telephone switchboard, and a general store. A Dutch immigrant built the mill in 1879 to grind grain into flour and cornmeal; it was later rebuilt here and electricity operates the 40-foot tall mill. Purchase admission for entire museum complex. Adults $4; seniors $3.50; students $1.

OLD DUTCH MILL

✳ **Green Space**

Mt. Mitchell Heritage Prairie (785-537-4385; audobonofkansas .org/mountmitchell/mountmitchell .html), approximately 5.5 miles north of the I-70 and KS 99 intersection and just off Mitchell Prairie Lane, outside of Wamego. See the faint outline of this monument installed high atop a 50-acre hilltop park from KS 99. A brass plaque commemorates the Connecticut–Kansas Colony/the Beecher Bible and Rifle Colony in honor of people who settled the Wabaunsee community beginning in 1856. Audubon of Kansas Inc. now operates the area, which also offers enormously diverse prairie landscape vegetation. Check for status of a self-guided walking tour of the area.

✳ **Lodging**

BED & BREAKFASTS ♿ **The Lodge—a prairie bed & breakfast** (785-499-5634), 705 KS 177, Council Grove. This lovely bed & breakfast with soaring ceilings and windows offers serene views across 20 acres of the Flint Hills. Dove gray and pale olive paint decorate three guest rooms with private baths on the ground floor. Facilities are available for dogs with advance notice. Full breakfast. No credit cards. $70.

♿ **1878 Sage Inn and Stagecoach Station** (785-256-6050; historicsage inn.com), 13554 SW KS 4, Dover. Once a thriving stagecoach station, it was built beside Mission Creek out of 18-inch native limestone by British immigrants—the Sage family, who are considered founders of Dover. The family operated the property as an Inn from 1865 to 1905. Surrounded by mature trees and set back from a quiet street, this home now offers six bedrooms with antique furnishings. Enjoy the morning paper, the terraced garden, or second-story deck. Full breakfast. $85–125.

(ᵗᵖ) **Holton House Bed & Breakfast** (785-364-4403; holtonhouse.com), 125 E. Fourth St., Holton. Four king rooms offer modern private baths in a graceful 1888 structure with wraparound porch. The first floor dining room, with full bar, accommodates approximately a hundred people. Stop by for their legendary family-style chicken dinners, 5–9 Fri.–Sat., 11–2 Sun. Continental breakfast weekdays; full breakfast weekends. $89.

♿ (ᵗᵖ) **The Barn Bed & Breakfast Inn** (785-945-3225; thebarnbb.com), 14910 Blue Mound Rd., Valley Falls. Stay in this 117-year-old barn that has been transformed to offer every modern amenity. Natural woodwork, ceiling fans, an indoor swimming pool, and gorgeous views of the surrounding countryside are only a few features at this casually elegant 21-room B&B inn. Full breakfast. $136.

(ᵗᵖ) **The Stein House B&B** (785-336-3790), 314 N. Seventh St., Seneca. Built by the great-great uncle of the current owner, who was a banker, city clerk, and founder of the local Knights of Columbus, the house became a B&B in 1996 and was put on the state's register of historic sites in 2004. Full breakfast. No credit cards. $60.

CABINS AND CAMPING (ᵗᵖ) **Crossroads RV Park and Campground** (785-221-5482; crossroads rvpark.com), 23313 S. US 75, Lyndon. Office open 8–8 Mon.–Sat., 2–8 Sun. Located near two Army Corps of Engineers lakes, this is a clean, neat campground. Walk your dog, play horseshoes, or do your laundry. Use the playground, nearby walking trails, and a visitor information center. 30/50 amp campsites $28.

(ᵗᵖ) **Millcreek RV Park** (785-636-5321), 22470 Campground Rd., Paxico. Situated beside the railroad tracks, this is a 50-year-old, AAA-rated park with playground equipment and a basketball hoop, picnic tables, and a storm shelter. You'll find a pop machine and laundry room, boats for rent, and full hookups. $28 or $168/week, plus electrical. Tents are welcome and there are three cabins available.

HOTELS AND RESORTS (ᵗᵖ) **The Cottage House Hotel-Motel** (620-767-6828; cottagehousehotel.com), 25

N. Neosho, Council Grove. This classy spot has served travelers for more than a century and received an AAA Diamond Award in 2010. All hotel rooms feature antique furnishings with private baths and individual climate control. Choose from a Victorian-decorated hotel room, a clean and comfortable motel room, or a honeymoon cottage with a living room area, minikitchen, and two-person Jacuzzi tub. $55–165.

&. ((ŋ)) **Red Rock Guest Ranch** (785-834-2552; redrockguestranch.com), 270th Rd., Soldier. Wild turkey and deer, stocked ponds, and 300–400 acres of land offer plenty of opportunities for hunting, fishing, hiking, and riding guests' horses at this 10-room B&B. Visitors can enjoy a hot tub room, gazebo picnic, or BBQ pit. A 1916 Sears Craftsman bungalow features a living room and a kitchen (guests here prepare their own meals), while another building features bunk space and a social area. Beginning May 1 the family's cattle return to the ranch, and guests can watch and/or participate in cattle activities. Full breakfast. $75.

The Gem Resort (785-449-2353; gemresort.com), 284 E. Flint Hills Dr., Lake Wabaunsee/Alma. A private screened deck, lake views, and plenty of space are several features of this five-bedroom lodge. Enjoy the on-site private club/sports bar or hire a professional masseuse. Add a lake activities package for $25 per person/per day, which may include boat fishing, skiing, tubing, and more. $80–150.

MOTELS AND LODGES &. ((ŋ))
Wamego Inn and Suites (785-458-8888; wamegoinn.com) 1300 Lilac Ln., Wamego. Once part of a discount

hotel chain, this privately owned, 43-room property offers all the modern basics in a clean and pleasant package, with a TV, refrigerator, and microwave in each room. There's also a pool and privileges to use an off-site fitness center. Expanded continental breakfast. From $75.

((ŋ)) **Starlite Motel** (785-336-2191), 410 N St./US 36, Seneca. Enjoy complementary coffee and snacks. Most rooms have a microwave and refrigerator. This is a neat, clean, and pleasant place to stay. Nothing fancy, but a great night's sleep. $55.

((ŋ)) **Main Street Loft** (785-770-0062), 514 Main St., Seneca. This beautiful, recently renovated loft apartment offers a fully equipped kitchen with eating bar, living room, and two bedrooms, plus modern decor and lighting, cable TV, and all linens. There's a fitness center downstairs, too. $85–100.

✳ Where to Eat

DINING OUT &. **The Willows Restaurant and Bar** (785-336-0201), 1921 N St., Seneca. Open 5–10 Mon.–Sat; bar open 4:30–10 Mon.–Thurs., 4–11 Fri.–Sat. Wide-open spaces meet wide-open interior in this family-owned restaurant set on 4 acres beside the local golf course. Appetizers include spinach artichoke dip, potato poppers, and crab cakes. Enjoy burgers, and sandwiches such as chicken ciabatta with sautéed onions and peppers, Swiss cheese, and honey mustard. Try rum-glazed salmon or Ryan's spicy Cajun pasta with mushrooms, peppers, onions, andouille sausage, and cream sauce. Moderate.

In Alma

Deb's Restaurant (785-765-2527), 327 Missouri Ave., Alma. Open 7–7:30 Mon.–Thurs., 7–8 Fri.–Sat., 11–2 Sun. buffet. Generally busiest at lunchtime, this family-owned restaurant has operated for four years. They're known for pies—especially coconut cream and strawberry when in season and fried-chicken dinners with mashed potatoes, salad/soup, vegetable, and toast or rolls. Inexpensive.

Smokin' G's Lakeside BBQ (785-449-2233), 18749 KS 99, Alma. Kitchen open 5–9 Mon.–Thurs., 5–10 Fri.–Sat., 11–2 Sun. This place constantly offers specials, from Friday night prime rib and seafood and $2 well drinks to ribs and chicken or a Mexican buffet with cheap beers or margaritas. Inexpensive–moderate.

Puffy's Cornerstone Café/Alma Food Mart (785-765-2212), 123 W. Third, Alma. Open 11–2 Mon.– Fri. Puffy's serves a lunch buffet and off the menu in a recently renovated room with knotty pine and rust-colored walls. On Thursday enjoy a chicken buffet and Friday, a steak buffet. Owner Jim Puff also owns the steak lover's paradise, Puffy's Steak and Ice House, in Maple Hill (puffys steakhouse.com) and has provided food service for the annual summer event Symphony in the Flint Hills. Inexpensive.

In Council Grove

♿ **Hays House Restaurant and Tavern** (620-767-5911; hayshouse .com), 112 E. Main St., Council Grove. Open 7–9 Sat., 7–8 Sun., 11–8 Tues.–Thurs., 11–9 Fri. Dine in the oldest continuously operating restaurant west of the Mississippi amid gorgeous woodwork, a stone fireplace, and period light fixtures. Opened in 1857 by Seth Hays, founder of Council Grove, it's a great spot for a weekend breakfast buffet, chicken-fried steak, or 12-ounce rib eye. Inexpensive–moderate.

♿ **Trail Days Café and Museum** (620-767-7986; traildayscafeand museum.org), 803 Main St., Council Grove. Open 11–8 Tues.–Sat., sometimes on Monday. Dine amid gorgeous antiques and lace. Check out the child's and parents' upstairs bedrooms filled with antique furniture, lamps, and quilts. There's also a log cabin next door. Inexpensive.

♿ **Santa Fe Diner** (620-767-2789), 212 W. Main St., Council Grove. Open 7–7:30 Mon./Wed.–Sat., 7–2 Sun. When one of the town's most popular lodging spots sends you customers, you must be doing something right. Menu favorites include homemade tacos, the Santa Fe Trail omelet (with steak), and the Santa Fe diner burger with jalapeños, hot sauce, and pepper jack cheese in the middle. Don't forget to try their homemade pies. Inexpensive.

Flint Hills Bakery and Smokehouse (620-767-6629), 318 W. Main St., Council Grove. Open 6–2 Tues.–Thurs., 6–8 Fri.–Sat. Choose a sandwich with pulled pork, brisket, meatloaf, chicken, or catfish ($5) with a side and drink for only $6. Then add coleslaw, BBQ beans, potato salad, cheesy potatoes, or macaroni and cheese. Or take out a meaty slab of ribs for $8–25. Inexpensive.

In Eudora

Jasmin Restaurant (785-542-1111), 719 Main, Eudora. Open 10:30–9

Mon.–Sat. Buddhas and sombreros, fried rice, and quesadillas mingle in this unusual restaurant on the town's main street. Enjoy daily Asian lunch specials or 10 Mexican lunch plates, plus large portions and small prices. Save room for fortune cookies or fried ice cream. Inexpensive.

& **Black Cat Café** (785-690-7084) 726 Main, Eudora. Open 7–2 daily, 5–9 Thurs.–Sat. This new café with orange walls and cat decor serves biscuits and gravy, French toast, or other breakfast favorites until 11 AM, followed by pork tenderloin, catfish sandwiches, or chef's salad, just to name a few. They're also known for fried chicken cooked to order. It takes 20 minutes to prepare but is worth every bite. Inexpensive.

In Holton
& ☗ **Boomers' Grill** (785-364-2468), 401 Colorado, Holton. Open 11–10 Sun.–Thurs., 11–11 Fri.–Sat. This is a comfortable, busy place with loads of appetizers such as guacamole and chips or zucchini sticks, classic Reubens, and The Boomer, a Philly steak sandwich piled high with caramelized onions and peppers, plus Swiss cheese. Inexpensive.

& **Big Mike's Diner** (785-362-6453), 316 Pennsylvania, Holton. Open 7–4 Tues.–Wed., 7–7 Thurs.–Fri., 7–4 Sat., 7–11:30 Sun. Don't let the decor fool you; what looks like a longtime diner is actually renovated to resemble a '50s eatery. Try the Big Mike breakfast, which includes eggs, home fries or hash browns, your choice of meat, and a biscuit and gravy or toast; a half-pound, open-faced burger topped with chili; or battered and deep-fried chicken liver and gizzard basket. Inexpensive.

All Around Sweets (785-364-3300), 317 Pennsylvania, Holton. Open 7:30–5:30 Mon.–Fri., 8–2 Sat. You can't go wrong with homemade pie, candy, or specialty espresso drinks. This family-owned sweetery also makes awesome cinnamon rolls for only $1 each. No credit cards. Inexpensive.

In Melvern
& **Legends** (785-549-3262), 129 SW Main St., Melvern. Open 11–9 Mon.–Thurs., 11–10 Fri.–Sat. This is a favorite spot for lake enthusiasts and locals who snap up fabulous Philly sandwiches and steak dinners with salad, choice of potato, and Texas toast for under $13. Made-to-order pizzas come with your choice of meats, plus mushrooms, olives, onions, green peppers, and even jalapeños. Inexpensive.

((ψ)) **Whistle Stop Café and Melvern Library** (785-549-3575), 117 SW Main, Melvern. Open 6:30–2 Mon.–Sat. Fifty-cent coffee and homemade pie for $2 are bargains. Try chicken or ham salad; other favorites include burgers, pork tenders, chili, and curlicue fries. After your meal, step into the adjacent Melvern Library. No credit cards, but there's an ATM available. Inexpensive.

In Osage City
& **The Muffin Top Cakery** (785-528-3140), 501 Market St., Osage City. Open 8–4 Tues.–Sat. Located beside the railroad tracks in the old Armand's hotel building, this spot is known for its scones, muffins, and cinnamon rolls, plus daily lunch specials such as homemade chicken salad on a croissant with a side and drink, all for under $6. Everything except the pastries is made-to-order, and there's nothing fried. Inexpensive.

Buzzard's Pizza (785-528-4900), 511 Market St., Osage City. Open 11–9 Mon.–Sat. Dinners are busiest at this family-run pizza joint with inventive pies like Roadkill—with BBQ beef, chicken, and bacon. Try their home-made breadsticks and enjoy Bud Light on tap. No credit cards. Inex-pensive.

In Paxico
& **J C's Pastries and More** (785-636-5149), 105 Newbury Ave., Paxico. Open 8–2 Tues.–Thurs., 8–4 Fri.–Sat., 12–3 Sun. Two-dollar cinnamon rolls, homemade broccoli soup, chicken wraps, and meatloaf are just a few of the favorites here. Buy pastries daily and enjoy an all-you-can-eat baked potato bar on Sundays. No credit cards.

& Y **Mill Creek Bar and Grill** (785-636-5559), 123 Newbury Ave., Paxico. Open 11–9:30 Mon.–Thurs., later on weekends. Burgers are thick and juicy and there's little on the menu for more than $5. No credit cards. Inex-pensive.

In Seneca
The Cornerstone Coffee Haus (785-334-4287), Fifth and Main Streets, Seneca. Open 7–5 Mon.–Sat; later in summer. This espresso bar, pastry hotspot, and breakfast/lunch destination occupies a beautifully restored bank building full of original stained glass, woodwork, and two unusual U-shaped ice cream parlor counters. Order a custom personal pizza or a chocolate malt. Inexpen-sive.

& **Lori's Café** (785-336-0059), 811 N St., Seneca. Open 5:30–1:30 week-days, 5:30–1 Sat. Farmers, truck driv-ers, businessmen, and locals chat over coffee near an open kitchen with a visible grill area. Try daily soups such as potato bacon; specials such as ham-burger steak with mashed potatoes, gravy, and corn; or pies that range from raisin cream to cherry and pecan. Inexpensive.

In Wamego
& & **Toto's Tacoz** (785-456-8090), 515 Lincoln St., Wamego. Open 11–2 Tues.–Sat., 11–7 Fri.–Sat. This fun restaurant is full of beach murals and multicolored umbrellas. The Califor-nia/Mexican menu includes Baja tacos, Dorothy's quesadilla, and Tin Man black bean burrito. Try the mammoth Hunk's burrito, which includes chicken, rice, beans, and some heat. Toto hides everywhere, from a painted surfboard to a wooden pup above the front door. Beer and children's portions are available. Inex-pensive.

The Friendship House Dutch Mill Bakery and Restaurant (785-456-9616; friendshiphouse.biz), 507 Ash, Wamego. Open 7–3 Tues.–Sat., 8–2 Sun. The *Topeka Capital Journal* voted this cute and cozy place the best bakery in northeast Kansas. There's a bakery case in the front room with lace and florals throughout adjoining rooms. *Bierocks* enthusiasts chow down on golden dough filled with seasoned ground beef and onion. During the annual tulip festival try their one-crust strawberry pie with a secret ingredient. Inexpensive.

& **Imperial Palace** (785-456-8880), 1701 Commercial Cir., Wamego. Open 11–9:30 daily. This is a large and spacious restaurant with granite tables and pale walls. Enjoy a Chinese buffet priced by the pound with stir-fried green beans, crab rangoon, veg-etable lo mein, and shrimp and chicken with vegetables. Or try popular roast pork fried rice, sweet and sour chicken, or beef with broccoli. Inexpensive.

Elsewhere

⅃ **Sommerset Hall Café** (785-256-6223), 5701 SW Douglas Rd., Dover. Open 7–4 Tues.–Sat., 5–8. Fri. This diner operates in an 1855 building once called the Sommerset Hall by people from outside of Dover, England, who settled here. ABC's *Good Morning America* named then house baker Norma Grubb's coconut cream pie America's best slice in 2008. Order pies with a day's notice, slices at lunchtime, or purchase one after 2 PM. Try the $4 third-of-a-pound Dover cheeseburger, jambalaya, or taco Tuesday. No credit cards. Inexpensive.

⅃ ⅄ **Guy and Mae's Tavern** (785-746-8830), 119 W. William St., Williamsburg. Open 11–midnight Tues.–Sat. This family-run restaurant has put tiny Williamsburg on the map. People travel for miles to enjoy pork rib slabs, thick meat sandwiches, smoky beans, and crunchy coleslaw. Have a brew, play some pool, and turn on the jukebox. No credit cards,

NORMA GRUBB'S COCONUT CREAM PIE AT SOMMERSET HALL CAFÉ WAS NAMED AMERICA'S BEST SLICE BY ABC.

but there's an ATM machine available. Inexpensive.

⅃ ⅄ **Bill and Ellie's E-Z Rock Café** (785-828-4612), 1304 Topeka Ave., Lyndon. Kitchen open 11–9 Tues.–Thurs., 11–10 Fri.–Sat.; karaoke Fri.–Sat. 8:30–1:30. There's zebra-print carpet on the bar face; fuchsia, turquoise, and canary-colored booths; and a sawed-off pink Cadillac in the corner. Enjoy sandwiches, salads, sides, and daily specials. Check out Mexican night on Tuesday, hot roast beef with mashed potatoes and gravy on Wednesday, and a full bar. Inexpensive.

Santa Fe Café (785-654-3555), 108 E. Santa Fe Ave., Burlingame. Open 7–2 Mon., 7–8 Tues.–Thurs., 7–9 Fri.–Sat., 7:30–2 Sun. This diner offers Biker BBQs every first and third Sun., March–Oct., and sponsors a motorcycle and car rally on the fourth Sun. But they're busy every day, whether they're serving veggie omelets with hash browns and toast, multilayer turkey club sandwiches, or burgers on homemade buns. They're also known for chicken-fried chicken and spicy cheese cubes. Inexpensive.

⅃ **Coffee Cup Café** (785-449-2818), 113 S. Main, Eskridge. Open 6–7 Mon.–Sat., 6–2 Sun. Dolly and Joe Mercer opened this café, previously called Anna Mae's, in 2009. They're known for Philly cheesesteaks, homemade pizzas, and a coffee group that gathers at around 10 AM most mornings. Inexpensive.

The Homeplace Café (785-924-3813), 303 Grant, Circleville. Open 7–2 Wed.–Sun. Opened in 1949, its new owners make everything from scratch. They're famous for the Homeplace omelet, served with your choice of meat, together with onions, green peppers, tomatoes, mushrooms, and cheese, plus hash browns and toast. Try homemade cinnamon rolls or a breakfast burrito. Lunch specials include pork loin chop with sides and a drink or the Homeplace chicken fried steak dinner. No credit cards. Inexpensive.

& **Trails Café** (785-364-2786), 606 Arizona, Holton. Open 10:30–9 Sun.–Thurs., 10:30–10 Fri.–Sat. Enjoy brunch, lunch, or dinner at this popular family-owned restaurant. Try a slice of pie, mouthwatering chicken-fried steak with country gravy, and a terrific salad bar, too.

Home Place Restaurant and Catering (785-985-3800), 102 S. Liberty St., Troy. Open 11–2 Sun.–Fri. Everything is made from scratch and a group of locals critique new recipes before they're served. Home Place is known for fresh breads, fried chicken (served on Sundays), and square pie, a tribute to the owner's experience working in public school food service. Try rhuberry or pear-berry pie with your spaghetti and meatballs. No credit cards. Inexpensive.

& Y **Branding Iron Restaurant** (785-793-2558), 301 S. Brownie Blvd., Scranton. Open breakfast, lunch, and dinner. This popular restaurant is known for chicken-fried steak, hamburgers, and chocolate chip pancakes, plus specials like hot beef sandwiches with mashed potatoes and gravy, pulled pork, or tacos. Inexpensive.

& **Bichelmeyer's Steakhouse Restaurant** (913-369-2337), 427 E. Fourth St., Tonganoxie. Open daily for lunch and dinner. In 1890 this brick building housed Zoeller Mercantile Co. Today it's a place to savor sandwiches, salads, fish, and, of course, premium meat, all beneath a

tin ceiling and vintage light fixtures. Inexpensive.

& **Breck's Green Acres Restaurant and Green Acres Pizza and Subs** (785-453-2166), 4961 E KS 268, Vassar. Restaurant open 5:30–9 daily. Pizza/sub shop open 11–9 Mon.–Wed., 11–10 Thurs.–Sun. The restaurant has served breakfast all day and broasted chicken for decades. Try their open-faced hot beef sandwich or breakfast (on weekends), lunch, and dinner buffets. Get a 14-inch chicken bacon pizza for under $15. Inexpensive.

& **Whiting Café** (785-873-3125), 308 Whiting St., Whiting. Open 6–2 Mon.–Sat. Serving breakfast all day, this family-owned café draws people from Atchison and Topeka for baby back ribs, served on each first Friday. Customers also love their homemade pies, pan-fried chicken, and real mashed potatoes. Order their homemade candy around the holidays. Inexpensive.

✳ Entertainment

Plumlee Buffalo Ranch (785-776-1271/539-2255), 29300 SW 99 Frontage Rd., Alma. Call about 60-minute tours. The Plumlees raise buffalo from birth and visit the herd on a daily basis. See these naturally curious creatures in open pasture. Late spring is a particularly good time to visit; calves are born weighing only about 40 pounds and light brown in color. Travel the ranch in four-wheel drive vehicles and learn all about this creature. Adults $20; seniors/military/children $10; children under five free.

Lazy Heart D Bison Ranch (785-456-9465), 17455 Pauling Run Rd., Westmoreland (outside Wamego).

Call for directions and tours. Ed Dillinger says that working with buffalo is about negotiation. They are very herd-oriented, have wool that they rub off themselves, and produce buffalo chips that burn like charcoal. He gladly takes small groups out to see them. Barn displays educate visitors about the many uses for buffalo and the health benefits of their meat. On a small knoll lies the original site for Wamego's Old Dutch Mill.

Jr.'s Hitchin' Post Opry (785-241-0489; hawkshaw5.tripod.com/id91.html), Fourth and Maple Streets, Quenemo (near Pomona Lake). Doors open 6 PM Sat.; 7 PM showtime; closed Jan.–Feb. On Saturday evenings this tiny town ignites with the sounds of hot country music, including percussion, guitar, vocal, and keyboards. Ralph "Junior" and Jane Wilson are opry managers/owners and official sponsors of mokanopry.com. A concession area sells burgers, dogs, fries, and popcorn. No credit cards. Adults $12; children 6–13 $6; seniors $11; extra $1 discount with ticket from previous week.

Annie's Country Jubilee (943-845-9600; anniescountryjubilee.com), 707 E. Fourth St., Tonganoxie. Doors open 6:30 PM Sat. ; 7:30 PM showtime; occasional special performances at different times. The nine-member Annie's Country Jubilee Band delights audiences with Nashville and other country-influenced music in a large, modern building located downtown. Adults $12.50; 55 and over $12; children under 13 $6.

Columbian Theatre (785-456-2029; columbiatheatre.com), 521 Lincoln Ave., Wamego. Open 10–5 Tues.–Fri., 10–3 Sat. Founder J. C. Rogers was a local banker and merchant who want-

ed a place to showcase art that he purchased at the 1893 World's Fair. After a $1.8 million restoration, completed in 1994, the theater again displays six magnificent, floor-to-ceiling murals Rogers bought from the government building rotunda at the fair, plus an eagle atop patriotic banners above a lobby door. The collection is worth more than $1 million. The 284-seat theater offers five locally produced musicals and two plays each year, and the gallery accommodates special events including dinner theater and brunch buffets. Free tours.

WINERIES BlueJacket Crossing (785-542-1764; bluejacketwinery.com), 1969 N. 1250 Rd., Eudora. Tasting room open noon–6 Wed.–Fri./Sun., 10–6 Sat. The tasting room at this rural winery outside of Lawrence is gorgeous and comfortable, with Southwestern-inspired decor, jewelry, and other local art pieces. In fact the wine label uses an original painting by Arapaho artist and impressionist painter Brent Learned. The winery received bronze medals in the 2010 Indy International Wine Competition for 2009 Seyval Reserve and 2009 Shady Betty. Try some for yourself. Free.

Davenport Orchards and Winery (785-542-2278; davenportwinery.com), 1394 E. 1900th Rd., Eudora. Tasting room open 4–7 Mon./Wed./Fri., 1–5 weekends. On a 1949 family farm the Davenports have made wine commercially since 1997. With German and Polish backgrounds, the couple uses Kansas-grown fruit to make sweet fruit wines, including peach and rhubarb, plus dry or sweet red or white grape wines. They also make rose and a sparkling wine.

& **Oz Winery** (785-456-7417; OzWineryKansas.com), 417 Lincoln Ave., Wamego. Open 10–6 Mon.–Sat., noon–5 Sun. Schedule private wine tastings for the back room. This operation creates wines from fermentation behind the shop. It's a bright, cheerful place, with multiple racks of wine and winery T-shirts. Start your wine tasting with a dry white and then move toward sweeter Emerald City Lights or Auntie Em's Prairie Rose. Try the Lion's Courage and Witch in a Ditch reds and special wine releases around OZtoberFest. Free.

Pome on the Range Orchards and Winery (785-746-5492; pomeonthe range.com), 2050 Idaho Rd., Williamsburg. Open 10–5 Mon.–Sat., noon–5 Sun. Apple wine is Pome's claim to fame, but there's also elderberry-, peach-, and blackberry-spiced wines and plenty of fresh produce. Check for several special events, including pottery and spinning demonstrations and a farmers' market. Kids will also love feeding the ducks a handful of food. Orchard tours and a pumpkin patch are popular fall activities.

& **Vin Vivante Winery and Poppyfield Gallery** (785-458-2930; vin vivante.com), 514 Lincoln, Wamego. Open 10–6 Mon.–Sat., noon–6 Sun. Part wine retailer and part art gallery, Vin Vivante has as much fun with labels as it does with its wines. Purple Crush is a red table wine that celebrates K-State, and Flint Hills Winery has license plate markings such as EAT BEEF or EAT BBQ. There's also Little Apple Winery and Off-Leash. Sample wine and view art from local and regional artists. Free.

✱ Selective Shopping

In Alma
Grandma Hoerner's (785-765-2300; grandmahoerners.com), 31863 Thompson Rd., Alma. Open 9–5

VIN VIVANTE WINES OFTEN HAVE HUMOROUS OR CUSTOM LABELS.

Mon.–Sat. You can see the bright red warehouse for this iconic company from the highway. Follow the gravel drive and purchase Grandma's big slice applesauce or salsa, watch production on weekdays, and sample, sample, sample.

Alma Bakery and Sweet Shoppe (785-765-2235), 118 W. Third St., Alma. Open Mon.–Sat., but with flexible hours; call ahead. Dark chocolate pecan toffee, black walnut brittle, and freshly baked cinnamon rolls are just a few treats you'll find here, in addition to cookies and special occasion cakes.

Alma Creamery (785-765-3522), 509 E. Third St., Alma. Open 8–5 Mon.–Fri., 9–3 Sat.; 20-minute tours of the creamery operation area available when they're not making cheese (due to health regulations). Perhaps best known for squeaky cheese curds, Alma Creamery has operated near the railroad tracks at the edge of town since 1946. Sample and then purchase a Colby-Jack moon or a small wheel of cheddar, plus other Kansas-made food products.

In Council Grove

&. **Aldridge Apothecary** (620-767-6731; apothecaryshops.com), 115–119 Main St., Council Grove. Open 9–5:30 weekdays, 9–5 Sat. One block deep, this shopping destination sells everything from KU and K-State T-shirts to crackle-glass vases, gourmet foods, and large purses. There's an original soda fountain with stone mosaic face and multiple stools believed to be from the 1920s. Try an old-fashioned root-beer float or double mocha frappé. Inexpensive.

&. **Trowbridge Classics** (620-767-6992), 113 W. Main St., Council

Grove. Open 10–5 Mon.–Sat., noon–3 Sun. Women will appreciate this classy store's inventory of knit pants and tops, plus purses and jewelry.

In Eudora

Quilting Bits and Pieces (785-542-2080; eudoraquiltshop.com), 736 Main St., Eudora. Open 9:30–5 Mon./Wed./Fri., 9:30–7 Tues./Thurs., 9:30–4 Sat. The co-owners of this lovely store have written five quilting books and created hundreds of quilt patterns. They emphasize appliqué and embroidery in their shop and also offer more than 2,500 bolts of quilting fabric.

DC Custom Crafted Cycles (785-542-1903), 726.5 Main St., Eudora. Open March–late Dec., 10–6 Tues.–Fri., 10–5 Sat., noon–3 Sun. Sip espresso and buy ammunition for your next hunting trip at this custom cycle shop that offers repairs and cycling accessories, from leathers for all ages to deerskin gloves and helmets.

In Holton

Bar S Tack and Western Wear (785-364-2150; barstackandfarrier.com), 108 W. Fifth St., Eudora. Open 9:30–5:30 Mon.–Fri., 9–4 Sat., or by appointment. Located on the north side of Holton's square, this store offers clothes, boots, jewelry, dishes, and more, all with a Western flair. Customers from northeast Kansas and Missouri and southeast Nebraska seek advice from the on-site farrier and purchase bits, ropes, and everything else needed to ride a horse.

Koger Variety (785-364-3321), 415 New York Ave., Holton. Open 9–6 weekdays, 9–5 Sat., 12–4 Sun. This is an old-fashioned five-and-dime store with many thousands of traditional five-and-dime items and an antique soda fountain serving sodas, malts, ice cream, and pop. New items come in frequently.

In Horton
The Electric City Emporium (785-548-6224), 113 W. Eighth St., Horton. Open 10–5:30, Tues.–Fri. 9–5 Sat. This variety store and flea market offers two floors packed full of new, used, and old merchandise of all types collected by the owner and more than 30 individual vendors. Oh, the treasures you'll find. No credit cards.

The English Leather Shop (785-741-0128), 119 W. Eighth St., Horton. Open 9–5 Tues./Wed./Fri., 9–noon Sat. Luke Pollock is a busy man between his leather shop and his farm. Services range from leather repair to custom hatbands, chaps, boots, belts, and buckles. He'll also repair a trunk or saddle, or hand-tool almost anything. No credit cards.

In Scranton
Four Corners Antique Mall (785-793-2325), 15791 Topeka Ave., Scranton. Open 10–5 Tues.–Sat., noon–5 Sun. Sassy the terrier is a well-behaved greeter. More than 15 vendors offer their wares in several buildings, including a life-size Dorothy mannequin with a straw hat, vintage Fiestaware, old ice-cream stools, Indian blankets, Depression glass, and antique saddles.

Happy Trails Antiques (785-793-2777), 307 Brownie St., Scranton. Open 11–5 Wed.–Sun. This is a bright, happy store with several completely packed rooms of books, small furniture, home decor, and more, and a definite Southwest vibe. Ask the owner about antique dolls and Mexican jewelry—she's an expert.

Elsewhere
Mom and I's Candy (785-548-7550), 521 Main St., Everest. Open 9–5 Mon.–Fri., Sat. mornings. This shop is known for Spoon Lov'n fudge sold in individual portion jars with a plastic spoon attached, as well as homemade toffee. They also stock seasonal home decor and Kansas-produced candles, jellies, and jams.

& **Kroeger's Country Meats** (785-887-6091), 505 Eisenhower Memorial Dr., Lecompton. Open 10–6 Mon.–Sat. For more than 25 years this family-owned meat market has sold heart-shaped Kansas City strips near Valentine's Day, homemade sausage and beef jerky, and hand-ground chuck. Select meats and cheeses by the pound, get gas, and buy beer. Visitors to Clinton Lake and Perry Lake also appreciate the grocery items available at this old-fashioned country store. Customers from as far away as Kansas City savor biscuits and gravy and other items, too.

Sports Mart (785-828-3293), 24131 S US 75, Lyndon. Open 6–8 Mon.–Sat., 7–6 Sun. Fill up your gas tank, then purchase camouflage jackets, fishing poles, foam coolers, guns, and cases. It's a popular and convenient stop for folks heading toward nearby lakes and wildlife areas.

Globe Art Glass (785-665-0110), 299 E. 550 Rd./US 56 at CR 1029 (12 miles west of US 56/US 59 intersection), Overbrook. Open when the owner is home; he lives in the back. Don't miss this workshop set back from the highway; look for a front window full of stained glass. Once a stop on the Santa Fe wagon train route with a full-service trading post, this spot now houses lovely stained-glass creations and an art class busi-

THE FRONT WINDOW AT GLOBE ART GLASS IS FILLED WITH MANY DESIGNS.

ness. Customers from 16 to 18 states purchase custom designs often created from photos and hand-drawn patterns.

Buggy Days (785-336-2271), 509 Main St., Seneca. Open 9–5 Tues.–Fri., 10–2 Sat. Antiques and collectibles range from an 1800s safe to an early 1900s ice box. The store once offered buggy repairs and a tin workshop upstairs. Ask to see the original rope-pull elevator. No credit cards.

Carriage House Antiques (785-456-7021), 212 Lincoln St., Wamego. Open 10–5 Wed.–Sat., noon–5 Sun. This little shop sells old and new items assembled to complement each other, from antique books to vintage-inspired clothing, imported decorative pottery, and gorgeous blown-glass orbs.

Schlaegel's Homegrown Popcorn (1-800-844-7494, popcorngifts.net), 31030 V Rd., Whiting. Open 8–12, 1–4 Mon.–Fri. The sign says SCHLAEGEL'S POPCORN TAX PREPARATION ACCOUNTING. But after selling plain unpopped popcorn for two decades, the Schlaegels entered the flavored popcorn market. They plant 10 acres of popcorn annually, create more than 30 flavors, and ship them nationwide. Caramel cheddar, strawberry, and even BBQ flavors line shelves in their on-site production facility. Stop by for a treat.

✳ Special Events

April: **Wamego Tulip Festival** (785-456-7849), Wamego City Park/Wamego. Join more than thirty-thousand people who visit vendors selling everything from pottery to

ANTIQUES PARADISE

Despite having a population of only two hundred, it's no surprise that Paxico is sometimes called the Antique Capital of Kansas. Behind vintage storefronts there are many antiques shops, including:

Mill Creek Antiques (785-765-2310). Specializing in beautifully restored antique stoves but offering several enormous rooms of furniture, 1900s chandeliers, and even old-fashioned bathroom fixtures.

R. J.'s Antiques and Collectibles (785-224-9543). You'll find hundreds of pieces of pristine Depression-era glass and other antiques or collectibles.

Yesterday's Rose, Too Antique Mall (785-636-5551). See 10 vendors with as many different antique and collectible treasure collections.

Old Woodman Antiques (785-608-4646). Specializing in fine, early American antique furniture, accessories, and tools.

W. B. Antiques (785-636-5122). A hat lover's paradise, plus jewelry, books, and linens.

Sisters and Co. (785-636-8400). With Jepson pottery and enamelware and other antiques/collectibles, plus sisters gifts.

Hidden Treasures (785-636-8933). Offers Americana and vintage home decor in addition to antiques and collectibles.

They're open on weekends, too.

MILL CREEK ANTIQUES SPECIALIZES IN BEAUTIFUL ANTIQUE STOVES.

homemade gourmet foods and laser-cut wood holiday ornaments. Try face painting and deep-fried strawberries.

May: **Wamego Country Club Cinco de Mayo Golf Tournament** (785-456-7849), Wamego Country Club, Wamego. Enjoy this four-person scramble at one of the state's top-rated courses with Mexican buffet and prizes that include cars, motorcycles, and vacations.

June: **Meatloaf Festival** (785-636-5577), Paxico. There's a meatloaf cook-off, vendors, live music, and games. **Prairie Band Potawatomi Pow Wow** (pbpindiantribe.com), Mayetta. Enjoy this celebration of American Indian culture with dances, artisans, and snacks.

July: **Kickapoo Traditional Pow Wow** (785-486-2131; ktick-nsn.gov /pow-wow.htm), Kickapoo Reservation, Horton. Enjoy American Indian food, arts and crafts, drummers, and dancers. **Fourth of July in Wamego** (785-456-7849). Double the normal population, a 140-year-old parade, antique car and tractor shows, and a festival lead up to one of the state's largest holiday fireworks displays. **Wah-Shun-Gah Days** (councilgrove .com), Council Grove. This three-day family festival honors the last full-blooded chief of the Kaw Nation and celebrates the long relationship of the Kaw Nation Native Americans with white settlers along the Santa Fe Trail. With Kaw Nation traditions, parades, carnivals, street dances, and food vendors.

October: **OZtoberFest** (785-456-7849), downtown Wamego. Travel the Road to Oz during this annual event with food, crafts, and activities. Meet Munchkins and relatives of the author and attend a special performance of the play at the Columbian Theater.

COME FLY WITH ME

Get a bird's-eye view of northeastern Kansas when you skydive with these companies:

Skydive Kansas LLC (785-840-JUMP; skydivekansas.com), Osage City. Weekends year-round and some summer days. The red metal warehouse that houses this 15-year-old operation has hosted more than thirty-three thousand jumps and offers examiner-rating training. Six hundred first-timers jump each year, including people from most states and several foreign countries. Directional signs near the runway point toward other skydive companies, including Skydive Kansas City, Missouri River Valley Skydivers, and Air Capital Drop Zone (ACDZ). Register online for $190 tandem first jump; military, college students, and other special rates may apply.

SkyDiveKState (785-456-8860/the drop zone on weekends only), Wamego Airport, Wamego. Open to the public and students every weekend. Solo or tandem jumps are available for people who weigh under 220 pounds. Feel the rush as you make your first jump from 10,000 feet. After training it's $165 for your first jump; repeat jumps range in price from $5–36.

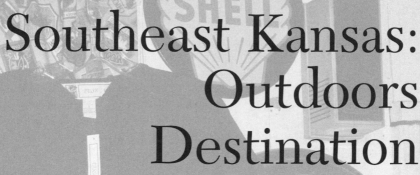

Southeast Kansas: Outdoors Destination

3

INTRODUCTION

Many people consider southeast Kansas the Little Ozarks region of the state. Adjacent to Missouri's Lake of the Ozarks area, this part of Kansas is far from flat, with roads that sometimes resemble roller coasters. Water is everywhere, from natural rivers and streams to man-made lakes and reservoirs, making fishing for crappie, bass, catfish, and other species—or boating for sport—favorite pastimes. Abundant wildlife includes hundreds of bird species, deer, and wild turkey, ripe for hunting throughout the area. You may even see an armadillo crossing the highway.

Folks often wear multiple hats in southeastern Kansas towns, and particularly in smaller locales. There's the realtor who helped to create a yellow brick road along city sidewalks and ushers tour bus groups around town; the couple that makes gorgeous pottery, runs a bed & breakfast, and helps promote the annual folk tour of decorated outhouses; plus the hunting outfitter who also sells insurance. And some of these folks create quite amazing things, from a private classic car museum with a glitzy '50s vibe to a restaurant so popular that people will drive for nearly an hour to enjoy the food.

Restaurants are known for amazing fried chicken, superb beef, and all types of homemade baked goods, including gargantuan cinnamon rolls and coconut cream pies. Every meal comes with a side of hospitality that extends to bed & breakfast establishments and small hotels where the owner lives nearby, checks in daily, and may even do the laundry. In fact, you'll find quite a few bed & breakfasts in this area, from the Victorian splendor of Lyons Twin Mansions in Fort Scott to the casual elegance of Pittsburg's Himmel House, set in a 1905 mansion. A number of renovated historical hotels also offer comfortable lodging.

Southeast Kansas was a hotbed of unrest during the nation's slavery conflict, and an area that attributes much of its early growth to the railroads. Murderous outlaws, globetrotting adventurers, and millionaires who built amazing mansions all have made their marks here. After the Kansas–Nebraska Act of 1854 created the Kansas Territory, voters had to decide whether to be a free or slave state. This was a particularly contentious issue in eastern Kansas, with its proximity to proslavery Missouri, and the town of Humboldt sustained several attacks during the Civil War. More than seven hundred soldiers died at Mine Creek in one of the War's largest cavalry battles.

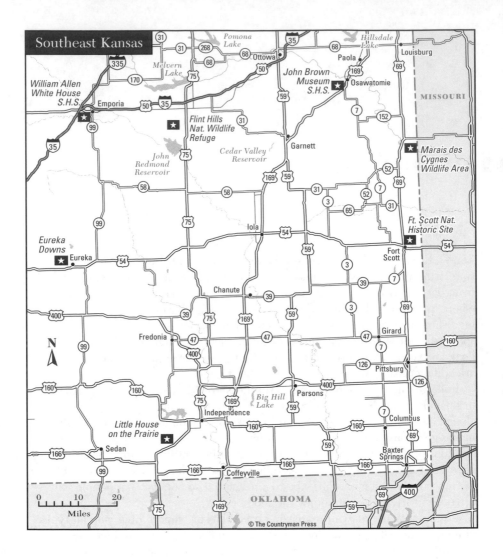

At one time the military post christened Fort Scott featured two hotels on opposite ends of the grassy plaza, with opposing views about whether slavery should continue. Today modern retail and dining options in the town of Fort Scott lie within sight of a fully restored and reconstructed fort. Many current residents exude enormous enthusiasm for the town and constantly seek ways to excite tourists, including a new focus on tours of the area's haunted properties. Gorgeous vintage homes are among them. Famous former residents include Gordon Parks and George Washington Carver.

Located along the Verdigris River, Independence was founded in fall 1869 and celebrated with a grand feast. Eighteen families arrived and the log Judson House hotel was built with businesses and a post office following soon afterward. Independence became an incorporated village in July 1870. By 1882, two flour mills, a woolen mill, and a canning company had also been established. The modern town has gained fame in several ways. Their annual Halloween-inspired event is a 10-day extravaganza called Neewollah—that's *Halloween,* spelled backward—and among the state's largest festivals. The theater world knows this town as the birthplace of playwright William Inge, and host of an annual international theater conference created in his honor. The downtown area bustles with activity along many original brick streets. History buffs will also enjoy a trip to the original Little House on the Prairie outside of town.

Coffeyville was the site of a horrific gunfight with the notorious bank-robbing Dalton Gang, which resulted in the deaths of several gang members and, more importantly, four local townspeople. The Dalton Defenders Museum commemorates local townspeople who died during the Dalton Gang gunfight. Fifteen historical murals created by local artist Don Sprague provide a visual history of Coffeyville, from a portrait of Chief Black Dog to Colonel Coffey at his trading post. The town was an early trading post, which is depicted in one of many historical murals created on buildings located throughout the downtown area. It's also a place where visitors can still see the splendor of the 1900s Brown Mansion, now a museum that still houses all of the family's original furnishings.

Chanute was a center for shipment of grain, corn, potatoes, and seed in the late 19th to early 20th century. The first natural gas well was drilled here in 1889, and oil was another major source of the community's wealth. Chanute gradually added zinc smelters, glass works, and cement factories to its economy, and the town became a major trade center in this part of the state. The city spawned several forward-thinking individuals that include flying enthusiast and Wright Brothers acquaintance Octave Chanute, for whom the town was named. Chanute was also a chief engineer and superintendent of LL&G Railroad. This is the hometown of Martin Johnson, too—world traveler and cultural archaeologist in the South Pacific, British North Borneo, and Africa—and his wife, Osa. Visit the Chanute museum that is dedicated to their travels and those of others who explored Africa. Today, the town has approximately ten thousand residents and is located in the Neosho River valley. Enjoy other cultures during the state's oldest Mexican Fiesta each fall. Or take a tour of Chanute's historic homes, plus the historic Santa Fe Depot and Flat Iron Building. Maps are available from the chamber of commerce.

The seat of Lyon County and one of southeast Kansas's larger cities, Emporia has more than twenty-six thousand residents. It's easy to reach from US 50, I-335, or I-35 and lies near the Neosho and Cottonwood Rivers. The town was founded in 1857 and its newspaper, the *Emporia Gazette,* was renowned for its quality with legendary newspaperman William Allen White at the helm. The first Veterans Day observance took place here in 1953, and the nation adopted this celebration the following year.

Fort Scott is the only major town in the state that remains after its establishment as a U.S. Army fort before Kansas became a territory. By 1869, 150 trains passed through daily. Carrie Nation busted up saloons here and George Washington Carver attended high school and did laundry here. Today the restored fort lies only blocks away from shops and restaurants. Townspeople have recently won Guinness World Records for the longest continuous line of coins in the world; the fastest mile of pennies laid; and the largest number of quarter-pound cheeseburgers eaten in two minutes. Fort Scott is also the hometown of legendary photographer and Renaissance man Gordon Parks.

The seat of Allen County, Iola was founded in 1859, and historical homes are still visible throughout town. Iola is located in the heart of farm country and offers a trailhead for the popular Prairie Spirit Trail. With the discovery of natural gas around 1895, the population boomed to more than eleven thousand. Today, approximately six thousand residents live here. Iola has the largest courthouse square in the United States and offers multiple historic sites, including the Veterans Memorial Wall and a Civil War Soldier statue in Old Iola Cemetery constructed of rare white zinc. See the Old Allen County Jail and Victorian Northrup House, both listed on the National Register of Historic Places, the boyhood home of noted botanist and explorer Maj. Gen. Frederick Funston, or take a ride on the historic Iola Trolley. There are more than one-dozen flea markets and antique, consignment, gift, and collectible stores here, as well as galleries, occasional theater and orchestra performances, and several restaurants.

With more millionaires than any other city in the U.S. until the Depression, Independence was the childhood home of playwright William Inge, who also attended Independence Community College, current site of an international theater festival in his honor. Each October the town's signature Neewollah event draws thousands of visitors who celebrate the Halloween season for 10 days along the town's brick streets. The first organized baseball game was played at night here in 1930, and Mickey Mantle played minor league ball here during his first season in 1949.

Parsons was also named for a railroad official, Judge Levi Parsons, who was president of the Missouri, Kansas, and Texas (MKT) Katy Railroad. Once a meeting place for the Osage Indians, it lies in the corner of Labette County near the Missouri and Oklahoma borders. Located very close to the Missouri and Oklahoma borders, this town of eleven to twelve thousand people prides itself on the enormous range of outdoor activities it offers. Hunters, fishermen, bird watchers, and hikers find gorgeous surroundings and abundant wildlife in every direction. Parsons was named among America's top 10 tails for hunting whitetail deer by *Outdoor Life* magazine in 2008.

In Pittsburg you'll find a modern town influenced by the Pittsburg State University. This large southeast Kansas city, with approximately twenty thousand residents, was founded in 1878 by Joplin businessmen and a Girard lawyer who persuaded the railroad to extend a line through Baker township to Joplin, Missouri, to serve the mining industry. Many grand old homes remain here and several historic buildings include Hotel Stilwell, built in 1889 by a Kansas City entrepreneur; the Historic Colonial-Fox Theatre; and the renovated Carnegie Library, built in the Prairie style followed by Frank Lloyd Wright. Over the years Pittsburg has also become known as the fried chicken capital of the world due to the presence of nearby restaurants that specialize in this favorite dish. More recently, Crawford County has cast itself as The Football Capital of Kansas due to its longstanding and successful athletic traditions. Pittsburg is also the location of the only Harley Davidson repair and restoration training facility in the nation, and wonderful fishing in area strip pits is another claim to fame.

Prepare for some pleasant surprises as you travel through southeast Kansas.

COFFEYVILLE, CHANUTE, EMPORIA, FORT SCOTT, IOLA, INDEPENDENCE, PARSONS, AND PITTSBURG

GUIDANCE Convention and visitors' organizations that serve this area include:

Chanute Area Chamber of Commerce and Office of Tourism (620-431-3350; chanutechamber.com), 21 N. Lincoln, Chanute. Open 8–5 weekdays (may close 12–1).

Coffeyville Area Chamber of Commerce (620-251-2550; coffeyvillechamber .org.), 807 Walnut, Coffeyville. Open 9–5 weekdays.

Emporia Convention and Visitors Bureau (620-342-1803; emporia.com), 719 Commercial St., Emporia. Open 8:30–5 weekdays.

Fort Scott Area Chamber of Commerce (620-223-3566; forthscott.com), 231 E. Wall St., Fort Scott. Open 8–5 weekdays, 10–4 Sat.

Iola Area Chamber of Commerce (620-365-5252), 208 W. Madison, Iola. Open 9–1 weekdays.

Crawford County CVB (620-231-1212; visitcrawfordcounty.com), 117 W. Fourth St., Pittsburg/Girard. Open 9–4:30 weekdays.

Independence Convention and Visitors Bureau (620-331-1890; indks chamber.org), 322 N. Penn Ave., Independence. Open 8:30–5 weekdays.

Parsons and Greater Labette County Tourism (620-421-7030; parsons chamber.org), 1715 Corning, Parsons. Open 9–5 weekdays.

GETTING THERE *By air:* You'll need a car to get from the airport to your destination. Major commercial flights are available at **Wichita Mid-Continent Airport** (316-946-47000; seven major carriers with a new terminal opening in spring 2013), 2173 Air Cargo Rd., Wichita; **Kansas City (Missouri) International Airport** (816-243-5237; 11 major carriers), 601 E. Brasilia Ave., Kansas City, MO; or **Tulsa International Airport** (918-838-5000; nine major carriers),

7777 E. Apache, Tulsa, OK. *By train:* No **AMTRAK** trains pass through this area. *By bus:* **Greyhound** serves the following southeastern cities: Chanute (no tickets sold here; 620-431-9540), 701 N. Santa Fe Ave./Pumping Petes; Coffeyville (620-251-9600), 1201 W, Eighth St./Muffler City; Emporia (620-340-0484), 2000 Industrial Rd./Short Stop Phillips 66; Iola (620-365-2611), 1700 E St./Jump Start Travel Center; Independence (no tickets sold here; 1-800-231-2222), 3024 W. Main St./Bailey's Corner.

GETTING AROUND Driving is the best way to get around this area.

MEDICAL EMERGENCY (arranged alphabetically by city name)

Neosho Memorial Regional Medical Center (620-431-4000), 629 S. Plummer, Chanute.

Coffeyville Memorial Hospital/Coffeyville Regional Medical Center (620-251-1200), 1400 W. Fourth St., Coffeyville.

Newman Regional Health (620-343-6800), 1201 W. 12th Ave., Emporia.

Mercy Health Center (620-223-2200), 821 Burke St./401 Woodland Hills Blvd., Fort Scott.

Mercy Hospital (620-331-2200), 800 W. Myrtle St., Independence.

Labette County Medical Center (620-421-4880), 1902 S. US 59, Parsons.

Mt. Carmel Regional Medical Center (620-231-6100), 1102 E. Centennial Dr., Pittsburg.

Via Christi Hospital (620-231-6100), 1 Mt. Carmel Way, Pittsburg.

✷ To See

HISTORIC PLACES, LANDMARKS, AND SITES

In Chanute

Octave Chanute-Wright Brothers Memorial (620-431-33500), 1 W. Main, Chanute. Always available. This replica of the 1896 Octave Chanute Glider commemorates how Octave Chanute was a mentor for the Wright Brothers. Wilbur Wright stated, "If he had not lived the entire history of progress in flying would have been other than it has been." Free.

Chanute Historic Homes, the Santa Fe Depot, and the Flat Iron Building (620-431-3350), 21 N. Lincoln, Chanute. Eighteen sites offer visitors a quick look at Chanute's historical structures in a self-guided tour. Free.

Historic Austin Bridge (620-431-3350), 3502 S. Santa Fe, Santa Fe Park/Chanute. Always open. Built in 1872 and moved here in 1999, this classic truss bridge now sits at the end of 3.5 hiking and biking trails, near a beautiful lake, and surrounded with plenty of picnic tables and playground equipment. Free.

In Coffeyville

Dalton Defenders Plaza, Death Alley, and Old Condon Bank, Eighth and Walnut, Coffeyville. The notorious October 5, 1892, attempt by the Dalton Gang to rob two banks here ended in death for three gang members. See the vault from the restored Condon Bank. Red paint, in narrow Death Alley, diagrams how the Dalton gang members were laid out near the tiny town jail. Free.

Elmwood Cemetery, off Eldridge and South Walnut Streets, Coffeyville. Always open. Three Dalton Gang members were buried near the railroad tracks where a pipe was the only grave marker until Emmett Dalton placed a headstone there. Frank Dalton, a U.S. Deputy Marshall killed on the job, is also buried here. Free.

Midland Theater (620-251-9251; midlandtheaterfoundation.org), 212 W. Eighth St., Coffeyville. Currently undergoing a massive renovation effort by the Midland Theater Foundation, this 1928 theater was a marvel for its time, with massive stained-glass windows in a second floor ballroom, a pipe organ, and plush, ornate decor throughout. Check website for its status. Free.

In Emporia
William Allen White House State Historic Site (620-342-2800; kshs.org /place/white), 927 Exchange St., Emporia. Open 9:30–5 Wed.–Sat., 1–5 Sun.; last tour begins at 4:30. Visit a legendary home restored to its 1920s grandeur where five presidents slept during the first half of the 20th century. When Emporia's best-known journalist, William Allen White, purchased the *Emporia Gazette* in 1895, he had this Queen Anne–style home built using red Colorado sandstone. The family lived here for 50 years and 90 percent of current furnishings are original, including three thousand books, a two-thousand-year-old vase from a Greek shipwreck, and White's beloved typewriter. Adults $3; children K–12 $1.

THREE MEMBERS OF THE NOTORIOUS BANK-ROBBING DALTON GANG ARE REMEMBERED AT ELMWOOD CEMETERY.

&. **All Veterans Memorial** (620-342-1803; emporiakschamber.org), 933 S. Commercial St., Emporia. Open daylight to 11 PM. America's first All Veterans Memorial, established in 1991. Other monuments include: Civil War Veteran Monument/Fourth and Union Streets; Civil War Veterans Monument/2000 Prairie St.; Hispanic American World War II Veterans Memorial/St. Catherine's Church/205 S. Lawrence St.; and Spanish-American War Memorial/S. Neosho St. and Kansas Ave. Free.

&. **Emporia Granada Theater** (620-342-3342; emporiagranada.com), 807 Commercial St., Emporia. Tour by appointment or attend an event here. Stunning doesn't begin to describe the incredible restoration work completed at this 1929 theater, once one of the state's largest movie palaces. Following a massive restoration effort, intricate, gilded plaster with faux jewels fills the lobby and decorates the auditorium, where red velvet curtains line the stage. Free to tour.

In Fort Scott

Fort Scott National Historic Site (620-223-0310), Old Fort Blvd., Fort Scott. Open April–Oct., 8–5 daily; Nov.–March, 9–5. In the 1800s this fort stood at the forefront of national history, from interactions with Osage Indians to participation in the Civil and Mexican Wars. During the 1850s the proslavery Western Hotel and antislavery Free State Hotel operated across the plaza from each other. See furnished officers' quarters, a commissary, and more in restored buildings. Call for tours. Admission 16 and up $3.

&. **The Gordon Parks Center for Culture and Diversity,** Danny and Willa Ellis Fine Art Center/Fort Scott Community College (1-800-874-3722, ext. 515; gordonparkscenter.org), 2108 S. Horton, Fort Scott. A $500,000 capital campaign will fund completion of this site. The center owns 25 boxes of Parks memorabilia, including his collection of *Life* magazines, and $5,000 from Bill and Camilla Cosby allowed the exhibit to acquire and ship Parks's desk from his NYC office. Call for hours and admission.

Gordon Parks Art Exhibit at Mercy Hospital (620-223-2200), 401 Woodland Hills Blvd., Fort Scott. See *Completely Unexpected.*

Fort Scott National Cemetery/ National Cemetery No. 1 (620-223-2840), 900 E. National Ave., Fort Scott. Open daily dawn–dusk. Thousands of headstones fan out across the

THIS PHOTO OF GORDON PARKS FILMING MOVIE FOOTAGE APPEARS AT THE GORDON PARKS CENTER FOR CULTURE AND DIVERSITY IN FORT SCOTT.

fairly flat site. It's one of 14 national cemeteries designated by Abraham Lincoln, with Union, Confederate, and buffalo soldiers—plus 16 Indians who served as military scouts—buried here. Free.

& **Lowell Milken Education Center** (620-223-9991), 4 S. Main St., Fort Scott. Open 8–5 Mon.–Fri., Sat. by appointment. This center teaches respect and understanding of all people and helps domestic and international students create dramas, films, websites, and exhibit boards. The Life in a Jar exhibit examines the relationship between students from a Kansas high school and Irena Sendler, a Polish Catholic woman who saved 2,500 children during the Holocaust. Learn about the local Sisters of Mercy and Andrew Higgins's invention of an amphibious boat used in the Normandy invasion. Free.

NATIONAL CEMETERY

In Independence

Little House on the Prairie (620-289-4238; littlehouseontheprairie.com), 2507 CR 3000, Independence. Open March 15–Nov. 31, 10–5 Mon.–Sat., 1–5 Sun.; summer hours, 9–5 Mon.–Sat., 1–5 Sun. Located 13 miles southwest of town, this site includes a replica of Laura Ingalls Wilder's 1870 cabin. See a one-room schoolhouse, a tiny antique post office, and a gift shop full of Wilder books and memorabilia. Free.

William Inge Collection (620-332-5468; ingecenter.org/ingecollection.htm), 1057 W. College Ave., William Inge Center for the Arts/Independence Community College/Independence. Call for an appointment. Renowned playwright William Inge lived here and attended the college. Today the library houses his Pulitzer Prize, plus hundreds of his manuscripts and books. The annual William Inge Festival draws theater enthusiasts from throughout the nation and world. Free.

Elsewhere

Oakwood Cemetery (620-421-7000), 200 S. Leawood, Parsons. Open 7–dusk. This 1872 cemetery is on the National Register of Historic Places. Antietam Circle No. 2 features dozens of Civil War veterans' headstones, plus a cast-iron gateway and a soaring flagpole with bronze statues of servicemen. Free.

Veterans Memorial Amphitheater (620-235-4762; psuvetmemorial.org), 1909 S. Rouse, Pittsburg State University campus/Pittsburg. Continuously open. This gorgeous amphitheater features a half-scale version of the Vietnam Memorial Wall, a reflecting pool, individual commemorative bricks, and a carved eagle in flight. Free.

Civil War Soldier Memorial and Statue (620-365-5252), 612 W St., Iola. A dapper soldier with his hand atop the rifle muzzle stands watch over Civil War soldiers buried beside the Neosho River (including the city's namesake, Iola Colborn). What makes him special is that this 1907 statue was crafted from rare white zinc. Free.

MUSEUMS

In Coffeyville

Dalton Defenders Museum (620-251-5448), 113 E. Eighth St., Coffeyville. Open 10–4 Mon.–Sat., 1–4 Sun. The notorious Dalton Gang were known as terrorists for several years, including three murders and a train robbery, before four of them met their demise during the 1892 Dalton Raid on Coffeyville. This museum commemorates four residents who also died during the encounter, with memorabilia that include Grat Dalton's Winchester rifle and an 1800s coffee mill. Adults $3; children 7–17 $1.

Aviation Heritage Museum (620-515-0232), 2002 N. Buckeye St., Coffeyville. Tours 10–4 Sat., 1–4 Sun., or by appointment. Located in a 1930s-era airplane hangar in Pfister Park, the museum introduces visitors to Coffeyville's importance as an aviation center during the 1900s. See small planes, pilot headgear, wartime newspapers, and much more. Volunteer guides are a wealth of information. Free.

Martin and Osa Johnson Safari Museum (620-431-2730; safarimuseum.com), 111 N. Lincoln Ave., Chanute. Open 10–5 Tues.–Sat.; also on Sun. in summer. Named the state's number one museum, it provides visitors information about Africa through permanent, rotating, and traveling exhibits. Bright green display case walls provide a gorgeous backdrop for African masks on the ground floor. The Johnson exhibit documents their adventures in Africa and other countries and their extensive photography and writings, including 10 of Osa's books— mostly for children. An on-site gift shop offers movies about their safaris on DVD. Adults $4; seniors/students/children 6–12 $2.

Major General Frederick Funston's Boyhood Home/Museum (620-365-3051), 14 S. Washington, Iola. May–Oct., Tues.–Sat. 12:30–4:30; Nov.–April, Tues.–Sat. 2–4. Frederick Funston explored the United States and spent two years in the Arctic. He served 18 months with Cuban insurgents in Latin America and became a lieutenant colonel. Funston returned to Kansas after an injury shortly before the Spanish-American War began and became colonel of the 20th Kansas Infantry. He oversaw capture of the commander of the Filipino army in 1901; became a brigadier general in the army at age 35; and in 1914 he was military governor and major general in the Mexican state of Vera Cruz. Funston died three years later. Free.

THIS IS A LIFE-SIZE MODEL AT THE MARTIN AND OSA JOHNSON SAFARI MUSEUM.

Iron Horse Museum (620-421-1959), 18th and Corning, west of Parsons Historical Museum, Parsons. Open May–Oct., 1–4 Fri.–Sun., or by appointment. The MKT railroad played a major role in the development of Parsons. Today visitors can see a wall clock from the MKT Roundhouse, actual conductor's uniforms, and a vintage *KATY* employee magazine. Learn more about the county's history next door. Free.

Crawford County Historical Museum (620-724-6460/Alden Allen; call ahead), Summit and Buffalo, KS 69, Girard/near Pittsburg. Open May–Oct., 2–4 Sun., or by appointment. From a fluting iron and an 1800s graduation dress to a mid-1900s working pipe organ, 1960s *Saturday Evening Posts*, and a grain anchor atop a mail cart, this little museum has all kinds of surprises. See a gorgeous stained-glass window in this one-time church that commemorates the life of a woman who died in the 1880s, and an antique fire hose cart. Free.

✳ To Do

BOATING AND FISHING Lake Fort Scott (620-223-0550), 2 miles south and 3 miles west of Fort Scott. Swim areas open 7–9. Hidden behind tall hills, this is a pretty lake where 360 water acres offer abundant fishing. $5 per day for two vehicles, per campsite.

Lake Parsons, 3 miles north on US 59 and 3 miles west on 20th Rd., Parsons. Nearly 1,000 acres of water, plus an additional 1,000 acres of land offer fishing, camping, picnicking, boating, and swim beaches galore.

Neosho River (620-421-7031), with access from Chetopa/Oswego. There are three public access boat ramps. Campsites and RV parking are also available near this great fishing spot that runs through Labette County.

Neosho State Fishing Lake (620-449-2539), St. Paul. For more than 80 years fishing enthusiasts have flocked to the first state lake constructed through funding from what is now known as the Department of Wildlife and Parks. There are 18 fishing piers. Camping, walking trails, and a shelter house are other features.

DAY SPAS Aveda Spa Salon, Courtland Hotel, Fort Scott (see *Lodging*). There are four therapy rooms—two that can accommodate couples and an enormous array of treatments. Sink into the luxury of a cleansing body wrap and enjoy a rain shower after your soothing River Stone massage. You'll also find manicures/pedicures, prenatal massage, and even temporary tattoos.

Heavenly Kneads Day Spa (620-431-3343, ext. 8), Tioga Suites Hotel, Chanute. Open 10–5 Fri., or by appointment. A licensed practical nurse, who also practices therapeutic massage, offers deep tissue or hot-stone massage, acupressure, and reflexology with aromatherapy and gentle music. $70 for 90-minute massage.

Lifestyle Therapies Massage (620-875-1212), 822B N. Broadway, beside Salon 9/Pittsburg. Licensed massage therapist Alice Burk offers seaweed minifacials, spa foot treatments, and hour massages. Call for rates.

Paradise, Lyons Twin Mansions, Fort Scott (see *Lodging*). Two rooms offer pampering options that include lymphatic body brushing, facials, intensive pedicures, and massage.

FARMERS' MARKETS Chanute Farmers' Market (316-431-3350), Main and Evergreen Streets, Chanute. Open May–Sept., 8–noon. Sat.

Coffeyville Farmers' Market (620-988-0808), Eighth and Walnut Streets, Coffeyville. Open 7–11 Sat., 4–7 Tues., beginning late May.

Emporia Farmers' Market (620-343-6555), Seventh Ave. and Merchant St., Emporia. Open May–Oct., 8–sellout Sat.; beginning mid-June, 5–sellout Wed.

Fort Scott Farmers' Market (620-223-0966), Skubitz Plaza, Fort Scott. Open May–Oct., 8–noon Sat., 4–7 Tues.

Independence, Kansas, Downtown Farmers' Market (316-352-5660), Penn and Myrtle Streets, Independence. Open 8–11 Sat.

Parsons Farmers' Market (316-421-7030), 1700 block of Washington St., Parsons. Open May–Oct., 7–sellout.

Pittsburg Area Farmers' Market (620-249-3011), 670 E. 600 Ave., Pittsburg. Open 7:30–sellout Sat., noon–sellout Wed.

GOLF Independence Country Club (620-331-1274; independence-cc.com), 2824 Country Club Cir., Independence. Open daily. There are men's and women's locker rooms and a pro shop at this popular Bermuda grass course, opened in 1940. Par 72, 18-holes, 6,118 yards.

Katy Golf Club (620-421-4532), 2307 N Blvd., Parsons. Open daily. This compact course offers long fairways lined with trees, chipping and putting greens, and a clubhouse. Par 36, 9 holes, 3,137 yards.

Countryside Golf Club (620-232-3654), 469 E. 520th Ave., Pittsburg. Play regulation holes on small fairways or use one of five tees on the driving range. Par 36, 9 holes, 3,075 yards.

Four Oaks Golf Course (620-231-8070), 910 Memorial Dr., Pittsburg. This pretty course with nice fairways opened in 1981 and offers 20 tees at the driving range. Par 65, 18 holes, 4,579 yards.

HIKING Prairie Spirit Rail-Trail extends from Ottawa through Garnett to Iola. This 51-mile system of trails follows railroad tracks last used by the Atchison, Topeka, and Santa Fe Railway Company. In Iola there's a park with several shelters and a merry-go-round, and another trailhead is near Garnett's restored train depot. The trail, which is perfect for hikers, cyclists, and nature lovers, intersects I-35 and US 59, 169, 68, and 31 highways. Visitors will find plenty of small towns and wildlife at every turn.

HUNTING Lil' Toledo Sportsmans Retreat and Lil' Toledo Lodge (620-244-5668; liltoledo.com), 10600 170th Rd., Chanute. Once a private fishing camp and located on more than 15,000 acres alongside the Neosho River, Lil' Toledo is ranked as the nation's #1 wing-shooting lodge, according to Orvis. Private baths, an event center, and hunts for waterfowl, upland game, wild turkey, and trophy deer are available, plus dog training, fishing and canoeing, or horseback rides. Enjoy trap and skeet shooting, plus nature trails and clubhouse. Contact them for package rates.

✳ Green Space

Gunn Park (620-223-0550), 1010 Park Ave., Fort Scott. Created in 1910, the park includes 155 acres and RV camping with water and electric hookups. Activities include Frisbee golf, horseshoes, fishing, multiple playgrounds, and enclosed shelters. Trout are added to Fern Lake each winter, with bass, crappie, and cat-fish, also. It's very hilly and gorgeous with fall foliage.

Mined Land Wildlife Area (620-231-3173), 507 E. 560th Ave., Pittsburg access. Covering approximately 14,500 water and land acres in southeast Kansas, this mining area turned wildlife haven offers grasslands, woodlots, and waterways full of blue herons, turtles, and cardinals—and that's only the start. Hunt, fish, camp, and hike here.

Parsons City Arboretum (620-421-7088), 2004 S. Briggs, Parsons. Comprising 19 acres in Glenwood Park, the nonprofit arboretum offers a wetlands area, daylily and wildflower beds, and a gazebo. Rotary club trails and a disc golf course are also in the park.

✳ Lodging
BED & BREAKFASTS

In Fort Scott
Lyons Twin Mansions (1-800-78-GUEST; lyonstwinmansions.com), 742 and 750 South National, Fort Scott. Over-the-top luxury is Miss Pat's focus. Enjoy DVDs, an outdoor hot tub or on-site fitness center, and off-street parking. Stroll through the property designated a Certified Wildlife Habitat by the National Wildlife Federation and enjoy free breakfast in the on-site restaurant. Schedule a massage or pedicure at the basement spa, too. $99–179; corporate rates available.

The Levine House Bed & Breakfast (620-223-3908; levinehouse.net), 747 S. National, Fort Scott. Each room has a private bath in this 1884 home. Eight fireplaces and period furnishings mix with Wi-Fi, complementary hot beverages, and robes. Enjoy breakfast on crystal and china. $90–120. Ask about the extended-stay executive suite.

Elsewhere
The Peaceable Inn B&B (620-431-3400; peaceableinn.com), 6180 183rd Rd., Chanute. Frank Lloyd Wright architecture, complementary afternoon and evening refreshments,

books, movies, games, puzzles, a pool, and a hot tub are available to all guests. Wi-Fi, turndown service, and terry robes add to the pampering. $75–135.

Molly Brown Inn Bed & Breakfast (620-331-1848; mollybrowninn.com), 417 Myrtle, Independence. With a picket fence and plenty of trees, the Molly Brown offers a Victorian vibe in rooms named for the owners' beloved canines. A tuxedoed ceramic dog with a plate of cookies greets guests. Enjoy private baths, a library, and a game room. $89–129.

Himmel House Bed & Breakfast (620-232-9494; himmelhouse.com), 402 W. Euclid, Pittsburg. Hand-carved wood and period wallpaper decorate the gorgeous entryway of this 1905 mansion, which offers casual elegance in three guest rooms. Breakfasts may include banana splits, Belgian waffles, brown sugar bacon, and egg casseroles. The largest room features a whirlpool tub, fireplace, balcony, and king bed. Enjoy television, movies, magazines, or a snack from the bright, airy sunroom. Secure Wi-Fi. $85–119.

HOTELS Tioga Suites Hotel (620-431-3343; tiogasuites.com), 12 Main

THIS TUXEDO-CLAD CERAMIC DOG IS A FITTING GREETER AT MOLLY BROWN INN BED & BREAKFAST, WHERE GUEST ROOMS ARE NAMED AFTER THE OWNER'S FAVORITE CANINES.

St., Chanute. This art deco hotel in the heart of downtown officially opened in September 1929 and was listed on the National Register of Historic Places in 1991. Recent renovations, with continued improvements in the works, help you to sleep, eat, and relax here. Full-size leather couches are in many suites with a desk, refrigerator, microwave, and two televisions. Visit the Main Street Family Restaurant or stop in at Grandma's Subs and Yogurt. Enjoy a sun-dappled lobby bar with original stone-faced fireplace and more luscious leather. Call for rates.

(ψ) **Courtland Hotel and Aveda Spa Salon** (620-223-0098; courtland hotel.com), 121 E. First St., Fort Scott. Current owners Frank and

Cheryl Adamson purchased this 1906, previously renovated building in 2004. This 15-room downtown hotel with wide upper hallway has hosted a basement speakeasy and high-stakes poker games. Today it offers casual surroundings with colors of the surrounding countryside. Eat continental breakfast beside the vintage-inspired lobby. The hotel features a dining room for special events for hosting up to 20 people. Check out their in-house Aveda Day Spa Salon with five treatment rooms. Continental breakfast. $59–99.

(ψ) **AppleTree Inn** (620-331-5500; appletreeinnhotel.com), 201 N. Eighth St., Independence. Quieter than a hotel along the highway, and within walking distance of Independence's downtown, this privately owned hotel constantly upgrades its facilities. There's a microwave, a small refrigerator, and a recliner in each room, plus a business center. Enjoy the indoor swimming pool with waterfall. Four suites have in-room hot tubs. $83–127.

✳ Where to Eat

DINING OUT ☟ **Tavern on the Plaza** (620-251-8700; tavernonthe plaza.com), 902 Walnut, Coffeyville. Open 11–2 Tues.–Fri., 5–10 Tues.–Thurs., 5–11:30 Fri.–Sat. Dark red and exposed brick walls, a white tin ceiling, and stained-glass chandeliers lend old-fashioned charm to this classy restaurant in an 1872 building. Order creamy fettuccine Alfredo for lunch and salad with honey mustard dressing and thick buttered toast. Sandwiches, beef, and seafood are other options. Musicians set the mood on some evenings, and there's a full bar. Inexpensive.

&. **The Buffalo Grill** (620-223-6400; thebuffalogrill.com) 3 W. Oak at North National, Fort Scott. Open 5–10 Tues.–Sat. Casual, modern elegance characterizes this lovely bistro with enormous windows and a large local following. The food will bring you back time after time. A fall seasonal appetizer was breaded calamari fingers with marinara and pesto sauces, and creamy mashed potatoes accompanied perfectly cooked salmon. Beef lovers will find fillets, rib eye, and Kansas City strip, and the spinach salad is delicious. Inexpensive.

EATING OUT

In Chanute

&. **Bench Warmers** (620-431-7733), 5 E. Main, Chanute. Kitchen open 11:30–1:30 Mon.–Sat., bar open 11:30–1:30. The decor features high ceilings, black-and-white linoleum, and a bar face. The lower walls are covered in corrugated metal, and there's a sports ball wallpaper border. Choose iceberg lettuce, spinach, or a mix of greens for the chef's salad, with small rolls of ham, egg slices, and more; and try the sweet/tangy sundried tomato vinaigrette. There's a full bar and multiple TVs broadcasting sports. Try the Bases Loaded potato appetizer; a Blackjack burger—blackened and seasoned with Monterey Jack cheese; or the deep-fried steak fingers basket with fries, Texas toast, and a side of gravy. Inexpensive.

Main Street Family Restaurant (620-431-3343), 12 E. Main St., Chanute. Open 6–9 Sun.–Thurs., 6–10 Fri.–Sat. This is a pleasant place with antique brick and plenty of light. Order breakfast all day, from egg sandwiches with choice of meat plus cheese on a biscuit to French toast

served with berries and whipped cream. There are also appetizers, soups and salads, half-pound burgers served with house-made fries, and steak, salmon, or smothered chicken. Inexpensive.

In Emporia

Amanda's Bakery and Café (620-340-0620), 702 Commercial St., #1fg, Emporia. Open 7–3 Tues.–Fri., 9–2 Sat. In only a few short years this little café has gained a reputation for delicious food, such as sandwiches served on inch-thick bread, filled with combinations such as red onion and pepper, cucumber, guacamole, and cream cheese. Try the creamy, crunchy broccoli salad with mayo, raisins, red onions, and almonds. And don't forget to buy a homemade cookie or brownie for dessert. Inexpensive.

AMANDA'S BAKERY AND CAFÉ IN EMPORIA IS KNOWN FOR TERRIFIC SANDWICHES AND SWEETS.

♿ **Casa Ramos** (620-340-0640), 201 Commercial St., Emporia. Open 11–9 Sun.–Thurs., 11–10 Fri.–Sat. Full-service bar. You won't feel like you're in Emporia as you dine on a daily special of chicken Milanese, nongreasy chicken taquitos, refried beans, Mexican rice, and creamy beans. There's a different special every day, and the place is packed for Sunday lunch. Have a beer or margarita with *carnitas uruapan,* another favorite. Inexpensive.

In Fort Scott

Rusty's Sports Bar and Grill (620-223-4777), 6 N. National, Fort Scott. Open 11–12 Mon.–Thurs., 11–2 Fri.–Sat. Customers love the beef vegetable soup, steak tips, corn fritters, juicy quarter-pound burgers, sampler appetizer platters, and the variety of sides, including skin-on fries or al dente vegetables. Check out live entertainment on weekends. With exposed brick, lots of wood, and sports memorabilia, the restaurant offers pool tables, a jukebox, and a third floor for private gatherings. Inexpensive.

♿ **Sugarfoot and Peaches BBQ** (620-223-2888), 1601 E. Wall, Fort Scott. Open 1:30–8 Tues.–Sat., 11:30–2 Mon.–Fri. $4.99 lunch specials. This loveable BBQ joint is quaint and cute on the inside. They're known for tender pulled pork and BBQ nachos with corn chips, pulled pork, Colby-Jack cheese, diced tomatoes, sour cream, jalapeños, and special BBQ sauce. Try savory and salty pinto beans and meat and pencil-thin sweet potato fries with ranch dressing and honey. Beer and lunch specials available. Inexpensive.

Bowman's Nu Grille (620-223-9949), 24 N. National, Fort Scott.

Open 6–8:30 Mon.–Sat., 7–2 Sun. Built in 1946 and expanded in recent years, this classic diner is renowned for its burgers and homemade fries, onion rings, and thick shakes. Huge chicken fried steaks come with salad, choice of potato, and hot roll or bread, and the pies are freshly baked. Inexpensive.

In Independence

♿ **Brothers Railroad Inn** (620-331-3335; brothersrri.com), 113 S. Pennsylvania Ave., Independence. Open 11–2, 5–9 Tues.–Thurs.; 5–10 Fri.–Sat.; 11–2 Sun. Build your own thin crust pizza with up to nine toppings at this family-owned restaurant with antique photos on the walls, or try a Philly cheesesteak or Reuben pizza. There are also sub sandwiches and large portions of classic Italian favorites such as veal parmigiana or baked fettuccine Alfredo. Enjoy the patio in nice weather. Inexpensive.

The American Soda Fountain and Sandwich Shoppe (620-331-0604), 205 N. Penn St., Independence. Open weekdays 7:30–6, 7:30–1 Sat. Sip on a thick made-to-order chocolate malt or a large cup of coffee for

SUGARFOOT AND PEACHES BBQ

only 50 cents and talk to locals at this old-fashioned soda fountain. Sample Toney's Coneys—small hot dogs with custom buns and a boatload of fixings—plus homemade pies, soups, and sandwiches, as well as breakfast sandwiches with bacon or sausage, one egg, and cheese. Inexpensive.

Ane Mae's Coffee House (620-331-4487), 200 N. Penn, Independence. Open 7–7 weekdays, 7–4 Sat. With a dozen tables and five counter stools, Ane Mae's offers daily specials, fresh sandwiches, soups, quiches, and baked goods made from scratch. But this spot is best known for its coffee, ordered fresh weekly from a seed-to-cup company with its own coffee plantation in El Salvador. You'll also find health supplements and whole foods to take home. Inexpensive.

In Iola

& **Sidelines Sports Bar and Grill** (620-365-8311), 112 S. Washington, Iola. Open 11–11 Mon.–Thurs., 11–12 Fri.–Sat. Bean fries, the Cornhusker Reuben and the Tiger—a deluxe turkey sandwich with avocado and bacon—are favorites at this bright and cozy eatery. Inexpensive.

El Charro (620-365-7771), 19 W. Madison, Iola. Open 11–9 Mon.–Thurs., 11–9:30 Fri.–Sat., 11–3 Sun. Walk into a Mexican village where a huge menu awaits you. The Tapatio burrito features rice, beans, and chicken or steak with red sauce and cheese dip, and the Jalisco features steak, chicken, and shrimp for under $10. Inexpensive.

In Parsons

& **Kitchen Pass Restaurant and Bar** (620-421-1907; kitchenpass.net/parsons/parsons.html), 1711 Main St., Parsons. Open 11–10 Mon.–Sat.; bar open 11–midnight Mon.–Thurs., 11–2 AM Fri.–Sat. In the heart of downtown Parsons, this cozy restaurant is a local hangout and visitor favorite. Try deep-fried beef ravioli with marinara and Southwestern egg rolls and house specialties such as Santa Fe chicken or beef quesadillas. Inexpensive.

Downtown Java (620-421-5282), 1800 Main St., Parsons. Open 7–7 Mon.–Thurs., 7–9 Fri., 8–9 Sat.; longer winter hours. You'll get a great mocha in this corner building that has received a gorgeous exterior facelift. Inside rust-colored walls, cavernous leather chairs, and free Wi-Fi create a delightful spot to unwind. Check out the back corridor to the bathroom; a hand-painted mural creates the feel of a French village street. Fresh pastries await in a display case near the register. Inexpensive.

El Pueblito Mexican Restaurant (620-421-3684), 1804 Main St., Parsons. Open 11–9 Sun.–Thurs., 11–10 Fri.–Sat. Walk into a Mexican village, replete with faux tile roofs, loads of archways painted to look like adobe bricks, and wall-spanning murals of Mexican street scenes. Add the food and you have the ingredients for a great dining experience. Lunch specials include a chile relleno with ground beef buried in cheese plus guacamole. All recipes are inspired by the cuisine of La Mocha, Guanajuato. You'll also find kid's and fajita plates, plus sopaipilla, flan, or fried ice cream for dessert. Inexpensive.

In Pittsburg

♥ **Chatter's Grill** (620-232-7277; mychatter.com), 2401 S. Rouse, Pittsburg. Open 11–10 Mon.–Thurs., 11–11 Fri.–Sat., 11–9:30 Sun. Pub, popular, and packed are three ways to describe this spot near Pittsburg State

University. They're known for daily buffalo wing specials (check hours) and classic pub fare—from spinach artichoke dip to pizza—plus pasta, fish, and great steaks and burgers. Full bar. Inexpensive.

Chicken Annie's (620-231-9460), 1143 E. 600th Ave., and **Chicken Mary's** (620-231-9510), 1133 E. 600th Ave., Pittsburg. Open 4–8:30 Tues.–Fri., 4–9 Sat., 11–8 Sun. Fried chicken reigns prominently side by side in these restaurants. Fried chicken, German potato salad, and crunchy coleslaw haven't changed in decades. At Chicken Mary's, enjoy your meal while sitting at a sheltered picnic table. At Chicken Annie's, enjoy a margarita, Blood Mary, or frozen fuzzy navel in the lounge and share your meal from a giant, midtable lazy Susan. This institution celebrated its 75th anniversary in 1934. Also, check out Chicken Annie's Girard (620-724-4090) and Chicken Annie's Pichler's (620-232-9260). Inexpensive.

Gebhardt's Chicken Dinners (620-764-3451), 124 N. 260th St., Mulberry (outside Pittsburg). Open 4–8 Mon., 4–9 Fri.–Sat., 11–7 Mon. Operating since 1946, this rural chicken destination is also famous for its fresh breaded catfish and livers and/or gizzards. Order a five-piece chicken dinner for only $10 with sides that include the very popular German coleslaw and potato salad and mashed potatoes with gravy. No credit cards. Inexpensive.

Otto's Café (620-231-6110), 711 N. Broadway, Pittsburg. Open 6–3 Mon.–Fri., 6–2 Sat. This candy-cane striped soda fountain has served appreciative customers since 1945 and everything is homemade. Breakfast is busiest and includes cinnamon rolls that are 9 inches across and three-egg omelets. They're known for pies, and entrées that come with a choice of three sides. Inexpensive.

Jim's Steakhouse and Lounge (620-231-5770), 1912 N. Broadway, Pittsburg. Open Mon.–Sat. 4:30–10. Beef lovers have flocked here for more than five decades. Some people think their steaks are the best available in southeast Kansas. Burgers, grilled pork chops, and fried chicken are other favorites. There's the feel of a vintage men's club with lots of dark wood. Inexpensive–moderate.

Elsewhere
& **Lanning's Downtown Grill** (620-251-8255), 111 W. Ninth St., Coffeyville. Open 7–3 Sat.–Thurs., 7–9 Fri. A spacious and airy diner with exposed brick walls, Lanning's makes its food from scratch, including crunchy fried chicken served with huge mounds of mashed potatoes, brown gravy, and creamy macaroni and cheese. Save room for homemade desserts. Inexpensive.

✳ Entertainment

In Fort Scott
& **The Liberty Theatre and Crooner's Lounge** (620-223-0098; fslibertytheatre.com), 113 S. Main St., Fort Scott. Call for an appointment. A historic single-screen movie theater with a second theater added has a new function as a venue for special events and live performances, including comedians, concerts, and big-screen sporting events. It's decorated with hand-painted murals depicting area history.

Trolley Rides (620-223-3566), 231 E. Wall, Visitors Center/Fort Scott. Open March–Dec., 11, 12, 1, 2, 3.

Enjoy a 1.5-hour tour that includes multiple gorgeous Victorian and several Frank Lloyd Wright–designed homes, many located along original brick streets. Heat porches on the third floor of mansions provided escape during the hottest part of the year. Adults $5; children 3–12 $4.

In Independence

Historic Homes Tour (620-331-1890), self-guided tour, Independence. Within 45 minutes and less than 2 miles, see nearly 30 beautiful homes built from the late 1800s to early 1900s.

Reichenberger Corn Maze and Pumpkin Patch (620-330-3031; indypumpkinpatch.com), 2570 W. 5000th St., off Peter Pan Rd., Independence. Call for hours. Marty and Amy Reichenberger expose visitors to agriculture at this beloved fall destination, which includes a 4-acre pumpkin patch and maze with 6-foot-tall corn.

Riverside Park and Ralph Mitchell Zoo (620-332-2512; forpaz .com), 1736 N. Fifth St., Independence. Open April–Oct., 9–8; Nov.–Mar., 9–5:30. This beautifully maintained park of more than 100 acres features a free zoo where you'll see a bobcat, an emu, and macaws. Ride the antique carousel (in season); picnic; play miniature golf amid a chapel, log cabin, and caboose; or ride the miniature railroad and enjoy the pool.

Riverside Beach Family Aquatic Center (620-331-4620; indyrec.com), 1501 N. 10th St., Independence. 1–7 Mon.–Sat., 1–6 Sun. A new facility, this cool pool, surrounded by huge beach umbrellas and featuring two mammoth slides, offers 388,979 gallons of wet and wonderful fun. $3 for children 3 and up.

Elsewhere

Toad Hollow Daylily and Iris Farm (620-343-8655), 1534 CR 170, Emporia. Stop by around Mother's Day or in late June. Open garden; can call for appointment. Drive down a county road to this official display garden of the American Horticultural Society since 2004. A truly lovely spot in the midst of blooming season—peach, magenta, and blue irises are only a few of the colors that bloom side by side, interspersed with lovely statuary. Hundreds of daylilies line terraced garden areas, too, in a wide array of colors.

Molly Trolley (620-365-5252; Iola Area chamber of commerce; iola chamber.org/trolley), 208 W. Madison Ave., Iola. This 1988 Boyerton Molly Trolley shows visitors historic Iola with special tour tickets for $5. Available for private rental at $75 for the first hour and $35 for each additional hour.

✳ Selective Shopping

In Chanute

Jodi's Attic (620-431-9422), 113 E. Main, Chanute. Open 10–5:30 Mon.–Thurs., 10–5 Fri.–Sat. You'll love the blackboard beside the front door of this home decor and kitchen store. There are also body care products, scarves, frames, and walking sticks available in this bright, airy space, packed to the gills with treasures. Ask about free giftwrap and shipping.

Bracelets Are Us (620-432-9919), 111 E. Main, Chanute. Open 10–5 weekdays, 9–5 Sat. During six years of operation owner Lisa Gant's inventory has grown to include purses, picture frames, and coffee mugs. It's worth stopping in just to see this place, painted in bright pastels and offering zebra print bags for your purchases

Summit Hill Gardens Soap Shop

(620-212-3878; summithillgardens .com), 2605 160th Rd., Chanute. Open by appointment. Owner Patsy Smeed's home was a school and a claim shanty from the 1800s. Her shop lies on the same property in a renovated farm building and she manufactures her goat's milk soaps nearby. Soap pricing is $1.75 per ounce and patchouli is the most popular scent. Find body-care products, aprons, vintage linens, and preserves here, too. No credit cards.

Feathered Nest (620-431-7764;

featherednestonline.com), 605 N. Santa Fe, Chanute. Open 10–5 Mon.–Sat. Billed as a big city store with small-town prices, it's a collection of everything from quilts to candles and picture frames. Get directions to this edge-of-town spot.

The Chanute Art Gallery (620-431-7807; chanuteartgallery.com), 17 N. Lincoln Ave., Chanute. Open 10–4 Mon.–Sat., or call for tours. Spread across four 90-year-old buildings, this volunteer-run gallery boasts a permanent collection with more than 600 works of art. Oil paintings in the window, carved wood near the front door, and pottery sculptures of all sizes are just a few items displayed here. Purchase a keepsake in the adjacent gift shop.

In Fort Scott

& **Life + Style** (602-223-2915; fslife plusstyle.com), 22 N. Main, Fort Scott. Open 10–6 Mon.–Sat., 12–5 Sun. Opened in 2009, this kitchen accessories store is also a great place to stop for a cup of coffee and perhaps a homemade cookie. The owners have created a bright, spacious spot out of a gutted and rehabbed downtown building where people can outfit their kitchens with the latest gadgets, sit and socialize, or learn to make the

TRAVEL DOWN A COUNTRY ROAD OUTSIDE OF CHANUTE TO FIND HANDMADE GOATS' MILK SOAPS AT SUMMIT HILL GARDENS.

perfect piecrust in the sparkling teaching kitchen.

The Iron Star (620-223-2929), 3 N. Main, Fort Scott. Open 10–5 Mon.–Fri. The downstairs offers antiques, baskets, tableware, quilts, and realistic silk florals. Upstairs find little girls' Sunday gloves and hats, a play kitchen, a velveteen and tulle ballet dress, plus women's blouses, earrings, slacks, and purses.

In Independence

&. **Magnolia Health and Home** (620-331-890; magnoliahealth&home .com), 106 N. Penn, Independence. Open 9–6 weekdays, 9–5 Sat. This is a gorgeous shop with more than 130 scents of hand-poured soy candles, 25 to 30 bath and body product lines, and dozens of loose-leaf tea varieties. Purchase essential and scented oils with custom labels. In chilly weather, sip a warm cup of tea as you browse.

Lillie's Classic Quilts (620-331-4690; lilliesclassicquilts), 113 W. Myrtle St., Independence. Open 10–5 Tues.–Sat. New and vintage fabrics, bedding, and accessories occupy this 1890s building. Operating since 2001, Lillie's was named one of the nation's top 10 quilt shops by *Better Homes and Gardens* and *American Patchwork and Quilting* magazine, and it was featured in the spring 2008 issue of *Quilt Sampler* magazine. Lillie's offers more than a thousand bolts of fabric, every tool that quilters need, and frequent classes and workshops (reservations suggested).

In Parsons

Smelly Good Stuffs (P620-421-3534; smellygoodstuffs.com), 1806 Main St., Parsons. Open 9–5 weekdays, 9–3 Sat. Offering the largest selection of incense in southeast Kansas, including

Wild Berry brand. Purchase shop-made incense (10 sticks for $1.25), plus soaps, paintball equipment, tie-dye T-shirts, lamp oil, lava lamps, and dozens of incense burners.

&. **Circle's Pecans** (620-632-4382; kansaspecans.com), 2499 US 400, McCune (near Parsons). Call for hours. Yes, pecans do grow in Kansas, and you'll find them in the shell, cracked, halved, or in pieces at this family-run operation that grows pecans in a three-thousand-tree orchard. Watch carefully because the building sits back from the road. It's a great place for pecan wood chips, too.

In Pittsburg

John's Sports Center (620-231-7740), 1806 N. Broadway, Pittsburg. Open 8:30–5:30 Mon.–Sat., 12–- Sat. For avid enthusiasts of the outdoors, John's offers everything from Justin Work boots and Wolverine shoes to Levis, Carhartt clothing, and Wrangler work wear. You'll find Browning gun safes, guns, clothes, and knives, hunting camouflage, dozens of fishing rods, water skis, and nylon towrope by the yard.

The Decorum (620-231-0926), 822 N. Broadway, Pittsburg. Open 10–7 Mon.–Thurs., 10–5 Fri.–Sat. Judy Dugan bills her shop as a little boutique where spirit and style meet and a girlfriends store that's not too serious. The biggest seller is jewelry, but you'll also find unusual greeting cards, baby gifts, candles, eclectic teacups, and formal aprons set amid purple walls, a red ceiling, and a leopard-print area rug. A visit here is pure fun.

Elsewhere

&. **Sweet Granada** (620-342-9600; sweetgranada.com), 805 Commercial

St., Emporia. Open 10–6 Mon.–Sat., 10–8 Thurs. Mother and daughter team Toni Bowling and Kim Reddeker studied chocolate making for a year before they opened in time for the 2004 holiday season. Four years later they received a 2008 Award for Excellence—Outstanding Merchant Kansas Main Street. The ladies make most items themselves, using white, milk, dark, and extra dark Guittard chocolate. Try the Amaretto chocolate swirl or lemon meringue fudge, the latter made with marshmallow cream.

✳ Special Events

January: **Albers Marine Fishing, Hunting, Indoor-Outdoor Show** (call Crawford County office), late January.

April: **William Inge Theatre Festival and Conference** (620-331-7768; ingefestival.org), see *Completely Unexpected.* **Civil War Encampment** (620-223-0310; nps.gov.fosc), Fort Scott National Historic Site, Fort Scott.

May: **Katy Days** (1-800-280-6401; katydays.com), Forest Park, Parsons. Celebrating a railroad heritage that began about 140 years ago, with a miniature train, model railroad show, Union Pacific Railroad Display, plenty of food and drink, and live entertainment.

June: **Prairie Days Festival at Little House on the Prairie** (1-800-882-3606), 13 miles southwest of Independence. **Southeast Kansas Antique Engine and Tractor Show** (620-231-1212), Pittsburg. See old gas engines, antique classic cars, and an old sawmill, plus turtle races and more.

July: **Blackberry Festival at Summit Hill Gardens** (620-212-3878), Chanute. Fresh blackberries, great soap, food, and more mark this annual event. **Four State Farm Show** (620-421-9450), Pittsburg area. See loads of farm machinery and equipment and agricultural products, plus daily haying demonstrations.

THE SWEET GRANADA

COMPLETELY UNEXPECTED
Brown Mansion (620-251-0431; brownmansion.com), Coffeyville. This early 1900s, 20,000-square-foot mansion has been a Coffeyville showpiece since 1906 when it occupied a 500-acre farm that also hosted a sanatorium. See family antiques, nine fireplaces, a 2,800-square-foot ballroom with fainting and smoking rooms, and a signed Tiffany chandelier.

Elk Falls Pottery Works (620-329-4425; elkfallspottery.com), Elk Falls. Some people call Elk Falls a ghost town. But Steve and Jane Fry have handcrafted ceramic pieces in the delightful studio/retail space beside their house for more than 35 years. Since 1980 they've also created up to a thousand mugs for Winfield's annual Walnut Valley Festival. Most work is custom, but visitors may purchase limited retail items.

JANE FRY CREATES A HAND-THROWN POT AT ELK FA POTTERY WORKS.

&. **Gordon Parks Art Exhibit at Mercy Hospital** (620-223-2200), Fort Scott. See the largest permanent display of Gordon Parks photography and poetry in the nation after the Library of Congress. Parks and onetime mayor Ken Lunt developed a close relationship, and when Lunt suggested that Mercy Hospital install a Parks display, they received 52 items from the family.

&. **Southeast Kansas Education Service Center—Greenbush** (620-724-6281; greenbush.org), Girard. This facility has a bioscience focus, providing children from Kansas schools with the opportunity to experience laboratory work that meets state standards. There's a mock space simulation area, a wind turbine, a paleontology dig area, and a community garden. Summer camp sessions are available and wetlands cabins are anticipated. The observatory offers free viewings through a research-grade telescope once each month.

Green's Service Station (620-378-3979), Fredonia. When was the last time you had Japanese food or salads made from organic ingredients in a service station dining room?

Try biscuits and gravy, Southwestern wraps, and fresh sub sandwiches at this family-run spot since 1946. And don't forget some fresh-baked pie.

Hollow Garden (620-725-4033), Sedan. Volunteers completely transformed this abandoned dumpsite near Sedan's main street. A boardwalk and footbridges lead through dense trees. You'll also see a waterfall, gazebo, carved statues, performance stage, and immaculate landscaping.

Little League Baseball Museum (620-856-3903), Baxter Springs. The Girls Little League World Series was held here and there's a collection of professional players' memorabilia, including a bat and pennant from Mickey Mantle, photos of Hale Irwin in football and baseball uniforms and teeing off, plus info about the founder of Little League Baseball, Carl Stotz.

Scotty's Classic Car Museum (620-347-8387), Arma. After more than three decades in the car business, Scotty and Phyllis Bitner have collected half a dozen restored antique cars and trucks in a sparkling space with the feel of a 1950s diner. There are also dozens of model cars, old bicycles, child-size play cars, and antique neon.

William Inge Theatre Festival and Conference (620-331-7768, ingefestival .org). This international theater festival honoring native son William Inge takes place every April at Independence Community College. It's the official theater festival of the state of Kansas with national and international participants, and previous honorees have included Edward Albee, Stephen Sondheim, and Arthur Miller.

CLASSIC CARS AND VINTAGE NEON ARE ONLY A FEW OF THE WONDERFUL THINGS TO SEE AT THIS PRIVATELY OWNED MUSEUM.

Pittsburg 4th of July Celebration (620-231-1212; visitcrawfordcounty.com), Lincoln Park, Pittsburg. Spectacular fireworks cap off a day of food, shopping, and activities.

September: **Little Balkans Days** (620-231-1000), Pittsburg. Golf and a 5K, a car and motorcycle show, an arts and crafts festival, and a chili cook-off are only the beginning of this annual event. **Taste of Fort Scott** (620-223-3566), throughout Fort Scott. Food, drink, entertainment and auction make a great event. **Annual Chanute Mexican Fiesta** (620-431-3350), Santa Fe Park Fiesta Grounds /Chanute. Professional musical and dance performances and loads of food characterize this celebration of Mexican heritage. **The Artist Alley Festival** (620-431-3350), Chanute. Enjoy a pancake feed, fine arts demonstra-tions, an antique car show, and a community theater presentation.

October: **Dalton Defender Days** (620-251-2550), Coffeyville. Historical reenactments, soap and broom making, an authentic chuck wagon, and a movie with popcorn are part of this annual event. **Balloons, Bikes, Blues and Barbecue** (620-421-6500), Parsons. The name says it all. **Neewollah** (*Halloween* spelled backward; 877-633-9655; neewollah.com), Independence. Kansas's largest annual festival began in 1919. Includes carnival rides and games, jalapeño corn dogs and buffalo burgers, and local and professional entertainment.

December: **Homes for the Holidays** (1-800-245-FORT), throughout Fort Scott. Tour Victorian homes and churches decorated for the holiday season.

OPERATING SINCE 1919, THIS ANNUAL HALLOWEEN-INSPIRED EVENT HAS BECOME ONE OF THE STATE'S LARGEST ANNUAL FESTIVALS.

THE VILLAGES OF
SOUTHEAST KANSAS

GUIDANCE Convention and visitors' organizations that serve this area include:

Caney Chamber of Commerce (620-879-5131; caney.com/chamber.htm), 312 W. Fourth St., Caney.

Cherryvale Chamber of Commerce (620-891-0072; cherryvaleusa.com/chamber/index.html), Cherryvale.

Columbus Chamber of Commerce (620-429-1492; columbus-kansas.com/chamber), 320 E. Maple, Columbus. Open 9–3 weekdays.

Greenwood County Economic Development Office (620-583-8177; greenwoodounty.org), 311 N. Main, Ste. 1, Eureka. Call ahead.

Friends of Elk Falls (620-329-4425 for Howard/Grenola/Elk Falls). Call for information.

Fredonia Area Chamber of Commerce (620-378-3221; fredoniachamber.com), 615 Madison, Rm. 1, Fredonia. Open 9–4 weekdays; sometimes closed at lunch.

Labette County Convention and Visitors Bureau (620-421-6500; parsons chamber.org/tourism.htm), 1715 Corning, Parsons. Open 9–noon and 1–5 weekdays.

Sedan tourist information **(620-725-5797, Nita Jones-Public Relations), 215 E. Main St., Sedan.**

GETTING THERE *By air:* Your exact location in southeast Kansas will determine which airport is closest, but you'll still need a car to get from the airport to your destination. Major commercial flights are available at **Wichita Mid-Continent Airport** (316-946-47000; seven major carriers with a new terminal opening in spring 2013), 2173 Air Cargo Rd., Wichita; **Kansas City International Airport** (816-243-5237; 11 major carriers), 601 E. Brasilia Ave., Kansas City, MO.; or **Tulsa International Airport** (918-838-5000; nine major carriers), 7777 E. Apache, Tulsa, OK. *By train or bus:* No **AMTRAK** trains or **Greyhound** buses reach these small cities.

GETTING AROUND Driving is the best way to get around this area.

Medical Emergency (arranged alphabetically by city name)

Coffey County Hospital (620-364-2121), 801 N. Fourth St., Burlington.

Fredonia Regional Hospital (620-378-2121), 1527 Madison St., Fredonia.

Girard Medical Center (620-724-8291), 302 N. Hospital Dr., Girard.

Rice County Hospital District #1 (620-257-5173), 619 S. Clark, Lyons.

Wilson Medical Center (620-325-2611), 2600 Ottawa Rd., Neodesha.

Oswego Community Hospital (620-795-2921), 800 Barker Dr., Oswego.

Sedan City Hospital (620-725-3115), 300 W. N St., Sedan.

✳ To See

HISTORIC PLACES, LANDMARKS, AND SITES

In Fredonia

& **South Mound Scenic Drive and Flag**, via Fifth or Seventh Streets, Fredonia. Always open. This 40" by 60" flag that marks a high hill becomes visible from US 400, a mile outside of town. Follow a winding road to the hilltop where you'll find playground equipment, benches, and a picnic shelter in need of paint. Free.

Clifton House (620-378-3268), 321 Eighth St., Fredonia. Call for appointment. Built in 1884 by the owner of the local newspaper, this is the town's oldest big house. The owners have worked for 15 years to create a place that pays homage to the young bride for whom it was built before her untimely death. Period dolls, loads of lace, and florals abound in this unusual spot. Free.

In Girard

Carnegie Library (620-724-4317), 128 W. Prairie, Girard. Girard was the smallest city in the nation to have a Carnegie Library when the structure was built in 1906. Newly painted architectural archways and stone walls delineate the original structure. Free.

Girard historic landmarks tour (620-724-4570), Girard. Always available. More than 20 stops on this self-paced tour range from the oldest business in Girard, still using its original equipment, to the Carnegie Library and private mansions. Free.

& **Kansas Vietnam Veterans Memorial** (316-724-4715), Prairie and Ozark Streets, Girard. Always open. Seven hundred and seventy-seven names of soldiers killed during the war mark this monument on the square. (Junction City's Kansas Vietnam Veterans Memorial includes 20 additional names of soldiers who died from their injuries after they returned.) Free.

St. Aloysius Church, located 7 miles west of Girard, in Greenbush. Always open. A huge shelter and pretty gazebo sit behind this ruined limestone church building. Legend has it that in 1859 a Catholic priest named Father Phillip Colleton found himself in a horrific thunderstorm; he hid beneath his saddle and vowed to build a church on the site, if he survived. The wood structure was destroyed by a storm in 1877 and a limestone structure replaced it 30 years later. Lightning struck and burned the second building, in 1982, long after it became a community building. The serene structure remains visible behind a wire fence. Free.

In Mound City

Old Sugar Creek Mission/Shrine of St. Philippine Duchesne, 727 Main, Mound City. Generally open. A statue of St. Philippine ministering to a kneeling American Indian fills an alcove in the mission chapel, which honors the missionary work of St. (Rose) Philippine Duchesne, who was declared a saint in 1988. It's located only a few miles from the original mission site, which is now situated in a park setting. Free.

Mound City Historical Park, Main St., Mound City. Located along the town's main thoroughfare, the site displays a log cabin replica of Fort Montgomery, a barn, an 1888 Mound City depot building, and an 1867 schoolhouse. Free.

Elsewhere

♿ **Seth Thomas Clock at Cherokee County Courthouse, Courthouse Square,** 110 W. Maple, Columbus. Always open. This giant 1919 clock was originally installed in the 1889 courthouse as a memorial to World War I veterans. The courthouse was replaced, and a local resident later restored the clock's operational capabilities. Today this Columbus icon in its 40-foot tower is the only one of its kind that still operates. Free.

1893 Iron Truss Bridge and The Falls (620-329-4425), Fourth and Montgomery Streets, about four blocks East of downtown Elk Falls (10-foot falls) at the Elk River. Always open. Donors purchased wood planks to give this landmark iron and steel bridge a facelift. A mill once stood near this favorite spot for enthusiasts of the outdoors and picnickers. Free.

♿ **Prudence Crandall Interstate Memorial Marker** (620-329-4425), Osage St. and KS 160, Elk Falls. After a school that Crandall established at Canterbury, Connecticut, became the first black female academy in 1831, she was imprisoned for violating Black Law. Crandall and her husband moved to Illinois after her release on a technicality. Following his death, Crandall and her brother moved to a farm in Elk Falls and Crandall purchased a house here after the Connecticut legislature granted her an annuity. Legal arguments used by her case were later considered in the Brown v. Board of Education case. Free.

Greenwood Hotel (620-583-7271; Heather Huntington Fuesz; greenwood hotel.org), 300 N. Main, Eureka. Call about tour/hours. This legendary hotel reopened with meeting rooms and a small museum late in 2010. Once a center for Flint Hills cattle trading, it's also where more than $1 billion traded hands during the teens and twenties of the 1900s. Oil business took place here and it served as a bus depot for 40 years. Free.

Walter Johnson Birthplace Memorial (620-473-2250), 900 W. Iowa Rd., Humboldt. This is the birthplace of baseball's Walter Johnson, one of the game's most successful pitchers and a player for the Washington Senators. Two miles north of US 169 and 1 mile along a gravel road is a cement and rock memorial near the farm where baseball great Walter Johnson was born. Learn more at the Humboldt Historical Museum at North Second Street, where news clippings and his stamp are displayed near information about another Humboldt native and baseball great George Alexander Sweatt, member of the Kansas City Monarchs, Chicago American Giants, and the Chicago Giants.

& **Oswego Downtown Murals,** Oswego. Twelve murals decorate this town. The best known, at Fourth and Commercial, depicts the Village of Little White Hair and Osage Indian culture.

Pioneer Bluffs (620-753-3484; pioneerbluffs.org), 695 KS 177, Matfield Green. Call for hours. In 2010 this 1859 historical site was the location of a documentary film celebration for the 20th anniversary of publication of *PrairyErth* with author William Least Heat-Moon. Visitors learn about ranching in the Flint Hills and tour a log cabin, a barn, and an on-site gallery (open 10–5 Fri.–Mon.). Educational talks about life in Kansas and a community-supported agriculture (CSA) garden are other features. Free, with program fees.

Swinging Bridge, north of KS 160/Fifth and Biddle, Moline. Always open. At more than 105 years old, this unusual bridge that spans Wildcat Creek is the oldest such structure in the state. Free.

St. Martin's Catholic Church (620-625-3235), Xylan Rd., Piqua. Open 24 hours. Beautiful brick and a tall spire that is clearly visible from US 54 characterize this church building, dedicated in 1922. Christmas Eve mass is one of the few remaining activities here. Free.

Mine Creek Battle Field State Historic Site (913-352-8890), near US 69 and KS 52, Pleasanton. First Wed. in April– last Sat. in Oct., 10–5 Wed.–Sat.; group tours by appointment. One of the Civil War's largest cavalry battles took place here on October 25, 1864, between 8,000 confederate soldiers and 2,500 Union troops. Six hundred Confederates were killed or wounded and there were 120 Union casualties. Americans with Disabilities Act (ADA) accessible. Adults $3; students $1; KSHS Inc. members and children five and under free.

WHEN BIG BRUTUS WAS BUILT IN THE 1960S, IT WAS THE WORLD'S LARGEST ELECTRIC SHOVEL, NOW VISIBLE FROM UP TO 4 MILES AWAY.

& **Yellow Brick Road** (620-25-5797; Jones Realty; skyways.org/towns /sedan), Main Street and surrounding streets, Sedan. Brooke Shields has one. So do Charlton Heston and Lawrence Welk. They're just a few celebrities who own bricks in the nation's longest yellow brick road. More than eleven thousand yellow cement bricks compose this unusual attraction that has drawn more than

YELLOW CEMENT BRICKS PAVE SIDEWALKS THROUGHOUT DOWNTOWN SEDAN IN THE NATION'S LONGEST YELLOW BRICK ROAD.

forty-five thousand visitors annually since it began in 1988. Bricks come from every state, 28 foreign countries, and sister city Sedan, France. Free.

Big Brutus Inc. (620-827-6177; bigbrutus.org/index.html), West Mineral. Always open. At 16 stories tall and 11 million pounds, the largest electric shovel in the world is visible above the tree line from 4 miles away when winter trees shed their leaves. Built in 1962–1963, it was used for the state's mining industry. Visitors center admission: adults $8; seniors $7.50; children 6–12 $5.

MUSEUMS Allen County Historical Museum (620-365-3051), 20 S. Washington, Iola. Open 12:30–4 Tues.–Sat. Previously the Old Allen County Jail, this museum displays four wedding dresses from 1912 to the 1940s, a teller window from the Savonburg State Bank, and dioramas about Territorial Kansas and the state during/after the Civil War. Donations.

Wilson County Museum (620-378-3965), 420 N. Seventh, Fredonia. Open 1–4:30 Mon.–Fri. Walk through county jail cell corridors where original cells display period clothing, children's toys, and antique quilts from the early 1900s. The sheriff and his family also lived in this historical house. Free.

Elevator Museum (620-358-3241; Dorothy Keplinger), Railroad Ave., Grenola. Call for appointment. This museum is housed in a 1909 grain elevator on the National Register of Historic Places, with a 1934 Chevrolet, a Civil War general's uniform, and a buffalo chip burner. See butter churn and straight razor collections plus two restored one-room schoolhouses with a classroom, an antique loom, and a vintage fire truck collection.

THIS 1879 POST OFFICE HAS BEEN RECREATED IN GRENOLA'S UNUSUAL ELEVATOR MUSE-UM, WITH ANTIQUE ITEMS DISPLAYED IN A 1909 GRAIN ELEVATOR.

Benson Museum (620-374-2142), 145 S. Wabash, Howard. Call for an appointment. A wall-spanning 1895 flag from an elementary school, period rooms with clothed mannequins, and wallpaper beads are just a few of the items in this volunteer-run museum. Visit the Country Schoolhouse and Teacher's Quarters and see farm implements at the Gragg Museum and Bertha's Dolls, a private collection with hundreds of dolls that occupy the first floor of a newly renovated building across the street. Free.

Humboldt Historical Museum Complex (620-473-5055), Second and Neosho Streets, Humboldt. Open June–mid-October 1:30–4 weekends, or by appointment. Five buildings include the Riverside Schoolhouse, a display of hand tools used by local farmers and tradesmen, old saddles, and a printing press. Visit the Open Pole Barn with its collection of horse-drawn farm equipment, The Stone House annex with historical memorabilia, or pictures and articles of Walter Johnson and George Sweatt, hall-of-fame baseball players born in Humboldt.

Norman No. 1 Oil Well and Museum (620-325-5316), First and Main, Neodesha. Call for appointment. A 65-foot oil derrick replica set back from the main street commemorates the first commercial oil well established in the Mid-Continent Oil Field. Visitors will also see Ringling Bros. and Barnum & Bailey memorabilia, Osage Indian artifacts, and more, regarding this area where oil was struck in 1892. A small RV park operates nearby.

The Buster Keaton Museum (620-468-2385), 302 Hill St., Piqua. Open 7:30–2 Mon.–Fri. They called him The Great Stone Face of Comedy, but Piqua calls him a native son. Take half an hour to see memorabilia that include his famous straw hat, dozens of black-and-white photos, movie posters, several original costumes, and buttons from the Iola Buster Keaton Film Festival. Donations.

Woodson County Historical Museum (620-625-2626), 204 W. Mary, Yates Center. Open 10–3 Mon.–Wed., Fri.–Sat. Much of this museum operates in the city's first Christian church, built in 1877. See a Civil War pup tent and a Studebaker box wagon. A country school and a small church are attached and an adjacent 1866 cabin was reassembled here in 1976. Visitors from China, Norway, New Zealand, and Africa have signed the guest blackboard. Free.

TOWNS Baxter Springs. Know as a gun toting preacher, John Baxter was also a businessman who moved his wife and eight children to this area in 1849. He ran an inn and general store that served travelers along the Military Road until his death during a land dispute shootout. Baxter Springs incorporated in 1868, honoring him and the spring that ran near his property.

Columbus. The second largest city in Cherokee County, and the county seat, this vibrant small city takes its name from Columbus, Ohio, the hometown of one of its founders. Before it became a town, this area was part of the 1803 Louisiana Purchase. Mining for coal, lead, and zinc were important in the development of Columbus and the region, as was agriculture. There's still an 1880s town square to visit, plus many historic churches and Victorian homes. And every October Columbus hosts their hot air balloon regatta.

Elk City. The oldest town in Montgomery County was established in 1868. It emerged on a site that was still within area where the Osage Indians lived and lies in a valley full of stone and oak trees, near US 160 and KS 39. Approximately three hundred residents live here. In 1998 a 123-pound catfish was caught in Elk City Lake.

Elk Falls. This town took its name from the falls located in the nearby Elk River. The Southern Kansas Railroad came through Elk County from Independence in 1879 but rail traffic dropped off significantly by 1890. Today some people consider Elk Falls a ghost town. Others call it the Outhouse Capital because of the annual tongue-in-cheek festival held each year for which residents enter decorated outhouses in competition.

Eureka. Located in Greenwood County, on US 54, this small town has approximately three thousand residents. Its name comes from when a pioneer to the area found a spring of cool, clear water near here in 1857 and exclaimed, "Eureka!" In 1872 the town became the Greenwood County seat. After two railroads arrived, Eureka became a favorite meeting spot for Texas cattle owners and Kansas City buyers. Today this area has a great reputation for hunting or fishing and is home to the legendary Eureka Downs horse race track.

Fredonia. European settlers first arrived here in the mid-1850s and the town was platted in 1868. By 1937 the town had a population of more than four thousand. Today, the chamber of commerce occupies the historic Gold Dust Hotel Building and a clock tower with 1886 clockworks anchors the square. Many remaining large homes were built more than a century ago. See houses on the National Register of Historic Places, plus The Bandstand, The Clocktower, and

Historic Fredonia Square with its 1932 bandstand. There's also a recently added veterans' memorial near the courthouse.

Humboldt. This town was attacked twice during the Civil War and almost burned to the ground. Twelve war sites include a stone at the center of town that reads CONFEDERATE SOLDIER WAS SHOT HERE OCT. 14, 1861 AS HE WAS TRYING TO REMOVE UNION FLAG. There are also sites in this area related to Underground Railroad activity. Once called Octagon City, Humboldt briefly hosted a vegetarian commune, too, that was created in 1856. Early residents vacated the area by 1857, largely due to its remote locale, lack of services, and harsh living conditions. Today, less than three thousand people live here. George Sweatt, who played with the Kansas City Monarchs baseball team, was once a Humboldt resident.

Mound City. The Linn County seat is where the French operated the first lead mines in Kansas and built a village along the banks of Nine Creek by the late 1830s. The mines were inactive for a time, switched to shaft mining by the 1870s, and then operated sporadically until 1947. This town was located along the western trail of the Underground Railroad to freedom, and a bust of John Brown—prominent in Kansas's antislavery movement—appears in the Linn County Historical Museum.

Neodesha. Oil shaped the early history of this town, located between the Verdigris and Fall Rivers, whose Indian name translates to "where the rivers meet." Today many 1800s buildings remain, including beautiful historic homes. See a replica of the first commercial oil well opened in the Mid-Continent (Oil) Field at the Norman No. 1 Oil Well Museum.

Oswego. This is the county seat of Labette County, renowned for its outdoor recreation—particularly hunting and fishing. The town lies near the Neosho River and has approximately two thousand residents.

Sedan. Location for one of the state's two yellow brick roads and a volunteer-run theater that shows current movies, Sedan is also home to renowned journalist Bill Kurtis, whose Red Buffalo Ranch is a favorite hunting spot. In addition, his Art of the Prairie Gallery showcases Midwestern artists. The famous clown Emmett Kelly was born here, too. Buildings from the early 1900s line the main street with multiple shops and dining options. The county seat of Chautauqua County is located at business US 166 and KS 99. Farming, ranching, and petroleum fuel the local economy, but tourism is becoming more important, with a small airport, parks, and a golf course.

✳ To Do

BOATING AND FISHING Bone Creek Reservoir (620-362-3022), CR 190 N and CR 690 E, Arma. Established in 1996, the reservoir offers many fish varieties, from walleye and crappie to enormous largemouth bass and catfish.

Big Hill Lake (877-444-6777), Little Ozarks, Cherryvale. One of the state's clearest lakes. About 8 miles west on US 400 and then 8 miles south of Parsons. You'll find camping with and without electricity, plus primitive sites. The lake is known for its fishing, picnicking, 17-mile-long Big Hill Horse Trail, hiking, swimming, and hunting, particularly whitetail, turkey, and squirrel.

Bourbon State Fishing Lake and Wildlife Area (620-449-2539), 8705 Wallace Rd., St. Paul. Fish for bass, crappie, walleye, and catfish, some of which reach trophy size. Fishing boats are allowed; so is primitive camping.

Fall River Lake and State Park (620-654-4445), 144 KS 105, Toronto. Contact Army Corps, especially regarding new cabins. **Fall River State Park** (620-637-2213). There's especially good bass fishing, plus camping, swimming, boating, skiing, and hiking. Canoe on the 2,450-acre reservoir, below the dam. Deer, turkeys, and prairie chickens occupy 8,000 acres of public wildlife area next door.

Woodson State Fishing Lake and Wildlife Area (620-637-2213), Fall River, northwest of Chanute. Enjoy picnic tables, toilets, dump stations, and 180 surface acres for fishing and motorboats. Hunting allowed with appropriate licensing.

GOLF Fredonia Golf Club (620-378-3270), 9711 Harper Rd., Fredonia. After playing 18 holes here, enjoy a full bar, sandwiches, and pizza at the 1930s clubhouse. Par 36, 9 holes, 2,574 yards.

Crawford Hills Golf Course (620-724-8855), 205 E KS 47, Girard. Play on Bentgrass greens at this popular nine-hole course. Par 36, 9 holes, 3,025 yards.

HUNTING

In Sedan

The Red Buffalo Ranch Hunting (925-812-0684), Sedan. Enjoy whitetail deer hunting on private land, plus accommodations for other local hunting/fishing. Ten thousand acres include gorgeous rocks, waterfalls, and, of course, wildlife. Day rate for guided hunts $200; 5–10 day packages also available.

Kansas Finest Outfitters LLC (620-205-0460; kansasfinest.com), 865 KS 99 (2 miles south of town), Sedan. Hunts are offered for deer, turkey, prairie chicken, and natural predators, with accommodations in a spacious, modern, fully equipped lodge. Though relatively new to Kansas, Sam Moore has been in the outfitting business for more than 13 years, previously in Illinois. Contact for rates.

Kansas Trophy Hunts (620-725-4011), 134 E. Main, Sedan. Offering semi- and fully guided deer, turkey, and other hunts on four ranches, in season, this outfitter also provides a lodge that holds up to 12 and is loaded with trophy mounts. Hunt packages include lodging and meals. Contact for rates.

Elsewhere

Buck Brush Adventures (620-328-3288; buckbrushadventures.com), 16091 Douglas Rd., Cherryvale. You'll find elk, whitetail, plus exotics such as water buffalo and sika.

Claythorne Lodge (620-597-2568; claythorne.com), 1329 NW 100 Rd., Columbus. Offering shooting, hunting (particularly birds), guides, dog kennels, lodging, a saloon, and conference and meeting facilities.

Flint Oak (620-658-4401; flintoak.com), 2639 Quail Rd., Fall River. With a five-star Rating from the National Association of Shooting Ranges, this outfitter offers hunting (particularly birds), fishing, and lodging to the public April 1–Sept. 30.

Eagle Head Outfitters LLC (620-358-3362; eagleheadoutfitters), 363 CR 8, Grenola. Hunt more than 21,000 acres and hunts for deer, quail, turkeys, geese, ducks, and doves. Lodge sleeps 15 comfortably.

Rim Rock Ranch (620-642-6402; huntrimrockranch.com), 2254 Antler Rd., Longton. Specializing in whitetail and turkey hunts, including guides, lodging, meals, and trophy field preparation. The staff has hunted in Africa, Italy, England, Zimbabwe, Mexico, and most U.S. states, and their trophies are everywhere at this comfortable modern lodge. Whitetail hunts $3,500–12,500; turkey hunts $1,610—add $500 per additional turkey.

Lazy W One Ranch (620-625-2056), 1208 Jay Rd., Yates Center. Lodging and meals are included in hunting packages for doves, ducks, geese, quail, and turkeys. Enjoy 8,000 acres and bring your own dog or borrow one and hunt on your own or with a guide. Deer hunting, bow hunting, and fishing are also available. Call for rates.

✴ Green Space

John Redmond Reservoir and Wildlife Area (620-672-5911), 2.5 miles north of Burlington on US 75. Located on the Neosho River, this long, narrow lake set amid rolling hills full of native grasses offers 9,400 acres of water and up to 12 feet of depth. Agricultural crops and heavy woods are also here. It's a great place to fish, with many varieties that include blue, channel, and flathead catfish, as well as largemouth, smallmouth, spotted, white, and striped bass, among others. Use the boat ramps or hike, bike, or ride horseback along Hickory Creek Trail. You can even camp out if you like.

Crawford State Park (620-362-3671), #1 Lake Rd., Farlington. RV sites plus tent campgrounds, a Laundromat, showers and restrooms, a swimming beach and marina, and even a fish hatchery are located here. Pick up a game of basketball or see a free Friday night movie. Cabins are also available; $45–90 per night, depending on season.

Elk City Reservoir, State Park and Wildlife Area (316-331-6295; kdwp.state .kss.us), near Independence. Amid seven thousand man-made marshes, plus natural lakes, rivers, and creeks you'll find more than two hundred bird species, including pelicans, egrets, birds of prey, and migrating ducks. There are water and electric hookups for RV camping and 4 miles of trails and good fishing are here, too. The area offers hiking and nature trails that have received national recognition. Two bike trails include South Squaw Bike Trail, a 3.3-mile trail near the south side of the lake, and the challenging 4-mile Eagle Rock Mountain Bike Trail.

Flint Hills National Wildlife Refuge (620-392-5553), Hartford. Office open 8–4:30 Mon.–Fri. You may see a bald eagle at this 18,500-acre refuge, administered by the U.S. Fish and Wildlife Service. Many other birds stay here, too,

AT THE TOP OF AN ENORMOUS HILL THERE'S A GORGEOUS VIEW FROM ELK CITY MEMORIAL OVERLOOK.

including wild turkeys, mallards, and wood ducks. November is the best time to see the largest number of migrating waterfowl. Hunting and fishing follows state regulations, and motor vehicles are only permitted on graveled or paved roads and parking areas.

Mined Land Wildlife Area No. 1 (620-431-0380), US 69 and US 160, north of Pittsburg. Covering 15,000 acres, this mining area turned wildlife haven offers grasslands, woodlots, and waterways full of blue herons, turtles, and cardinals— and that's only the start.

✳ Lodging

BED & BREAKFASTS Smittle House (620-429-2420; smittlehouse .com), 426 S. Kansas, Columbus. Step from the wraparound porch into this elegant 1907 Victorian home with original stained glass, lush furnishings, and three guest rooms—one with an attached bath and whirlpool tub. This pair of world travelers also offers multicourse exotic dinners that require reservations at least 3–4 months in advance. $70–85 for two.

Sherman House B&B (620-329-4425; elkfallspotter.com), 10th St., Elk Falls. Elk Falls Pottery founders Steve and Jane Fry also own this cozy, serene little place where their restaurant experience shines in multicourse breakfasts. The building served as an eating house near the railroad from 1879 through 1890. Although the B&B has been for sale, this pair plans to create new local lodging, so call to check their status.

Cattle Baron Inn Bed & Breakfast (316-374-2503; bbonline.com/ks/cattle), 516 E. Randolph, Howard. This 1910 Victorian home full of antiques offers two guest rooms, each with a private bath down the hall. Enjoy original millwork and stained glass and comfortable modern amenities. Rooms are $65–90.

Grandma's House (918-766-5314), 219 S. Montgomery, Sedan. Quilts in three bedrooms, DSL Internet and a computer, and a fully equipped kitchen are just a few amenities at this lovingly maintained 1930s house. There's also a kennel available and movie rentals. Sleeps six. $70 and up.

CABINS AND CAMPING Mound Valley Campsite (620-336-2741), Cherryvale. There are 90 campsites and the following amenities: a dump station, showers, restrooms, water, boat ramp and dock, hiking, picnic area, group shelter, beach, and equestrian trail.

Spring Creek Guest House/Double Arrow C Ranch (620-583-7271; doublearrowc.com), 1209 P Rd., Eureka. Enjoy this private 1920s two-bedroom home with original kitchen cabinets and a hidden Prohibition cabinet. Located on 20,000 acres that have been in co-owner Heather Fuesz's (pronounced "Fees's") family for 25 years, it offers a fully equipped kitchen, a renovated bath, and wooded walking trails. It's a nice spot for small groups, fishing enthusiasts, and bird watchers. From $65.

Camp Hunter (620-473-3232 or 620-473-2341), near Ohio and Second Streets, Humboldt. Closed midnight to sunrise. Wooded at the edge, with lots of large trees, the park has gravel roads. Contact Humboldt city hall or police department for a permit. $5 per night per camper and cabin; camper and cabin rental available.

The River Cabin at Red Buffalo Ranch (620-725-4022; theredbuffalo.com), 118 S. Jackson St., Sedan. This cabin offers casual comfort with a spectacular river view, a fully equipped kitchen, and a loft bedroom. It's near the entrance of this 10,000-acre ranch, owned by renowned photographer Bill Kurtis, and a favorite spot for whitetail hunting. And be sure to visit the 14-foot Butcher Falls nearby. Or call for availability of the Butcher Falls Bunk House, or the Stone House and Garden in Sedan. River Cabin is $125 per night.

HOTELS AND MOTELS Little Brick Inn (at Café on the Route, 620-856-5646; thelittlebrickinn.com), 1101 Military Ave., Baxter Springs. It's located near the state's only remaining 13 miles of the legendary Route 66, with upstairs rooms that flank a super-wide hallway in a historic bank building robbed by Jesse James in 1876. Eat breakfast in a bright, cheerful upstairs dining area. Rooms $50–75.

Maple UnCommon Hotel (620-429-3130; mapleuncommon.com), 120 E. Maple, Columbus. Each suite, created in what was once a department store, offers bedroom and lounging space; several feature Southwestern colors and artwork. The two-story lobby with soaring ceiling houses a rotating art gallery beside a large banquet room with French doors. Rooms $68–125.

((ŋ)) **Crooked Creek Lodge and Swinging Bridge Café** (620-647-4055; molinecrookedcreek.com), 304

Walnut, Moline. Once a care facility, this building now offers rooms on the inn side (from $51) and lodge rooms with private baths (from $85). All rooms have cable. The bear room sleeps six, offers a refrigerator, and is decorated with a wall-spanning hand-painted mural. Eat breakfast, lunch, or dinner on-site at the café. (See *Eating Out.*)

((ψ)) **Country Haven Inn** (620-364-8260; countryhaveninn.com; also in Hillsboro), 207 Cross St., Burlington. This bright, comfortable, small hotel offers queen beds, refrigerators, microwaves, and desks in every room. Expanded continental breakfast. $70.

& ((ψ)) **Fredonia Inn** (620-378-4419), 901 N. Second St., Fredonia. Rooms are newly remodeled, clean, and comfortable, with microwaves and refrigerators in each one. $49.

RESORTS AND LODGES Big Hill Lodge (877-244-4455; bighilllodge .com), 415 S. Liberty, Cherryvale. Opened in 2003, the property offers individual wood-paneled rooms, 6-person suites with kitchens and quilts, cabins, and even a three-bedroom house that sleeps 14 and seats 8 at the dining table. $69–129 for four. Weekly/monthly rates available.

✻ Where to Eat

DINING OUT & Café on the Route/Little Brick Inn (620-856-5646; thelittlebrickinn.com),1101 Military Ave., Baxter Springs. Open 11–2:30 Mon.–Sat., 4–8 Mon./Tues./Thurs., 4–6 Wed., 4–9 Fri.–Sat. (reservations encouraged), 11–2 Sun. buffet for $9. Featured on the Food Network's *Diners, Drive-ins and Dives*, Café on the Route is known for contemporary comfort food, such as highly addictive fried potato salad with a mustard glaze. You'll get a lot of food for a great price. Enjoy light-as-air corn muffins, homemade croutons, and refreshing cranberry-orange salad dressing. Inexpensive–moderate.

EATING OUT

In Fredonia
Tri-Mee Drive In (620-378-2624), 1017 Washington St., Fredonia. Open 11–9 Mon.–Sat. When customers come here for a burger rather than buying a steak somewhere else, they must be pretty terrific. Get a 5-ouncer for under $2 on Mondays. Add a peanut butter/hot fudge shake and you won't need to eat again until tomorrow. Inexpensive.

El Puerto (620-378-2525), 1400 N. Second St., Fredonia. Open 11–9

CAFE ON THE ROUTE

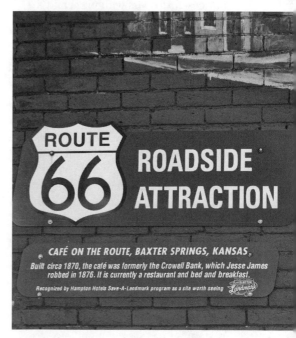

Mon.–Thurs., 11–10 Fri.–Sat., 11–3:30 Sun. Try the Jalisco burrito, a huge tortilla with chicken (or beef), beans, and cheese, plus sides of guacamole, sour cream, and *pico de gallo* in a fried tortilla bowl; or beef steak ranchero served with rice, beans, and flour tortillas. Order shrimp quesadillas and lunch specials. Inexpensive.

Stockyard Restaurant (620-378-2563), 360 W. Madison St., Fredonia. Open 11–2 Mon./Thurs./Fri., 9–2 Tues. (after cattle sales at the adjacent auction house), 5–8 Thurs., 5–9 weekends. Best known for their Friday prime rib special and their steaks, this restaurant near the stockyards also serves seafood, chicken, and pork dishes, as well as premium burgers and sandwiches. Inexpensive.

In Howard

Howard's Poplar Pizza (620-374-2525), 202 S. Wabash, Howard. Open 11–9 Tues.–Thurs., 11–10 Fri.–Sat., 11–2 Sun. Also in Andover, Poplar's entices customers with pizza and a buffet that includes fried chicken, BBQ meatballs, and Salisbury steak. Gingham-checked tablecloths add a homey touch. Inexpensive.

Toot's Drive-In (620-374-2345), 1251 KS 99, Howard. Open 10–9 Sun.–Mon., 6–9 Tues.–Sat. Pancakes and hash browns are local favorites during breakfast, served until 10 AM But you haven't lived until you've tried a fudge monkey. Take the largest foam cup you've seen and then fill it with two layers of soft serve, bananas, hot fudge, and nuts, if you want. No credit cards. Inexpensive.

Elsewhere

Prairie Nut Hut (620-568-2900), 1306 Quincy St., Altoona. Open 4–9 Tues.–Fri., 11–8 Sat. This landmark restaurant has served mountain oysters for more than 50 years, as customers belly up to a bar made from outlaw Frank Dalton's bowling lane. Throw your peanut shells on the floor, because the natural oils are good for the ancient wood. You can also buy big juicy burgers, award-winning chicken-fried steak, and bottled beer. On Tuesdays it's only $1 a bottle. Inexpensive.

Barto's Idle Hour (620-232-9834), 210 S. Santa Fe, Frontenac. Open 4–10 Tues.–Sat. Great chicken with all the fixings and a lounge that's opened a little bit longer await customers at this popular eatery. But you'll also find Italian and Slavic-inspired items on the menu, paying homage to local immigrants. Inexpensive.

Linda's Diner (620-678-333), 106 S KS 99, Hamilton. Open 6–8 Sun.–Thurs., 6–noon Fri.–Sat. People come from as far away as Emporia for karaoke nights at this spacious diner, known for homemade coconut cream and crunch-top pies, biscuits and gravy, and hot beef sandwiches with meat cooked for 12 hours. Inexpensive.

&. **Two Sister's Café** (620-439-5333; twosisterscafeks.com), 106 N. Commercial St., Kincaid. Open 7:30–2:30 Tues.–Thurs., 7:30–8 Fri.–Sat., 7:30–2 Sun. Cute and spacious with a country feel, a gumball machine, and quart-size iced tea, this place is known for piping hot, perfectly crisp fried chicken. Enjoy a huge breast piece with cut green beans, white or brown gravy, a homemade roll, and a trip to the salad bar, and then try some fresh cobbler or pie. No credit cards. Inexpensive.

&. **Swinging Bridge Café** (at Crooked Creek Lodge; see *Lodging*;

620-647-4055; molinecrookedcreek
.com), 304 Walnut, Moline. Open 6–8
Mon.–Sat., 11–2 Sun. This yellow-
walled café offers specials such as
BBQ chicken sandwich with potato
salad or beef tips over mashed potatoes. Even the smallest burger is juicy
and flavorful. Choose from beer and
other bottled alcoholic beverages or
try a big slice of apple, strawberry
rhubarb, or chocolate fudge pecan
pie. Inexpensive.

Everybody's (913-795-2306), 534
Main, Mound City. Open 11–9
Tues.–Fri. Also serving Opie's Pizza.
They're known for the largest tenderloins in Linn County and spicy, meaty
chili, with seven cobblers and pies
daily, game trophies and a big-screen
TV. No credit cards. Game trophies
and a big screen TV. Inexpensive.

Gebhardt's Chicken (620-764-
3451), 260 Rd., Mulberry, 4 miles east
of US 69 and KS 47. Open Mon. 4–8,
Fri.–Sat. 4–9, Sun. 11–7. Set back
from a country road, this restaurant
has served a family recipe of chicken
with cream gravy and green beans
since 1946. No credit cards. Inexpensive.

Josie's Ristorante (620-479-8202),
400 N. Main, Scammon. Open 5–8
Wed.–Thurs. and 5–9 Fri.–Sat. People
from miles around enjoy Italian food
based on recipes brought from Josie
Saporito when she her husband,
Frank, moved to the U.S. In 1986
Josie's grandson Mike and his wife,
Sally, began to cook Josie's amazing
recipes for the public at their new
restaurant. Pasta is made daily and
fried ravioli and lasagna are frequent
crowd-pleasers. No credit cards.
Moderate.

Scipio Supper Club (785-835-6246),
CR 2350 and Nebraska Rd., Scipio.

Open from 6 AM Mon./Wed./Fri–Sun.
This unassuming building located
about 2 miles off US 59 has offered
breakfast from 7:30–11 on summer
Sundays; Wednesday fiesta nights
with $1 tacos and margaritas on the
rocks and weekly Mexican specials;
and bike nights on first and third
Mondays. Full bar. Steaks and their
famous potato chips are favorites.
$5–19. Inexpensive– moderate.

&. **Buck's BBQ** (620-725-5025), W
US 166, Sedan. Open 11–9
Mon–Thurs., 11–10 Fri.–Sat. Bar
opens after 5. Spacious yet cozy, this
spot has become a favorite of hunters
and locals, particularly for their BBQ
ribs, pulled pork, and steaks—all of
their meat is cooked on a smoker. But
they also make a great chef's salad.
Inexpensive.

✳ Entertainment

&. **Eureka Downs** (620-583-5528;
eurekadowns.com), 210 N. Jefferson,
Eureka. Gates open 11:30 on summer
race days, 1 pm post time; contact for
race schedule. Enjoy fast-paced
excitement at this track that has
offered live quarter horse and thor-
oughbred races for nearly 140 years.
The facility also boards horses, and
you may see them exercising on the
track or near the barn on nonrace
days. Adults $7; seniors and children
under 14 $5.

Camptown Greyhound (620-230-
0022), 313 S US 69, Frontenac. Call
to learn if this popular entertainment
venue is offering races again.

Rawhide Arena and Co. (785-867-
2369; rawhidarena.com), 31983 NE
Utah Rd., Greeley, May–Nov. Enjoy
rough stock practice Wednesday
nights, team roping practice on
Thursday nights, and ranch sort

EUREKA DOWNS

practice ($20) on Tuesdays. Special events are offered by the Missouri Kansas (MoKan) Youth Rodeo, Kansas Junior Bullriders Association (KJBA), Christian Youth Rodeo Association (CYRA), and the National Federation of Professional Bull Riders (NFPB), and include mutton busting and ranch rodeos. Visiting cowboys named Rawhide Arena the 2006 Missouri Rodeo Cowboys Association (MRCA) Rodeo of the Year. The arena also works with youth groups and offers ponies for special events.

Humboldt Speedway Inc. (620-473-3694; humboldtspeedway.com), 1663 Georgia Rd., Humboldt. Open Fri. evenings, beginning in April and on Sat. for go-kart races. Gates open at 6 PM and racing begins at 8. For fast-paced racing action, visit this rural 0.375-mile oval track where hundreds of spectators gather. The track accommodates race-modified and street stock cars, e-mods, and bombers. Adults $9; children 6–12 $4; Pit Pass $25 for adults, $10 for kids. Takes place on Saturdays.

Thomas H. Bowlus Fine Arts Center and Cultural Center (620-365-4765), 205 E. Madison, Iola. On any given day you'll hear children's voices and dancing feet in the building. A 750-seat auditorium and 120-seat recital hall host dozens of performances, each year. Call about their schedule and stop by the art gallery.

Kansas Rocks Recreation Park (ksrockspark.com), 2051 130th St., Mapleton. Open 8–7 Sat. and 8–5 Sun. in summer; 8–5 Sat. and 8–4 Sun. in winter. The park offers 240 acres of beginner, intermediate, and expert trails for hikers, mountain bikers, and four-wheel drive vehicles This is the place to challenge yourself, in hilly, rocky trails designated for

4WD vehicles and dirt jump/skill areas for bicycles. There are toilets, picnic shelters, grills, and a play area available, too. Opened since 2003, the park offers daily and annual passes.

✳ Selective Shopping

In Fredonia
Julie's Antique Flower Factory (620-378-3131), 922 E. Washington, Fredonia. Open 11:30–5:30 Mon.–Fri., 9:30–4 Sat. This is a delightful spot near the edge of town, packed from floor to ceiling with antiques, quilts, and large metal wall stars. You could easily spend hours here.

Back Porch Gift Shop and Bakery (620-378-3000), 630 Madison St., Fredonia. Open 9:30–4 Tues.–Thurs., 9:30–5 Fri., 9:30–12 Sat. What began as a gift shop with baked goods has become a destination for daily specialty items, from caramel pecan rolls to *kolaches* or *bierocks*. Shop for gift items that include candles shaped like individual pies.

In Humboldt
Patrick Haire Cabinet Maker (620-473-2348), 118 Eighth St., Humboldt. Open when the doors are open. In this 1866 building Haire has fully restored the 19th-century woodworking machinery that he uses daily to create primarily historically inspired furniture. This is Haire's second completely restored historical mill building, and he has also taught restoration in Colorado. No credit cards.

Terry's Flower Shop, Home Décor and More (620-473-3747), 107 S. Ninth St., Humboldt. Open 10–5 Mon.–Sat. Find the largest selection of unusual lamps in southeast Kansas at this giant store full of high-end

home furnishings, fountains, and, of course, floral designs.

In Sedan
Red Buffalo Gift/Coffee Bar (620-725-4022; theredbuffalo.com), 107 E. Main St., Sedan. Open 9–5 Mon.–Sat. This long, narrow store is a treasure trove of Indian blankets, Western decor, and homemade jams and jellies, with ice cream, plus premium coffee offered near the back; gourmet and dessert coffees are also available by the bag.

Leota's Gifts and More (620-725-4949), 110 E. Main St., Sedan. Open 9–5 Mon.–Wed./Fri., 9–7 Thurs., 9–4 Sat. You'll like the handmade local jewelry and 12 flavors of ice cream or handmade smoothies. But the motorized figures in this shop make it an extra special place.

Elsewhere
Bilke's Western Outlet (620-856-5707), 1041 Military Rd., Baxter Springs. Open 9–6 weekdays, 9–4 Sat. For 30 years this shop has carried Western clothing, dozens of saddles, Stetsons, and cowboy boots. Ask to tour the cowboy museum upstairs— an incredible collection of Western memorabilia by co-owner Jim Bilke.

S&S Western Outfitters (620-922-3613), 101 N. Delaware, Edna. Open 10–6 weekdays, 9–1 Sat. This store is full of rustic wood furniture, Western-inspired pillows, and Native American Indian art, plus cowboy hats, clothing, and multicolored Olathe boots. It's an offshoot of the long-established original in Joplin, Missouri.

Tonovay Antique Mall (620-583-5242), 1698 KS 99, Eureka. Open 9–6 Mon./Tues./Fri./Sat., 1–6 Sun. What looks like an old warehouse has become an antique and collectibles emporium packed from floor to ceiling with ceramic Santas, 1950s table lamps, dozens of ball jars, hundreds of mismatched coffee mugs, and thousands of paperbacks. Ceiling fans cool this place during summertime.

Frontenac Bakery (620-231-7980), 211 N. Crawford, Frontenac. Open 7:30–sellout Sun. This bakery established by Italian immigrant George Vacca still uses the original 110-year-old oven that was retooled in 1976. The current owners are known for cinnamon rolls and pillow-soft bread, baked Wednesday through Sunday mornings, and they use 3,500 pounds of flour per week. No credit cards.

Red Barn Soap Company (620-374-2500; redbarnsoapcompany), 144 E. Randolph St., Howard. Usually open 10–4:30 Tues.–Fri., 9–noon Sat. Bars are handcrafted using olive oil, coconut palm kernel and palm oil, shea and avocado butter, and goat's milk in luscious scents such as oatmeal-honey-almond, fresh lemon, milk and honey, and spearmint.

& **The Derrick** (620-325-3000), 502 Main St., Neodesha. Open 9–5 weekdays, 10–3 Sat. Gorgeous home decor and gift items, beautifully displayed, characterize this multiroom store on Neodesha's main drag.

Oswego Fudge Factory/Oswego Drug Store (620-795-2233), 413 Commercial, Oswego. Open 9–1 and 2–6 weekdays, 9–1 Sat. Made upstairs every Thursday, this creamy fudge comes in butter pecan, vanilla praline, or peanut butter chocolate flavors. Fall holiday flavors may include maple nut or pumpkin pie. They also ship.

Eisler Brothers Old Riverton Store (620-848-3330), US 400/old US 66, Riverton. Open 7:30–8 Mon.–Sat.,

noon–7 Sun. Browse through US 66 T-shirts, shot glasses, books, and flags, plus items from the animated feature *Cars* (the design crew took inspiration from Eisler and its spot along the route). Then buy a sandwich from the old-fashioned deli. Food is inexpensive.

Needle in a Haystack (620-736-2942; needleinahaystack.com), 207 Q Rd., Severy. Open 9–5 Mon.–Sat., 1–5 Sun. Look for a water tower west of KS 99 and US 400. This barnlike structure with soaring ceilings offers more than three thousand bolts of fabric, including a camouflage pattern, precut fat quarters, and lots of quilting tools. Individual vendors also offer their wares, many made with fabric, but also soap, yarn, and candles.

✳ Special Events

May: Annual **Cherry Blossom Festival** (620-891-0072), Logan Park, Cherryvale. Several hundred people attend this signature spring event, which features music, arts and crafts, a car show, and fireworks. **Elk County Ranch Rodeo** (620-374-2405), rotating locations. Watch open ranch-style bronc riding and competitions in cow milking, branding, and more. Annual **Yellow Brick Road Festival** and **Chautauqua Hills Blues Festival** (620-725-5650), Sedan. Chow down at the mountain oyster cook-off and parade and/or on fabulous BBQ. Enjoy dozens of professional performances during this 10-year-old event.

June: **Flint Hills Rodeo** (620-273-6480; flinthillsrodeo.com), Strong City. For 75 years this event has offered guests the best in rodeo performances, from cowboys and cowgirls as they perform rope tricks to rides on bucking broncos and navigating barrels on horseback. There's also a parade and cowboy dances. **Bike Across Kansas** (bak.org), crossing the state. Since 1975 biking enthusiasts have participated in this popular event. Participating cities in 2010 included Goodland, Colby, Hill City, Osborne, Minneapolis, Herington, Osage City, Eudora, and Leavenworth. **Chautauqua County Fair and Rodeo** (620-725-5650), June or July, at Sedan City Park and Fairgrounds, Sedan. Enjoy a parade, talent shows, carnival rides, a restored and antique car show, and a sanctioned rodeo. **Fredonia Flag Festival** (fredoniachamber.com). Includes the **Ole' Glory BBQ Challenge**, a beer garden, cooking contests, and much more.

July: **Yates Center Mardi Gras** (620-625-2118), Yates Center. Enjoy a KCBS (Kansas City Barbecue Society) BBQ cook-off, American Legion Riders bike show, and much more.

August: **Linn County Fair and Rodeo** (includes annual PRCA championship rodeo, 913-795-2591; linncountyfair.org), Mound City. This event includes a truck and tractor pull, rodeo and demolition derby, draft horse pull, gospel show, and mutton busting.

October: **Biblesta** (620-473-3374), first Saturday, in Humboldt. See the world's only parade based on the Bible with floats, walking entries, and biblical costumes. **Columbus Day Festival and Hot Air Balloon Regatta** (620-429-1492; columbusday balloons.com), Columbus. Weekend before Columbus Day. This is one of southeast Kansas's fastest-growing festivals in which dozens of hot-air balloons make night and day ascents, while visitors also enjoy a scarecrow contest, pancake breakfast, bean feed, parade, car and motorcycle show, antique tractor show, and children's activities.

November: **Cattlemen's Day** (620-583-8177; greenwoodcounty.org), Eureka. What better way to celebrate ranch heritage than with pancakes, a parade, and daylong exhibits. Cap off the day with a banquet and dance. **Elk Falls Outhouse Tour** (620-329-4425; outhousetour.com), Elk Falls. What began as a tongue-in-cheek addition to the town's fall festivities has been a signature event since 1996. **Pecan Fest** (620-236-7371),Chetopa. This annual event features an arts and crafts show, vendors, pecan demonstrations, and cooking contest, plus children's events and games, singing competitions, and other activities.

North-Central Kansas: Melting Pot

4

INTRODUCTION

You'll find a little bit of everything in north-central Kansas, from ethnic enclaves to quirky art, historic sites, and beautiful countryside. Visit Little Sweden USA in Lindsborg or Kansas's Czech Capital in Wilson. This is where you'll see the World's Largest Ball of Twine and the longest sculpted brick mural ever created. The town of Lucas is full of unusual art such as the renowned Garden of Eden, with enormous cement sculptures and a family mausoleum, Frances Deeble's backyard art, or fanciful porcelain pieces created by renowned artist Eric Abraham.

North-central Kansas is home to President Dwight D. Eisenhower, candy baron Russell Stover, and several important pony express sites. Coronado explored this area, the song "Home on the Range" was created near Nebraska, and, for a brief time, the Kansas Territory's first capitol operated here, too.

The variety of terrain in north-central Kansas includes sprawling agricultural areas, rolling hills, and gorgeous river valleys and creek beds. Hunting, fishing, and appreciation of wildlife are common activities at multiple reservoirs, lakes, and designated wildlife areas. See massive rock structures that seem plucked from another world at Mushroom Rock and Rock City. This area also features both the Geographic Center of the 48 States and the Geodetic Center of North America.

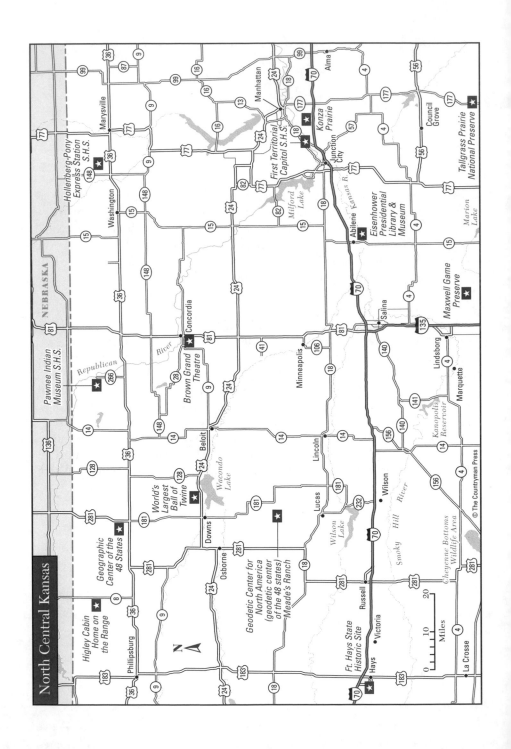

North Central Kansas

EAST OF SALINA

Abilene is located along modern-day I-70. It's also the childhood home of Dwight D. Eisenhower. During pioneer days, longhorn cattle traveled from Texas to Abilene along the Chisholm Trail, and the town began when the Hersey family established a stagecoach stop here in 1857. Old Fort Riley served as a cavalry post protecting settlers and the railroads on which they traveled.

By 1867 the Kansas Pacific Railroad reached Abilene, and growth began. Before long it became known as a typical Wild Western town, full of saloons and gambling houses. As cattlemen became prosperous, Abilene grew wilder. When the town incorporated in 1869 it was time for change. Wild Bill Hickok became city marshal after the first city marshal was murdered as he tried to restore law and order. Hickok was thought of as fearless and was an expert with his twin pistols. In 1871 Abilene's one-time mayor, T. C. Henry, introduced townspeople to his first crop of winter wheat, launching Kansas's enormous participation in the nation's wheat production.

With more than six thousand residents, Abilene is the current seat of Dickinson County. Visit the Eisenhower museum and grounds or catch a glimpse of old wealth at the Historic Seelye Mansion, Gardens, and Patent Medicine Museum, once owned by a local physician and inventor. Dine on chicken that has been nationally known since World War II or in a converted mansion, or pat the head of a champion racing greyhound.

Approximately twenty thousand people call Junction City home. Three towns were planned for the intersection of the Smoky Hill and Republican Rivers before the area was christened Junction City. The city served as a mainline railroad stop during its heyday and turned 150 in 2009. Renowned photographer Joseph Judd Pennell made Junction City one of the most photographed cities in the western United States; four thousand of his glass negatives are currently housed at the University of Kansas.

Junction City is easy to navigate. All north–south streets are named after presidents; all east–west streets are numbered or named after trees. Located in the heart of the Kansas Flint Hills, it's also a great spot for outdoor activities, especially in its highly popular Milford Lake area, and hunting of all kinds is available. You'll also find hunting—and fishing—at Fort Riley, and you're close to the Konza Prairie, with 7 miles of public trails and endless views of wildlife.

Initially built to provide protection for new settlers who came to the area by wagon train and to protect the railroads, nearby Fort Riley was a cavalry post. Many buffalo soldiers operated out of the fort. The pandemic Spanish flu also began here in 1918, and there was a trolley station on post from 1901 to the early 1930s. Today, 101,000 acres compose this military city and more than eighteen thousand soldiers are associated with the fort. In spring 2010, seven thousand Fort Riley soldiers were serving in war efforts.

Known as the city of beautiful sunsets, Milford is a paradise for lovers of the outdoors. It has grown up around Milford Reservoir, with its 163 miles of shoreline and 15,700 surface acres of water.

GUIDANCE Learn more about cities in this chapter from these organizations:

Abilene Convention and Visitors Bureau (785-263-2231; abilenecityhall), 201 NW Second St., Abilene (Enterprise/Herrington). Open 8–5 weekdays.

Washington County Tourism (785-325-2116; Gloria Moore), 199 N. Main St., Barnes.

Geary County Convention and Visitors Bureau (785-238-2885; junctioncity .org), 823 Washington St., Junction City (and Milford). Open 8–5.

Marysville Chamber of Commerce (785-562-3101), 101 N. Tenth, Marysville. Open 9–12, 1–5 weekdays; visit Koester House Museum, April–Oct., 10–4:30 Sat., 1–4:30 Sun.

Waterville Chamber of Commerce (785-363-2515; at the Weaver Hotel), 126 S. Kansas St. Call and then stop by the hotel.

GETTING THERE AND GETTING AROUND North–south highways east of Salina include US 77, -KS 148, KS 9/15, and KS 43. Highways that travel primarily east–west and generally toward Salina include US 36, KS 9/148, US 24, KS 18, KS 4, and US 56. *By air:* Junction City is the largest metropolitan area in this section of north-central Kansas, but there is no commercial air service available, so driving is your best bet here. Some taxis are available, in town. *By bus:* **Greyhound** (785-238-3161) serves Junction City from 122 E. Flint Hills Blvd.

MEDICAL EMERGENCY (arranged alphabetically by city name)

Memorial Hospital (785–263-6676/2100) 511 NE 10th St., Abilene.

Clay County Medical Center (785-632-2144), 617 Liberty, Clay Center.

Geary Community Hospital (785-238-4131), 1102 St. Mary's Rd., Junction City.

✳ To See

HISTORIC PLACES, LANDMARKS, AND SITES

In Abilene

& **Greyhound Hall of Fame** (785-263-3000; greyhoundhalloffame.com), 407 S. Buckeye, Abilene. Open 9–5 daily. When visiting this site, located near the National Greyhound Association, you'll likely meet retired greyhounds Jade and the renowned Talentedmrripley, who sits atop a special pillow. You'll learn that greyhounds were dogs of aristocracy during the Middle Ages and began racing during the 1920s. There's loads of information about dog racing, from weigh-in and lead out to finish line, as well as the history of pari-mutuel wagering. Plaques describe individual dogs and people who have shaped the sport. Opened in 1973. Free.

The Heritage Center of Dickinson County (785-263-2681; heritagecenterdk .com), 412 S. Campbell, Abilene. Open in winter, 9–3 Mon.–Fri., 10–5 Sat., 1–5 Sun. Open Memorial Day through Labor Day until 4 PM Fri. and 8 PM Sat. At the historical museum, learn about the prairie before westward expansion began and how the area has changed since that time. In the museum of independent telephony, see the first commercial telephones and phones through the years. An original C. W. Parker carousel is gorgeously painted and still operates. Adults 16 and older $4; $2 carousel rides.

In Junction City

Ġ **Buffalo Soldier Memorial,** 18th and Buffalo Soldier Dr., Junction City. The red small houses at this location are what remain of government quarters built during segregation for buffalo soldiers. When segregation ended these soldiers were able to buy these houses, and descendants live there today. One remaining buffalo soldier lives in Junction City.

Heritage Park, Sixth and Washington Streets, Junction City. This park is home to a Civil War memorial arch, the Kansas Vietnam Veterans Memorial, and a Junction City /Geary County law enforcement memorial.

Elsewhere

Hollenberg Pony Express Station and Visitors Center (785-337-2635, kshs.org/places/hollenberg), 1 mile east of KS 148 on KS 243, Hanover. Open first Wed. April–last Saturday Oct., 10–5 Wed.–Sat. There's a lovely visitors center and a Conestoga wagon without a roof at this historic site. Adults $3; students $1; children under five free.

MUSEUMS

In Abilene

Ġ **Dwight D. Eisenhower Presidential Library and Museum** (785-263-6700; eisenhower.archives.gov), 200 SE Fourth St., Abilene. Open 9–4:45 daily. Administered by the National Archives and Records Administration, this site of five buildings could keep visitors occupied for a full day. See family furnishings from the 1940s in the modest 1898 Eisenhower Home, which housed Dwight's boyhood family of seven sons for 13 years. The museum showcases Eisenhower's West Point uniform, the D-day planning table, and a D-day display. You'll find Mamie Eisenhower's wedding dress and head-of-state gifts such as gilt candelabras here, too. The presidential library, a large statue of Eisenhower, and a meditation chapel where he, Mamie, and son David are buried are also found here. Adults 16–61 $8; seniors (62 and up) $6; ages 8–15 $1.

Historic Seelye Mansion, Gardens, and Patent Medicine Museum (785-263-1084), 1105 N. Buckeye, Abilene. Tours begin 10–4 Mon.–Sat., 1–4 Sun.

DWIGHT D. EISENHOWER PRESIDENTIAL LIBRARY AND MUSEUM

A BUFFALO HEAD DECORATES THE
ENTRANCE TO THE EISENHOWER LIBRARY
IN ABILENE.

(last tour at 3). Built for $55,000 in 1905, this 11,000-square-foot Georgian-style home displays the best household decor available from the 1904 St. Louis World's Fair, plus the most complete private library in Kansas. See Edison lights, a Tiffany mosaic fireplace, and four thousand pieces of Haviland china. Owner Dr. A. B. Seelye created and sold more than a hundred medicinal and other products; see related artifacts, the third-floor ballroom, and beautifully restored gardens. Adults $10; children 6–12 $5; groups of 10 or more $7.50; youth groups $5.

In Belleville

Boyer Museum of Animated Carvings (785-527-5884), 1205 M St., Belleville. Open May–Sept., 1–5 Wed.–Sat., or by appointment. Paul Boyer is a self-taught artist who uses soft pine, cedar, and walnut to create animated hand-carved figurines including people, animals, cars, and engines that range from humorous to beautiful. The detail and creativity in each piece is astounding. Adults $5; children 6–12 $2; children 5 and under free.

In Chapman

The Kansas Auto Racing Museum (785-922-6642), 1205 Manor Rd., Chapman. Open 9–5 Mon.–Sat., Sun. by appointment. This classy little museum provides a history of motorsports in Kansas through displays of vehicles, trophies—including the first NASCAR trophy awards at Charlotte Speedway—and other items. See a hall of fame for drivers, too. Free.

In Marysville

Pony Express Original Home Station No. 1 Museum (785-562-3825), 106 S. Eighth St., Marysville. Open April–Oct., 10–5 Mon.–Sat., noon–4 Sun. The pony express route ran from St. Joseph, Missouri, to Sacramento, California, and back, from April 1860 to October 1861, with riders changing horses every 12–15 miles during the 10-day trips. The advent of the telegraph caused this vital service to end. At the museum, see antique vehicles, dozens of period rifles, and equipment for making horseshoes.

Koester House Museum (785-562-2417; Marysville chamber of commerce), 10th and Broadway, Marysville. Call for a tour or information. This lovely mansion in downtown Marysville is still furnished with belongings from the banking family that lived here before the turn of the 20th century after moving here in 1850. A stunning wall of handcrafted woodwork holds the family's personal library, and rare white bronze zinc sculptures decorate the yard. The family eventually developed an entire block of the town, which the heirs gave to Marysville in 1977.

& **Doll Museum** (785-562-3029), 912 Broadway, Marysville. Available by appointment. This collection of more than a thousand dolls, toys, and history has

SEELYE MANSION EXTERIOR

RACE VEHICLES AND TROPHIES ARE JUST A FEW MEMORABILIA AT THE KANSAS AUTO RACING MUSEUM.

received national recognition. The dolls are made of papier-mâché, modeling clay, china, bisque, wax, and wood. Visitors will also see miniatures, old rocking horses, pedal toys, and dollhouses here.

TOWNS Clay Center. The first settlers to permanently locate in what is now Clay County arrived in 1856, and many settlers arrived over the next couple years. But the 1860 drought ended immigration here until after the Civil War, as well as a number of good harvests. The first log schoolhouse was built in 1864 on government land. Today Utility Park and Zoo provides a shady oasis for residents and visitors.

Concordia. This town was founded in 1871 along the Republican River in the Smoky Hills region of the Great Plains. Nature was not kind to Concordia during the early years. Major floods annihilated the town in 1902 and 1915, and a major blizzard struck in 1912. Current summers are hot and humid with cold, dry winters.

Approximately six thousand people live in this small town that has a big history. Carry A. Nation visited Concordia, which is well known for its participation in the Orphan Train Movement; a museum is now housed in the Union Pacific Railroad Depot. But there was also a German prisoner-of-war camp here, and the original guardhouse remains. In addition, the Brown Grand Theatre is a spectacularly restored 1907 venue that now hosts performing arts programs.

Marysville. Founded in 1854, the town of Marysville was home to the first pony express route west of St. Joseph, Missouri. Today, visitors can visit the Pony Express Original Home Station No. 1, which has become a museum that commemorates this short-lived method of mail delivery, including the original stable. It is a thriving agricultural area and also home to the stunning red brick Historic Marshall County Courthouse, completed in 1892.

Washington. During summertime, soybean fields are deep green in the morning and almost white later in the day because of lack of water. In Washington County there are spring and fall turkey hunts, pheasant hunts begin in November, and deer hunts take place from September through early December.

FORT RILEY SITES

U.S. Cavalry Museum (785-239-2737). See gear used to protect horses from chemical warfare in 1942, edged weapons and hand arms in the weaponry room, and cavalry uniforms dating from 1776 to 1950. Self-guided tours typically last up to an hour.

First Territorial Capital of Kansas. Drive by the tiny building that served as the state's first territorial capital, which held that distinction for only a few days before it was moved to Lecompton.

Custer House (785-239-2737). This house dates back to the 1850s and replicates quarters where Custer lived at the fort. The only unaltered quarters from that time period featured high ceilings, which made it cooler in summertime, and an enormous master bedroom featured a walk-in closet with a window. See antique dolls and Noah's Ark in a child's bedroom, plus a simply furnished bachelor's room.

1st Infantry Division Museum. Allow 30 to 45 minutes for a tour. Fort Riley soldiers have assisted in military conflicts across the globe, including in Africa, Sicily, Normandy, the Balkans, and Yugoslavia. See a mannequin in a foxhole and a bunker made of 1-inch twigs like those created during World War I in a narrow, dark passageway. There's information about the Vietnam War and the Iraq conflict, and a video informs visitors about the function of military transition teams in Iraq and Afghanistan.

St. Mary's Chapel. The state's first stone church was used by Episcopalians who lived on the fort, which included many officers. It later functioned as a schoolhouse and ammunition storage site before becoming a Catholic chapel in 1938.

✳ To Do

BOATING AND FISHING Milford Lake/Milford State Park/Milford Reservoir (785-238-4010), 3612 State Park Rd., Milford. A favorite of fishing enthusiasts, this is the state's largest lake, where walleye, crappie, bass, and catfish are plentiful. Seven campgrounds offer electric/water hookups and about one-third of campsites have sewer hookups; primitive campsites and cabin rentals are available. There's an active yacht club with the feel of a 1950s summer camp and an off-road vehicle area. Includes Quimby Creek and Steve Lloyd wetland areas.

Milford Nature Center (785-238-5323). Touch animal furs, see wildlife dioramas, and enjoy live animal exhibits. Walk the nature trails or visit the bird-watching wall. Milford Fish Hatchery offers tours at 1 PM on weekends or by appointment.

GOLF Great Life Golf and Fitness at Chisholm Trail (785-263-3313), 645 2400 Ave., Abilene. A retired optometrist built this pasture golf course featured in *Golf Course News, Golf World,* and *Golf Digest.* Plum thickets, narrow fairways, and wind can make play here challenging. Par 72, 18 holes, 6,568 yards champion.

Rolling Meadows Golf Course (785-238-4303), 6514 Old Milford Rd., Milford. Designed by nationally recognized architect Richard Watson, this popular course received 4.5 stars from *Golf Digest* as a top place to play golf in the state. Grass fairways, sand bunkers, and six lakes add excitement to playing here. Par 72, 18 holes, 6,370 yards.

HUNTING Boone's Cabin (785-223-1332, boonescabin.com), P.O. Box 186, Milford. One of the state's top-rated hunting and fishing venues according to *Outdoor Life* magazine, this site offers fully guided turkey and deer hunt packages that include meals. The lodge and cabins can accommodate 24 people. Check out their biggest buck contest in January and children's hunting/fishing programs. Seven-day archery hunting package $2,800; seven-day muzzle load hunt package $3,200; 2.5-day turkey hunt $450. Fishing trips run $300/day per boat, which accommodates up to four people.

✳ Green Space

Clay County Campground and Park at Milford Lake (785-461-5774), 201 Second St., Wakefield. There are hundreds of RV slots at this nicely maintained 40-year-old campground full of sheltered picnic tables and trees. There's a large swimming pool nearby and playground equipment with seesaws. RVs $16; tents $10.

Washington State Fishing Lake (785-461-5402), Washington County. Enjoy 65 water acres stocked with bass, catfish, bluegill, and crappie, plus 352 acres of land ripe for hunting everything from quail and pheasant to white-tailed dear and turkey. Picnic, grill, and even try primitive camping here, too.

Washington City Park. See an 1882 log cabin plus a rose garden, fountain, shaded playground, and an overlook on Mill Creek Dam. Complete hookups are available, for $10 per night, plus primitive camping, and a new pool offers water features. The delightful Munchkin Land playground was built nearby in 2000.

Utility Park (785-632-5674), Fourth St., across from the power company/Clay Center. This is a beautifully landscaped park set below road grade with a fountain, a stone picnic shelter, and a huge playground apparatus. There's a small zoo with many birds, plus gray fox, coati, and lemur.

Dexter Park (785-632-5674), Sixth and Grant, Clay Center. See a donated M-60 tank and a small 1934 band shell in this park along the town's main thoroughfare. Enjoy disc golf and playground equipment.

✳ Lodging

BED & BREAKFASTS Abilene's Victorian Inn B&B (785-263-7774; abilenesvictorianinn.com), 820 NW Third St., Abilene. This pale purple 1900 heritage home offers three rooms and three suites with private baths. Sleep with a carousel horse that honors carousel builder C. W. Parker in the Parker suite, which accommodates four and has a private sunroom. Enjoy soothing pastels and florals and a private balcony in the Eisenhower room. Owner Adrian Potter serves gourmet fare such as coconut pecan French toast with baked bacon and warm syrup. Borrow a bicycle or browse the gift shop. $79–129; additional guests extra.

Windmill Inn (785-263-8755; access -one.com/windmill), 1787 Rain Rd., Chapman. Watch gorgeous sunsets across the prairie from the wraparound porch of this lovely home on a family farm. Enjoy a private bath, an honor bar, and perhaps an attached sitting area (available with some rooms). For extra pampering schedule a hot-stone massage; minimum two required. You won't want to leave this country oasis. Full breakfast. $99–125.

Gloria's Coffee and Quilts (785-763-4569), W KS 9, Barnes. Stay in a turn-of-the-century home where large rooms and complementary chocolates and ice water are standard and two/three rooms have private baths.

Gloria can also tell you everything about Barnes and surrounding towns. Full breakfast. $75–100.

Sun Rock Ranch Resort (785-238-2728; sunrockranch.com), 6260 Skiddy Rd., Junction City (check the address; country road addresses sometimes change unexpectedly). Guests from France and Germany have found this 1,700-acre retreat south of I-70. Watch heifers birth their calves or read a book in the sitting room. Enjoy a supervised horseback ride, go fishing, or take a hayrack ride (prearranged). The pioneer room, with twin beds and an antique rocker, dates back to 1877 when the original house was built. A 1990 renovation added two more rooms. Full breakfast. $70.

CABINS AND CAMPING Flagstop Resort and RV Park (785-463-5537; flagstoprvpark.com), Eighth and Whiting, at Milford Lake. With laundry facilities and a small grocery store, a white sand beach near a play area, a boat ramp, and its own Anchor Inn Bar and Grill (open May to October), this is a great place to camp. Enjoy walls of windows and a deck area, with burgers, shrimp baskets, beer, and wine coolers. Campsites $25; cabins $60–95; tents and no-hookup campsites $10; fees for overnight and day-use visitors; locked RV/boat storage $1 per day.

SUN ROCK RANCH RESORT IS A B&B SET ON A 1,700-ACRE RANCH IN JUNCTION CITY.

HOTELS AND MOTELS Weaver Hotel (785-363-2515; weaverhotel .com), 126 S. Kansas Ave., Waterville. Sleep amid turn-of-the-century furnishings in this fully restored 1905 hotel once favored by railroad travelers and crews. This town of under seven hundred people contributed $600,000 to refurbish individual rooms and construct private bathrooms, and the names of donor families appear on each door. Architect Bruce McMillan received a historical preservation award for his work. Stay in a room or suite, and purchase candles, Oz figures, or gourmet foods in the gift shop. $65–150.

The Clyde Hotel (785-446-2231), 420 Washington St., Clyde. From the outside this 1870 hotel is reminiscent of New Orleans with beautiful wrought-iron details. Inside, rich col-

THE WEAVER HOTEL IN WATERVILLE HAS BEEN FULLY RESTORED TO ITS 1905 GRANDEUR.

ors, original woodwork, and vintage-style furnishings create a soothing environment. Larger rooms offer private baths. Breakfast served in your room. $60 and up.

(ᵞ) **Herington Inn and Suites** (785-597-4581), 565 US 77, Herington. Stay near historic Council Grove. Traveler basics in rooms at this recently built spot include microwaves, refrigerators, and personal voice mail, and there's even a lounge located next door. Pets are allowed in smoking rooms and pet carriers only. Expanded continental breakfast provided. $67–92.

✳ Where to Eat
EATING OUT

In Abilene
Brookville Hotel (785-263-2244; brookvillehotel.com), 105 E. Lafayette, Abilene. Open 11:30–2 and 5–7 Sun., 5–7:30 Wed.–Fri., 1:30–2 and 4:30–7:30 Sat. Initiated in the 1870s, Brookville became legendary for its family-style chicken dinners during World War II. The hotel moved to Abilene in 2000 and received a 2007 James Beard American Classic Award. Gold-painted tin ceilings, antique-looking lighting fixtures, and beautifully carved woodwork will send you back in time. The classic meal includes relishes, sweet and sour coleslaw from a family recipe, cottage cheese, fried chicken, mashed potatoes, gravy, cream-style corn, baking powder biscuits, and home-style ice cream. Inexpensive.

Kirby House Restaurant (785-263-7336; kirby-house.com), 205 NE Third St., Abilene. Open 11–2, 5–8 Mon.–Sat. Banker Thomas Kirby built this gorgeous Victorian home for his wife and daughter in 1885. It underwent a massive restoration in 1987 before it reopened as a restaurant. Brocade doorway drapes, hand-carved woodwork, hardwood floors, and an original tin ceiling decorate this enormous restaurant; ask about the couple's table in the cupola. Enjoy homemade quiche, a fried-chicken dinner or grilled steak, and three-layer carrot cake for dessert. Moderate.

ENJOY LUNCH OR DINNER AMID THE 1885 SPLENDOR OF THE KIRBY HOUSE RESTAURANT IN ABILENE.

Mr. K's Farmhouse Restaurant (785-263-7995, mrksfarmhouse.com), 407 S. Van Buren St., Abilene. Open 11–2 Tues.–Sun., 5–9 Tues.–Sat. In a country setting only minutes from downtown, dine where the Eisenhowers and Jimmy Stewart enjoyed meals at the legendary Lena's. Mr. K's has become a legend in its own right. Highlights include pan-fried chicken, a sweet Italian vinaigrette house dressing, and homemade pies including coconut cream. Inexpensive.

In Junction City
Seoul Restaurant (785-238-3387), 204 Grant Ave., Junction City. Open 11:30–8 Thurs.–Tues., 11:30–2 Wed. Sharing a doorway with Seoul Oriental Supermarket, this family-owned restaurant is a particular favorite of Fort Riley soldiers. Fried mackerel served with fresh vegetables is a big seller; so are *kimbap* (rice with vegetables rolled in seaweed) and *bulgogi* (BBQ beef marinated with coriander). Inexpensive.

In Milford
Milford Tropics (785-463-5551), 103 11th St., Milford. Open 11–2 daily; check for evening hours. Don't let the plain white siding and blue tin roof fool you; inside you'll find a tropical paradise with grass huts and fake parrots. Order shrimp and veggie kabobs with rice; Jamaica jerk steak with fries, veggies, and rice; Black Angus cheeseburgers; and huge, soft onion rings. Everything tastes fresh, and there's a full bar. Inexpensive.

In Marysville
Wagon Wheel Café (785-562-3784), 703 Broadway St., Marysville. Open 6–9 daily. There's a cozy diner atmosphere here with friendly staff and good prices. Try their fried cheese balls or steak with a side of fried baked potato wedges and have a cocktail. Inexpensive.

Hong Kong Chinese Restaurant (785-562-2715), 410 Broadway St., Marysville. Open 11–3, 5–8:30. Everything served here is ultrafresh, and the buffet offers loads of choices, from General Tso's chicken to fried rice, lo mein, and shrimp with vegetables. Their crab rangoon is crunchy and sweet/savory. Inexpensive.

In Clay Center
Dragon House (785-632-2788), 407 Lincoln St., Clay Center. Open 11–9:30, Tues.–Sun. This restaurant is easy on decor but clean, neat, spacious, and soothing, with about three-dozen buffet items. Menu favorites include roast pork lo mein, sweet and sour chicken, and beef with broccoli. Inexpensive.

Maury's Family Restaurant (785-632-3223), 521 Sixth St., Clay Center. Open 6–2 Mon.–Sat., 7–2 Sun. There's always a buffet available in this cheerful place. From the menu, try a patty melt on grilled rye or hot beef sandwich with mashed potatoes. Many people complement their pancakes, and the chocolate peanut butter pie is a local favorite. Inexpensive.

Tasty Pastry Bakery (785-632-2335), 511 Court St., Clay Center. Open breakfast through lunch. Buy a dozen homemade potato rolls for less than $2 or an enormous nut roll for under $1. There's been a bakery here since the 1920s, and the current owners worked for the previous owners. They have carried on a baking tradition that includes glazed maple sticks and generations-old drop cookie recipes. Try a third-of-a-pound burger on a homemade bun or a chicken strip basket for lunch. Inexpensive.

Elsewhere

Our Daily Bread Bake Shoppe and Bistro (785-763-4269; barnesks .net/dailybread.html), 23 N. Center, Barnes. Open 11–2:30 weekdays. Dine amid garden murals and original tin ceilings, where locals flock for lunch and buy their favorite pies. Inexpensive.

Two Doors Down Restaurant (785-729-3633), 307 Baird St., Cuba. Open 11:30–1:30 Mon.–Sat., 5–9 Wed.–Sat. Whatever else you order, make sure to get a *kolache,* a homemade poppy seed Czech roll, or a huge caramel roll. It's a cute place with barn wood on the walls and red accents, where the owner greets you at the back counter. No credit cards. Inexpensive.

Ricky's Café (785-337-8903), 323 W. N St., Hanover. Open 7:30–9 Mon.–Thurs., 7:30–9:30 Fri.–Sat., 8:15–2 Sun. Operating for 25 years, this little restaurant decorated in red, white, and black draws people from nearly an hour away. Buy breakfast, a third-of-a-pound cheeseburger, or a house-made chicken-fried steak dinner. No credit cards. Inexpensive.

SNACKS Tompers Perk (785-238-0111; tompersperk.com), 318 E. Chestnut, Junction City. Open 7–7 Mon.–Thurs., 7–9 Fri.–Sat. Named after a childhood nickname, this small, cozy, spot operates near the back of Rivendell Bookstore. There's a gurgling fountain, a wall-spanning mural, and a dining gazebo with twinkling lights. Enjoy half-price frozen drinks from 2–4 Tues.– Sat. Try their caramel macchiato with a homemade cinnamon roll or breakfast sandwich or a Tuscan chicken wrap at lunch. Inexpensive.

✱ Entertainment

In Washington

Marcon Pies (785-325-2430), 124 W. Eighth St., Washington. Call for a tour. After 25 years this amazingly small operation makes five hundred pies per day, typically Monday through Thursday. Pies go out the day after they're baked, except during holidays—when baking takes place seven days a week and pumpkin and pecan pies are frozen because of their popularity. Then they're made and delivered daily throughout the central United States.

Kansas Specialty Dog Services (KSDS) Inc. (785-325-2256; ksds .org), 124 W. Seventh St., Washington.

LOCATED IN WASHINGTON, KANSAS SPECIALTY DOG SERVICES INC. RAISES DOGS TO BE SERVICE COMPANIONS.

Visit by appointment. With Labrador and golden retrievers in house for training, the nonprofit KSDS raises dogs from birth for use as service companions that assist clients who have disabilities. Kansas State University and Hills are two major veterinary room supporters. Pups spend 18–20 months in foster care before their release to clients, who also receive training with the dogs. Kansas Lions organizations cover the cost of student housing and meals.

Herrs Machine Memory Lane Collection (877-525-2875), F and College Streets, Washington. Open 8–5 weekdays or by appointment. Lawrence and Cara Herrs have collected vintage vehicles, which Lawrence restores, for decades. They proudly share this unusual collection with visitors, from a 1926 Model T Speedster to a 1930 Model A Roadster, a 1918 IHC Model KL fire truck, and a model of 1907 IHC Mogul tractor. Their passion is infectious and the craftsmanship is spectacular.

✳ Selective Shopping

In Abilene

&. **Cypress Bridge** (785-263-1963; cypressbridge.com), 110 NW Third St., Abilene. Open 9–6 Mon.–Wed., 9–7 Thurs., 9–6 Fri., noon–5 Sun. This is one of only two Kansas stores that carries kitchen items from the Culinary Institute of America, and their Winter Warmth candles appeared in gift bags distributed during the 2005 Billboard Music Awards. In fact they're perhaps best known for candle making and custom-scented body care products. You'll also find bath linens, Mexican pots, gourmet foods, and greeting cards here, too. The owners believe that everyone

AMERICAN INDIAN GALLERY BASKETRY

should be able to afford pretty things, including complementary votive candles.

American Indian Art Center (785-263-0090), 206 S. Buckeye, Abilene. Open 9:30–5 Mon.–Sat., 11–4 Sun. This husband and wife team grew up near Nebraska—he within the Iowa Tribe of Kansas and Nebraska, also known as the Ioway. They opened in the 1990s, with fine art crafted by tribally enrolled people. Today they sell award-winning basketry, sand painting, sterling jewelry, and dozens of books and music that reflect American Indian culture.

&. **Russell Stover Candies** (785-263-0463, russellstover.com), 1993 Caramel Blvd./exit 272, off I-70), Abilene. Open 9–6 Mon.–Sat., 10–5 Sun., except major holidays. Chocolate lovers will adore 8,000 square feet of chocolates and other candy with views of the production area. More than 500 plant employees produce 125,000 pounds of candy daily, with a 1-acre freezer for recently outdated candy sold at a significant discount. Many holiday items are at least 50 percent off, plus there are cheap seconds and plenty of samples.

Rittel's Western Wear (785-263-1800), 1810 N. Buckeye, Abilene. Open 9–7 Mon.–Sat., 1–5 Sun. This Western store offers saddles from $1,400, nylon rope, Bailey straw hats, and more than two hundred pairs of boots by Fatbaby, Dingo, Justin, and Laredo, to name a few. Purchase men's and women's shirts and jeans and men's Western-style suits and jackets.

Treasures by Tracine (785-263-7700) 300 N. Broadway, Abilene. Open 10–5 Mon.–Sat. Black-and-white graphics decorate this shop full of Archipelago Botanicals, stuffed animals, flameless pillar candles, tote bags, and the owner's signature jewelry—some of which received recognition during Salina's Smoky River Festival. The gorgeous tin ceiling was completely restored in 2009 after it fell into and demolished the store.

In Junction City
Gatherings on the Prairie LLC (785-238-7300; gatheringsonthe prairie.com), 615 N. Washington, Junction City. Open 10–6 Mon.–Fri., 10–4 Sat. This store offers affordable home and garden items and changes the mix frequently. Purchase gourmet food items, frames, table lamps with an antique look, and dozens of aprons. During the last weekend in September a Christmas wonderland transforms the shop from floor to ceiling.

Barnes Mercantile (785-763-4400, barnesmercantile.com), 108 N. Center St., Barnes. Open 10–5 Mon.–Sat., Sun. by appointment. This little shop features goods from 110 vendors: Kansas landscape photographs, Kansas-made jams and salsa, and much more. Find pine-needle baskets, stained-glass windows, and small cabinets made by a retired woodworking teacher, all at astonishingly low prices. No credit cards.

The Clay Gourmet (785-632-5534), 432 Lincoln Ave., Clay Center. Open 9:30–5:30 Mon.–Fri., 9:30–5 Sat. There's a huge display of Fiestaware here with five times that inventory available. Purchase bulk coffee, tea, and spices. Enamelware coffeepots and Bundt pans and a large selection of Wilton cake decorating accessories are other finds.

✳ Special Events
March: **Cuba Rock-A-Thon** (785-729-3632), Main St., Cuba Community Hall/Cuba. Celebrate this tiny town's Czech heritage with 315 hours of entertainment, food, and craft vendors and rocking around the clock.

July: **Fort Harker Days** (785-472-4526), Kanapolis. Sand volleyball and a hamburger feed kick off this annual event, which includes a parade, car show, turtle races, food, and other activities.

August: **Pony Express Festival** (785-337-2635), Hanover. Located on the Oregon Trail and pony express route, this event offers demonstrations of soap and candle making, horseshoeing, pony express reenactment, and a catered noon meal. **El-Kan Western Riders Rodeo**

(785-472-3350), Ellsworth. It's the perfect mix of bronco and bull riding, clowns, and cowboys, with entertainment and dancing.

September: **Fort Riley Apple Days Fall Festival** (785-239-6398). Enjoy historical reenactments, equipment displays, food/drink vendors, and fresh apple pie. **US 36 Treasure Hunt** (785-877-3968; ushwy36.com/treasure.htm). This 400-mile event begins in Washington and offers yard sales, collectibles, and food all the way to the KS 15/US 36 border.

October: **Annual Chisholm Trail Day Festival** (785-263-2681), Abilene. Enjoy historical presentations and folk craft demonstrations, an antique farm show, and live entertainment designed to celebrate Dickinson County's role in massive cattle drives (particularly in the Abilene area).

December: **Christmas Tour of Area Historic Homes** (785-263-2681), throughout Abilene. Tour many of the county's stately late 1800s to early 1900s homes decorated in their holiday finery.

THE PONY EXPRESS FESTIVAL TAKES PLACE IN HANOVER EACH AUGUST.

SALINA, CONCORDIA, AND WESTWARD

With a population nearing fifty thousand, Salina is the largest city in north-central Kansas. *BusinessWeek* magazine has called Salina the best place in the entire state to raise children. It's also a great place to capture Kansas's strong wind currents. Smoky Hills Wind Farm operates approximately 10–20 miles west of Salina, and each enormous windmill has three long, silver-gray pointy arms that resemble elongated propeller blades. Surrounded by wide-open spaces, Salina is ripe for severe thunderstorms, too, with strong winds and damaging hail or tornadoes. In fact, an F-3 tornado hit the town in September 1973, and another one brushed Salina's south side in June 2008. Weather can change quickly, so visitors should be prepared. But in good weather, check out the city's 25 parks. Other activities include wine tasting, visits to Rolling Hills Wildlife Adventure, and performances at the renovated Stiefel Theatre for the Performing Arts. Shop Salina's antiques stores or other shops, and choose a restaurant for any taste.

From the 1850s to 1860s Salina's trading post drew immigrants, prospectors, and American Indians, but many men from this area joined the U.S. Army at the time of the Civil War, leaving the town vulnerable to Indian and other attacks. The Union Pacific Railroad arrived, followed by the city's incorporation, in 1870. Soon afterward cattle became big business here, and wheat production grew enormously, too. Alfalfa became part of Salina's agricultural landscape, followed by milling operations. The arrival of three railroads cemented the city's important role in state agriculture. Salina remains a major commercial player in north-central Kansas, particularly with its proximity to I-70 and I-135 and its overall location 81 miles north of Wichita and 164 miles west of Kansas City.

With less than six thousand residents, Concordia lies along the Republican River in the Smoky Hills region and along US 81. Founded in 1871, Concordia hosted many traveling entertainers, including Wild Bill Hickok and Ringling Bros. Carry Nation brought her temperance crusade here, too. The city sustained major damage in 1902 when the river flooded the dam, and to a lesser degree in 1915. An enormous blizzard struck in 1912, and a massive fire destroyed the rail depot in 1913. Perhaps Concordia's most historically important site is the National Orphan Train Complex, which commemorates efforts by two charity institutions to relocate two hundred and fifty thousand children between 1854 and 1929 who were homeless or whose parents could no longer afford to care for them.

GUIDANCE **Beloit Travel and Tourism Committee** (785-738-2717), 123 N. Mill St. Open 8–5 weekdays.

Cloud County Convention and Tourism (785-243-4304), 130 E. Sixth St., Concordia. Open 9–noon and 1–5 weekdays, 10–1 Sat.

Ellsworth-Kanopolis Chamber of Commerce (785-472-4071; ellsworthkschamber.net), 114.5 N. Douglas, Ellsworth. Open 10–12, 1–4 weekdays.

Lincoln Area Chamber of Commerce (785-524-4934), 144 E. Lincoln Ave., Lincoln. Open 9–3 Mon.–Thurs.

Lucas Area Chamber of Commerce (785-525-6288), 201 S. Main, Lucas (also Wilson).

Minneapolis Area Chamber of Commerce (785-392-3068), 200 W. Second St., Minneapolis.

Lindsborg Convention and Visitors Bureau (785-227-8687), 104 E. Lincoln, Lindsborg. Open 8–5 Mon.–Fri.

City of Marquette (785-546-2205), 113 N. Washington, Marquette. Open 9–12 and 1–4 Mon.–Tues./Thurs.–Fri.

Visit Salina (785-827-9301), 120 W. Ash, Salina. Open 8–5 weekdays.

GETTING THERE AND GETTING AROUND *By car:* You'll want your car for most travel to and through north-central Kansas, where major highways include US 81, I-135, I-70, US 281, US 26, US 34, KS 18, and KS 4. *By air:* Seaport Airlines offers daily flights at **Salina Municipal Airport** (785-827-3914), 3237 Arnold Ave. Flights also travel to and from **Kansas City International Airport** (in Kansas City, Missouri). *By train:* There is no **AMTRAK** service available in north-central Kansas. *By bus:* **Greyhound** serves Salina (785-827-9754), 671 Westport Blvd., AMOCO Travel Plaza.

MEDICAL EMERGENCY (arranged alphabetically by city name)

Mitchell County Hospital (785-738-2266), 400 W. Eighth St., Beloit.

Cloud County Health Center (785-243-1234), 1100 Highland Dr., Concordia.

Ellsworth County Medical (785-472-3111), 1604 N. Aylward Ave., Ellsworth.

Lincoln County Hospital (785-524-4403), 624 N. Second St., Lincoln.

Lindsborg Community Hospital (785-227-3308), 605 W. Lincoln St., Lindsborg.

Ottawa County Health Center (785-392-2122), 215 E. Eighth St., Minneapolis.

Russell Regional Hospital (785-483-3131), 200 S. Main, Russell.

Salina Regional Health Center (785-452-7000), 400 S. Santa Fe Ave., Salina.

Smith County Memorial Hospital (785-282-6845), 614 S. Main St., Smith Center.

✳ To See

HISTORIC PLACES, LANDMARKS, AND SITES

In Concordia

&. **The Whole Wall Mural** (785-253-7210; Cloud County Convention and Visitors Bureau), Sixth St. and US 81, Concordia. Always open. The longest sculpted brick mural in the nation is a gorgeous picture of this area's history. Commissioned by the Cloud County Historical Society, it depicts the Sisters of St. Joseph Nazareth Convent, whose Motherhouse is listed on the National Register of Historic Places, as well as the Brown Grand Theatre, the 1934 iron truss Republican River Bridge, pheasants, a field of sunflowers, and a massive locomotive that seems to steam outward from the wall. You could spend hours picking out all the beautiful details.

&. **National Orphan Train Complex** (785-243-4471; orphantraindepot.com), 300 Washington St., Concordia. Open 9:30–noon and 1–4:30 Tues.–Fri., 10–4 Sat. Listed on the National Registry of Historic Places, this beautifully restored building documents mass migrations of youngsters whose families could no longer support them during the Depression. See black-and-white photos and window scrims of children transported through this site and a map showing the number of children from each state placed by the Children's Aid Society between 1854 and 1910. Adults $5; children under 12 $3.

&. **Brown Grand Theatre** (785-243-2553, browngrand.org), 310 W. Sixth St., Concordia. Call for an appointment. This 1907 building was restored as a stunning performing arts center in rich shades of deep green and gold leaf in 1980. Four original curtains remain; the Napoleon curtain is a reproduction by the company that crafted the original curtain, and 30 original playbills decorate upper lobby walls. More than 50 events per year draw thousands. Tours by donation; call for show schedule and ticket prices.

In Lindsborg

Old Mill Complex Heritage Center (785-227-3595, oldmillmuseum.org), 120 Mill St., Lindsborg. Open Mon.–Sat. 9–5, 1–5 Sun., except holidays. A dry goods store stocks antique hats and tiny post office boxes. See farm tools that include a saddle and harness stitcher, a potato planter, antique tractors, and a fire truck. The Swedish Pavilion building debuted at the 1904 St. Louis World's Fair and was later donated to Lindsborg in honor of Bethany College president Carl Swensson. Moved to the museum complex in 1969 and partially restored, it became a site for annual heritage events. Adults $2; children 6–12 $1.

The Red Barn Studio (785-227-2217; redbarnstudio.org), 212 S. Main, Lindsborg. Open 1–4 Tues.–Sun. or by appointment. Lester Raymer was a prolific artist in most mediums who considered painting his primary art until his death in

1991. His bright and airy home and studio were remodeled almost completely with recycled materials, as were many art projects. The year 2010 marked the 50th anniversary of the first decorative toy he made for his beloved wife, Ramona. Free.

& **The Birger Sandzén Memorial Gallery** (785-227-2220; sandzen.org), 401 N. First, Lindsborg. Open 1–5 Tues.–Sun. This gallery was created in memory of Sven Birger Sandzén, who died in 1954 after teaching at Bethany College and a career in painting. His oil on canvas landscapes hang in several rooms, with rotating exhibits by guest artists. Ask about seeing his adjacent studio, too. Free

& **Wild Dalas of Lindsborg** (888-227-2227; call about a map), Lindsborg. Always available. The Dala horse is perhaps Sweden's best-known icon. Lindsborg residents have created a herd of these tail-free fiberglass horses, painted in bright colors with inventive designs; dozens are placed throughout town. Look for Yankee Doodle Dala, Dalamation, Salvador Dala, and more. Free.

Elsewhere

World's Largest Ball of Twine (913-781-4713), Wisconsin St., Cawker City. Always visible, this ball of sisal twine has been famous since it weighed in at 14,687 pounds in 1988. One of the nation's top ten roadside attractions sits beneath a metal roof structure and is surrounded by several commemorative benches. People continue to enlarge the legendary twine ball, which remains the biggest in existence. Free.

St. Fidelis Church (785-735-2777; stfidelischurch.com), 601 10th St., Victoria. Open continuously. Known as the cathedral of the plains, St. Fidelis has become a much-sought-after historical landmark in this small, rural town. The fourth church built on this spot began in 1908 and was completed three years later,

WILD DALA HORSES WITH INDIVIDUAL NAMES AND DESIGNS APPEAR THROUGHOUT LINDSBORG.

using native limestone. Thick walls and two 141-foot towers shielded a magnificent interior that is 220 feet long and up to 110 feet wide. Archways and an ornate altar give it the look of an antique European sanctuary. It was added to the National Register of Historic Places in May 1971 and underwent massive restoration during the 1990s. Reflecting the Catholic faith of German settlers who reached the area in 1875, the structure underwent major repairs and restoration in 1994, with interior painting contributed by the third generation of the Linenberger family to have painted inside the church. Ornate detail at the altar, ceiling carvings, and stained glass create a calm, gorgeous space. Free.

Denmark Evangelical Lutheran Church (785-524-4934; lincolnkansas chamber.com; call for specific contact information), Denmark/Lincoln area. On the first day of pheasant season this little church hosts a hunter's luncheon and bazaar at the church hall, a lovely structure with a narrow, wood plank ceiling. A small congregation still holds Sunday services in this 1880 limestone church, listed on the National Register of Historic Places. The surrounding countryside is truly beautiful, but you will travel on gravel roads. Free.

Ellsworth Historical Walking Tour (785-472-4701; Kanopolis chamber of commerce for maps), 1141.5 N. Douglas, Ellsworth. This self-guided walking tour takes visitors to 17 historic sites within about four blocks of the historic downtown district. See the locations of Mueller's Boot Shop in the 1870s, the 1873 county jail, and the town's first building, Seitz Drug Store, founded in 1868, as well as the Kansas Pacific Railroad Depot.

1867 Historic Fort Harker Guardhouse Museum Complex (785-472-3059), 308 W. Ohio, Kanapolis. The Ellsworth County Historical Society maintains four original buildings, including this fort that was built to protect rail, wagon train, and other travelers on the Smoky Hill and Santa Fe Trails. See an original guardhouse, junior officer's quarters, and a depot with salt mine and various history exhibits. $3 includes the Hodgden House Museum Complex.

1873 Victorian Hodgden House Museum Complex (785-472-3059), 104 SW Main St., Ellsworth. Call for tour. This large complex features an 1880s livery stable and church, a 1912 one-room school, and a small log cabin, plus a general store, 1900s train depot and caboose, and a turn-of-the-century wooden windmill. The signature building is an 1878 home. $3 includes historic Fort Harker.

The Marshall-Yohe House (785-524-4934), 316 S. Third St., Lincoln. Call for appointment. This Queen Anne Victorian house is another of Lincoln's gorgeous 1885 homes, with a broad front porch and well-maintained wood ornamentation. See original furnishings, plus 1900 period furniture from the two prominent local families who owned it. Tours $5.

Heym-Oliver House (785-483-3637), 503 Kansas St., Russell. Open Memorial Day weekend–Labor Day weekend, 11–4 Sat., 1–4 Sun., or by appointment. Located on a corner lot, this two-story home, no bigger than several car lengths, housed a family of seven children. See period furnishings in this historic house. Call for ticket prices.

Russell Stover Birthplace. Eleven miles south of Russell on CR 657 is an Osborne County Historical Marker that reads BIRTH SITE OF RUSSELL STOVER

MAY 6, 1888 FOUNDER OF RUSSELL STOVER CANDIES. See where a sweet story began.

Berens Antique Farm Machinery (785-735-9364), 704 Grant, Victoria. Tours by appointment only. Dozens of John Deere tractors from the 1930s to 1950s, doctor buggies from the early 1900s, and the Midwest's largest collection of horse-drawn wagons for hauling grain are among the vehicles that Vernon Berens began to restore in 1985 after a teaching career—work he continues to do while farming. Free.

Union Pacific Gravesite, Old US 40 historical marker, Victoria. A plaque on this small stone monument erected by the Union Pacific Railroad Company commemorates six Union Pacific track laborers who were massacred by Cheyenne Indians in 1867.

Rock City (785-392-3068), N. Rock St., Minneapolis. Open dawn–dusk. This 5-acre park displays an unusual collection of Dakota sandstone concretions. Some of them are as much as 27 feet in diameter; others are nearly the size of the guest information center and gift shop. Admission $3.

MUSEUMS

In Lincoln

Post Rock Scout Museum (785-524-5388, postrockscoutmuseum.com), 161 E. Lincoln Ave., Lincoln. Open 1–5 most afternoons. Housed in an 1881 building, this collection features Girl Scout uniforms from many decades, international flags, 1960s-era canteens, and even a royal-blue sari from a Girl Scout conference. The museum also displays memorabilia from Girl Guides, Pioneer Girls, Camp Fire Girls, and Girl Reserves. Part of nonprofit organization the Crispin Antiquarian Foundation. Free.

Crispin's Drugstore Museum (785-524-5383, crispinsdrugstoremuseum.com),

THESE IMMENSE BOULDERS LIE ON A 5-ACRE SITE AT ROCK CITY, OUTSIDE OF MINNEAPOLIS.

THIS FABULOUS PRIVATE COLLECTION OF SCOUT UNIFORMS AND MEMORABILIA IS IN LINCOLN AT THE POST ROCK SCOUT MUSEUM.

161 E. Lincoln Ave., Lincoln. Open 1–5 most weekdays. Part of the Crispin Antiquarian Foundation, this museum was established to preserve and share historical artifacts from the pharmaceutical field, especially from 1880 to 1920. Every bottle, display case, and wall decor item comes from this period, including dental floss and home remedies. Free.

Kyne House Museum and Topsy School (785-524-4614), 214 W. Lincoln Ave., Lincoln. Open 2–4, Tues./Thurs., 1–4 Sun. See a room dedicated to artist, cartoonist, and graphic designer Frank Cooper, cavalry artifacts from fights with Indians along Spillman Creek, and uniforms from the Spanish-American War. There's a period doctor's office and a display about Anna Wait, the first woman to vote in Lincoln County. Visit the attached 1885 limestone Kyne House with mannequins in period dress and 1800s furniture. Free.

In Salina

Central Kansas Flywheels Yesteryear Museum (785-825-8473; yesteryear museum.com), 1100 W. Diamond Dr., Salina. Visit a one-room schoolhouse, tiny church, sawmill, barbershop, and general store that replicate life in the 1800s to 1900s. Then check out the museum, showcasing farm equipment that includes John Deere tractors and enormous hauling trucks. Check for special events. Admission $4.

&. **Smoky Hill Museum** (785-309-5776), 211 W. Iron, Salina. Open noon–5 Tues.–Fri., 10–5 Sat., 1–5 Sun. This city-owned museum is beautifully designed and informative, from the Prairie Education Lab where visitors learn to build a log cabin and tepee to displays about wheat and its components or an old-fashioned, hands-on mercantile. Ask about special events. Free.

Elsewhere

Highbanks Hall of Fame National Midget Auto Racing Museum (785-527-2526; highbanks-museum.org), US 81 and 12th St., Belleville. Open Oct.–May 31, 11–4 Wed.–Sun.; June 1–Sept. 30, 10–5 Tues.–Sun. The Belleville High Banks racetrack has hosted racing from horses to motorcycles since 1910 and become known as the world's fastest half-mile dirt track. There's a lot to see at this nearby museum, from a 1940 Ford midget car to Indy vehicles, driver uniforms, and information on High Banks Hall of Fame members such as A. J. Foyt. Free.

Pawnee Indian Museum State Historic Site (785-361-2255), 8 miles north of US 36 on KS 266, near Republic. Open 9–5 Wed.–Sat., 1–5 Sun., or groups by appointment. Enter this large round building surrounding part of an earth lodge used by the Pawnee Indians during the 1820s. A lodge model exposes a structure with wood beams that was nearly twice the height of its inhabitants. Depressions from other lodges are clearly visible outside, remnants of an entire village that, at one time, contained more than a thousand people. The recorded voice of a Pawnee elder describes Pawnee customs and culture. Adults $3; students $1; children five and under free.

Oil Patch Museum (913-483-6640), Fossil St. and Access Rd., Russell. Open Memorial Day weekend– Labor Day weekend 4–8 or by appointment. If you see outdoor drilling rigs, derricks, and other equipment, you'll know you're in the right place. Learn about how cable and rotary tools operate and how oil is transported to a refinery. See different sizes of rotary heads and horse-drawn cement mixers and saltwater pumps. Free.

THE KANSAS MOTORCYCLE MUSEUM IN MARQUETTE COMMEMORATES A KANSAN WHO RACED FOR MORE THAN FIVE DECADES, AND DISPLAYS MANY OTHER BIKES, TOO.

Kansas Motorcycle Museum (785-546-2449; ksmotorcyclemuseum.org), 120 N. Washington, Marquette. Open 10–5 Mon.–Sat., 11–5 Sun. See more than a hundred vintage motorcycles, minibikes, and bicycles, including the motorcycle named Lucille that Jim Oliver road around the world in 60 days, as well as a 1930 Harley Davidson VL-74 and a 1950 Harley Davidson panhead. Much of the museum commemorates Stan "The Man" Engdahl, a local dirt-track racer renowned throughout the U.S. for more than five decades. Stan and LaVona Engdahl were instrumental in opening the museum. Free.

Ottawa County Museum (785-392-3621), 110 S. Concord, Minneapolis. Open 10–noon, 1–5 Tues.–Sat. Ottawa County in the 1880s was a place where African Americans voted, attended schools with whites, organized a church, obtained marriage licenses, and participated in many town activities. See a large display about one-time resident George Washington Carver, who had many friends in town and ate several Sunday dinners with a white classmate. Learn about the little girl from Delphos, Kansas, who suggested that Abraham Lincoln grow a beard, and see rare Kansas dinosaur bones. Free.

TOWNS Cawker City. Home of silent movie actress Claire Windsor, the town became official when its plat was recorded in 1871. It was named after a hand of poker among the three founders resulted in a win for E. H. Cawker. Located within the north–south flyway of Canadian snow, blue and white front geese, and many duck species, this area is prime for bird hunting.

Ellsworth. The business area of this little city is recognized as a historic downtown district. Plaza walking tours introduce visitors to Ellsworth's history through its buildings (call the chamber of commerce). Fort Ellsworth was established in 1864, before it became Fort Harker and moved to present-day Kanapolis. General Sheridan planned the winter Indian campaign here in the late 1860s and Generals Grant, Sherman, Hancock, Miles, and Custer also visited or worked from here. The town was founded in 1867 when immense buffalo herds roamed nearby, and it served as the main location for Texas cattle trade. The plaza area witnessed hundreds of thousands of cattle driven to the stockyards, and gambling houses and saloons lined the streets, where gunfights happened frequently. A self-guided historical tour includes 17 sites with interpretive signs.

Glasco. Four churches located within several blocks of each other display stained-glass windows in various styles. See 1900s windows in the Catholic church, 1960s windows in the Lutheran church, plus the United Methodist and Christian churches. And check out the local soda fountain inside the drugstore, too, in operation since the early 1900s.

Lincoln. Once known as Lincoln Center and still considered the post rock capital of Kansas, Lincoln lies near the intersection of KS 14 and KS 18 and overlooks the Saline River. There are gorgeous post rock limestone buildings throughout the town of approximately 1,200 residents, including the 1900 county courthouse and side-by-side scouting and drug store museums. Quarrying quartzite continues to be a major source of local jobs. International explorer Martin Johnson is a famous native son, and the town commemorates Abraham Lincoln's birthday with large community celebrations. There's also an annual Lincoln Reenactment Day.

Lindsborg. Broomcorn was once a major crop here; wheat and sunflowers now occupy many acres. Of 13 original colonies established in the Smoky Valley, Lindsborg is the only one that remains and offers full services, from shopping, dining, and lodging to gas stations and medical care. Local high school and college students are tennis fanatics, and full orchestra and band begin during fourth grade in the public school. Bethany College was founded 13 years after the town was founded, with a labyrinth and beautiful gardens.

Lucas. Less than five hundred people live in this farming community located north of Wilson Lake, but the town is legendary for quirky art. Built by Civil War Veteran S. P. Dinsmoor, the Garden of Eden has drawn curious visitors since 1907, mostly because of the massive cement sculptures that decorate the entire property. The Grassroots Art Center mentors and displays the art of self-taught Kansas artists who work in a wide array of mediums, while Flying Pig Studio and Gallery offers whimsical porcelain art by a nationally known artist. The World's Largest Things exhibit and Florence Deeble's Rock Garden are other don't-miss sights.

Minneapolis. Developer of multiple uses for peanuts, George Washington Carver spent early years in Kansas, and the Ottawa County Historical Museum hosts one of the nation's top collections of Carver memorabilia. It also houses rare dinosaur bones discovered in Kansas. Nearby, Rock City is an otherworldly collection of dark gray rock concretions with several trail areas available.

Osborne. Historical buildings in this small town include the 130-year-old Main Street Drug, the 1924 Sunflower Inn—once considered one of the finest hotels between Denver and Kansas City—and the 1906–1908 Osborne County Courthouse, listed on the National Register of Historic Places. A 10-block walking tour or a self-guided driving tour titled Sod House Days offer glimpses of Osborne's historical buildings and homestead sites. Limestone and shale make up the scenic Blue Hills, and the nearby North and South Fork Solomon Rivers flow into Waconda Lake.

Russell. Located in the heart of post rock limestone country, this town began as a melting pot of cultures, with immigrants from Bohemia, Germany, Ireland, Wales, England, Germany, and Volga Russia. Russell was named for Avra P. Russell, who raised a company for the 2nd Kansas Infantry and eventually became a captain under Lincoln. When the railroad was under construction the town was known as Fossil Station. From 1930 to 1940 the population more than doubled due to oil discoveries. This is also the boyhood home of Senators Bob Dole and Arlen Specter.

Wilson. This small town located just south of I-70 lies between Salina, Hays, and Great Bend and only 7 miles from Wilson Lake, called the clearest lake in Kansas. It is also home of the Kansas Originals Market and the recently renovated Midland Hotel, featured in the movie *Paper Moon*. In 1865 a Butterfield stagecoach station operated near the current town. Early names for Wilson were Attica and Bosland before the U.S. Post Office renamed it in 1873. During the 1870s Czechoslovakian immigrants came to work on the railroad, bringing their unique culture with them. In 1974 Wilson was named the Czech Capital of Kansas.

✳ To Do

DAY SPAS Oasis Salon and Spa (785-243-4500), 136 W. Sixth St., Concordia. Open noon–7 Mon., 10–7 Tues.–Fri., 10–5 Sat. This sleek new spot opened in 2010; certified massage therapists offer hot-stone massage and back treatment as well as traditional massage. They're known for giving great pedicures and offer all traditional hair and nail services, plus tanning, facials, and makeup application. Call for rates.

GOLF Russell Memorial Park/Municipal Golf Course (785-483-2852), 1054 E. Second St., Russell. This is clearly the place where Russell residents go to play, with a veterans memorial, skate area, huge playground apparatus, disc golf course, picnic shelters, ball fields, and public pool. Par 36, 9 holes, 3,141 yards.

Salina Municipal Golf Course (826-7450; salinamuni.com), 2500 E. Crawford, Salina. Find rolling blue grass fairways with bent grass greens and four tee boxes, a dedicated driving range, and a clubhouse. Par 70, 6,500 yards, 18 holes.

Riverbend Golf Course (785-452-9333), 4701 Ohio, Salina. This is a popular course located in the country. Par 27, 1,190 yards, 9 holes.

Lindsborg Golf Course (785-227-2244), 1541 Svensk Rd., Lindsborg. Enjoy cheap greens fees and friendly staff. Par 69, 5,414 men's yards for 18 holes, 9 holes.

✳ Green Space

Wilson Lake (785-658-2551; Army Corps of Engineers; wilson-lake.org). Before you reach the access road you'll see bright blue water in a shallow valley with some beautiful rock outcroppings. There's a full-service marina in Wilson State Park/Sylvan Grove, a switchgrass mountain bike trail with enormous hills, and great opportunities for camping, hiking, hunting, and fishing—including channel catfish, white perch, and bass. Overlooking the lake, the Knotheads shop sells bait and fishing/camping supplies and rents pontoon and paddle boats. Camping $12–18 (877-444-6777).

Waconda Lake (785-545-3345), 2131 180 Rd., Glen Elder. This area is a winter favorite for large water birds and bald eagles. With 100 miles of shoreline and a surface area of 12,586 acres, this reservoir is the state's third largest. Overlook the lake while camping at the nearby Glen Elder State Park.

Jewell State Fishing Lake (620-672-5911), outside of Jewell. This long lake with one arm offers 57 surface acres and many fish species, including walleye, largemouth bass, channel catfish, black crappie, and saugeye.

Kanopolis State Park (785-546-2565) 200 Horsethief Rd., Marquette. See American Indian petroglyphs on Faris Cave walls in Kansas's first state park, established in 1955. Fish for crappie or channel catfish and rent one of more than 300 campsites. Hike or ride horseback amid the rolling, wooded Smoky Hills region. Boating and swimming are also available.

Greeley County Wildlife Area (620-227-8609), 11 miles north of I-70. Open Sept. 1–Jan. 31. Hunters will find abundant white-tailed and mule deer and ring-necked pheasant in season at this 900-acre grassland wildlife area. Other game species include rabbits and mourning doves.

Coronado Heights Park (888-227-2227), 3 miles northwest of Lindsborg, off KS 4. Open 8–11. Spanish explorer Francisco Vázquez de Coronado reached this area in 1541 while seeking the legendary Seven Golden Cities of Cíbola and lived with Kaw Indians for two years. A 1988 marker commemorates his visit. A rough asphalt road leads to where a Works Progress Administration (WPA) castle still stands, with a breathtaking view. Free.

Välkommen Trail, Lindsborg. Children under 18 not allowed from midnight–5 AM. Once the site of Missouri–Pacific and Union Pacific rail beds, this lovely 2.5-mile bicycle and pedestrian trail opened in summer 2006. Enjoy the natural beauty and admire a refurbished railroad bridge. Free.

Viking Valley Playground (785-227-3355), 400 block of North Main in Swensson Park, Lindsborg. This community-built playground was created after polling pint-size residents, and volunteer workers used largely donated tools and materials. Kids enjoy a tree house, a rocket ship, a castle with a turret, and a climbing wall. Local artists contributed free decorative murals. Free.

✳ Lodging

BED & BREAKFASTS & (ᵍⁱ) **Howell House Bed and Breakfast** (785-454-3888, howellhousebandb.com), 701 Blunt St., Downs. Stephen and Joan Heide offer four guest rooms in this completely renovated 1883 Italianate-style home listed on the state historical register. May is crazy for them, particularly Memorial Day weekend. Each room has a separate bath. There are no phones or TVs in rooms, but one has a whirlpool. Weekend full breakfast; continental breakfast on weekdays. $80.

& (ᵍⁱ) **Seasons of the Fox** (785-227-2549, seasonsofthefox.com), 505 N. Second St., Lindsborg. An elevator, hot tub, and gorgeous terraced garden are extra features at this luxurious, restored 1905 house. Breakfast is a multicourse event presented with great fanfare. Choose from four seasonally decorated rooms with private baths and enjoy afternoon refreshments plus evening sweets. You'll want to return soon. $90–125.

(ᵍⁱ) **Riverbend Bed & Breakfast** (785-346-5217; riverbend-retreat .com), 745 CR 388 Dr., Osborne. Enjoy luxury accommodations in what was once co-owner Joe Hubbard's private home. Located along the south fork of the Solomon River, it's a great spot for anyone who wants a quiet retreat, with plush carpet and Wi-Fi, plus river views from each bedroom. A large public area is perfect for meetings, and visitors enjoy the fire ring and river walk. Co-owner Laura McClure is a walking encyclopedia about the area. Full breakfast. $80.

(ᵍⁱ) **Endiron Estate Bed & Breakfast** (785-452-9300), 100 S. College Ave., Salina. Soothing colors, sumptuous linens, and gorgeous woodwork fill this lovely 1884 home. Beveled leaded glass windows, original fireplaces and light fixtures, and period antiques add to the ambience. Full breakfast. $65–165.

Trader's Lodge Bed & Breakfast (785-488-3930; traderslodge.com), 1392 210th Rd., Wells (north of Salina). This lovely country lodge offers themed rooms such as the Southwest room with hanging chiles and a bed made from logs, plus a common TV area with animal skins and antique posters. Enjoy the arbor and garden, sauna, and exercise equipment. Neal Kindall creates bowie knife and American Indian artifact replicas and offers informational programs about American Indians and mountain men, while Kay Kindall is an expert baker known for her terrific cinnamon rolls. $70–90.

((ψ)) **Simple Haven B&B** (785-658-3814; simplehavenbandb.com), 615 27th St., Wilson. Sue and Joe Curtiss enjoy hosting guests in this antique-filled 1885 house. Choose from five bedrooms with private baths and small TVs, such as the Bird room or Grandma's room. Socialize in the sunny common lounge and enjoy a hot breakfast in the casual dining room. $85–110.

CABINS AND CAMPING Triple J RV Park (785-483-4826), 187 E. Edward Ave., Russell. Picnic tables and shelters, BBQ grills, and a playhouse on stilts are only a few features of this nicely maintained park. Enjoy miniature golf, a 24-hour Laundromat, cable, Wi-Fi, and plenty of trees. There's even a storm shelter. $28 full hookup.

Harlow Lodging (785-525-7725), 239 Kansas, Lucas. Billy and Janiss Harlow maintain this house, located south of their own home, which includes two full-size beds, three twins, a TV, a full kitchen with microwave popcorn, and a coffeepot. Enjoy the front porch, located half a block from the Garden of Eden. Nothing fancy, but it's clean, neat, and offers plenty of room. No credit cards. One person $25.

HOTELS ⅃ **Historic Midland Hotel and Restaurant** (785-685-2284), 414 26th St., Wilson. This beautifully restored 1899 building was largely funded through the Wilson Foundation—a group of local people who wanted to help preserve it. Every room has its own bath and craftsman-style furnishings. In the lobby see photos from *Paper Moon,* which was partially filmed here. There's a full-service restaurant on the main floor, and Drummers Tavern operates in the basement. $65–130.

((ψ)) **The Swedish Country Inn** (785-227-2985; swedishcountryinn.com), 112 W. Lincoln, Lindsborg. Enjoy a traditional breakfast with Swedish meatballs, pickled herring, apple rings, and waffles with lingonberries after sleeping in your comfortable room with quilts and a small TV. There's always free coffee in the lobby, too. $69–95.

MOTELS AND LODGES Sportsman's Lodge (785-658-3814; sportsmenslodge.net), 2523 Ave. E and Main St., Wilson. The front door to Sincerely Yours—a gift, floral, and bakery shop—doubles as a day entrance for this wonderful little lodging spot. Decorated with animal heads, trophy fish, and outdoor themes, it offers four double beds,

THIS 1800S RENOVATED ENDIRON ESTATE BED & BREAKFAST IS SALINA'S ONLY B&B.

two folding couches, a fully equipped kitchen, and a large TV room. There's also a basement dog kennel and a private entrance with security door. $35 for one; minimum $70.

Mill Street Inn (785-392-7232), 419 W. Second St., Minneapolis. This two-year-old inn is a revelation, with spacious suites that have kitchenettes or full eat-in kitchens, private ceramic tile baths, and an enormous common area featuring a pool table, large flat-screen TV, and four-tap bar. Choose from the Serenity suite, Swanky suite, Sportsman's suite, or Stardust suite. $75–100; spare bedroom $50.

Kansas Creek Inn (785-243-9988), 1330 Union Rd., Concordia. Stay in a limestone home with a large addition in the midst of a working farm with a spacious dining room and shared bath. There's a swing set available, plus a large deck and loads of sunflowers in season. Full breakfast. $65.

Spillman Creek Lodge (785-277-3424; spillmancreek.com), Denmark/Lincoln. Richard and Brenda Peterson have created a spot that caters to pheasant and waterfowl hunters and anyone who appreciates a quiet country setting, and they treat guests like family. Two small lodges on their family's working grain farm each offer private bedrooms and two private baths with fully equipped kitchens. $60 lodging or $280–400 for bird hunting packages with lodging and meals.

Rancho Milagro (785-472-4850, ranchomilagrokansas.com/aboutus .html), 2366 Ave. K, Brookville, near Mushroom Rocks State Park. Jesse James may have kept a hideaway in a 75-foot canyon on this ranch where wagon trains once stopped. Previously used in large part for hunters, the venue now offers historical and horseback tours and weekend chuck wagon dinners. Enjoy a fully equipped kitchen, laundry facilities, sitting areas, and continental breakfast. Each guest room has an outdoor entrance to a balcony. $70.

& ((y)) **Post Rock Motel** (785-524-4424), 1907 E KS 18, Lincoln. Recently renovated, clean, and comfortable, this small motel has a lot going for it, including refrigerators and microwaves in each room, a friendly owner, and a great location. $43–58.

& **Camelot Inn** (785-346-5413), 933 N. First St. #281 at the intersection of KS 281 and 24, Osborne. It's a clean, neat motel, with some upgrades made during the past 10 years. Upstairs rooms have refrigerators and microwaves. $57–59.

& ((y)) **Viking Motel** (785-227-3336), 446 Harrison, Lindsborg. Affordable and pleasant, this motel offers two beds, a microwave, a refrigerator, and even an outdoor pool. Continental breakfast. $60.

& ((y)) **Coronado Motel and RV Park** (785-227-3943), 305 N. Harrison, Lindsborg. Old and new wings of this motel lie across the street from each other. Each clean, neat, and comfortable room features a refrigerator, coffeemaker, iron, and ironing board. Or rent one of 18 RV slots beneath the trees with full hookups and pull-throughs. $63.

& ((y)) **West Lake Inn** (785-454-3345), E KS 24, Downs. Fourteen rooms have the feel of a moderately priced chain motel with a TV, refrigerator, and microwave in each one. This is a pleasant highway option at bargain prices. There's also a game-cleaning station available. $38–46.

Lakeside Lodge (785-781-4719; lakesidelodgekansas.com), 817 Oak St., Cawker City. Offering fully equipped motor homes or cabins with cable TV, washer/dryer facilities, towels, and bed linens. There's a fish- and game-cleaning house available and a lighted airstrip nearby. The Lake family offers guide service, boat and RV storage, outside or private inside stalls, goose blinds, RV hookups, and a trap range, too. No credit cards. Call for rates.

✳ Where to Eat

EATING OUT

In Beloit
&. **Plum Creek Meats** (785-738-3893), 118 E. Court St., Beloit. Open 11–9 Mon.–Sat. What began as a deli is now a full-service restaurant with the lunch menu written on a chalkboard. On Thursdays fried chicken is the lunch focus. Call for hours for the new adjacent sports bar, Down Under. Inexpensive.

The Shop (785-738-9902), 209 E. Main, Beloit. Open 6:30–2 Tues.–Sat., 5–8 Fri.–Sun., 9–1:30 every first/second/fourth Sun. Try a Porter Sunrise—a ciabatta-bread sandwich with your choice of cheese and meat plus eggs. There's homemade hot chocolate and pasta with garlic bread dinners for under $8. Try a lunch wrap like their chicken cordon bleu (with chicken, ham, Swiss cheese, lettuce, and tomato) and then enjoy the dessert of the day. Inexpensive.

In Concordia
&. **Heavy's BBQ** (785-262-4132; heavysbbqnck.com), 103 W. Seventh St., Concordia. Open 11–10

Sun.–Thurs., 11–11 Fri.–Sat. The Big Huey sandwich comes with your choice of brisket, turkey, smoked sausage, pulled chicken, or ultratender pulled pork. Try the creamy, sweet coleslaw and smoky beans. It's a pleasant place with plenty of appetizers, chicken dishes, and their famous ribs. Inexpensive.

The Huckleberry Tea House (785-243-7832), 512 State St., Concordia. Open 11–2 Tues.–Sat., 2–3 for tea and dessert. There are teacups and pots for sale at the entryway and lace tablecloths and flowers on every table. Twenty sandwiches come with soup and salad, such as the Andrew (chicken breast with cheddar, bacon, and ranch dressing on grilled sourdough), or try the spinach quiche. Save room for homemade carrot cake or other desserts. No credit cards. Inexpensive.

&. **Jitters** (785-243-4630), 221 W. Sixth St., Concordia. Open 7–9 Tues.–Thurs., 7–12 Fri.–Sat. A coffee shop since 2008, this spot has become a very busy full-service restaurant and bar, offering 30 wines and imported beers. Try their popular hummus dip or Italian sandwich. Inexpensive.

El Puerto (785-243-6165), 217 W. Sixth St., Concordia. Open 11–9 weekdays, 11–10 Sat., 11–3 Sun. Freshly made tortillas are the foundation for favorite dishes that include enchiladas verdes and flautas. The taco salad and combination dinner (one burrito, taco, and enchilada) also receive rave reviews. Inexpensive.

In Lincoln
✐ &. **Happy Days Diner** (785-524-4933), 116 S. Fifth, Lincoln. Open 11–10 Mon.–Sat., 11–8 Sun. This place is a lot of fun, with red, white, and black decor and vintage Coke

signs, bottles, and memorabilia. Order the crispy chicken salad, Philly steak wrap, or triple-stack burger. Twisters are shake-like beverages with candy or other items mixed in. Inexpensive.

& **Hungry Hunter Restaurant** (785-524-5246), 109 W. Lincoln, Lincoln. Open 6–2 Sun.–Wed., 6–8 Thurs.–Sat. You'll see loads of hunting and fishing trophies and country decor in this pleasant little place on Lincoln's main street. Enjoy huge portions; terrific omelets and pancakes are favorites. Inexpensive.

Lincoln Grocery (785-524-4401), 123 S. Fourth St., Lincoln. Hot deli open by 10. This store offers something unusual—meaty, crispy fried chicken served from a deli case in the back room. Add skin-on fried potato wedges or mashed potatoes with gravy, coleslaw, and biscuits, all for less than $7. Inexpensive.

In Lindsborg

Öl Stuga (785-227-8762; olstuga .com), 119 S. Main St., Lindsborg. Open 4–2 AM Mon., 11–2 AM Tues.–Sat. When Mikhail Gorbachev visited Lindsborg he wanted to eat with locals at this longtime eatery. Try the Brent Nelson sandwich with sausage, BBQ sauce, smoky sharp cheese, hot pepper cheese, and onions on a submarine bun, or create your own sandwich with your choice of bread, meats, cheeses, and condiments. Have a beer and play some cribbage. Inexpensive.

& **The Brick House Grill** (785-227-4800; formerly the Swedish Crown), 121 N. Main St., Lindsborg. Open 11 AM daily; closes 8 Wed.–Thurs., 9 Fri.–Sat. ; bar open until midnight; 9–2 Sun. breakfast. Enjoy Swedish favorites such as the *smörgås* open-faced sandwich with a wonderful

mustard-dill sauce, try a side of ultra-creamy coleslaw, or order pizzas with hand-tossed crust and homemade sauce. Play pool in the bar at the rear. Inexpensive.

Scandinavian Pastries and Emporium (785-227-2680), 101 N. Main St., Lindsborg. Open 7–5 Tues.–Sat. Ten-inch cinnamon rolls and flaky kringle are just a few of the delightful pastries you'll find here. Lunch is also available, including Lindsborg chicken salad on marble bread. Inexpensive.

& **Jalisco Mexican Restaurant** (785-227-8987), 107 N. Main St., Lindsborg. Open 11–9 Mon.–Thurs., 11–10 Fri.–Sat., 11–3 Sun. Order fajitas *texanas* or a combination dinner in this cheerful restaurant or try the especial el Jalisco: beef steak with cooked onions, bell peppers, and tomatoes, plus rice, beans, and flour tortillas. Inexpensive.

& **The Butcher, Baker, and Candlestick Maker** (785-227-8904), 130 N. Main St., Lindsborg. Open 7–5 Mon.–Sat. Offering mostly baked goods made from scratch, including Swedish pancakes and waffles, this local coffee shop also has soft-serve ice cream, candles, and body care products. Or purchase freshly butchered meats and jerky.

In Russell

& **Meridy's Restaurant and Lounge** (785-483-4300), 1220 S. Fossil St., US 281, Russell. Open 6–10 Mon.–Sat., 7–9 Sun. This pleasant place is packed at noon and most people choose the buffet, from onion rings and fried chicken to sausage and potatoes, and a big salad bar. The open-faced roast beef sandwich, with an enormous helping of mashed potatoes and dark brown gravy, is a popular menu item. Breakfast offerings range from waffles to omelets. Inexpensive.

Old 40 Highway Gifts and Treasures (785-483-5538), 1205 W US 40, Russell. Open 7:30–5:30 Tues.–Fri., 9–1 Sat. (closed first Sat. of every month), 11–2 for lunch. Purchase home decor and gift items in this quaint and cozy spot that is also well known for its *kolaches* and *bierocks*, pecan caramel rolls, or luscious four-layer chocolate torte cake. Lunch specials include Italian or Mexican dishes and BLTs or sandwiches and salads on the menu. Inexpensive.

In Salina

& **Martinelli's Little Italy** (785-826-9190), 158 S. Santa Fe, Salina. Open 11–10 Mon.–Sat., 11–9 Sun. At night this looks like a romantic spot. At any time, people enjoy this largely Italian menu, including stuffed mushrooms; calamari strips; tilapia piccata; Martinelli's pasta with Alfredo sauce, mushrooms, and grilled chicken; and Martinelli's pound cake, with a glass of wine. Inexpensive–moderate.

& **4 Bears Café and Catering** (785-827-3837; 4bearcafe.com), 1700 E. Iron Ave., Salina. Open 7–3:30 Mon.–Fri. Located inside the board of trade building, this cute place has offered made-from-scratch biscuits and gravy, pulled-pork sandwiches, *bierocks,* and much more, since 1999. Save room for apple pie. Inexpensive.

Russell's Restaurant (785-825-5733), 649 Westport, Salina. Open 24/7. Enjoy breakfast anytime, including Bob's special hash browns with peppers, onions, mushrooms, sour cream, and Swiss cheese. Other favorites include the Our Pride chuck burger or open-faced hot beef sandwich. Inexpensive.

& **Hickory Hut BBQ** (785-825-1588), 1617 Crawford, Salina. Open 11–8:30 Mon.–Sat. This cheerful spot full of old license plates and black-and-white photos has operated for more than 25 years. Try a Slammer sandwich with Polish sausage, beef, pork, Slammer sauce, and your choice of side. Voted a readers' choice winner by the *Salina Journal.* Inexpensive.

& **Imperial Garden Express** (785-309-1688), 2259 S. Ninth #152, inside Central Mall, Salina. Open during mall hours. This food-court restaurant serves great food, including crisp egg rolls packed with flavor and dishes such as Snow White chicken or hot braised pork. Inexpensive.

Elsewhere

Renaissance Café (785-822-6750; renaissancecafeassaria.com), 210 N. Center St., Assaria. Open 5–9 Thurs.–Sat. Dinner is served in a century-old high school gym and includes gourmet dishes with an Italian flare, such as seared duck and cherries, spinach lentil soup, and pork piccata. Save room for dark chocolate bread pudding with bourbon and cream sauce. Inexpensive–moderate.

& **Circle Inn Restaurant** (785-346-9444), 1106 W US 24, Osborne. Open 6:30–8 Tues.–Sat., 6:30–2 Sun. A fire and a tornado were not enough to kill this business, where the co-owner is famous for his green chile sauce. Try it on a giant smothered chicken burrito or order other breakfast and dinner items. No credit cards. Inexpensive.

Paden's Place Restaurant (785-472-3643), 120 N. Douglas Ave., Ellsworth. Open 11–8:30 Mon.–Thurs., 11–9 Fri.–Sat.; bar open 11–midnight Tues.–Thurs., 11–2 AM Sat. Operating for 20 years, this little bar with Western art is known for Mexican dishes and chicken-fried steaks. Inexpensive.

Ⓨ **Trappers Bar and Grill** (785-593-6678), Simpson. Open 8–10 Tues.–Sat. This restaurant off US 24 draws steak lovers from all over, and some say their prime rib is the best in the state. There's beer, burgers, and sandwiches, or try fried alligator or their bull fries. Inexpensive.

♿ **Heartland Restaurant and Bohemian Culture Club** (785-984-2388), 202 Mill St., Alton, outside Osborne. Open 11–2 Tues.–Fri., 8–2 Sat. This popular restaurant operates in the Bohemian Culture Club building, established by early settlers to this area. Co-owner Nedra Auer has been told her pies are to die for, and coconut cream is a favorite. The restaurant is known for hand-breaded chicken-fried steaks, hefty chicken club sandwiches, and sandwich wraps. Inexpensive.

Banner Restaurant (785-738-5751), 720 N. Bell, Beloit. Open 6–8 daily. There are daily specials, homemade pies and rolls, and a burger bar at this popular restaurant. They're very busy on Sundays when they serve fried-chicken dinners. No credit cards. Inexpensive.

GREEN CHILE SAUCE, USED IN MANY DISHES AT CIRCLE INN RESTAURANT, IS AN OSBORNE FAVORITE.

♿ **Made from Scratch** (785-658-3300), 527 27th St., Wilson. Open 7–9 Mon.–Sun. Owner Jayne Reilly wins awards for her pies, such as coconut cream and rhubarb, often served with homemade vanilla ice cream. Chickens decorate the large room, where customers also love the biscuits and gravy and *bierocks*. Inexpensive.

Corner Bar and Grill (785-781-4940), 804 Oak St., Cawker City. Open 11:30–1:30 and from 5 PM Mon.–Sat. Known far and wide for KC strip or rib eye steak dinners and their beef enchilada plate, this casual little place also serves a Western BBQ burger and mini corn dogs. Enjoy beer on tap or bottled and well or mixed drinks.

♿ **K-18 Café** (785-525-6262), 125 N. Greeley Ave., Lucas. Open 6–10 daily. Try the 8-ounce KC strip steak for breakfast with two eggs, hash browns, toast, and coffee for just over $10. There are also breaded pork sandwiches, Black Angus burgers, and chicken gizzards. Save room for homemade pie. Inexpensive.

♿ **Mity Kwik** (785-392-3415), 218 W. Third St., Minneapolis. Open 5–10 daily. This convenience store offers freshly prepared sandwiches and daily specials. On Friday try the enchilada with ground beef, cheese sauce, and shredded cheese, plus lettuce, tomato, and sour cream, with jalapeños on request. It's a cheap, filling lunch. Inexpensive.

SNACKS ♿ **Espresso, Etc.** (785-445-4055), 718 N. Main, Russell. Open 7–7 Mon.–Fri., 9–5 Sat. Come for a caramel macchiato or a steamer. Stay for a freshly made panini, salad, soup, or a smoothie made with green tea. With upholstered chairs, dark woods, and a chalkboard menu, this coffee shop offers Wi-Fi and recently added ice cream, including home-made vanilla. Inexpensive.

Hodge Podge (785-568-2542), 113 E. Main St., Glasco. Open 9–5 Mon.–Fri., 9–noon Sat. Have a choco-late malt beside a 1951 soda fountain counter and a 1927 back bar. Buy a little bit of everything here but leave your credit cards at home.

✳ Entertainment

In Salina

&. **Salina Community Theatre** (785-827-3033; salinatheatre.com), 303 E. Iron, Salina. Box office open 11:30–5:30 weekdays. After 50 seasons of comedy, drama, music, and mystery, this theater will open a brand new facility in 2011. See shows like *Annie, Hello Dolly,* and *The Sunshine Boys.* Adults $24–27; seniors $21–24; stu-dents $16.

The Stiefel Theatre for the Performing Arts (785-827-1998), 151 S. Santa Fe, Salina. Open for individual performances. Built in 1931, this beautiful theater was restored to its former grandeur and has become a favorite performance venue for regional and national artists since 2003. Shows range from per-formances by the Black Crowes to the Salina Symphony and a production of *The Lion, The Witch and the Wardrobe.* Call for prices.

Smoky Hill Vineyards and Winery (866-225-2515; kansaswine.com), 212 W. Golf Link Rd., Salina. Open 10–6 Mon.–Sat. View vineyards from this family-operated winery that has won numerous awards. The state's largest grape-producing winery offers red, white, port, and specialty fruit wines such as red raspberry. Taste them in a large, lovely tasting and event space.

✧ &. **Rolling Hills Wildlife Adventure** (785-827-9488), 625 N. Hedville Rd., Salina. Open 9–5 win-ter; 8–5 summer. Walk through beau-tifully landscaped grounds with spacious enclosures for a hundred animal species and enjoy a cafeteria-style restaurant and picnic area. There's also a wildlife museum with a children's exploration center and trav-eling exhibit displays. Zoo admission: adults $11; children 3–12 $6; seniors $10. Museum admission: adults $10; children 3–12 $5; seniors $9. Combo tickets are $14/$8/$13.

✧ **Kenwood Cove** (785-826-7430; kenwoodcove.com), 701 Kenwood Park Dr., Salina. Open daily in sum-mer, 12:30–8 Mon.–Sat., 12:30–6 Sun. Caribbean foliage and crashing waves decorate 1,400 feet of slides, a chil-dren's play area, an inner-tube glide, and more. There are concessions and free parking. Adults 18–61 $5; chil-dren 3–17 $3; seniors 62 and up $2.

&. **Salina Art Center** (785-827-1431; salinartcenter.com), 242 S. Santa Fe, Salina. Open noon–5 Wed.–Sat., 1–5 Sun. Art for all tastes, a hands-on area, activities such as glass blowing, and contemporary and international film showings are all part of this mul-tipurpose center. Free.

Elsewhere

✧ **Lakeside Recreational Park** (785-667-5795; lakesiderec.org), 1288 E. Lapsley Rd., Assaria. Call for access and admission. In addition to the outdoor pool and 400-foot water slide, this park offers outdoor grills, a basketball court, campfire spots, and even a family paintball game area. Grab a snow cone, rent a paddleboat, or hit the beach.

LUCAS ARTS

♿ **Grassroots Art Center** (785-525-6118; grassrootsart.net). The Kansas Grassroots Art Association mentors artists in 17 Kansas counties who create art, mostly to please themselves. Small displays introduce visitors to ordinary people who are self-taught and do not teach their craft. See 51 years of limestone and composition rock sculptures by Inez Marshall, a life-size car made from soft-drink can tabs, and Glenn Stark's Americana-inspired wood figures.

♿ **World's Largest Collection of the World's Smallest Versions of the World's Largest Things** (785-760-0826; worldslargestthings.com). Erika Nelson runs this nonprofit organization, which reflects things she likes to study—what she describes as "roadside attractions, kitsch, visionary art environments, and the world's largest things." Her hand-painted pickup has carried rocking horses and plenty of other treasures, and an old school bus is filled with miniature displays that replicate unusual roadside attractions from throughout the country.

Florence Deeble's Rock Garden and Garden of Isis (785-525-6118). See miniature versions of an Indian pueblo, Mt. Rushmore, and the Cathedral Group from within the Teton Range, all crafted from cement in Deeble's backyard since 1906. Inside Deeble's house there's unusual creative work by Lawrence visual artist Mri-Pilar, who incorporates doll bodies, kitchen utensils, and other recycled materials.

Flying Pig Studio and Gallery (785-525-7722; ericabraham.net). World-renowned artist Eric Abraham sells inventive porcelain pieces with unusual names like Mr. and Mrs. Pig Went to the Opera and Heard the Fat Lady Sing, and can craft a custom sink with mirror in three to six months.

The Garden of Eden (785-525-6395; garden-of-eden-lucas.kansas.com/index .html). This property represents the vision and work of Civil War veteran S. P. Dinsmore. In the late 1800s he built the limestone home with the town's first indoor plumbing. One hundred and fifty exterior cement sculptures include a concrete U.S. flag, limestone mausoleum, and cement and wire cages for wild animals. At age 81, Dinsmore married his second wife, a 20-year-old. Two surviving children include an 83-year-old son—the youngest surviving son of a Civil War veteran.

ERIC ABRAHAM CREATES AND SELLS HIS PORCELAIN ART AT FLYING PIG STUDIO IN LUCAS.

& **Lincoln Art Center** (785-524-3241, lincolnartcenter.org), 126 E. Lincoln Ave., Lincoln. Open noon–4 Tues.–Fri., 10–1 Sat. Primarily modern and contemporary two- and three-dimensional art adorns this bright and airy, white-walled space. It's a lovely surprise and a nationally recognized arts destination.

& **Ellsworth Area Arts Council Gallery** (913-472-5658), 204 N. Douglas, Ellsworth. Open 12:30–4:30 Mon.–Sat. This lovely gallery primarily features regional artists, with a common theme in each show such as Western art.

& **Karpov Chess School** (785-227-2224; anatolykarpovchessschool.org), 106 S. Main St., Lindsborg. Call for information and camps. World-renowned chess player Anatoly Karpov has founded 15 chess schools throughout the world, including this one, the first in the U.S.

Vonada's Stone Quarry (785-526-7391); vonadastone.com), 532 Quail Ln., Sylvan Grove. Call for appointment. Request a demonstration at this family-owned stone quarry and learn about the area's post rock limestone tradition. Purchase post rock art, including sundials, benches, personalized signs, and more. Tours $7.

& **Deines Cultural Center** (785-483-3742, deinesculturalcenter.org), 820 N. Main, Russell. Open 12:30–5:30 Tues.–Fri., 1–5 Sat.–Sun. All of the art in this bright, modern space comes from within a 60-mile radius. See handmade quilts, a majestic wood carving of buffalo, acrylic paintings, hand-thrown pots, and more. Free.

& **ArtSpace Contemporary Art** (785-546-2455, artspaceusa.com), 115 N. Washington, Marquette. Open 10–5 Tues.–Sat., 1–5 Sun. With artis-

tic displays by the delightful Rich Thibodeau, his daughter and Bethany College–graduate Nicole, artist Mri-Pilar, and more, this 1888 dry goods store turned gallery and studio offers paintings, sculpture, and fine art prints. Displays change quarterly.

Kuhn's Pumpkin Patch (785-735-2219), 1130 350th Ave., Victoria. Open through the month of October. There are several pumpkin varieties here, from minis to hundreds of pounds, plus gourds, straw bales, and milo—and they're all within view of St. Fidelis's twin steeples.

& **Prairie Wind Art Gallery** (785-454-3847), 810 Morgan Ave., Downs. Call for hours. Billing his work as wildlife-Western-rustic, artist Peter Ozias sells paintings in gold wood frames, with titles such as *Autumn Cottonwoods and Winter Wheat* or *Last Light on the Farmstead.* He also offers framing services and customer seating.

Long's Collectible Showplace and Gift Shop (785-822-7185), 768 Broadway, Salina. Open 6–8:30 Tues.–Thurs., 1–6 Sat., or by appointment. This amazing display features more than a thousand Barbie dolls and four thousand Hot Wheels die-cast cars. Tour the collection and then buy one to take home. Over age 12 $2.

❋ Selective Shopping

In Cawker City
Great Plains Art and Antique Gallery (785-781-4344), 719 Lake Rd., Cawker City. Call for hours. Lottie Herod offers antiques and collectibles, but she also sells her oil paintings of rural Kansas and, more importantly, custom ceramics that celebrate the Ball of Twine. She has cre-

ated ceramic Ball of Twine Christmas ornaments, coffee mugs, toothpick holders, and shot glasses and will even autograph your purchase. No credit cards.

The Little Bait Shop (785-781-4246; littlebaitshop.com), 1017 Ninth St., Cawker City. Open March–Oct., 7–7 daily. Tom and Marty White house eight 600-gallon bait tanks in their red metal building just off Cawker City's main street. With some of the largest bait available in this part of Kansas, they sell leaches, worms, crawdads, goldfish, salties, perch, and even bait shrimp. Buy soft drinks, tackle, croppie jigs, sandwiches, pizzas, and homemade jerky here, too.

In Concordia

Essentials and Fabric Essentials (785-243-4755), 118 W. Sixth St., Concordia. Open 9–6 Mon.–Wed./Fri., 9–7 Thurs., 9–5 Sat. This shop stocks more than five thousand quilting bolts, plus stitchery and sewing books. There are also health foods, supplements, and teas, plus candles and greeting cards. See Christmas decorations upstairs year-round.

Coppoc Sports (785-243-4284), 126 W. Sixth St., Concordia. Open 9–5 Mon.–Sat.; closes 8 Thurs. This is more than the average sports-gear store. Purchase a huge selection of children's logo athletic wear, an enormous variety of athletic shoes, and even medical scrubs.

In Ellsworth

Ellsworth Village Mall (785-472-4659), 210 N. Douglas Ave. Ellsworth. Open 7:30–5 Mon.–Sat. Marvel at an 1887 Roosevelt pipe organ and 10-foot-tall nutcrackers or buy a used book. Antiques and collectibles, baby books, a booth for making stuffed bears, and a holiday

store are several offerings. Savor a sub sandwich or fresh fruit smoothie in an area that feels like a '50s diner. Inexpensive dining.

Old West Trading Post (785-472-3919), 123 N. Douglas, Ellsworth. Open 9–5 Mon.–Sat. This Western-inspired store is a popular destination for folks who want straw or felt cowboy hats, bleached longhorn skulls, and hundreds of cowboy boots. Buy antique chaps and bridles or framed Western art; treasures abound.

Elsewhere

& **The Feathered Nest** (785-527-5524), 1914 M St., Belleville. Open 8–6 Mon.–Fri., 8:30–5 Sat. Secure Wi-Fi, smooth jazz, a soothing fountain, and lingering coffee regulars are just the start of this wonderfully diverse shop on Belleville's main street. Buy everything from bamboo sleepwear and stuffed chairs to jewelry, glass table lamps, and ceramic vases. Home-decor lovers could spend hours here.

Stuff 'n' Such (785-454-3416), 801 Morgan, Downs. Open 9–5:30 Mon.–Sat. Located in an old railroad hotel where Walt Disney slept, this never-ending store offers lodging upstairs. Shop for gourmet foods, greeting cards, stuffed animals, and diffuser oils, and browse three rooms of fabric, equipment, books, and patterns. One lodging unit offers beds for six, two bathrooms, living room with dining area, galley kitchen, and television. Call for lodging rates.

Village Lines (785-524-5133, village lines.com), 139 W. Lincoln Ave., Lincoln. Open 9:30–5:30 Mon.–Sat. Operating since a major downtown commercial influx in the mid-1980s, this shop offers everything from art

IN BELLEVILLE, THE FEATHERED NEST OFFERS MULTIPLE ROOMS OF UPSCALE FURNISHINGS AND ACCESSORIES.

with American Indian themes to embroidered pillows and books galore. Most items are Kansas products and half are consigned. Enjoy coffee and snacks at the dining table that has become a neighborhood destination.

& **Brant's Meat Market** (785-525-6464), 125 S. Main, Lucas. Open 8–5:30 weekdays, 8–6 Sat. Doug and Linda Brant continue a tradition that began with Doug's grandfather in 1922. Sample their all-natural, wood-smoked, savory beef jerky and soft homemade bologna, and then buy some to enjoy at home.

City Sundries (785-546-2234), 104 N. Washington, Marquette. Open 10–7 weekdays, 10–6 Sat., noon–6 Sun. Buy cards, aspirin, and balloons and then enjoy lunch or dessert at the original soda fountain. Savor a mini

peanut éclair with soft-serve ice cream, chocolate sauce, peanuts, gobs of whipped cream, and a cherry, or a homemade shake for less than $3. Grilled chicken wraps and three-cheese sandwiches or burgers are also on the menu. Inexpensive.

T&H General Store (785-461-5267; thgeneralstore.com), 674 Sunflower Rd., Wakefield. Open 9–6 Thurs.–Sat. This is a great place to get live minnows, crawfish, and other bait, plus lake maps, firearms, ammunition, and even sporting licenses. Buy snacks, cast-iron cookware, hardware, and more. Enjoy a cup of coffee or a beer, and rent space in boat/camper storage.

& **Kansas Originals Market and Gallery** (785-658-2602; kansasoriginals.com), 233 KS 232, Wilson. Open 9–6 Mon.–Sat., 11–6 Sun. See work from more than three hundred Kansas artists in this enormous building just off I-70. Sip complementary coffee as you peruse a handmade wooden airplane with a moving propeller, a flag-shaped braided rug, decorative metal sheaves, and Kansas sunflowers everywhere.

✳ Special Events

April: **Kansas Storytelling Festival** (kansasstorytelling.com), Downs. Experience two evening concerts and loads of individual storytelling sessions, workshops, and music for every taste—from homespun tales and poetry to historical portrayals and stories for children. Storytellers from across the nation participate.

May: **Fidelisfest** (785-735-2777), Memorial Day, Victoria. Experience a German wedding-style dinner, plus a country store with homemade baked goods and handmade items created by parishioners, as well as a beer garden, brat and burger stand, and an auction of more than two hundred items. **Denmark Heritage Day** (402-434-5348) every third year in Lincoln.

June: **Flatland Blues Fest** (785-483-3742), Russell. Sponsored by Deines Cultural Center, the event features loads of musical entertainment. **Smoky Hill River Festival** (785-309-5770), Oakdale Park/Salina. The three-day event offers concerts, food, shopping, and kids' activities. **Midsummer's Festival** (888-227-2227; midsummersfestival.org), Lindsborg. Little Sweden USA shares its heritage with food, concerts, costumes, and dancing.

July: **Czech Festival** (785-658-2211, wilsonkansas.com/czech-festival.htm), Wilson. This annual event celebrated its golden anniversary in 2010. It features a beer garden, ice-cream social, parade, dances, a carnival, car and tractor shows, sports tournaments, and more.

August: **Herzogfest** (785-735-2352), Victoria. After almost 30 years this event in the German Capital of Kansas features concerts, a polka mass, a free signature concert, and fireworks, plus an auction and car show. **Cawker City Picnic and Twine-A-Thon** (skyways.lib.ks.us /towns/cawker/twine), Cawker City. This event includes the Twine-a-Thon, where people add twine to the famous Ball of Twine. There are also food stands, a car show, and even a street dance. **Thor's Roar Motorcycle Rally** (785-227-8687 for visitors information), downtown Lindsborg. This Saturday event features a bikers breakfast and bike show, kids' games, and, of course, many vendors. Many bikers stop through before or after visiting Sturgis.

October: **Svensk Hyllningsfest** (888-227-2227), Lindsborg. Activities include the Dala Daze and Viking Knights Parade, Swedish folk dancing and other entertainment, area artist and craft booths, and a traditional Swedish smorgasbord.

November: **Lighted Christmas Parade and Weihnachtsfest** (785-483-6960; chamber of commerce), downtown Russell. Enjoy Russell's signature holiday events on Thanksgiving weekend.

SHOPPING IN LINDSBORG

Anderson Butik (785-227-3864, andersonbutik.com). It has been nearly 40 years since Dean and Charlotte Anderson opened this Main Street gift shop full of Swedish maps and books and Dala horses, plus Swedish lingonberries, cheeses, and herring. Charlotte will tell you all about Lindsborg while you shop.

Aunt Agda's Attic (785-227-2966). Most handcrafted Swedish items in the store are made by the owners' daughter, but you'll also find antiques and collectibles.

Smoky Valley Rare Coins (785-227-2966; smokyvalleycoins.com; behind Aunt Agda's Attic). Ron Johnson has collected coins for 60 years, and this is the only coin store between Topeka and Wichita. He buys and sells coins and has an inventory of fifty thousand, most from the U.S. and many certified. See a 1909 VDB Lincoln cent worth $1,400 and a 1916 D dime worth $3,000.

Hemslöjd Inc. (1-800-779-3344; hemslojd.com). From Swedish table runners and door harps to imported and house-made Dala horses, this shop has something for every Swedish cultural enthusiast.

Clogs 'n' Such/Dala Clogs (785-227-2951). Maud and Thomas are passionate about their clogs, which they make and ship all over the U.S. and half of Europe. Their custom work has appeared in national magazines, and Maud is expert in traditional Kurbits painting. They also stock other clog brands.

♿ **Wild Dala Winery** (785-617-0036; wilddalawine.com). Call for hours. In cooperation with Vin Vivante Winery from Wamego, Wild Dala Winery offers nearly a dozen different wines. Enjoy tastings at the granite bar atop massive wine casks while surrounded by lovely art.

Small World Gallery (785-227-4442, smallworldgallery.net). If you're lucky you'll meet renowned *National Geographic* photographer Jim Richardson between his photo trips. Enjoy his breathtaking images and greeting cards, plus jewelry made by his wife, Kathy, using beads and metals collected during their worldwide travels. Custom designs are available.

Elizabeth's (866-344-0005, hand-woven.net). Since 1984 Elizabeth Walker has sold her handwoven wearable art in downtown Lindsborg. She also offers custom design services. Scarves, casual poncho cuts, and dramatic capes are made from rayon, chenille, and cotton in deep rich colors.

Laura May's Cottage (785-227-3948). Bamboo, alpaca, and silk are just a few all-natural fibers in this yarn inventory. The owner teaches others in her tiny shop, where customers can purchase handmade scarves, shrugs, and sweaters, plus knitting and needlepoint books.

Wichita and Beyond: From Cowboy Country to Air Capital

5

THE CITY OF WICHITA

Located on the Arkansas River, and with a population of more than three hundred and fifty thousand, Wichita is Kansas's largest city. It has topped *Forbes*'s online list of most affordable cities in the Midwest and ranked third in AAA's list of most affordable U.S. cities to visit. Highways that lead into the city of Wichita include I-135, I-35, US 54/400, KS 254, KS 96, KS 42, and KS 15.

Spanish explorer Francisco Vázquez de Coronado met Indians here, whom he called the Quiviras. The city incorporated in 1870, became a railhead for cattle drives from southwestern areas of the country, and hosted plenty of rowdy cowboys. For a true taste of Wichita's Old West roots, hit the boardwalk at the multibuilding Old Cowtown Museum. By the 1890s the town had grown to become the state's third-largest metropolitan area. Carrie Nation brought her temperance crusade to Wichita, and the discovery of oil got the city's aviation industry underway.

The city transformed from Cowtown to Air Capital of the World in a little over a hundred years, in part through the efforts of such pioneers as Clyde Cessna, Walter Beech, and Bill Lear. The early aviation industry and the city's population grew exponentially as Wichita plane manufacturers began to provide equipment during World War II. Today more than 45 percent of general aircraft in the world are constructed here, where Cessna and Hawker Beechcraft remain, with the addition of Learjet, Spirit AeroSystems, Airbus, and Boeing.

Located between Wichita and suburban Derby, McConnell Air Force Base is a large employer for the area and the only Total Force base, providing air refueling and airlift services across the globe. The annual Wichita Flight Festival is a highly popular summer event at the base, and several small airports outside of the city offer occasional fly-in breakfasts that draw enthusiastic crowds.

Wichita has recently undergone a renaissance in its Old Town area, which the American Planning Association has designated as one of the top 10 great neighborhoods in the US. Once an industrial corridor and warehouse district with ties to railroad activities, the revived and thriving neighborhood is now a combination of renovation and new construction, offering the biggest concentration of nightlife in the city, plus museums, shopping, and loads of restaurants. With its funky, fun vibe, the Delano neighborhood offers more shopping opportunities, including Hatman Jack's, which creates custom-crafted hats, Al's Old and New

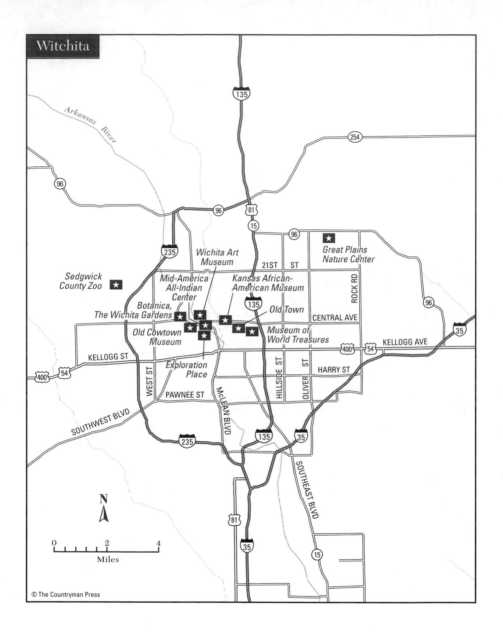

Arkansas River

254

96

135

96

81

15

96

Great Plains
Nature Center

Wichita Art
Museum

21ST   ST

Sedgwick
County Zoo

Mid-America
All-Indian
Center

Kansas African-
American Museum

ROCK RD

Botanica,
The Wichita Gardens

135

Old Town

CENTRAL AVE

96

235

Old Cowtown
Museum

Museum of
World Treasures

35

KELLOGG AVE

KELLOGG ST

400

54

Exploration
Place

WEST ST

HILLSIDE ST

OLIVER ST

HARRY ST

400

54

PAWNEE ST

McLEAN BLVD

SOUTHWEST BLVD

235

135

35

SOUTHEAST BLVD

N

81

0   2   4

35

15

Miles

© The Countryman Press

Bookstore, and Wichita Tobacco and Candy Co. Once a town in its own right,
Delano was annexed into Wichita during the late 1870s.

There are seemingly endless dining options in Wichita, with more than a
thousand restaurants to choose from. Nu Way Café has been renowned for its
ground meat sandwiches, and Scotch and Sirloin for its steaks, over many
decades, while multicultural cuisine is reflected in the menus at Café Bel Ami or
Connie's Mexico Café.

Notable Wichita residents include William C. Coleman, who created the
Coleman Arc Lamp and gradually expanded his business to feature the coolers

and camp stoves for which the Coleman Company has become legendary. Enthusiasts of the outdoors appreciate deep discounts on Coleman products at the Wichita outlet store. Other major businesses that began here include Pizza Hut, White Castle, and Taco Tico.

Explore Wichita's history with a trolley tour. Visit the Kansas African American Museum to learn about the rich African American tradition and community in Wichita, where the Dockum Drug Store sit-in drew attention to the fact that the owner refused to serve African Americans. Today a stirring life-size replica of the lunch counter and patrons occupies a downtown pocket park near the drugstore's original location. The Wichita Art Museum, Museum of World Treasures, and the county historical museum are other popular destinations.

Wichita is a city that honors its American Indian roots, from pylons at either end of a bridge on 13th Street that feature carved portraits of American Indians (and buffalo) to the stunningly beautiful Keeper of the Plains statue at the intersection of the Arkansas and Little Arkansas Rivers, and the educational Mid-America All Indian Center with its annual summer powwow.

The center is just one of multiple attractions located in the vibrant Wichita riverfront area, including the Wichita Art Museum, Botanica, the Wichita Gardens—a gorgeous oasis near the edge of town—the Old Cowtown Museum, and Exploration Place, a terrific spot for children of all ages to explore and experience the natural and man-made world, from aviation to Renaissance castles.

A vibrant performing arts community offers something for every taste, whether you prefer drama with your dinner or classical opera. The Music Theatre of Wichita has offered musical theater performances for more than four

OLD TOWN

decades and jumpstarted the careers of several well-known professional performers, including Kristin Chenoweth, and the INTRUST Bank Arena frequently hosts concerts and special events.

Efforts to keep residents and visitors in touch with the natural world include
the beautifully designed and maintained Sedgwick County Zoo, Botanica, and
Great Plains Nature Center, where visitors learn about native vegetation and animals. Just west of town is the privately owned Tanganyika Wildlife Park, where
rare and endangered animals are cared for and shared with the public.

This is also a great place to play golf. Five municipal courses offer a wide
range of terrain and challenge levels at great prices, and there are 28 more public, private, and semiprivate courses available.

Wichita has more sunny days than Miami. The area also experiences frequent
thunderstorms, particularly from early spring to early summer. It is known for
severe weather, which spawns large hailstorms and tornadoes. F-5 and F-4 tornadoes struck in the Wichita area during 1991 and 1999, and there was tornadic
activity here during the May 2010 outbreak that hit the Oklahoma City area.

Wichita is much more than an air capital. This large Kansas city offers small-
town charm coupled with excitement for the present and for future development. Give yourself at least three or four days to fully appreciate its charms and
treasures.

AREA CODE 316

GUIDANCE Learn about the city through the **Go Wichita Convention and
Visitors Bureau** (316-265-2800; gowichita.com), 515 S. Main, Ste. 115, Wichita.
Open 7:45–5:30 weekdays.

GETTING THERE *By car:* Drive to the Wichita area from Kansas City to
Wichita in about three hours, primarily on I-35. *By air:* Wichita hosts a full-service airport that is the state's largest. **Wichita Mid-Continent Airport** (316-946-
4700) recently received a $10 million facelift, too, from the ground up.

GETTING AROUND Car travel is easy here; locals say that you can get anywhere in Wichita in 20 minutes or you're lost. The beautiful Wichita Transit
Center also transports locals and visitors on 51 buses and offers a wheelchair-lift
van and paratransit routes.

MEDICAL EMERGENCY Via Christi Regional Medical Center (316-268-
5000), 929 N St. Francis, Wichita.

Wesley Medical Center (316-962-2000), 550 N. Hillside, Wichita.

Susan B. Allen Memorial Hospital (316-321-3300), 720 W. Central, Wichita.

✳ **To See**

HISTORIC PLACES, LANDMARKS, AND SITES Keeper of the Plains,
650 N. Seneca St., Wichita. Closed midnight–5 AM. This breathtaking sculpture
raises its hands toward the sky and Great Spirit beside the intersection of the Big

and Little Arkansas Rivers. Standing 44 feet tall, the Keeper of the Plains has become a symbol of the city, a sacred gathering place for American Indians, and the central feature of an eight-year restoration and river beautification project that cost $20 million. It's lit at night and surrounded by plantings that include prairie grasses and cacti. A ring of fire burns at night during daylight saving time.

& **Mid-America All Indian Center Inc.** (316-350-3340; theindiancenter.org), 650 N. Seneca St., Wichita. Open 10–4 Tues.–Sat. Antique moccasins, feather fans, and portrait art of American Indians are just a few things you'll see here in recognition of the impact of Indian tribes from this area. At the small gift shop, purchase American Indian jewelry and pottery, plus books, music, and videos. Adults $7; seniors $5; children 6–12 $3.

Veterans Memorial Park/John S. Stevens Veterans Memorial Park, 503 W. Central Ave., Wichita. The nonprofit Veterans Memorial Park of Wichita Inc. maintains this expansive park, which includes 16 out of 40 veterans memorials erected throughout Wichita. It's lush and shady with rolling hills, nighttime spotlights, and easy access to the river walk.

MUSEUMS **Frank Lloyd Wright's Allen-Lambe House/Allen-Lambe House Museum** (316-706-9286; allenlambe.org), 255 N. Roosevelt, Wichita. Open 10–5 Mon.–Sat., noon–5 Sun. Call for tours 10 days in advance; closed on all major holidays. Designed in 1915 for prominent journalist and later governor Henry J. Allen and his wife, Elsie, this is the state's only private residence designed by Wright and the last of his Prairie-style houses. The museum celebrated its 20th anniversary in 2010, which included a lecture by Wright's grandson Eric Lloyd Wright. Photos are allowed of the exterior. Tours $10, 5–20 people required. Adults $8; seniors 60 and up $7; children 4–12 $6.

OLD COWTOWN MUSEUM BUILDINGS PROVIDE A VIEW OF WHAT WICHITA MAY HAVE LOOKED LIKE FROM THE 1860S TO 1880S.

Kansas African-American Museum (316-262-7651; tkaamuseum.org/index
.html), 601 N. Water St., Wichita. Gallery open 9–5 Tues.–Fri., 2–6 Sat. Built
more than 90 years ago, the brick and columned Calvary Baptist Church played
a critical role in the lives of Wichita's African American community for many
years. See photographs from and of Gordon Parks, plus stunning images of area
jazz and blues performers and early years among black Kansans, as well as
African tribal masks and statues and art pieces from young black artists. Adults
$5.50; youth 5–17 $2.50; seniors $4.50; group rates available.

Kansas Aviation Museum (316-683-9242; kansasaviationmuseum.org), 3350 S.
George Washington Blvd., Wichita. Open 10–5 Mon.–Sat., 12–5 Sun. Housed at
McConnell Air Force Base, this museum occupies the original Wichita Municipal Airport terminal building, which has been fully restored. It chronicles the
growth and development of general aviation in Kansas and displays aircraft and
aviation-related artifacts. Adults $8; seniors $7; children 12 and under $6.

✒ ♿ **Museum of World Treasures** (316-263-1311; worldtreasures.org), 835 E.
First St. N, Wichita. Open 10–5 Mon.–Sat., 12–5 Sun. Touch fossil clams from
Colorado, see an entire room of Buddha statues, and enjoy wall-spanning photos
of ancient Mayan buildings. There's a Civil War soldier encampment with a
trunk, saddle, and musket; a redcoat coat and vest; and an exhibit about black
pioneers in aviation. Three reconstructed dinosaur skeletons positioned in battle
will amaze you. An entertainment area features the Scarecrow's pitchfork from
The Wizard of Oz and *Young Frankenstein* photos signed by the actors. Adults
$9; seniors $8; children 4–12 $7.

THE AIR CAPITAL OF THE WORLD KICKS OFF ITS ANNUAL RIVERFEST WITH A GRAND
PARADE.

THE MUSEUM OF WORLD TREASURES FEATURES A MASSIVE DISPLAY ABOUT ANCIENT EGYPT.

🖉 **Old Cowtown Museum** (316-219-1871; oldcowtown.org), 1865 Museum Blvd., Wichita. Open mid-Dec.–mid-April, 10–4 Tues.–Sat.; mid-April—mid-Dec., 9:30–4:40 Wed.–Sat., and noon–4:30 Sun. The museum's centerpiece is a town with reproduction buildings that simulate how Wichita looked during its Old West days from 1865 to 1880. Travel the boardwalk past the Southern Hotel, Fritz Snitzler's Saloon, and much more, often with reenactors adding authenticity. Adults 18–61 $8; seniors 62 and up $6.50; youth 12–17 $6; children 4–11 $5.50; children under 4 free; group rates available.

♿ **Wichita Art Museum** (316-268-4921; wichitaartmuseum.org), 1400 W. Museum Blvd., Wichita. Open noon–5 Sun., 10–5 Tues.–Sat.; café open 11–2 Sun., 11–3 Tues.–Sat. The largest art museum in the state of Kansas mixes old and new, including art from the late 1800s in a hexagonal room, a glittering display of art glass from Steuben to Tiffany, and low-lit sepia-tone American Indian images. There's also an art study library. In the Muse Café, try homemade soups such as sweet potato bisque, mixed-green salads with house dressing, or quiche with fresh fruit. Adults $7; seniors 60 and up $5; students with ID and youth 5–17 $3; children under 5 free; free admission Sat. Café is inexpensive.

♿ **Ulrich Museum of Art at Wichita State University** (316-978-3664; ulrich.wichita.edu), 1845 Fairmount St., Wichita. Open 11–5 Tues.–Fri., 1–5 Sat.–Sun. Six thousand works of modern and contemporary art include an iconic 1991 red and blue LOVE piece, a thesis exhibition by four students (held twice a year), and a sculpture of trees made from old shoes. The Martin H. Bush Outdoor Sculpture Collection features more than 70 pieces sprinkled throughout the campus. Look for visitor parking on Fairmount Street, near the centipede sculpture. Free.

& **Wichita-Sedgwick County Historical Museum** (316-265-9314; wichita history.org), 204 S. Main, Wichita. Open 11–4 Tues.–Fri., 1–5 Sat.–Sun. Constructed as a city hall in 1892, this limestone structure with bell tower, antique beveled windows, and turrets resembles an urban castle. Tour four floors of this city's history about Wichita Indian tribe members, who were the area's earliest inhabitants, and the city's transformation from Old West town to Air Capital of the World. See a 1916 Jones Six automobile created by local Ford dealer John Jones, a fully furnished Victorian home display, and even a 1910 drugstore. Adults $4; children 6–12 $2.

Kansas Sports Hall of Fame/Sports Museum (316-262-2038; kshof.org), 515 S. Wichita, Wichita. Open 10–4 Mon.–Fri. The hall of fame and museum recently reopened following renovations at the Wichita boathouse. View a video that showcases great moments, players, and coaches throughout the state's history, and learn about approximately 200 stellar athletes, from Barry Sanders to Maurice Green and Wilt Chamberlain. Free.

✳ To Do

DAY SPAS & **Salon Knotty and Day Spa** (316-636-4400; inside Genesis Health Club; second location in El Dorado), 1447 N. Rock Rd., Ste. 200, Wichita. Open 8:30–8:30 Mon.–Fri., 9–6 Sat. This is a sleek, modern place, where special packages may include an herbology body polish or a workout with a personal trainer. The 3.5-hour Knotty Girl spa package is a client favorite, which features a facial, makeup session, deluxe pedicure, and shampoo and style for $145.

GOLF MacDonald Golf Course (316-688-9391), 840 N. Yale, Wichita. This course offers several water features, tree-dotted rolling hills, well-maintained fairways, and a full-service pro shop. Par 17, 18-holes, 6,958 yards.

Tex Consolver Golf Course (316-337-9494), 1931 S. Tyler, Wichita. Golfers who like to challenge themselves will appreciate six holes with water and loads of trees, plus a clubhouse. Par 72, 18 holes, 7,361 yards

L. W. Clapp Golf Course (316-688-9341), 4611 E. Harry, Wichita. Wichita's smallest course is nicely landscaped with a creek that creates challenging play. Par 70, 18 holes, 6,043 yards.

Auburn Hills Golf Course (316-219-9700), 443 S. 135th St. W, Wichita. One of the best municipal golf courses in the Midwest area, it offers a pro shop and a course with 52 sand traps and 14 lakes. Par 72, 18 holes, 7,169 yards for longest tees.

Arthur B. Sim Golf Course (316-337-9100), 2020 W. Murdock, Wichita. This fairly simple course operates near downtown Wichita with tree-lined fairways. Par 71, 18 holes, men: 5,867 yards; women: 5,012 yards.

OUTDOORS & **Botanica, The Wichita Gardens** (316-264-0448; botanica .org), 701 N. Amidon Ave., Wichita. Open 9–5 Mon.–Wed./Fri.–Sat., 9–8 Thurs., 1–5 Sun. Nearly 25 years old, this 9.5-acre site has grown into a multifaceted park full of gently rolling terrain; beautiful gardens; lush, natural forest areas;

and soothing waterfalls, fountains, and sprinklers. Most paths are paved, with some covered in wood chips. Visit the Downing Children's Garden (after summer 2011), a learning environment with elements of play, or the xeriscape garden. You may even find college students painting here. Adults 13–61 $7; seniors $6; youth 3–12 $3.

& **Great Plains Nature Center** (316-683-5499; gpnc.org), 6232 E. 29th St. N, Wichita. Center open 9–5 Mon.–Sat.; park open sunrise– sundown daily. The GPNC provides environmental education for visitors. Large dioramas depict Kansas wildlife such as prairie dogs and buffalo, and visitors can compare their hand size to cast animal tracks. Other exhibits discuss wetlands, riparian habitat, and woodlands. Follow 2.5 miles of paved trails that will introduce you to more than 100 wildflower species, nearly 40 tree and shrub varieties, 13 fish species, and 160 bird species. You'll also see loads of reptiles, amphibians, and fish. Fishing allowed with a valid Kansas license. Free.

Naftzger Memorial Park (316-268-4361; city hall), Douglas and St. Francis, Wichita. Open 6–midnight. Located across the street from Old Mill Tasty Shop, this gorgeous, shady park has a waterfall and brick walkways, plus wrought-iron wall accents and benches, picnic tables, and gates.

SPECTATOR SPORTS ICT Roller Girls (no phone listed; ictrollergirls.net), 1900 E. Macarthur, Skate South/Wichita. This all-female team of flat track roller derby enthusiasts has grown to include more than 30 women. The nonprofit

A LOCAL ART STUDENT PAINTS AT BOTANICA, THE WICHITA GARDENS.

GREAT PLAINS NATURE CENTER

group practices weekly and shows off their skills from Lincoln, Nebraska, to Columbia, Missouri, and Colorado Springs. Recently named an official Women's Flat Track Derby Apprentice League, the group will eventually be allowed to participate in regional and national competitions. Admission $9; check in advance.

& **Wichita Wingnuts** (316-264-NUTS; wichitawingnuts.com), 300 S. Sycamore, Lawrence Dumont Stadium/Wichita. Enjoy fast-paced AA professional baseball. Members of the North Division of the American Association of Independent Professional Baseball, the team won the division title for the first half of the 2009 season. Adults $6–12; senior/youth/military $8–11; children two and under free.

WICHITA AREA FARMERS' MARKETS Old Town Farmers' Market (316-992-0413), First St. and Mosley, Old Town/Wichita. Open early May–mid-October, 7–noon Sat. and 3:30–6:30 Wed. at Andover Central Park.

El Dorado Farmers' Market (316-320-4150), N. Main and 12th Streets, Wichita. Open June–Sept., 7:30–noon.

Derby Farmers' Market (620-782-3125), 800 N. Baltimore, Derby. Open May–Oct., 8–noon Sat.

Central Park Farmers' Market (316-992-0413), Central Park, Andover. Open June–Aug., 3:30–6:30 Wed.

✴ Lodging

BED & BREAKFASTS ((ᵞ)) **Vermillion Rose B&B** (316-267-7636; vermillionrosebb.com), 1204 N. Topeka Ave., Wichita. Stay in this classic 1887 home, where every room has a different character, from the Desert Rose with Southwestern decor and an original brick fireplace to the Garden Rose with four-poster bed and curtain-draped tub. Each room has a private bath and television. Enjoy the expansive dining room, plus teas, coffees, books, and magazines at any time. Full breakfast. $85–105; 10 percent deposit.

College Hill Bed & Breakfast (316-612-4577; collegehillbedand breakfast.com), 3308 Country Club, Wichita. Sink into a cozy wicker chair on the sunporch as you enjoy a full hot breakfast, or sip tea or coffee brought to your room while you relax in a cozy robe. Romance is key at this B&B with a white picket fence. It's full of quilts and luxurious linens; one room and the private cottage have whirlpool tubs; and there are little touches such as turndown service, stocked refrigerators in each room, and guest umbrellas. $99–169; $169 for the private cottage.

HOTELS AND LODGES ⚹ **The Castle Inn Riverside** (316-263-9300; castleinnriverside.com), 1155 N. River Blvd., Wichita. Little did Burton Harvey Campbell know, when he built this 1888 Scottish-inspired castle, that it would later become a 14-room inn. At night hundreds of white lights line the turret and high-peaked roof. Restored to its former grandeur, the inn features gorgeous antique–filled rooms that go by names such as Kansas Suite, Native American,

Scotland Yard, and Olde English. Play chess or borrow a book from the library. Wines, cheeses, and soft drinks and other beverages available 5–7 Fri.–Sat.; desserts, coffees, teas, and liqueurs served 7–10. Full breakfast. $125–275.

⚹ ((ᵞ)) **The Hotel at Old Town** (316-267-4800; hotelatoldtown.com), 830 E. First St. N, Wichita. Rooms honor the building's early 1900s roots while offering a full kitchen, CD player, and 37-inch TV in every room. Sip free coffee in the Victorian-style lobby. Look at sepia-tone photos of old Wichita in the hallways and the largest collection of Keen Kutter memorabilia in the nation. There's a fitness center, hotel cupboard, free enclosed parking garage, conference center, and piano bar. Walk to plenty of restaurants within a few blocks. From $109.

✴ Where to Eat

DINING OUT ⚹ **Chester's Chophouse and Wine Bar** (316-201-1300; chesterschophouse.com), 1550 N. Webb Rd., Wichita. Open 4:30–9 daily. Think of wood, leather, and stone fireplaces, and windows that overlook historic Beech Lake. Start with red pepper hummus and crunchy flat bread dusted with steak seasonings and end with edible or drinkable desserts. Try the maple mustard salmon, oak grilled pork chops, spicy BBQ calamari, or prime bone-in cowboy rib eye steak. The restaurant uses local produce whenever possible, changes the menu often, and offers a *Wine Spectator*–recognized wine list. Moderate.

⚹ ♈ **Larkspur** (316-262-5275; lark spuronline.com), 904 E. Douglas Ave., Wichita. Open 11–10 Mon.–

Thurs., 11–11 Fri.–Sat., 4–9 Sun. Housed in the circa 1914 to 1922 James C. Smyth Hyde building, this restaurant offers dinner favorites such as fresh crab cakes and grilled lamb chops over fresh garlic and rosemary balsamic reduction. Original brick, natural wood, and an expansive patio with arbor characterize Larkspur. Live piano enhances weeknight meals, and live jazz plays on weekend evenings. The restaurant offers free Wi-Fi and daily food and beverage specials. Moderate.

& ♈ **Oeno Wine Bar** (316-440-5000; oenowine.com), 330 N. Mead St., Wichita. Open 4–2 AM Mon.–Sat. Come enjoy one of the largest bars in the state. Sleek and sexy, with dark wood and plush seating, this Old Town spot offers dozens of American and imported wines plus champagnes. But they're also known for martinis like lime luxury and mojito pitchers. Appetizer or tapas plates include cheese flights, pear and blue cheese bruschetta with caramelized red onion, a hummus trio, or prosciutto-wrapped quail. Moderate.

& **Scotch and Sirloin** (316-685-8701; scotchandsirloin.net), 5325 E. Kellogg Dr. S (across the highway from the Robert J. Dole VA Medical Center), Wichita. Open 11–3 Mon.–Sat. lunch, 5–10 Sun.–Thurs., 5–11 Fri.–Sat. It's been more than 40 years since Scotch and Sirloin began serving Sterling Silver beef, and they're still known for their prime rib special. With the vibe of a bygone era and white-and-black table linens, this restaurant offers enormous portions and amazing blue cheese dressing. For a light meal try the Scotch salad with steak that features chickpeas, tomato wedges, red onion and pepper

rings, pepper Jack cheese, black olives, and two egg halves, topped with steak slices. To take some of their signature meat home, check out S&S Meats across the parking lot. Moderate.

& ♈ **Sabor Latin Bar and Grill** (316-201-4880; saborwichita.com), 308 N. Mead St., Wichita. Open 11–10 Mon.–Thurs., 11–11 Fri.–Sat., 4–9 Sun. With the motto Tango with Your Tastebuds, this spacious, hip, and modern place offers dishes from Puerto Rico, Cuba, Venezuela, and others, including South American paella, lobster tacos, Salvadorian *pupusas,* and slow-roasted Adobo pork. Add a mojito or a margarita and enjoy a solo vocalist/guitarist from 7 PM Fri.–Sat. Moderate.

& **Café Bel Ami** (316-267-3433; cafebelami.biz), 229 E. William St., Ste. 101, Wichita. Open for lunch Mon.–Fri., dinner Mon.–Sat. White tablecloths and rich jewel tones decorate this classy restaurant, known for its Mediterranean cuisine and attentive servers. Try grilled Halloumi cheese with Roma tomatoes and olive oil; shrimp ravioli with onions, leeks, and mushrooms in lobster cream sauce; or braised lamb shank with vegetables over rice. Moderate.

EATING OUT & **Connie's Mexico Café** (316-832-9636; conniesmexico cafe.com), 2227 N. Broadway St., Wichita. Open 11–8 Mon.–Sat. Wichita's oldest family-owned Mexican restaurant has operated since 1963. Outside it's an unassuming brick building; inside it's a clean, comfortable place to dine with Mexican paper decorations. Burritos are the house specialty, but you'll also find fajita Monterey and chorizo with eggs and beans. They're located in El Barrio, the city's traditional Mexican neighborhood. Inexpensive.

& **Old Mill Tasty Shop** (316-264-6500; oldtownwichita.com/old-mill-tasty-shop), 604 E. Douglas Ave., Wichita. Open 11–3 Mon.–Fri., 8–3 Sat. Black-and-white photos of old Wichita line the walls at this longtime eatery, where the marble soda fountain is original, the chicken salad is famous, tortillas are fried with a light touch, and some waitresses have worked for decades. Try the triple club sandwich with ham and bacon, spinach salad with hot bacon dressing, a towering slice of carrot cake with light cream cheese icing, or an ultrathick malt. Inexpensive.

& **River City Brewery** (316-263-2739), 150 N. Mosley St., Wichita. Open 11–10 Mon.–Sat., noon–9 Sun. Wichita's only remaining brewery is a fun and lively place with a big menu. Stop by Wednesday for all-day $6 pizza, try Big Sid's baby back ribs served with rough-cut fries, or share some Southwest chicken pinwheels. There are also salads, a homemade chicken noodle soup, and entrées such as River City fish and chips. Inexpensive.

& **The Beacon** (316-263-3397), 909 E. Douglas Ave., Wichita. Open 6–3 daily. The Beacon offers "breakfast the way you remember it" all day, including the traditional, an open-faced English muffin, two eggs, your choice of ham or bacon, and cheese melted on top—plus hash browns or country fried potatoes. The egg cook has actually received thank-you notes for his omelets. Other options include burgers, roast beef, meatloaf, meal-size salads, steak, catfish, or liver and onions. Inexpensive.

Nu Way Café (316-684-6132; nuway cafe.com), 1416 W. Douglas Ave., Wichita. Open 10:30–9 daily. This is the original spot where Wichita residents learned to love Nu Way's signature crumbled meat sandwiches with loads of mustard, pickles, and onion since 1930. They're also known for homemade root beer—available by the half gallon—curly fries, ultra thick malts, and chili, served plain or with beans. Belly up to the black Formica counter or slide into a bright red booth and chow down to the sounds of classic rock 'n' roll. Inexpensive.

ANTIQUE BLACK-AND-WHITE PHOTOS ARE PART OF THE DECOR AT OLD MILL TASTY SHOP.

& ⍦ **Hangar One Steak House**
(316-941-4900; hangaronesteakhouse
.com), 5925 W. Kellogg Dr., Wichita.
Open 4–10 Mon.–Thurs., 11–11
Fri.–Sun; longer lounge hours. Dine
and drink near the airport in a building that resembles an airplane hangar.
Enjoy fried hot pickle bomber wheels
with honey mustard sauce or spitfire
bacon-wrapped BBQ shrimp on the
Crash Pad patio with its outdoor bar.
Savor a Star Fighter sirloin or a Piper
pork chop; cigars are available outside. Mostly inexpensive.

& ⟨⟩ **Mead's Corner** (316-201-1900;
meadscorner.com), 430 E. Douglas
Ave., Wichita. Open 7–10 Mon.–
Thurs., 7–midnight Fri.–Sat., 10–6
Sun. Owned by the First United
Methodist Church, this fair trade coffeehouse on an Old Town corner is
known for coffee and other beverages,
plus local musicians who perform on
some evenings. Read a book while
sinking into the leather sofa. Inexpensive.

Aida's Coffee House (316-262-
6721), 920 E. First St., Wichita. Coffeehouse lunch 11–3; coffee served
10–4:30. This pleasant spot operates
in the mezzanine at Aida's upscale gift
shop, full of Brighton accessories,
Vera Bradley, Wilton Armetale, Crab-
tree & Evelyn, and other well-known
brands. Order toasted ham or California club sandwiches, quiche with
salad, fresh soup, and bread made
fresh daily. And, of course, there are
mochas, lattes, and other coffee
drinks available, too. Inexpensive.

✳ **Entertainment**

All Star Adventures (316-682-3700;
allstarwichita.com), 1010 Webb Rd.,
Wichita (affiliated with All Star
Sports; 316-722-7529; 8333 W. 21st

N, Wichita). Summer hours 10–10
Mon.–Thurs., 10–midnight Fri.–Sat.,
noon–8 Sun. (with shorter hours at
other times). This spot offers Wichita's only permanent carnival, with a
turbo slide, a tilt-a-wheel, old-fashioned carnival music, and a food trailer selling cotton candy, popcorn, and
ice cream. Enjoy an arcade, miniature
golf, bumper cars, batting cages, a
driving range, and go-karts in the
bright and busy building. Unlimited
two-hour fun pass for weekends and
holidays: over 48 inches $18.95; under
48 inches $14.95; individual attraction
tickets also available.

✐ & **Sedgwick County Zoo** (316-
660-9453; scz.org), 5555 W. Zoo
Blvd., Wichita. Beginning March 1,
open 8:30–5 daily; beginning Nov. 1,
open 10–5 daily. Uncaged giraffes
munch on vegetation in their habitat.
Tree-tall bamboo lines a path to the
chimp and orangutan habitat. Walls of
windows offer views of massive tigers
and chimps. Glimpse a grizzly and
watch prairie dog antics in North
America. Miniature villages full of
authentic buildings and music transport you to Asia and Africa. In the gift
shop, purchase notepads made from
handcrafted recycled elephant dung
paper and then grab pizza, yogurt, or
a corn dog at Beastro. Adults 12–61
$11.50; seniors 62 and up/children
3–11 $7.

✐ & **Exploration Place** (316-660-
0670; exploration.org), 300 N.
McLean Blvd., Wichita. Open noon–5
Sun.–Mon., 10–5 Tues.–Sat. The
Sedgwick County Science and Dis-
covery Center was 10 years old in
2010 following a merger of a science
center and a children's museum.
Internationally recognized architect
Moshe Safdie designed the stunning

COOL VIEWS

Downtown sculptures. Look west along Douglas and you may think there's a stray dog down the street, but it's only one of the sculptures scattered between Topeka and Main. A businessman reads the paper while walking barefoot in a sidewalk fountain, and a little boy pours water into his sister's outstretched cup. Perhaps the most impressive sculpture lies in Chester I. Lewis Reflection Square Park between Broadway and Market Streets. It's a life-size depiction of the Wichita lunch counter where several black citizens were first served a meal in what had previously been a diner that only served whites. Free.

Wichita Transit Center (316-265-7221), 214 S. Topeka, Wichita. Open 6–6:30 Mon.–Fri., 7–5:30 Sat. Each year the city's transit authority transports locals and visitors on 51 buses and 43 wheelchair-lift van and paratransit routes. Located near the INTRUST Bank Arena, Wichita's primary transit center is beautiful, too, decorated in shades of turquoise, salmon, and white, with plenty of sheltered bench seating and an expansive tile mural along one wall of the main building.

ON A HOT SUMMER DAY, THIS FELLOW READS HIS NEWSPAPER BAREFOOT IN DOWNTOWN WICHITA.

building. See a permanent display depicting human flight since its inception, stand in tornado-force winds, or visit AgMagination, which teaches visitors about the science of producing food. There's a three-story stone castle, plus a miniature display of Kansas that depicts state landmarks throughout the 1950s. See a movie and learn about everything from sea monsters to Egypt or visit the café and gift shop. One-quarter of displays are traveling exhibits, such as BODIES and Titanic. Adults 12 and up $9.50; seniors 65 and up $8; youth 4–11 $6; children under 4 free.

♀ **Clifton Wine and Jazz** (316-686-5299; cliftonsquare.com), 3700 E. Douglas Ave., Clifton Square/Wichita. Open 4–midnight Wed.–Sat.; participates in the Friday Art Crawl. The only wine and jazz bar in College Hill, this spot is hopping. A hair salon, a medical spa, and a café surround the pretty little house-turned-entertainment-venue. The club also sponsors field trips, such as to area wineries during harvest time.

& **Starlite Drive-In Theatre** (316-524-2424), 3900 S. Hydraulic, Wichita. A new season begins each March. Watch a double—or even a triple—feature movie extravaganza. Experience this classic spot, built as a -first-class operation and '50s-style drive-in in 1973. Visit the drive-through ticket booth and then listen to movie sounds from pole-mounted speakers or your FM radio, and from the comfort of your car or lawn chair. A neon-lined snack bar sells hot dogs, popcorn, malts, and root beer. If you'd rather bunk down nearby, check out several hotels/motels within a five-minute drive of the theater and ask for Starlite Drive-In rates. Adults $8; children 5–11 $2.

SEE A MINIATURE TORNADO AT EXPLORATION PLACE, A SCIENCE CENTER AND MUSEUM.

& **Warren Old Town Theater Grill** (316-691-9700; warren theatres.com), 353 N. Mead St., Wichita. Open for Sat.–Sun. matinees plus evening shows. More than 800 people can watch movies simultaneously in 7 theaters. A director's suite offers 22 recliner seats. Each theater features small dining tables or attached trays. Order Southwestern egg rolls, a 0.5-pound Black Angus burger, a Warren Mobster pizza, or a bite-size bananas Foster and a cocktail. Admission $10 plus $3 for 3-D features or $5 for the director's suite, not including food/beverage.

Wichita Ice Center (316-337-9199; wichitaicecenter.com), 505 W. Maple St., Wichita. Open 9–10 daily. The center features Olympic- and NHL-size rinks. Public skating sessions, lessons, special events, broomball, and speed skating are just a few activities here. Get your skates sharpened, choose a locker, and grab a bite from the snack bar. Admission for three-hour public session $6; for family of four $25; skate rental $2.

✸ Selective Shopping

& **Cero's** (316-264-5002; ceroscandy .com), 1108 E. Douglas Ave., Wichita. Open 10–5 Mon.–Fri., 10–4 Sat. This landmark candy manufacturer celebrated 125 years of continuous operation in 2010 but became an arm of the local Mental Health Association more than a decade ago. The association acquired all of the old recipes, wood paddles, and copper kettles

THE ORIGINAL COLEMAN ARC LAMP WAS FIRST SOLD IN 1901, AND NUMEROUS LAMP DESIGNS FOLLOWED.

from family members, changed some packaging, and added bows plus chocolate popcorn and logo chocolates. Watch candy makers at work and take a treat home.

COLEMAN STORE

WICHITA'S PERFORMING ARTS

& **Crown Uptown Theatre** (316-681-1566; crownuptown.com), 3207 E. Douglas Ave., Wichita. This 30-something-year-old theater offers four tiered table levels. Guests choose buffet items that include entrées, eight side dishes, soup, a salad bar, rolls, and beverages. There's also a full bar, and desserts are available for an additional charge. Adults $27–34; children 12 and under free.

& **Mosley Street Melodrama Dinner Theatre** (316-263-0222; mosleystreet.com), 234 N. Mosley, Old Town/Wichita. For more than 45 years this beloved melodrama company has offered dinner theater shows full of villains and good guys. Guests enjoy a home-style buffet dinner by Pig In! Pig Out! BBQ (vegetarian option available with advance request). Purchase alcoholic/nonalcoholic beverages and desserts such as fantasy fudge or lemon Bundt cake. Then settle in for an evening of laughter-inducing melodrama followed by a musical comedy revue.

& **Music Theatre of Wichita** (316-265-3253; musictheatreofwichita.org), 225 W. Douglas Ave., Ste. 202, Wichita. Entertainment that initially provided a summer break from the symphony season celebrates 40 years of operation in 2011. This nationally known theater company produces five musicals every year, with a mix of equity and nonequity performers, including some from Broadway and Los Angeles. Alumni of the theater, including Kristin Chenoweth, perform in almost every Broadway show. The Disney Company let this theater be one of the first to perform *Beauty and the Beast,* so their sets have been subsequently used across the nation. Must be five or older to attend.

& **Wichita Grand Opera Inc.** (316-262-8054; wichitagrandopera.org), 225 W. Douglas Ave., Century II Performing Arts Center and Concert Hall/Wichita. The professional season includes a wide range of shows, from *The Mikado* and *Carmen* to a performance by the Ukranian National Dance Company and of the comic ballet *Coppélia*. Call about events and ticket prices.

& **Wichita Symphony** (Box office, 316-267-7658; wso.org), 225 W. Douglas Ave., Century II Performing Arts Center and Concert Hall/Wichita. Check for calendar and pricing. The symphony began in 1945 and offers five to six musical series each year, from pops to classical, and blue jeans concerts, plus large free concerts during the holiday season and at the end of Riverfest.

& **INTRUST Bank Arena** (316-440-9000; intrustbankarena.com), 500 E. Waterman St., Wichita. Built with Kansas limestone, glass, steel, and brick, this constantly busy entertainment venue was initially supported by founding sponsors INTRUST Bank, Spirit AeroSystems, and Cessna, and a local sales tax. Holding up to 15,500 guests for center-stage concerts or basketball games, as well as

CROWN UPTOWN THEATRE

many smaller venues, the facility offers the Budweiser Brew Pub, Papa John's Pizza, Carlos O'Kelly's Mexican Café, and 162 beer taps throughout the arena. Party and other suites are also available.

♿ **Diamond W Chuckwagon Supper at Old Cowtown** (866-830-8283; diamondwchuckwagon.com), Old Cowtown, Wichita. Step back in time at the Old Cowtown Museum Empire House Theater as the Diamond W Wranglers serve an old-fashioned all-you-can-eat brisket dinner and beverage on tin plates and cups. Groups also may choose breakfast or lunch packages. Find your assigned seat, say the Pledge of Allegiance, hear a blessing, and chow down as you enjoy these internationally renowned performers of Western music. Drums, bass, guitar, fiddle, and vocals in close harmony characterize renditions of "Mariah," "Orange Blossom Special," and "Yellow Rose of Texas." They've played Carnegie Hall twice and have also performed in China and Germany. Ask about rates.

& **Coleman Factory Outlet and Museum** (316-264-0836), 235 N. St. Francis, Wichita. Open 9–6 Mon.–Fri., 9–1 Sat. William C. Coleman began to sell his Coleman Arc Lamp in Wichita in 1901. Between 1905 and 1927 he manufactured numerous varieties, including the Coleman Model R reading lamp. See early lamps, irons, and a coffeemaker in the tiny museum of this store, which is 1 of only 10 across the nation. Then marvel at modern coolers, tents, and camp stoves sold at discount prices to customers from around the world who make this a Wichita destination. There's even a Coleman lamp pictured on the New Guinea coin.

& **Hatman Jack's** (316-264-4881; hatmanjacks.com), 601 W. Douglas Ave., Wichita. Open 10–5:30 Mon.–Fri., 10–5 Sat. Jack Kellogg learned to make custom hats during high school and never looked back. Luciano Pavarotti, Merle Haggard, Mickey Spillane, and cast members from *Dr. Quinn, Medicine Woman* have all worn his one-of-a-kind creations. Kellogg still uses some 1890s tools to create individual hats but also stocks an endless array of men's and women's hats from all over the world and particularly from Italy and England. Two rooms showcase hundreds of colors, styles, and sizes.

& **Chilton Billiards** (316-262-3539), 300 S. Topeka St., Wichita. Open 9:30–5:30 Mon.–Sat. Pool players will love this place. The 84-year-old billiards shop offers an astonishing array of pool cues, plus deluxe pool tables, bar stools, and other adult game room equipment spanning 150,000 square feet.

HATMAN JACK'S

& **Paramount Antique Mall** (316-722-0500; paramountantiquemall .com), 13200 W. Kellogg Ave., Wichita. Open 10–7 Mon.–Fri., 10–6 Sat., noon–6 Sun; closed Thanksgiving and Christmas. Named the best antique mall in mid-America in 2004, 2006, 2007, and 2008 by Discovery Publications Inc., this antique emporium has roughly two hundred vendors who sell everything from 1950s women's coats to Coca Cola Classic bottles with their original brew and Waterford crystal. There's also a lounge area that offers a couch, TV, and free coffee and water. Check the schedule for monthly outdoor flea markets, too, from March to June.

& **Watermark Books and Café** (316-682-1181; watermarkbooks .com), 4701 E. Douglas Ave., Wichita. Open 8–8 Mon.–Fri., 8–5 Sat.–Sun. (café opens 7 AM). Book lovers have flocked to this landmark independently owned bookstore since 1977. The company also has a rare book depository downtown. They staff the store with readers, and their philosophy is, If We Don't Have It, We Can Order It. Special features include Watermark Staff Recommends—slips placed in books that staff members love—art shows, and a café whose tomato bisque and homemade focaccia are legendary.

&. **The Spice Merchant** (316-263-4121; spicemerchant.com), 1308 E. Douglas Ave., Wichita. Open 9–5:30 Mon.–Fri., 9–5 Sat. This Wichita classic has roasted premium coffee since 1985. Customers buy dozens of bulk spices and teas, watch as an employee custom-grinds their coffee from more than 60 varieties, or purchase salt and pepper mills and teapots of every shape and size. You'll find Torani syrups, panko bread crumbs, and kalamata olive spread, as well as incense and candles near the front door.

&. **City Arts** (316-337-9088; wichita arts.com), 334 N. Mead St., Wichita. Open 9–9 Mon.–Thurs., 9–8 Fri., 10–4 Sat. One large room on the first floor primarily serves as a gallery, with most adult and youth art classes and workshops taking place upstairs. Purchase hand-crocheted scarves, hand-thrown pottery, hand-strung bead necklaces, prairie burn photos, or wood wall decor cut with a scroll saw, in the small gift shop.

✳ Special Events

May: **PBR Wichita Invitational** (316-785-SEAT; pbr.com), INTRUST Bank Arena, Wichita. Enjoy cowboy showmanship during one important stop on this national professional bull riders' circuit. **Cinco de Mayo** (316-644-0714), Old Town, Wichita.

CHILTON BILLIARDS

Authentic Mexican dishes, *tejana,* Mexican folkloric music, and even a jalapeño-eating contest are part of this three-day event. **Riverfest** (877-WFIFEST; wichitariverfest.com), Wichita. Wichita's biggest party offers something for everyone. Watch the opening night parade, ethnic dancing, enormous firework displays reflected in the river, and live music. Vendors serve every kind of food imaginable, and there's a contest for every skill during this nine-day extravaganza.

July: **Mid-America All Indian Center Pow Wow** (316-350-3340), Mid-America All Indian Center, 650 N. Seneca, Wichita. Join thousands of people who enjoy singing, dancing, shopping, and food that reflect the best of American Indian culture.

August: **Wichita Black Arts Festival** (316-262-7651; call to confirm), Wichita. A parade is only the beginning at this annual celebration of African American culture.

September: **Wichita Flight Festival** (wichitaflightfestival.com), Wichita. See aircraft demonstrations including U.S. Air Force Thunderbirds, veterans ceremonies, and much more.

October: **Asian Festival** (316-689-8729; indoasian.org/waa), Century II Performing Arts Center and Concert Hall, Wichita. Wichita's Asian community has offered this festival for more than 30 years. Enjoy dances, songs, 35 food booths, and special events that include calligraphy and face decoration. **Tallgrass Film Festival** (316-974-0089), around Wichita. Billing itself as Films on the Fringe, this event has celebrated independent films since 2003.

SUBURBAN WICHITA

Suburban and small towns ring Wichita's urban core. To the south you'll find Derby, named by *Family Circle* magazine as one of the top 10 best towns for families. *U.S. News and World Report* calls it one of the best places to retire, and it's been designated a Tree City USA by the Arbor Day Foundation. The town touts its friendly neighborhoods, high-quality schools, and recreation opportunities, and more than twenty-two thousand residents call Kansas's 17th largest city home.

Railroads once provided the main source of income for the adjacent town of Mulvane. Learn about the early years at the Mulvane Historical Museum in a former renovated Santa Fe Depot. Founded in 1879, it's near five Santa Fe railroad lines. Approximately 5,500 residents live in this southern Wichita suburb.

A 1999 tornado destroyed several historical buildings in the town of Haysville, which lies at the southern edge of Wichita. The tornado eliminated a 1914 blacksmith shop and Haysville State Bank, but a replica of the building now surrounds the original vault. Today this southern suburb is experiencing a growth spurt, with more than eleven thousand residents in 2010.

Only a little over 60 years old, Park City encompasses about 6 square miles on Wichita's north side and has approximately eight thousand residents. Named for its location on the Arkansas River, Valley Center is another northern suburb. It was incorporated in 1885 and has a population that hovers around five thousand people.

The western suburb of Goddard is a town of approximately two thousand people and named for J. F. Goddard, a vice president of the Atchison, Topeka, and Santa Fe Railway in the 1880s. It's also home to Lake Afton, a popular spot for all kinds of water activities and host of the Midwest's largest music festival.

Items listed below have N, S, E, or W compass points in front of them to indicate their approximate direction from downtown Wichita.

✳ To Do

WINERIES ♿ **(S) Windswept Winery and Storey Vineyards** (620-782-3952; windsweptwinery.com), 1227 92nd Rd., Udall. Open 1–7 Mon.–Fri., 10–7 Sat., 1–7 Sun.; closes 6 PM in winter. Pick up some fresh blackberries with your wine at this family-owned operation that grows more than 5 acres of French hybrid grapes. The first vines were planted in 1999 and new offerings include Land Rush White and Land Rush Red, which pay homage to the Oklahoma Land Rush. Purchase apple and blackberry wine here, too.

& (S) **Wyldewood Cellars Winery** (316-554-9463, wyldewoodcellars.com), exit 33 off Kansas Turnpike I-35, Mulvane. Open 9–6 Mon.–Sat., noon–5 Sun. This winery currently produces more than 40 different types of wine that have received more than 300 international awards. They're particularly well known for elderberry and elderberry-blend wines, whose berries come from 18 growers, but you'll also find such varieties as Prairie Sunset wine—a white grape blend with hints of apple, pear, and citrus, and Elderflower wine, a recent favorite in Europe. Purchase sand plum gourmet jelly and root-beer fudge, plus other food items made specifically for the winery.

✳ Green Space

(W) **Cheney State Park/Cheney Lake** (316-542-3664; stateparks.com/cheney .html), 16000 NE 50th, Cheney. One of central Kansas's favorite state parks is the perfect spot for everything from sailing and swimming to fishing and hunting. It is well marked, beautifully maintained, and bicycle friendly. There's plenty of shady camping available and seven rentable cabins. Construction of Cheney Reservoir in 1965 created 9,600 lake surface acres. State park hunting and fish-

ALTHOUGH BEST KNOWN FOR THEIR ELDERBERY WINE, WYLDEWOOD CELLARS WINERY ALSO PRODUCES MANY OTHER VARIETIES.

ing licenses/permits are required. Daily vehicle fees are around $4; call for camping/cabin rates.

(S) Udall City Park (620-782-3512), Udall. Located on a ridge overlooking the Walnut/Arkansas River valleys and about 7 miles from Windswept Winery, this recently restored park features a beautiful gazebo, plenty of trees, and playground equipment. Restrooms, pavilions, and a rock blocks structure are also in the city's site improvement master plan.

✳ Lodging

BED & BREAKFASTS & **(S) Aunt Sue's Restaurant and Bed & Breakfast** (316-777-1232; auntsues mulvane.com), 1134 N. River Rd., Mulvane. This country retreat offers three log cabins, a red barn banquet facility, and an open-air chapel. Stay in the loft with its star quilt and antique furnishings; in a cabin with its queen bed, shower/bath, microwave, and in-house movies; or the secluded cottage. Get to know fellow travelers around the campfire pit or soak in a private hot tub. The Friday-only restaurant menu changes monthly but may feature parmesan chicken breast or low-fat honey-teriyaki salmon and several sides. $90–130 for lodging.

CABINS AND CAMPING ((ψ)) **(W) All Seasons RV Park** (316-722-1154; allseasonscampground.com), 15520 W. Maple St., Goddard. Located just off US 54, about 10 miles from downtown Wichita, this nicely maintained park offers 48 RV and 5 tent campsites in a rural area with plenty of trees. Wi-Fi, some groceries, propane, and laundry facilities are available. There's also a walking trail entrance, a pet walking area, and a playground on site. Reservations recommended. RV sites from $27; tent sites from $10.

✳ Where to Eat

DINING OUT (S) Luciano's (316-777-0045; restaurantlucianos.com),

216 W. Main St., Mulvane. Open 11–4 Wed.–Mon., 4–9 Mon./Wed.–Sat., 4–8 Sun. Enter an Italian vineyard, which has become an area favorite. Born in Italy, Luciano met and married an American and then settled here, where local wheat fields and sunflowers reminded him of his home in Tuscany. Enjoy calamari over greens with herbs and spices, baked lasagna, choice-grade Angus beef, and tiramisu. Try handmade gnocchi on Wednesdays, hear live music on Sundays, and pair Italian wines with your meal. Dinner reservations recommended. Moderate-priced entrées.

EATING OUT & **(N) Red Stone Grill** (316-821-9696), 5355 N. Broadway St., Park City. Open 7–8 Mon.–Sat., 7–2 Sun. Southwest murals and colors decorate this popular spot that offers such specials as blackened chicken breast with Cajun shrimp and two sides for under $10. Other favorites include their burgers and onion rings or nachos. You can also order pasta, chicken, and fish dishes, salads of all sizes and varieties, and even steaks. Inexpensive.

& **(N) Bravo's Italiani** (316-755-9966), 218 W. Main St., Valley Center. Open 11–9 Tues.–Thurs., 11–10 Fri.–Sat., 11–9 Sun. A restaurant is doing something right when a soldier asks about shipping their pizza to

Iraq. Customers also like their potato gnocchi, hot subs, and lasagna, plus other pasta, chicken, and seafood dishes. There are daily lunch specials, plus wine and limited bar offerings. Inexpensive.

♂ ♿ **(N) Big Larry's Burgers** (316-755-9858) 328 S. Meridian, Valley Center. Open 11–8 Mon.–Sat. This cheerful spot with a diner feel is known for their fresh-cut fries offered with cheese or chili and cheese. Add fries and a drink to your mushroom Swiss or bacon cheddar burger order for about $3. Or try their Philly cheesesteak with a butterscotch malt. Inexpensive.

♿ **(N) Auntie C's** (316-744-7244), 425 E. 61st St., Park City. Open 6–2 daily. Dine on chile *rojo* with eggs, hash browns, Spanish rice, and beans amid Western decor, from cowboy photos to bleached skulls. Or try andouille sausage with eggs, hash browns, and toast or a biscuit. You'll also find lunch and dessert specials here. Inexpensive.

♿ **(S) Mija's Café** (316-788-8922), 120 N. Baltimore, Derby. Open 7–2 Mon.–Fri., 7–11 Sat. Homemade hash browns and fresh-cut fries are claims to fame at this longtime eatery with a diner vibe. At dinnertime try chicken-fried steak or *bulgoki*—an Asian stir-fry dish. You'll also find plenty of breakfast options and sandwiches, plus some kid-friendly items. No credit cards. Inexpensive.

♿ ⛾ **(S) Little Busters Sports Bar** (316-788-1299), 457 N. Baltimore Ave., Derby. Open 11–2 AM weekends, 11–11:30 PM weekdays. Known as the home of Derby's best burger, this is also a great spot for Reubens and Phillies, enchiladas, or ribs. Food and drink specials are often available,

with Friday karaoke and Saturday evening bands.

♿ **(S) Talliano's Pizzeria** (316-788-8315), 408 N. Baltimore, Derby. Open 11–10 daily. Enjoy lunch or dinner buffets with a pizza bar and salad bar and create your own pizza with your choice of crust, sauce, and toppings. Specialty pizzas include From the Garden and Taco-Taco-Taco. It's a cozy, yet large restaurant in a small strip mall. Inexpensive.

♿ **(W) Gerrard's Restaurant** (316-0794-8606), 20201 W. Kellogg Dr., Goddard. Open 6–9 daily. Gerrard's has served great breakfasts and more for about 30 years. There are daily specials and a daily buffet with breakfast available anytime, including the popular 2 x 4 special with two griddle-cakes, two eggs, two sausage patties, and two bacon slices. Quarter-pound burgers, tuna melts, or breaded catfish filets are other favorites. Sepia-tone photos of 1916 school girls, an African queen, and old aviation shots surround customers as they enjoy strawberry rhubarb pie.

✳ Entertainment

♂ ♿ **(W) Tanganyika Wildlife Park** (316-794-8954; twpark.com), 1037 S. 183rd St. W, Goddard. Open April and Oct., 9–5 Fri.–Sun.; May–Sept. 9–5. What began as a zoo supply business has evolved into a privately owned park where visitors interact with endangered animals in an open, natural setting. Jim and Sherri Fouts have 75 years experience in the wildlife industry, and this is the largest breeder of snow leopards in the world. Lemurs adopt a Zen-like lineup, tigers snooze in the sun, and kids interact with large turtles. Pat a kangaroo or take a camel ride. Then

IF A KANGAROO APPROACHES AT TANGANYIKA WILDLIFE PARK, IT'S OKAY TO PET HIM.

✈ **(S) Rock River Rapids Aquatic Park** (316-788-POOL; rockriver rapids.com/#), 1900 E. James St., Derby. Open late May–mid-August. You can see this water park's mammoth, two-story slide from blocks away. There are additional slides, plus a tree-house-themed play structure with an emptying 1,000-gallon water bucket, and multiple pools. Adults 18 and older $8; children 3–17 $7; children 2 and under free with adult admission.

♿ **(N) Prairie Rose Chuckwagon Supper** (316-778-2111; prairierose chuckwagon.com), 15231 SW Parallel St., Benton. Open Thurs.–Sat., every second/fourth Sun. The Prairie Rose is a huge place, with a 30'- x- 50' pavilion, an RV park, and an opera

visit the snack bar or gift shop. Strollers, wagons, wheelchairs, and electric scooters are also available. Adult $12; children 3–12 $8; children under 3/seniors 90 and up free; seniors 60–89 $9; military discount with ID.

✈ **(W) Lake Afton Public Observatory** (316-978-3191; webs.wichita .edu/lapo), MacArthur Rd./39th St. S and 247th St. W, Lake Afton County Park, Cheney. Check for schedule of public programs. A 16-inch telescope operated by Wichita State University's Fairmount Center for Science and Mathematics Education anchors the center of this long, one-story museum building. Look at Kansas meteorites, try out astronomy-based computer games, and enjoy programs such as "The Moon and Gas Giants" or photography events. No credit cards. Adults $4; children 6–12 $3; family rate available.

PRAIRIE ROSE CHUCKWAGON SUPPER

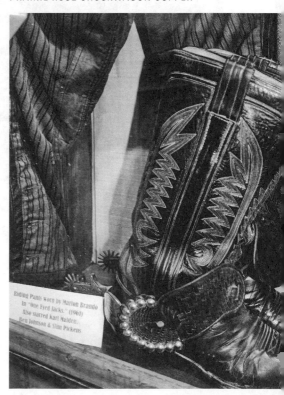

FLY-IN FUN

& **Stearman Field** (316-778-1035, stearmanfield.com), 14789 SW 30th St., Benton. Inside a metal hanger there's a modern restaurant and bar full of air memorabilia such as an antique Sinclair Aircraft gas pump. Every third Saturday watch fly-ins while savoring a giant breakfast burrito or visit free, all-day events with bands and fireworks in June and October. This is a great place for flight training and the menu is so popular that pilots fly here for lunch from all over. Hear smooth jazz from the parking lot while two flat-screen TVs offer flying scenes inside.

& **Beaumont Hotel Fly-Ins** (620-843-2422; hotelbeaumontks.com), 11651 SE Main, 45 miles east of Wichita on US 96/400. Established in 1879, this one-time stagecoach station has become a favorite spot for fly-in breakfasts, which take place on occasional Saturday mornings. Pilots taxi along main street and then park in front of the hotel, utilizing its own 2,600-foot grass airstrip in the midst of 66 rural acres.

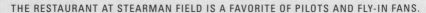

THE RESTAURANT AT STEARMAN FIELD IS A FAVORITE OF PILOTS AND FLY-IN FANS.

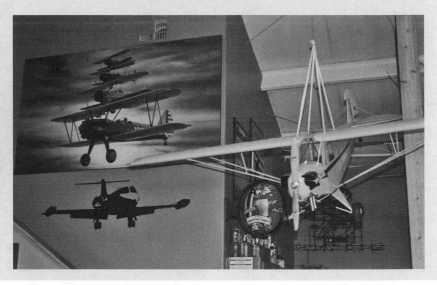

house that seats 330. Catch a Hopalong Cassidy movie or browse riding pants worn by Marlon Brando and a dozen Buck Jones posters. Enjoy dinner and a Western stage show in the Prairie Rose Opera House. Supper show for adults $30; children 6–12 $10; children 3–5 $5; reservations required.

(N) 81 Speedway (316-755-1781), 7700 N. Broadway, Park City. See championship dirt track auto racing, from sprint cars to stock cars, with the traveling O'Reilly/National Championship Racing Association and its various teams. The speedway also hosts numerous special events. Ages 10 and up $9; children 6–10 $5.

(S) Derby's Bronze Sculptures (316-788-1559), 611 N. Mulberry, city hall/Derby. A dozen bronze sculptures are located throughout town depicting family-friendly activities such as children flying kites and playing baseball. Locations are shown on a map available at city hall.

✳ Selective Shopping

&. **(W) Goddard Gunnery** (316-794-3333; gunnery.com), 20410 W. Kellogg Dr., Goddard. Open noon–6 Mon.–Fri., 9–5 Sat. This old-fashioned gun shop with an up-to-date inventory recently moved to a spacious new facility just north of US 54. Purchase firearms such as Smith & Wesson and Winchester or check out dozens of fishing poles, camouflage gear, and gun safes as tall as a small man.

✳ Special Events

April: **Prairie Rose Western Days** (316-778-2121; prairierosechuck wagon.com), Prairie Rose/Benton, late April–early May. This entertainment extravaganza features cowboy songs around the fire, mountain man and cowboy encampments, wagon rides, a petting zoo, Mexican *charros* on horseback wearing beautiful costumes, a black powder shoot, gunfights, and more.

June: **Frisco Water Tower Festival** (620-843-2591), downtown Beaumont. First weekend celebrating this 1885 historic site. Enjoy a catfish dinner and a pancake breakfast at the Beaumont Hotel, a parade, antiques and crafts, and a street dance.

July: **Midwest Rockfest** (877-442-3301; midwestrockfest.com), Lake Afton, Goddard, third weekend. Kansas's and the Midwest's largest outdoor rock festival. Major artists such as Styx and Twisted Sister rock out at this two-day event where many visitors also camp.

EAST OF WICHITA

Butler County is known as the Prairie Chicken Capital of the World, making this a favorite hunting destination from November to January. It's also a water-lover's haven, with El Dorado State Lake in the neighborhood. The town of Augusta has approximately 8,500 residents. Today, a new brick and concrete roundabout and Americans with Disabilities Act (ADA) curb cuts complement original brick streets in this Kansas Main Street City. There are also five parks, including the 26.3-acre Garvin Park and the 265-acre Augusta City Lake. C. N. James established a log trading post here that still exists as part of the local museum. A contest was held to name the town between his wife, Augusta, and Henrietta, the name of a local business owner. Augusta's Red Brick District was established along State Street in 1868, and the first train arrived here in 1881 as livestock production and agriculture activities increased. By the 1900s, the Santa Fe and Frisco railroads served the town, and discoveries of oil and natural gas offered additional employment opportunities. The Augusta Oil, Gas, Mining, and Prospecting Company was formed in 1904, and the oil industry was a driving force in the town's continued development. Historic landmarks include the art deco Augusta Theatre, the Vietnam War memorial at Elmwood Cemetery, and the Kansas Museum of Military History, a huge building full of more than ten thousand vehicles, articles, and permanent displays relating to military life. One of Augusta's most famous citizens, Payne Dunham, was on the honor roll when she graduated from Augusta High School and died two days before her grandson, Barack Obama, was elected president.

The town of Augusta hosted a trading post by the late 1800s, followed by a hotel and a general store. Vincent Smith filed his land claim nearby in 1869, and other settlers began to arrive the next year. The Frisco Railway was completed through the township in 1880, and G. M. Pattison received title to what would later become Andover.

After platting of the original town site, the town name was changed from Cloud City to Andover. Other businesses operating in Andover during the late 1880s and early 1900s included a hotel, a bank, a lumberyard, a blacksmith shop, a millinery shop, and a post office. The first school arrived in 1882. Passenger trains traveled through the town from 1885 through 1960. In 1968 Andover added a major annexation, growing the population from five hundred to two thousand residents. By the 1990s the population had grown to include more than four thousand people.

A devastating F-5 tornado swept through Andover in April 1991, killing 13 people and leaving nearly a third of its residents homeless. In all, more than 300 homes, 10 businesses, and 2 churches were destroyed. Offers of help poured in from surrounding cities and organizations and the town began to rebuild. A small memorial lies near the edge of town.

In 2005 Andover passed a sales tax increase that helped fund construction of a new library at Andover's Central Park. As part of Butler County, the town also offers easy access to big-city amenities.

The town of El Dorado has approximately 12,500 residents, and its name is Spanish for "the gilded." The first party of settlers arrived here in 1857, and the town grew quickly due to agricultural crops and raising livestock. El Dorado serves as a gateway to the Kansas Flint Hills and offers enormous outdoor opportunities at El Dorado Lake and State Park. The downtown area provides dining and shopping options, plus a series of bronze sculptures depicting everyday life, a 10' x 25' Flint Hills mural, and a terrific art gallery in a historical building. There's also a delightful student art gallery at Butler Community College. In addition, El Horse is home to the popular Iron Course Concert Hall, with energetic weekend music performances by artists from all over. Arts are so prevalent, in fact, that the then governor Kathleen Sebelius named El Dorado a City of the Arts in October 2006.

Kansas once produced approximately 9 percent of the world's oil and many oil wells still operate in the El Dorado area, with related service industries and a refinery. This is also where you'll find the Kansas Oil Museum (and Butler County History Center), which provides a clear summary of the industry in this area.

AUGUSTA RED BRICK DISTRICT

GUIDANCE Andover Area Chamber of Commerce/Convention and Visitors Bureau (316-733-0648; andoverchamber.com), 1607 E. Central, Andover.

Augusta Chamber of Commerce/ Convention and Visitors Bureau (316-775-6339; chamberofaugusta .org), 112 E. Sixth Ave., Augusta.

A DISPLAY AT THE KANSAS OIL MUSEUM EDUCATES VISITORS ABOUT THE FORMATION OF OIL IN THE EARTH.

El Dorado Convention and Visitors Bureau (877-858-5600; visit eldoradoks.com), 201 E. Central, El Dorado. Open 8–5 weekdays.

✳ To See

MUSEUMS

In El Dorado

& **Kansas Oil Museum and Butler County History Center** (316-321-9333; kansasoilmuseum.org), 383 E. Central Ave., El Dorado. Open 9–5 Mon.–Sat. Allow some time to tour this fascinating museum, which also tells the story of ranching and farming in the county. A research center features genealogy information and rare books. Learn about Grasshopper Year 1874 and El Dorado's Stapleton Well, which produced twenty-five thousand barrels of oil daily from around 1916 to 1917. Operate scale models of oil rigs and then visit a replica oil town including full-size rigs, a fully equipped doctor's office, and a period home. Adults $4; seniors $3; students 6–18 $2; children 5 and under free.

Coutts Memorial Museum of Art (316-321-1212), 110 N. Main St., El Dorado. Open 9–5 Tues./Thurs., 1–5 Wed./Fri., noon–4 Sat. This museum inventory features a thousand original works that include an enormous collection of Frederic Remington's bronze sculptures, plus many examples of Prairie Print Makers art and local artists' work. Admire a magnificent chandelier on the main floor, where you may also see a painting with three-dimensional geese springing from the surface. Free.

Elsewhere

Augusta Historical Society and Historical Museum (316-775-5655), 303 State St., Augusta. Open 11–3 Mon.–Fri., 1–4 Sat.–Sun.; tours avail-

REMINGTON SCULPTURE

able. Volunteers staff this museum, which includes the C. N. James Trading Post log cabin, erected in 1868, and the town's first building. It previously housed the store of C. N. James, a post office, a Masonic Lodge, Baptist and Methodist services, and a public school. The Gary Kroeker Blacksmith Shop was established in 2009 in honor of local resident Gary Kroeker, who enjoyed teaching people about the blacksmithing craft. Free.

✳ To Do

BICYCLING El Dorado Bike Trails (316-321-7180), 618 NE Bluestem Rd., El Dorado State Park/El Dorado. Four cycling trails travel through this 12,500-acre area of water and parkland. It's a great place for camping or renting a cabin. Use the full-service marina and swimming beaches, plus horseback and hiking trails, too. Mountain bike trails range from 0.75 mile to 12 miles.

BOATING AND FISHING El Dorado State Park and Lake (316-321-7180), 618 NE Bluestem Rd., El Dorado. With 8,000 acres of water, this army corps project was completed in 1981. Air-conditioned cabins lie in a grove of trees at Shady Creek with campsites available at Walnut River and several other campgrounds. Swimming beaches and shower, restroom, and laundry facilities, plus ADA-accessible playgrounds, are also available. Boulder Bluff Horse Campground sites offer individual horse corrals. There's a large marina, rolling hills, bike and walking paths, and a private sailing club that offers reciprocal use to members from any other sailing club in Kansas.

Butler State Fishing Lake (620-876-5730), 1 mile north and 3 miles west of Latham. It's hard to believe this is a man-made lake after 50 years, with its dense vegetation and loads of native grasses. Catch a catfish or bass from one of three fishing piers. Hunters appreciate the quiet and beautiful marsh area, which is a great spot to shoot waterfowl.

GOLF Prairie Trails Golf and Dining (316-321-4114; prairietrails.com), 1100 Country Club Ln., El Dorado. Open 7–sunset. Built as a private club, this compact but challenging 18-hole course is now owned by the city. In the clubhouse, enjoy the Friday prime rib special and try a burger, vegetarian pasta, or Reuben at lunch. Inexpensive dining. Par 71, 18 holes, 6,438 yards.

Cedar Pines of Andover (316-733-8070), 1208 W US 54, Andover. There's a teaching focus at this course and a swing trainer available for use during lessons. Green number 5 features an artificial surface after sustaining serious damage. Play two rounds in less than two hours. Par 33, 9 holes, 2,280 yards.

✳ Green Space

In Augusta
Augusta City Lake and Garvin Park (316-775-4510), North Washington St., Augusta. With approximately 26 acres, this park is a favorite for strolls through nature or playing Frisbee. It also features four baseball diamonds, an amphitheater, playground equipment, and a picnic shelter. The 265-acre lake offers fishing and sailing opportunities.

PlayPark Pointe (316-755-4510), N. Ohio St. near Augusta City Lake, Augusta. Multiple turrets and slides make this a great playground where kids can blow off steam.

Central Park (316-733-6940), 1607 E. Central Ave., Andover. Take a walk along the paths that travel through this 80-acre park or catch a fish from the dock. Located in the park, the new Andover Public Library and its in-house coffee shop provide another break.

✳ Lodging

HOTELS AND MOTELS ♿ ((ʘ))
Augusta Inn (316-775-5979), 712 W. Seventh Ave., Augusta. Each room offers a refrigerator and microwave with coffee in the lobby. It's clean and comfortable with a pleasant staff. Enjoy a continental breakfast each morning. $60.

✳ Where to Eat

EATING OUT

In Augusta
Miller's Five Drive-In (316-775-9989), 330 State St., Augusta. Open 10–8:30 Mon.–Sat., 10–6 Sun. An Augusta landmark for 47 years, this tiny burger joint's facade and menu haven't changed much over the decades, and pricing is still terrific. Enjoy your milk shake at one of four street-side picnic tables. Inexpensive.

♿ ((ʘ)) **Red Brick Inn** (316-775-1200), 403 Walnut, Augusta. Open for breakfast, lunch, and dinner. From the moment Tim Kasting and Steve Barlay opened their restaurant they wanted to be part of the community. Special activities include dances for high school students, mystery dinner theater, and live music on Friday nights. Customers love the new patio area for outdoor dining and appreciate the bar. The eggs Benedict is a breakfast favorite. Try their awesome Reuben, Maui burger, chef salad, or steak, too. Inexpensive–moderate.

In El Dorado
♿ **Susie's Chili Parlor** (316-321-2242), 124 S. Main, El Dorado. Open 6–8 Mon.–Fri., 6–3 Sat. Barack Obama's grandmother once worked at this El Dorado landmark, which is now just as famous for its pies. Try the decadent coconut cream or peanut butter pie. Lunch choices include

MILLER'S FIVE DRIVE-IN HAS OFFERED BURGERS AND ICE-CREAM TREATS FOR ALMOST 50 YEARS.

tuna melts, chef salads, and giant cheeseburgers. There's also a huge breakfast menu, including the breakfast special with two slices of bacon or a sausage patty, an egg, hash browns, toast, and coffee. Inexpensive.

Y **True Lies** (316-320-9255), 607 N. Oil Hill Rd., El Dorado. Open 5 AM–2 AM daily. Go for the small town atmosphere and start your day with a ranch scrambler or biscuits and gravy. Or join the crowd on weekend evenings to hear live music while eating hand-cut Kansas steaks and comfort food such as chicken-fried steaks, liver and onions, burgers, or shrimp, plus daily lunch specials. Mostly inexpensive.

Elsewhere
Y **Timbuktu Bar and Grill** (316-733-5630), 1251 N. Andover Rd., Andover. Open 11–midnight. Many people know this spot as home of the best burger in the world since 1982. It's also a favorite local hangout, with poker and bike nights and free popcorn days. The original burger is half a pound, topped with American cheese and fried onions. Try their jalapeño bottle caps or minitacos with an ultracold beer in a mason jar mug. Inexpensive.

✳ Entertainment

In El Dorado
𝄞 **Flint Hills Overland Wagon Train Trips** (316-321-6300; wagon trainkansas.com), El Dorado. Leave your electronics at home and return to a simpler time. Panoramic views of the Flint Hills are a big part of these one-day and weekend tours, designed to give guests a true glimpse of pioneer life. You'll also enjoy hearty pioneer meals, singing, and storytelling

around the campfire and an all-around unforgettable daylong or weekend experience. Check for rates.

& Y **Iron Horse Concert Hall** (316-321-6348; The Flinthills Music Guild; shorock.com/ironhorse), 315.5 S. Main St., El Dorado. Check website for schedule. Tucked in behind the Circle Gallery and open on Saturday nights, this surprising concert hall seats 88 people who travel from all over the state to enjoy bluegrass, folk, country, Celtic, and other music during about 10 months of the year. Iron Horse has operated here for 10 years. Adults $12 and up; senior rate available; children under 12 free.

& **El Dorado Main Street Sculpture Program** (877-858-5600), multiple locations, El Dorado. Bronze sculptures placed throughout the downtown area represent multiple individual donations and depict everything from three children balancing on a log to the Little Fisherman statue and a mother sitting cross-legged on the ground while embracing her young daughter. Location maps are available from the El Dorado Convention and Visitors Bureau.

& **Butler Community College Erman B. White Gallery** (316-322-3325), 901 S. Haverhill Rd., El Dorado. Open 10–4 weekdays. A large room of student art ranges from hand-thrown pottery to captivating pencil drawings. The college also offers a permanent exhibit called Sculpture without Walls—a series of sculptures scattered throughout the campus—with a map available. Ten art shows are held each year.

Elsewhere
Stone Arch Bridges of Butler County Tour (1-800-278-3697; tour

butlercountyks.com), throughout Butler County. Nearly a dozen spectacular stone arch bridges are sprinkled throughout the county. Obtain directions through tourbutlercountyks .com, and then wear comfortable shoes to access slopes and the best views of some bridges.

Augusta Historic Theatre (316-775-3661; augustahistorictheatre.com), 523 State Council, Augusta. Movies shown 7:30 Fri.–Sat., 2 Sun.; additional summer hours and special events. This 75-year-old theater is known far and wide as the first whose interior was lit entirely by neon. It joined the National Register of Historic Places in 1999. Each individual letter outside has its own neon color, and sunbursts decorate the upper marquee. Built by private owners for $70,000, the 633-seat art deco theater also features wall-spanning, hand-painted murals, and handmade ornamental plaster. The Augusta Arts Council acquired the theater in 1989 for use as a movie house and community arts center.

✳ Selective Shopping

In El Dorado
&. **Walter's Flowers and Interiors** (316-321-1740), 124 N. Main St., El Dorado. Open 8–6 Mon.–Sat. This delightful 9,000-square-foot shop has won awards for its floral and interior design and works with customers from across the nation. You could easily spend an hour or two looking at the beautiful furniture and hundreds of home accessories amid brightly painted walls.

&. **Circle Gallery and Frame Shop** (316-321-2105), 315 S. Main St., El Dorado. Open 10–6 Mon.–Fri., 10–2 Sat., 6–10 Sun., and when the Iron

Horse Concert Hall (see *Entertainment*) is open in back. It's been more than 36 years since this gallery and frame shop began to offer custom framing services. The long, narrow space features handmade jewelry, paintings, scroll saw carving, and much more, mostly by regional artists. Framing services are a big part of what they do, and there's some consignment art on hand.

District 142, 142 N. Main St., El Dorado. The town's newest retail and dining group includes Beyond Napa Private Cellars (316-321-2345), Salon Knotty and Day Spa (316-322-0211), Satchel Creek Steaks (316-320-1937), and Scooter's Coffee House (316-322-0211). Look for more additions as construction progresses.

In Andover
Andover Antique Mall LLC (316-733-8999), 656 N. Andover Rd., Andover. Open 10–6 Mon.–Sat., noon–6 Sun. Visit 30,000 square feet with 60 dealers, some of whom have multiple booths. You'll find enormous variety here at reasonable prices, and you'll need a couple hours to take a good look. Choose from guns, china, loads of antique furniture, a jukebox, a craps table, and old Fisher Price toys; there's something for everyone.

In Augusta
Pigeon's Roost Mall (316-775-2279), 601 State St., Augusta. Open 10–5 Mon.–Sat., 12–4 Sun. Tour two huge floors of antiques and collectibles in this expansive treasure house, plus some items in the basement. They sell everything from kitchen iron shelf fixtures to antique sewing machines and table lamps. Take the elevator or enjoy the furnishings decorating each stair landing.

EL DORADO LAKE IS A MAJOR RECREATION DRAW IN THIS AREA.

✳ Special Events

May: **Jazz, Blues, and Swing Festival** (316-321-3088), El Dorado. Three stages offer performances by local, professional, high school, and college musical artists, and there's even a dance contest.

June: **Chautauqua Art Fair** (316-321-3088), downtown El Dorado. Regional artists gather to help promote public appreciation of art and sell their work. Classes and demonstrations are also available.

July: **Prairie Port Festival** (316-321-1841), El Dorado. What a way to celebrate the holiday! Four days of activities include a pageant queen contest, bingo, a large parade, and celebrity concert, plus food and arts/crafts vendors.

October: **Augusta Historical Museum's Yesteryear Fair** (316-775-5655), Augusta. Call for specific date. See blacksmithing, log hewing, a Walnut Valley Muzzleloaders display, steam engines, and narrow gauge trains, or ride on a horse-drawn buggy. See 19th-century crafts inside the museum cabin.

November: **Celebration of Freedom** (316-321-3150), El Dorado. For a full week El Dorado offers activities for veterans and speakers, plus concerts, social gatherings, and loads of food.

December: **Annual Christmas Parade of Lights and Holiday Home Tour** (316-775-6329), Augusta. Augusta's celebration of the Christmas season has become a beloved annual tradition.

South-Central Kansas: Flint Hills Country

6

INTRODUCTION

Once you've reached the edge of the Kansas Flint Hills several times, it's easy to recognize the change in terrain. During springtime the hills turn brilliant green and are strewn with wildflowers as far as the eye can see.

When shallow seas receded from this area many millions of years ago, limestone, shale, and plenty of fossils remained. Zebulon Pike christened the Flint Hills in the early 1800s after noticing the large concentration of flint in this rolling, undulating landscape. This is the nation's only remaining area of tallgrass and a true Kansas treasure. In fact, author William Least Heat-Moon recognized their beauty in his book *PrairyErth*.

EAST OF HUTCHINSON

Arkansas City has grown up where the Arkansas and Walnut Rivers intersect and lies at the intersection of US 166 and US 77. However, despite the spelling of its name, this *Arkansas* is pronounced differently than the state name. In this area, pronunciation of the river's and the town's name is Ar-KAN-sas, with the second *s* also said aloud. Because this pronunciation can be confusing, many people simply call the town Ark City.

White settlers gradually moved into the area beginning in the 1860s, and the town was supposedly established by 1870. When the Cherokee Strip Land Run began in the 1890s, the city's population briefly leapt to one hundred and fifty thousand, a number that quickly dropped to five thousand after the run ended. Famous and infamous folks also came through town in the late 1800s, including Buffalo Bill Cody and a band of outlaws called the James-Younger Gang.

After railroads reached Ark City, the town prospered for many years until railroad activity dwindled substantially by the 1980s. Today major employers include Creekstone Farms Premium Beef and Wal-Mart, and the city is working to improve its downtown area. The city's population is about the same as that of nearby Winfield—around twelve thousand people—with a median household income of approximately $30,000.

A million-dollar Main Street face-lift is transforming the small town of Caldwell, at the edge of the Chisholm Trail, where few empty commercial buildings remain. The KanOkla telephone company is headquartered here, and the town of approximately 1,200 residents offers multiple restaurants.

McPherson was named after Gen. James McPherson, a Union general who died during the 1864 Battle of Atlanta. It was incorporated in May 1872, and by 1879 the Santa Fe and Union Pacific Railroads arrived. The Missouri Pacific and Rock Island Railroads came along soon afterward. Oil was discovered in the county right before the Great Depression, saving it from economic challenges faced by many other towns.

Today nearly fourteen thousand residents call McPherson home, where there's a vibrant downtown full of restaurants, shops, and the restored McPherson Opera House, plus 12 city-maintained parks. McPherson is a Kansas Main Street City. It's also the home of the first Olympic basketball champions from 1936, who are the subjects of a new mural painted by local high school students.

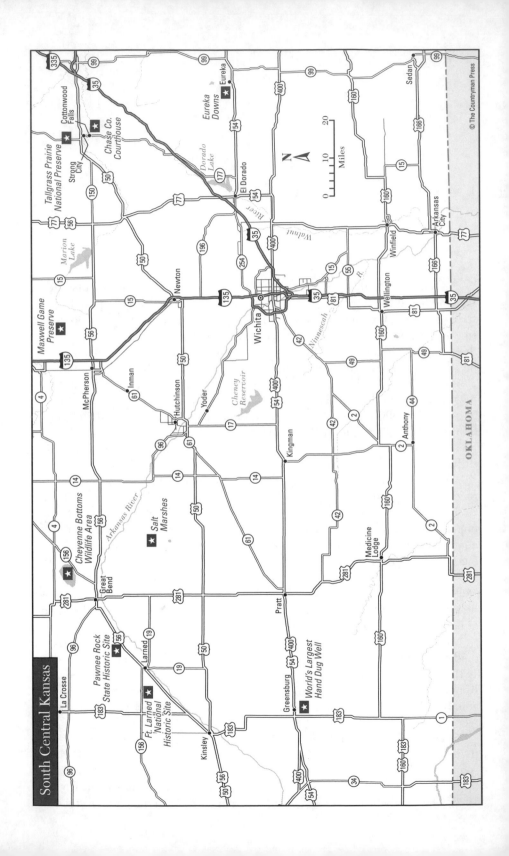

South Central Kansas

© The Countryman Press

Located at US 81/I-135, McPherson is close to two large cities—Hutchinson and Salina.

You'll see hundreds of grazing buffalo and elk at Maxwell Wildlife Refuge outside of nearby Canton, and huge flocks of migratory birds at the McPherson Valley Wetlands. And, for a wonderful information resource about the state, visit the Kansas Sampler Center in nearby Inman.

This small town has several historical spots, from the Santa Fe Trail Marker just north of town to the tiny white 1906 Telephone Office and the faded red Historic Flour Mill, built in the 1890s. It is also home to the Kansas Sampler Foundation, whose mission is to preserve and sustain rural culture. Foundation activities include the annual Kansas Sampler Festival, which showcases the talents of state residents, and 8 Wonders of Kansas, a program that recognizes the state's best restaurants, historical attractions, natural beauty, and more. Stop by their barnlike office building for informational brochures. See a Stan Herd mural that depicts the town in 1910, a beautifully maintained 1957 Rock Island Caboose, and the fully equipped 1887 Rock Island Depot.

Situated north of Wichita and along I-135, the town of Newton has nearly twenty thousand residents whose median income is approximately $40,000. Throughout several blocks of the downtown area, there are many restaurants and coffee shops, plus retail establishments selling office supplies, books, and antiques.

What is now a peaceful and calm urban environment was considered one of the wickedest western towns during the early 1870s, largely because of a gunfight that resulted in the deaths of eight men. Many Mennonite immigrants followed the Bernhard and Wilhelmina Warkentin family here, where they built a magnificent Victorian home that is currently a museum and listed on the National Register of Historic Places.

By 1872, Newton benefited from its distinction as a railhead for the Chisholm Trail, plus western terminal for the Atchison, Topeka, and Santa Fe Railway. In fact, Newton remained a major dispatching center for the railroad until the mid-1980s. A military presence was especially strong here during World War II, when the U.S. Navy acquired the city's airport for use as a naval air station.

Surrounded by blue stem grass and located in the heart of the Kansas Flint Hills, Winfield is a music-loving town that lies 17 miles north of Oklahoma at the intersection of US 77 and US 160. Nearly twelve thousand people call this prosperous small south-central city home, and residents have a median family income of more than $50,000.

Native Americans and white settlers both traveled through the Walnut valley for many years before the Santa Fe Railroad line arrived in 1879. Only 20 years later, Winfield's population had reached nearly six thousand, with all of the amenities expected in a growing town, such as newspapers, banks, flour mills, and schools.

The discovery of oil and helium in the surrounding area also enhanced Winfield's growth, with eight oil fields operating nearby in 1925. After the Depression and during World War II the War Department built Strother Field here, with an influx of air force families to the area until the war ended.

A flurry of building marked Winfield's 100th birthday in 1973, including an expanded hospital, a new courthouse and high school, and use of Strother Field as a municipal airport. The now internationally renowned acoustic and bluegrass Walnut Valley Festival was getting started at about this time, and news spread that Winfield was a town that loved music. By the early 1990s, Winfield was named number 56 among the best small towns in America. A small four-year college, community theater, 18-hole golf course, and winery, plus restaurants and shops, all contribute to the city's quality of life.

Eli Yoder founded the small town that bears his name in 1889, near the center of surrounding Amish communities. It remains a small picturesque town where Amish horse-drawn buggies juxtapose with thriving modern businesses, from furniture and antique stores to bulk foods and mercantile shops.

GUIDANCE These organizations serve communities in south-central Kansas:

Arkansas City Chamber of Commerce (620-442-0236), 106 S. Summit, Arkansas City. Open 9–5 weekdays.

Chase County Chamber of Commerce (620-273-8469), 318 Broadway, Cottonwood Falls. Open noon–4 daily.

City of Inman (620-585-2122; inmanks.org), 104 N. Main, Inman.

McPherson Convention and Visitors Bureau (620-241-3340), 306 N. Main., McPherson. Open 8–5 weekdays.

Newton Convention and Visitors Bureau (316-283-7555; thenewtonchamber .org; ask for Jennifer Muller), 500 N. Main St., Newton. Open 8–5 Mon.–Thurs., 8–4 Fri.

Wellington Kansas Chamber of Commerce Convention and Visitors Bureau (620-326-7466; whscrusaders.cc), 207 S. Washington, Wellington.

Winfield Area Chamber of Commerce/Convention and Tourism (620-221-2421), 123 E. Ninth St., Winfield. Open 8–5.

GETTING THERE *By air or train:* The nearest full-service airport is in Wichita. **AMTRAK's Southwest Chief** serves Newton (414 N. Main St.) and Hutchinson (North Walnut and East Third Streets). *By bus:* The nearest **Greyhound** stop serves Emporia (620-340-0484). Go to 2000 Industrial Rd./Short Stop Phillips 66.

GETTING AROUND Your best bet is a personal car with good ground clearance that will allow you to easily navigate some rugged roads, which lead to select natural wonders.

MEDICAL EMERGENCY (arranged alphabetically by city name)

Smith County Memorial Hospital (785-282-6845), 614 S. Main St., Arkansas City.

South Central Kansas Regional Medical Center (620-442-2500), 216 W. Birch, Arkansas City.

Sumner County Hospital (620-845-6492), 601 S. Osage St., Caldwell.

Memorial Hospital (620-241-2250), 1000 Hospital Dr., McPherson.

Sumner Regional Medical Center (620-326-7451), 1323 N. A St., Wellington.

William Newton Memorial Hospital (620-221-2300), 1300 E. Fifth Ave., Winfield.

✴ To See

HISTORIC PLACES, LANDMARKS, AND SITES

In Newton

Warkentin House (316-283-3113), 211 E. First St., Newton. Open 1–4:30 Sat.–Sun. (longer summer hours). Built for Bernhard and Wilhelmina Eisenmayer Warkentin, between 1886 and 1887, this stunning, fully furnished 20-room home serves as a museum and lies in the state's largest residential historical district. After moving his family here, Warkentin encouraged Mennonite farmers to follow. This was the first home in Newton with an electric elevator. Etched leather on the walls looks like masonry, and the dining room table has 12 leaves. Czech chandeliers and built-in wood cupboards surrounding one fireplace are other custom features. Adults $3; children 5–12 $1.50.

Newton AMTRAK Station, 414 N. Main, Newton. Open midnight–8 AM weekdays, 1:30 AM–4 AM weekends. Closed for ticketing on weekends. This beautifully maintained massive brick building was originally built in 1929 to serve the Atchison, Topeka and Santa Fe Railroad. There's an 1871 drinking well out front that was considered the city's best water source for several years after it was built.

Elsewhere

Chase County Courthouse (620-273-8469), 300 Pearl St., Cottonwood Falls. Open 8–5 Mon.–Fri. (no holidays). Tour the oldest operating courthouse in Kansas. Built in 1873, this lovely limestone building sits near the edge of downtown. Guided tours $4; 12 and under free.

Roniger Memorial Museum (620-273-6310), southwest corner of Courthouse Square, Cottonwood Falls. With more than ten thousand American Indian artifacts, the collection of arrowheads here is the largest in the state. A flood in 1951 unearthed many of these artifacts, left behind in an abandoned Indian camping area. George and Frank Roniger created the museum from their extensive artifact collection. Other items include many stuffed animals and wild birds from this area and historical memorabilia. Free.

The Mennonite Settlement Museum (620-947-3775), Hillsboro. Open 10–12 and 1:30–4 Tues.–Fri., 2–4 Sat.–Sun.; for guided tours only. Beginning in 1874, Russian and Polish Mennonites built more than a dozen settlement villages in Marion and McPherson Counties, including buildings at this complex. See the Jacob Friesen Mill, whose windmill arms have an open structure, and a fully furnished early one-room schoolhouse. Reflected in an adjacent pond, the 1876 Peter Paul Loewen House is constructed with clay bricks and a straw-burning combination of oven and furnace; it is the last of its kind in North America. Adults $3; students $1; preschool free.

Pioneer Bluffs (620-753-3484), 695 KS 177, Matfield Green, near Strong City. In 2010 this historical site and 1895 farm property was the location of a documentary film celebrating the 20th anniversary of the publication of *PrairyErth* with author William Least Heat-Moon. At other times, visit the art gallery located in a renovated 1908 home or attend events that celebrate the tallgrass prairie and Flint Hills area.

MUSEUMS **Cherokee Strip Land Rush Museum** (620-442-6750), 31639 US 77, Arkansas City. Open 10–5 Tues.–Sat.; tours available. On September 16, 1893, there was a major land rush in the area. The museum honors that momentous event and preserves the history of the town, plus south-central Kansas and north-central Oklahoma. See antique photos of the Boomers Camp at Ark City, a fully furnished one-room schoolhouse, and an American Indian grass home. Ask about the annual Mountain Man Encampment, too. Adults $4.50; seniors $3.50; children 6–12 $2.

THIS CONDOLENCE LETTER FROM JOHN F. KENNEDY AT THE STARS AND STRIPES MUSEUM IN CANTON IS DATED THE DAY BEFORE HIS ASSASINATION.

THE WHITE HOUSE
WASHINGTON

November 20, 1963

ear Mr. and Mrs. Everhart:

t was with deep regret that I learned of he death of your son, Sergeant First Class illiam J. Everhart, United States Army, while serving in Viet Nam.

While I realize that there is little that can be said to lessen your grief, I want you to know that your son had an excellent military record. From the time he entered the service in 1948, to his most recent assignment, he exhibited outstanding leadership and devotion to duty. These attributes, together with his many fine personal traits, won for him the respect and admiration of those with whom he served.

It is my sincere hope that the memory of William's devoted service will be a source of comfort and pride to you. Your son's valiant service is attested to by the award of the Purple Heart from a grateful Nation.

Mrs. Kennedy joins me in extending our heartfelt sympathy to you in your tragic loss.

Sincerely,

Mr. and Mrs. Frank L. Everhart
Box 288
Canton, Kansas

Stars and Stripes Military Museum (620-628-4484; at Three Sisters Victorian Tea, for access to the museum), 14 W. Allen, Canton. Call for appointment. This little museum houses some real treasures. See a condolence letter from John F. Kennedy to the local Everhart family, whose son had died—written the day before his assassination and likely his final personal correspondence. Learn about six Minear brothers who all served in the military but returned home safely. Uniforms and personal items from soldiers in most major military conflicts also fill the space. Free.

Mennonite Heritage Museum (620-367-8200), 200 N. Poplar, Goessel. Open March/April/Oct./Nov., 12–4 Tues.–Sat.; May–Sept., 10–5 Tues.–Sat., 1–5 Sun. Eight buildings give visitors a clear picture of Mennonite life a hundred years ago in this small town. They include a one-room school, a blacksmith shop, and a barn full of antique vehicles. See vintage dresses, portraits, and washboards in displays about individual families, a late-1800s kitchen, and a liberty bell crafted from Turkey Red wheat straw by two hundred Kansas Mennonites. Commissioned by the Smithsonian, it required two thousand man-hours. Adults 13 and older $4; children 7–12 $2.

McPherson Museum and Arts Foundation (620-241-8464; mcpher sonmuseum.com), 1130 E. Euclid, McPherson. The 1920 house itself is a historical treasure, with silk wallpaper and period furnishings. You'll also see fossils, Native American artifacts, and pioneer history exhibits. Open 1–5 Tues.–Sat. Adults $3; children under 13 $1; students $2.

♿ **Kansas Sports Museum** (316-804-4686; kshof.org), 601 SE 36th St., Chisholm Trail Center/Newton. Open 10–5 Mon.–Sat., 1–6 Sun. Tour an astonishing 22,000 square feet chock full of sports memorabilia in this museum that is a division of the Kansas Sports Hall of Fame. You'll see photos, signed balls, trophies, uniforms, and more, from and about high school, college, and professional sports. Adults $7; K–12 $6; seniors/military/AARP/AAA members $6; children under 6 free.

♿ **Chisholm Trail Museum** (620-326-3820), 502 N. Washington Ave., Wellington. Open mid-April–end of May, 1–4 weekends; June–Oct., 1–4 daily; Nov., 1–4 weekends. Tour three stories and 40 rooms in the old 1916 Hatcher Hospital full of photographs going as far back as the Civil War and the 1870s cattle train, plus artifacts. See antique dolls and carriages and travel to the third floor on an 80-year-old elevator that is one of the state's oldest still in use. Visit antique sewing, weaving, barber, and schoolroom vignettes, and more. On the second floor, antique furnishings decorate several rooms depicting a typical period home. Free.

✴ To Do

BOATING AND FISHING Chase State Fishing Lake (620-767-5900), 1130 Lake Rd., near Cottonwood Falls. Hikers will appreciate shady trails, a gorgeous waterfall, and wildflowers near this 109-acre lake. Camp on 23 acres; hunt for game birds or deer; and fish for crappie, catfish, bluegill, walleye, and bass.

Cowley State Fishing Lake (620-876-5730), 20467 US 166, Dexter. This pretty 197-acre lake nestles in a shallow valley just south of US 166 near Ark City. Extremely clear water offers plenty of channel catfish, bass, bluegill, walleye, and more. There are 113 acres available for hunting, particularly quail, rabbits, and squirrel, with some waterfowl.

GOLF Turkey Creek Golf Course (620-241-8530; golfturkeycreek.com), 1000 Fox Run, McPherson. This popular course with undulating landscape is packed on weekends and parking is at a premium. There's a driving range and a full-service snack bar, too. Par 70, 18 holes, 6,241 yards.

The Links at Pretty Prairie/Pretty Prairie Golf Course (620-459-4653, pretty prairiegolf.com), 1 Power Dr., Pretty Prairie. Gently rolling, beautifully maintained terrain awaits players at this country golf oasis. Par 70, 9 holes, 3,010 yards.

Wellington Golf Course (620-326-7904), 1500 W. Harvey Ave., Wellington. One of the nation's toughest short courses features manicured rye grass and rolling terrain and fairways framed by many hardwood and pine trees. You'll need to focus on accuracy versus shot length to play successfully here because of the many water hazards and tight fairways. Par 70, 18 holes, 6,201 yards.

Quail Ridge Golf Course (620-221-5645), 3805 Quail Ridge Dr., Winfield. Check for hours. This lovely course annually receives 4.5 stars from *Golf Digest's* Places to Play listing. Ponds and creeks and doglegs provide challenging play amid native grasses. Par 72, 18 holes, 6,826 yards.

✳ Green Space

Tallgrass Prairie National Preserve (620-273-8494), near Cottonwood Falls. Open 9–4:30 daily, except in inclement weather. This National Park Service Property features the tallgrass prairie of the Kansas Flint Hills, part of nearly 4 million acres between southern Nebraska and northern Oklahoma. Tour an 1880s mansion built by a cattle baron, plus a barn and outbuildings. Hike amid hundreds of bird and plant species and dozens of reptiles, amphibians, and mammals. Orientation video and information sessions available. Free.

Maxwell Wildlife Refuge (620-628-4455), near west border of McPherson State Fishing Lake, and Canton. This is a 2,800-acre wildlife refuge plus a fishing lake accessed via a 45-degree gravel road that ends at the edge of a geographical bowl filled with a lake. Fish for bass and catfish, camp, follow the nature trail, or have a picnic. Adults $8; children under 12 $5; children under 4 free. Visitors center with prairie displays, snacks, and small gift items.

Eureka Lake (620-583-5858), 2000 P Rd., Eureka. This was a hot spot during the local oil boom of the 1920s and '30s. Today there's a heated fishing dock, a bait shop with small menu, and the Phillips Cabin available for rent. At Eureka City Lake Spillway, visitors get a rare look at a tall rock wall from the Pennsylvania era, where a waterfall plays. Rock-strewn ground leads from P Road back to the falls—a favorite spot for photographs.

✳ Lodging
BED & BREAKFASTS

In Winfield
Iron Gate Inn (620-221-7787; iron gateinnks.com), 1203 E. Ninth Ave., Winfield. If you want to stay at this lush B&B, you'll have to think ahead. Proprietor Diane Cook books her four guest rooms up to seven or eight months in advance. Lace and linen, rich woodwork, and canopied and draped beds complement dozens of gorgeous antiques. The 1885 mansion was built by John Peter Baden, who also founded the nearby Southwestern College. $80.

((ᵩ)) **The Barns at Timber Creek** (620-221-2797; timbercreekbarns .com), 14704 91st Rd., Winfield. A gravel road and driveway lead to this rural retreat, which looks like a standard barn until you reach the front door and step into the spacious yet cozy living and dining room. Relax in the country quiet, choose a lovely room full of antiques with its own bath, and enjoy satellite TV. Full breakfast. $95.

((ᵩ)) **Bluestem Bed & Breakfast** (620-221-0735; bluestembedandbreak fast.com), 13292 172nd St., Winfield.

This spacious, modern home in the country has become a luxury bed & breakfast with enormous vistas and plenty of opportunities to bird-watch while hiking amid native grasses and wildflowers or walking the labyrinth. On-site therapeutic massage and meeting space is also available. Full breakfast. $125–150.

Elsewhere

((ᵠ)) **The Campus Cottage** (620-837-4791, the campuscottage.com), 2420 Goerz Ave., North Newton. The Campus Cottage occasionally has long-term renters; call well in advance. Everything about this little two-bedroom house says calm, from earth tones in the living room to lace-draped windows and a small rear screened porch. No credit cards. Self-serve breakfast and snacks. $80 for one bedroom; $100 for two bedrooms.

((ᵠ)) **Sunflower Inn of Yoder** (620-465-3664), 3307 Switzer, Yoder. You'll feel like you've stepped back in time from the moment you see the pitcher and bowl on a washstand inside, kerosene-style lamps, handmade quilts, and wood rocking chairs on the porch. Three bedrooms each have private baths. No credit cards. Call for current rates.

HOTELS AND RESORTS Grand Central Hotel & Grill (620-273-6763; grandcentralhotel.com), 215 Broadway, Cottonwood Falls. This abandoned historical hotel received a remarkable renovation before reopening in 1995. This AAA Four Diamond Historic Country Inn features a casual western vibe with gourmet cuisine and luxury accommodations. $160.

& ((ᵠ)) **Beaumont Hotel** (620-843-2422; hotelbeaumontks.com), 11651 SE Main, 45 miles east of Wichita,

Beaumont. Comfortable log furnishings decorate the lobby. Enjoy a large sunporch, exercise room, '50s-style diner, or Prairie Fire (dining) room with picture-window views of the Elk River Wind Farm. In nice weather, enjoy your meal on the wooden deck. There's a refrigerator, microwave, and coffeemaker in each room. Sleep below a black-and-white photo of a vintage airplane in the guest suite or standard rooms. The hotel was completely renovated in 2001 with private baths. Call for rates.

MOTELS, LODGES, AND INNS Millstream Resort Motel & Campground (620-273-8114), 401 Mill St., Cottonwood Falls. This lovely little property recently received a complete makeover with rustic decor and coffee pot, refrigerator, microwave and WiFi in each room or suite. Ask about the private cottage or RV and campsites. Rooms are $62–99.

((ᵠ)) **Country Haven Inn** (620-947-2929; countryhaveninn.com), 804 Western Heights, Hillsboro. This relatively new lodging is small and offers a lot of features for the money. Enjoy an in-room refrigerator, 20-inch televisions, private telephone voice mail, and desks with tilt chairs. There's also a king suite with Jacuzzi. Continental breakfast with waffles. $62–80.

((ᵠ)) **Blue Stem Lodge** (620-583-5531), 1314 E. River St., Eureka. New rooms feature microwaves, refrigerators, 26-inch LCD televisions, a hide-a-bed, and individual temperature controls. Every room has a coffeemaker, a hair dryer, and an outside door, and there's a small outdoor pool out front. It's clean and neat with comfortable furnishings. $44–49.

Spring Creek Guest House /Double Arrow C Ranch (620-583-7271; doublearrow.com), 1209 P Rd., Eureka. Heather Fuesz (pronounced "Fees") delights in sharing this rambling cottage with guests. Enjoy a huge living room, dining room, and kitchen, plus two bedrooms in this antique house set amid 20,000 acres full of wildlife. There's even a snack basket on hand. $65–100 for 2–4 people.

Pilgrim Ranch Retreat, LLC (620-273-8445 in evening; pilgrimranch.com), 1895A 180th Rd., Cottonwood Falls. Enjoy a fully equipped 1940s-era cottage with three bedrooms, or the bunkhouse, set amid a 3,000-acre ranch. Hunt, fish, ride trails with your horse, and more. Call for rates.

✴ Where to Eat

EATING OUT

In Caldwell

Last Chance Bar and Grill (620-845-2434), 30 S. Main St., Caldwell. Open 11:30–2 Tues.–Fri., 5–9 Tues.–Sun. Locals say this chef knows what to cook and how to cook it; try the Reuben sandwich or pork chops. There's a full bar and a good dose of small town hospitality. Inexpensive.

✐ **Steve's Place** (620-845-6464), 1 S. Main St., Caldwell. Open 11–9 Mon.–Fri. and Sun. night. This is a cheerful spot to eat great pizza, from garden Alfredo to German pie, cattleman's BBQ, or meatball. You'll also find a dozen pasta dishes, sandwiches, burgers, and ice cream. Try the garlic bread with cheese appetizer, too. Inexpensive.

Red Barn Café (620-845-2171), 624 S. Main St., Caldwell. Open 6–8

Mon.–Sat., 6–2 Sun. People take photographs of this spot's huge, fluffy omelets, and small chef's salads are the size of a dinner plate. Try house favorites like the farmer's breakfast with sausage, onion, hash browns, and Swiss cheese, smothered in gravy, or the chili. No credit cards. Inexpensive.

In Cottonwood Falls

Emma Chase Cafe/Emma Chase Country Store (620-273-6020; emmachasecafe.com), 317 Broadway, Cottonwood Falls. Open 9–2 daily and 5–8 Fri. The community gathers here for home-cooked food and camaraderie, savoring the daily salad bar and quart glasses of iced tea. Purchase Kansas handcrafts, jams, and kitchen items in the store, and enjoy music "jams" with dinner, every Fri. evening—the audience sometimes fills the street! No credit cards. Inexpensive.

The Gallery at Cottonwood Falls & Friendly D's Coffee Shop (620-273-6100), 313 Broadway, Cottonwood Falls. Open 12–5 Wed.–Thurs. and Sun., 10–5 Fri.–Sat., closed Jan.–Feb. except by appointment. From lattes and Italian sodas to quiche and deli wraps, this eatery set in a store full of antiques offers a delightful spot for a quick bite. Inexpensive.

In Eureka

Copper Kettle (620-583-5716), 815 River St., Eureka. Open 6:30–8:30 Tues.–Fri., 7:30–8:30 Sat., 7:30–2:30 Sun., 6:30–2:30 Mon. A dining landmark since 1968, this restaurant is especially known for its omelets and homemade baked goods, including fresh sandwich buns and cinnamon rolls, but they serve a broad lunch menu, too. Inexpensive.

In McPherson

Amics Mediterranean Café and Tapas Bar (620-241-1833), 120 N. Main St., McPherson. Open 11–2 Mon.–Sat., 5–10 Thurs.–Sat.; closed Sun. Crusty bread and herbed olive oil begin your meal at this bright and welcoming bistro. Tapas, such as gazpacho, which tastes like summer, and tortilla *espanola*, rules, but also choose from entrées including baked polenta or pesto chicken pizza. Add some homemade sangria for a complete Spanish experience. Inexpensive.

Neighbor's Café (620-241-7900), 204 S. Main St., McPherson. Open 6–2 Tues.–Sat., for breakfast 6–1 Sun. The $4.50 cinnamon roll or pancakes fill a dinner plate, and hash browns are freshly prepared in this long and narrow diner. Breakfast is big here, but there are also sandwiches, plus dinners such as roast beef or chicken-fried steak. Inexpensive.

Main Street Deli (620-241-1888), 108 S. Main St., McPherson. Open 10:30–9 weekdays and 10:30–8 Sat. The line is eight deep on sunny summer days. Build your own wrap or try ham and Swiss quiche or a classic chicken salad sandwich. Ask for a sample of homemade fudge while you peruse the chalkboard and shop the small boutique in front as you wait for lunch. Inexpensive.

Tres Amigos (620-245-0505), 121 W. Marlin St., McPherson. Open 11– 9 weekdays; closes 10 Fri.–Sat. There's plenty to like on this classic Mexican menu, including the popular *molcajete*—grilled chicken, steak, chorizo, shrimp, and bacon, plus peppers, onions, tomatoes, mushrooms, and pineapple, all topped with melted cheese. It comes with rice, beans, lettuce, sour cream, guacamole, *pico de gallo*, and tortillas. Inexpensive.

Bella Casa (620-245-5104), 900 W. Kansas Ave., #1, McPherson. Open 11–9:30 Mon.–Thurs., 11–10 Fri.–Sat., 11–9 Sun. Customers particularly enjoy this cozy yet spacious restaurant's veal dishes, chicken Alfredo, and lobster ravioli. With a bowling alley next door you can sometimes hear pins dropping. There's a full bar at the back, run by the folks who operate the bowling alley. Inexpensive.

In Newton

&. (ᵗᵖ) **Karen's Kitchen** (316-804-4573; karenskitchennewton.webs.com), 701 N. Main St., Newton. Open 7:30–3:30 Mon.–Sat. The breakfast quiche, burrito, or pancake platter are under $5 at this pleasant restaurant with original tin ceiling and local art. Try the grilled chicken pretzel roll—a tasty combination of grilled chicken breast, bacon, cheddar, lettuce, tomato, and mayonnaise—or the house favorite, strawberry cake. You'll also find a bakery case full of goodies. Buy wind chimes, jewelry, or Western cast-iron items, too. Inexpensive.

&. **Prairie Harvest Market and Deli** (316-283-6623; prairieharvest newton.com), 601 N. Main St., Newton. Open 9–6 Mon.–Fri., 9–5 Sat. With the slogan whole foods for a whole community, this store offers deli foods beginning at 11:30 AM, including hummus, sausage and cheese plates, chicken wraps, meal-size salads, and chocolate cake. Everything is made from scratch using locally and/or organically grown ingredients whenever possible. Sandhill Plum jam, barley malt, and more than three hundred bulk food items await customers, too.

& **Jacky Chen III** (316-283-3388; jackiechen.ucraa.org), 512 N. Main St., Newton. Open 11–9:30 Mon.–Thurs., 11–10:30 Fri.–Sat., 11:30–9:30 Sun.; closed Wed. Six buffet tables crowd the self-serve buffet room in this Newton favorite decorated with Chinese lanterns and wall fans. Choose from more than 120 Chinese, Japanese, Mexican, Italian, and American items, or order Chinese menu items, from chow mein and fried rice to roast pork with Chinese vegetables. Inexpensive.

& Y **Reba's Restaurant and Bar** (316-284-9800; rebasrestaurant.com), 301 N. Main St., Newton. Open 11–2 Tues.–Fri., 5–9 Wed. (burger night), 5–9 Thurs.–Sat. This restaurant offers big city food in a cozy vintage building. Thick, juicy pork chops arrive in an apricot/horseradish glaze, and sweet potato risotto accompanies macadamia nut–crusted salmon. Try some tapas, Black Angus burgers topped with Greek olives and pepperoncini, or other combos, or luscious carrot cake decorated with edible flowers. Moderate.

In Winfield

Burger Station (620-221-9773), 113 E. Seventh St., Winfield. Open 10:30–8 Mon.–Sat. There's just enough room to stand as you wait for your order, where the Crow family has served customers since 1965. They grind and patty their own meat, make potato salad and baked beans in-house, and are known for their double cheeseburgers. No credit cards. Inexpensive.

& (ɰ) **College Hill Coffee** (620-229-8155; collegehillcoffee.com), 403 Soward, Winfield. Open 6:30–6:30 Mon.–Thurs., 6:30–11 Fri., 7:30–3 Sun. Of course you can get a terrific latte or café Americano here. But you'll also find a great grilled Reuben, homemade soup served in a bread bowl, and fresh salads. And it's all wrapped up in a delightful old house turned coffee destination. Inexpensive.

Elsewhere

& **La Cabana** (620-947-0260), 117 S. Main, Hillsboro. Open 11–9 Mon.–Sat., 1–3 Sun. You won't soon forget this restaurant, with its bright orange and green walls, sombreros, and serapes. Try the $4 weekday lunch special, lime margaritas on the rocks for about $2, fajitas *tapatias*—marinated beef with red peppers, onions, beans, pico de gallo, sour cream, cheese, and flour tortillas—or *taquitos* Mexicanos. Inexpensive.

Bull's Eye Grill (620-465-BULL), 3408 E. Red Rock Rd., Yoder. Open 11–8 Mon.–Sat. This is a small place with an enthusiastic owner and third-of-a-pound build-your-own burgers with nearly two dozen cheeses, toppings, and condiments available. Try fried green beans or corn nuggets, a club sandwich, or a chicken-fried steak sandwich. Inexpensive.

Hitchin' Post (620-753-3471) 201 Reed St., Matfield Green. Open 11–9 Tues.–Thurs., until 10 Fri.–Sat. Tie up your horse and grab a beer at this popular hangout. They'll even cook your fish or hunting catch. No credit cards. Inexpensive.

Kountry Kafé (620-654-3500), 220 E US 56, Galva. Open 6–2 Mon.–Sat., 6–8 Thurs. With special dinners such as fried chicken or brisket. Home cooking includes pies and cinnamon rolls made from scratch. Most sandwiches, salads, sides, and baskets are under $5, and the breakfast crowd is usually large. Try homemade corn-bread with sausage gravy for only $4.99. No credit cards. Inexpensive.

SNACKS

In McPherson

Java John's International Coffee (620-241-0500; javajohns.net), 209 N. Main St., McPherson. Open 7:30–5:30 weekdays, 9–4 Sat. Welcoming from the moment you enter, Java John's is McPherson's local coffee roaster, with a delightful coffeehouse on Main Street. Sit beside an old-fashioned street light with a cappuccino or a four-berry smoothie, and then take a pound of beans home with you. Inexpensive.

The Cake Lady and The Old Muffin Factory (620-241-9900), 217 S. Main St., McPherson. Open 8:30–5:30 weekdays, 9–3 Sat. They offer three flavors of freshly baked muffins on weekdays and bake fresh cookies every other day. Order a muffin and a cup of coffee for under $3 and shop for gourmet food items. Inexpensive.

✳ Entertainment

In McPherson

McPherson Opera House (620-241-1952; mcphersonoperahouse.org), 219 S. Main, McPherson. Call for a tour, event schedule, and ticket prices. Built in 1888, this national historic site is in the midst of restoration, and the 900-seat auditorium already has returned to its former grandeur with period murals, heavily draped private balconies, and perfect acoustics. Events in 2010 included *The Wizard of Oz*, the Glenn Miller Orchestra, and a Summer of Love event that featured a concert by The Family Stone.

McPherson Waterpark (620-245-2578; mcphersonwaterpark.com), 511

N. Lakeside Dr., Lakeside Park/ McPherson. Open 1–7 Mon.–Thurs./ Sat./Sun., 1–8 Fri. With many lights for night use, a three-story relaxed spiral slide, and a lap swim area, this water park offers 600,000 gallons of summer fun. Adults $4; children 4–7 $1; children 8–17 $3; seniors 62 and up $2.

Antique Auto Restoration Program (620-241-3340), 1600 E. Euclid, McPherson. Tours by appointment. Classic car enthusiast Jay Leno supports two scholarships to this unusual program at McPherson College, the only college in the world that offers a four-year bachelor's degree in automotive restoration. Students conduct historical research and learn hands-on restoration skills.

Model Train Displays (620-241-8464; mkmrclub.org), 1111 E. Kansas Ave., McPherson. Open 1–5 weekends or call for tours. This huge display sponsored by the Mid Kansas Model Railroaders features multiple layouts plus historical photos of old train depots of McPherson and the surrounding area. Adults $2; children 3–12 $1.

Starlite Lanes (620-241-1200; starlitelanes.com), 900 W. Kansas Ave., McPherson. Open 6–9 weekdays, 1–midnight Sat., 1–6 Sun. McPherson residents have bowled for 50 years in this small but tidy bowling alley. All games $2.95; 6–close Fri.–Sat. all games $3.10; cosmic games $3.30; 1–6 Sat.–Sun specials: $2.50 per game or $5.50 for three games; shoe rental $3, or $2 for children size 1–4.

In Newton

Blue Sky Sculpture (316-283-8027; philepp.com/public.htm), 12th and Kansas, Newton. Look for the water tower painted with a cloud-studded blue sky; the sculpture lies nearby in Centennial Park. Made of ceramic tile to honor local resident Jacqueline Smith, the multistory twin ceramic paneled sculptures seem to fade into the true sky on a sunny day. Free.

& **Carriage Factory Art Gallery** (316-284-2749, carriagefactorygallery .com), 128 E. Sixth St., Newton. Open noon–5 Tues.–Fri., 11–2 Sat. Listed on the National Register of Historic Places, this antique building, with an exposed original stone wall, houses multiple exhibits, such as art quilts, Kansas-themed oil and acrylic paintings, and pieces created by well-known regional artists. Albert Krehbiel's renowned impressionist oil paintings are the centerpiece of this collection.

Elsewhere
Flying W Ranch (620-274-4357); flinthillsflyingw.com), Rt. 1, Cedar Point. Josh and Gwen Hoy are passionate about sharing the Flint Hills on the 9,000-acre family ranch where they raise cattle, host chuck wagon suppers and prairie burns, and offer hiking, fishing, and riding. Lodging and meals are available. Call for rates and prairie burn calendar.

The Storey Vineyards and Windswept Winery (620-782-3952; windsweptwinery.com), 1227 92nd Rd., Udall. Open 1–6 weekdays, 10–6 Sat., 1–6 Sun.; ask about vineyard tours. Travel 2 miles south on 21st Road and then 1.75 miles west on 92nd Road to reach this family-owned operation based on 5.5 acres of French hybrid grapes initially planted in 1999. Taste the results in the small, modern tasting room and gift shop, which also offers made-in-Kansas products, gift baskets, and more.

Winfield Community Theatre (620-221-6270; winfieldcomm theatre.com), Meyer Hall at St. John College, Winfield. More than 40 years after it began, this performing arts group still offers several shows each year. After many seasons in The Barn, they moved to renovated space at the college in 2003. Recent offerings have included *The Sound of Music, The Foreigner, Jacques Brel Is Alive and Well and Living in Paris,* and *A Little Piece of Heaven.* Admission $9.

❋ **Selective Shopping**

& **Three Sisters Victorian Tea Room and Treasures Gift Boutique** (620-628-4484), 105 N. Main St., Canton. Open 11–4 Tues.–Sat. Serving food and beverages for monthly themed tea events and special occasion dinners, this pretty place on Canton's main street has multiple holiday home decor displays in front, and the delightful little tea room anchors the back end. Enjoy cookies and cocoa with Mrs. Clause on the first Sat. in December. Inexpensive meals.

Henry's Candies (620-876-5423), KS 15, Dexter. Open 8–5 Mon.–Sat., 9–5 Sun. See a candy-making business that has operated for more than 50 years. Founder Tom Henry invented what is now known as the Oh Henry! candy bar while he worked at Ranney-Davis Candy Co. in Arkansas City. This company has the copyright for Mallowmilk chocolates, and the Better Mousetrap brand features chocolate with pecans and almonds. There are dozens of candies to choose from and a window into the factory.

In Cottonwood Falls
& **Jim Bell and Son Clothing Co.** (620-273-6381; jimbellandson.com),

322 Broadway, Cottonwood Falls. Open 9–6 Mon.–Fri., 10–5 Sat. Dozens of cowboy hats surround a giant stuffed buffalo near the entrance of this store that opened its doors in 1927. Hundreds of cowboy boots fill another corner and there are women's, children's and reenactor clothing upstairs. Buy custom chaps from resident leather artisan Bruce Brock or the prefect pair of jeans.

& **Flint Hills Gallery LLC** (620-273-6454), 321 Broadway, Cottonwood Falls. Open 10–3 Mon.–Sat. Most of the art here is landscapes in beautiful oils by the family who owns it. This is a gorgeous space, too. No credit cards.

& **The Gallery at Cottonwood Falls** (620-273-6100), 313 Broadway, Cottonwood Falls. Open noon–5 Wed.–Thurs., 10–5 Fri.–Sat., noon–5 Sun. This multifaceted business offers rustic wood furniture and home decor on two floors, with a coffee shop in front.

In Galva (near McPherson)
Marci's on Main (620-654-3751), 220 S. Main St., Galva. Open 10–5 Mon.–Fri. Candles, mugs, kitchen serving dishes, Gooseberry cookbooks, and cut crystal bowls are just a few of the home goods available in this pretty little store across from the fire station.

Galva Emporium (620-654-3393), 540 S. Main St., Galva. Open 11–5 Mon.–Sat. *Vintage Life* magazines, paper Coca Cola ads, and dozens of 1950s children's books are just a few of the treasures here. Old coal buckets, antique dining chairs, and crystal-edged chandeliers hang from the ceiling. Be sure to look for lace-covered and silk-fringe-decorated lampshades made by the owner to echo Victorian decor.

& **M&M Choppers** (620-654-3142), 300 S. Empire, Galva. Open 10–6 Tues.–Thurs., 10–5 Fri., 10–2 Sat. Four motorcycles are parked on the black-and-white linoleum floor. There's a small area of leathers, T-shirts, and hats, as well as motor oil and other necessities. Shoot the breeze with fellow bikers over a cup of coffee at the dining room table.

In McPherson
& **Krehbiels Meat Market and Deli** (620-241-6565, healthymeats .net), 2212 E. Kansas Ave., McPherson. Open 8–7 Mon.–Sat. The aroma of BBQ and smoked meats begins at the front door. From their own butchering plant to signature baby back ribs and German sausage, meat is king here. Try a Kobe beef or buffalo burger for lunch, too. You'll also find gluten-free frozen baked goods, Amish wedding juice concentrate, and health and wellness meals created in cooperation with the local hospital. Inexpensive meals.

& **The Bookshelf and The Hidden Closet** (620-241-6602), 206 N. Main, McPherson. Open 9–8 weekdays, 9–5 Sat. (Hidden Closet closes at 6 weekdays). This is a full-service bookstore that often hosts author book signings and talks. On the other side, purchase gently used designer wear from Louis Vuitton, Prada, Coach, and others at a fraction of the normal cost.

& **A5 Western** (620-241-2660), 102 N. Main, McPherson. Open 10–6 Mon.–Fri., 10–4 Sat. Opened in 2010, this store stocks mainly boots, lots of jeans, and some Western-inspired home decor items. It's nicely arranged, with enthusiastic staff.

The Cook's Nook (620-241-7180), 219 N. Main, McPherson. Open 9–8 weekdays, 9–5 Sat. Home cooking

MAKING MUSIC

Symphony in the Flint Hills (620-273-8965; symphonyintheflinthills.org), rotating locations within the Flint Hills region, near Emporia. It's been more than 15 years since Matfield Green rancher Jane Koger, hosted her 40th birthday celebration at Homestead Ranch, with entertainment provided by orchestra members from as far away as Denver and St. Louis. Today thousands of people purchase tickets and make their hotel reservations up to a year in advance for the event that features the Kansas City Symphony. Patrons bring lawn chairs and purchase sandwiches or burgers and beer/wine with event tokens. Shuttle buses, a silent auction, a Cherokee storyteller, an observatory tent with telescopes, and live country-western music are other features. Put a flag on the car, bring a flashlight and bug spray, and wear comfortable shoes, then settle in for a one-of-a-kind musical experience. Aaron Copland's music never sounded more at home than it does here. General admission: adults $60; children 12 and under $40; food and beverage extra.

Walnut Valley Festival (620-221-3250; wvfest.com), Winfield. Most people who know about this 40-year-old music extravaganza simply call it Winfield. Residents know where to go, but there may not be clear signage to the event site, so ask for directions if you haven't attended before. There are performances on multiple stages and impromptu evening jam sessions in the camping area. A musician plays Beatles tunes on his electrified acoustic guitar, following another soloist on hammered dulcimer, and before a trio with vocals, guitar, and two dulcimers. Sometimes an unusual instrument headlines a set, such as the Chapman Stick—the equivalent of two guitars mounted side by side—played by a Wichita resident. But this event

enthusiasts will enjoy browsing 4,000 square feet of floor-to-ceiling cooking gadgets, tableware, pans, and much more. After 22 years the owner has just the right mix at reasonable prices.

& **Sassy Bags** (620-755-6223), 302 N. Main, McPherson. Open 11:30–5:30 weekdays, 10:30–4 Sat. Bright pink and black create a fun, welcoming spot to buy purses of every shape and size, plus jewelry and shoes. Find a colorful diaper bag or backpack or even a child's tutu.

In Newton

Anderson Book and Office Supply (316-283-3570), 627 N. Main, Newton. Open 9–5:30 Mon.–Sat., 9–8:30 Thurs. This family business has operated in Newton for five generations and in its current location since 1938. Find everything from gym shorts and local school T-shirts to puzzles, stuffed animals, and much more.

& **Kitchen Corner** (316-283-4253), 607 N. Main, Newton. Open Mon.–Fri. 10–5:30, Sat. 10–5. This downtown store offers fresh fudge and packaged is also about competition, such as the seven-hour International Finger Style Guitar Championships. There are endless food and beverage choices, loads of crafts and trinkets, and a huge collection of sheet music for sale. Full festival $80 in advance/$90 at gate; Fri.–Sat. $60 advance/$70 at gate; Sat.–Sun. $50/$60; Fri. or Sat. $35. Children 6–11 $5, payable only at gate; children under 6 free with paid adult. Advance ticket mail orders must be postmarked approximately three weeks before the event.

EACH JUNE THE KANSAS CITY SYMPHONY PLAYS OUTSIDE AT A FLINT HILLS RANCH DURING THE DAYLONG SYMPHONY IN THE FLINT HILLS.

gourmet chocolates. There are decorator-quality plastic plates, tabletop fans in the shapes of animals, and a huge array of insulated plastic cups from a popular manufacturer, for starters.

In Yoder

& **Yoder Furniture Co.** (620-465-2220), 3405 E. Switzer Rd., Yoder. Open 10–6 Mon.–Fri., 10–4 Sat. This store sells mostly oak and some cherry furniture, including beds, bedroom suites, rolltop desks, and corner cupboards in a cavernous, light, airy, and inviting two-story building. Purchase

candles, fruit preserves, and butters and fresh salsas, too.

& **Yoder Meats and Kansas Station** (620-465-3807; yoderkansas.com/yoder_meats.htm), 2509 E. Switzer Rd., Yoder. Buy fresh buffalo meat from $12.99/pound and elk from $5.99/pound, plus farm-raised rabbit and chicken. This is a sleek, modern shop with plenty of preserves, salsa, and jerky. Browse the gift shop where Kansas-made products include gourd birdhouses, wheat weavings, lace table runners, and homemade noodles.

✳ Special Events

May: **C.A.R.S. Show** (620-241-0731), McPherson. Enjoy this annual event hosted by the Automotive Restoration Students Club at McPherson College campus.

April: **Mountain Man Living History Encampment** (620-442-6750), Cherokee Strip Land Rush Museum, Arkansas City. The encampment depicts life before 1840. Throw a tomahawk, learn to do beadwork, watch American Indian dancers, and listen to music from the era.

Prairie Fire Festival (620-273-6020), Cottonwood Falls Dam and Bridge, Cottonwood Falls. The six-day event honors Flint Hills ranchers, who participate in annual prairie burnings, with seminars, art and quilt displays, and the Friday evening blue grass jam session with dozens of musicians performing.

June: **Flint Hills Rodeo** (620-273-6480; flinthillsrodeo.com), Strong City. This 75-year-old event features cowboy and cowgirl performances, a parade, and dances. River Suite (620-273-8469), Cottonwood Falls. Enjoy food, a cash bar, and music during this event, which is held on a bridge the day before Symphony in the Flint Hills.

The Winfield Country Roundup (620-221-2112; winfieldcountry roundup.com), Winfield. Enjoy country entertainment, including top entertainers such as Charlie Daniels, Ronnie Milsap, the Outlaw Junkies, and Matt Engels. Great campsites are available, too.

August: **When Pigs Fly BBQ Contest and Fly In** (620-241-3303), McPherson Airport, McPherson. This is a Kansas City BBQ Society–sanctioned contest, with plane rides and parachute jumps, a car show, and loads of great food.

September: **Scottish Festival** (1-800-324-8022; macfestival.org), Lakeside Park, McPherson. Enjoy highland dancing, bagpipe competition, classes, and other traditional entertainment during this annual event. **Hillsboro Arts and Crafts Fair** (620-947-3506; artsandcraftsfair.org), Hillsboro. See work from dozens of vetted artists and 16 states in this daylong, 40-year-old event.

October: **Flint Hills Folklife Festival** (620-273-6020; flinthillsfolklifefestival.cm/), Cottonwood Falls. Reenactors portray life in the mid-1800s.

Mountain Man Rendezvous (620-628-4455), Maxwell Wildlife Refuge, McPherson. Explorers and trappers from the 1800s come to life in this historical rendezvous event. **Taste of Newton** (316-283-7555; the Newton Chamber), Newton. This evening event is the largest food festival south of Chicago, with a dizzying array of items to try.

November: **Chase County Country Christmas** (620-273-8469), Cottonwood Falls. Enjoy a special breakfast, gingerbread-decorating contests, a visit from Santa, and the lighting of the 1873 Chase County Courthouse.

HUTCHINSON AND WEST

Reno County's largest city and the county seat, Hutchinson, is located at the intersection of US 50, KS 96, and KS 61, near the Arkansas River, and approximately 39 miles northwest of Wichita. The population of more than forty thousand swells to upward of three hundred and fifty thousand people each September as the city hosts the 10-day Kansas State Fair, Kansas's largest annual event.

But visitors find plenty to do anytime they visit Hutchinson, from the Kansas Cosmosphere and Space Center to the amazing Underground Salt Museum and a downtown area with plenty of restaurants, antique shops, and other retailers. However, you should be aware that many businesses in Hutchinson are closed from Sunday to Monday.

Local residents have a median household income above $30,000, with the largest number employed by Promise Regional Medical Center, Hutchinson public schools, and Dillon Companies, a grocery store chain that was founded here.

Hutchinson was incorporated in 1872 to take advantage of the Santa Fe Railway's crossing over the Arkansas River. The Burlington Northern Santa Fe Railroad, the Southwest Chief route of AMTRAK, and the Union Pacific Railroad continue to serve the city. Benjamin Blanchard discovered salt in Reno County in 1887, and the Carey Salt Company began to produce rock salt here more than three decades later. Today, two additional companies operate salt plants in the area.

Great Bend was part of the Wild West in the 1870s, with plenty of crime, drinking, and licentious behavior. It was named for its proximity to a large bend in the Arkansas River.

But after its cowtown phase ended, the city emerged as a regional trade center, partially due to oil found in the region and later when a major World War II army air corps training base operated here. Raising cattle has remained an important source of the city's income since its early days.

The current city is located at the intersection of US 281 and US 56, approximately 235 miles from the Kansas City area. Other major roadways include KS 96 and KS 156. Between fifteen and sixteen thousand people call Great Bend home and have a median household income above $30,000. Famous Great Bend residents include jazz singer Karrin Allyson, film director Oscar Micheaux, and Jack Kilby, the 2000 Nobel Prize winner in physics.

Great Bend's downtown area has recently seen major renovation and growth thanks in large part to the influence of MyTown, an organization of investors determined to jumpstart the neighborhood's economy. Young businesses in the MyTown district include gift shops and boutiques, restaurants, and a gorgeous, full-service salon and day spa.

Hunting is also big business around Great Bend. More than 60,000 acres of public hunting area lie within 60 miles of this city, and Kansas Wildlife and Parks lease 50,000 private acres near town for walk-in hunting. They include acreage in Cheyenne Bottoms Wildlife Area, Wilson Wildlife Area, Kanopolis Reservoir, Quivira National Wildlife Refuge, Pratt Sandhills Wildlife Area, Texas Lake Wildlife Area, and Hodgeman State Fishing Lake (SFL) and Wildlife Area. Greyhound racing began here in 1887. Visitors can learn about the sport's history and meet several champion dogs at the Greyhound Hall of Fame.

At about 17 miles west of Medicine Lodge the first of many gypsum hill out-croppings becomes visible. Soon, a breathtaking red-rock vista unfolds before you. It's part of the 300,000-acre Gypsum Hills, most of which are in Oklahoma.

With approximately two thousand residents and located near US 160 and US 281, Medicine Lodge is where Carrie Nation lived and began her temperance crusade. It's also where the U.S. government signed the historic Medicine Lodge Peace Treaty with five American Indian plains tribes in 1876. When Indian raids continued, despite the peace treaties, a stockade was constructed for protection. The town incorporated in 1879, and current industries include agriculture, natural gas, and gypsum.

Pratt was organized in 1873 and became known as the Gateway to the High Plains by the mid-1880s. The population reached more than eight thousand by 1890, but growth peaked in the 1930s. Today, this small city is known for great hunting and outdoors activities.

GUIDANCE **Greater Hutchinson Convention and Visitors Bureau** (620-662-3391; hutchchamber.com), 117 N. Walnut St., Hutchinson. Open 8–5 weekdays.

Great Bend Convention and Visitors Bureau (620-792-2750), 3007 10th, Great Bend. Open 9–5 weekdays.

Kingman Area Chamber of Commerce (620-532-1853; kingmancc.com), 322 N. Main St., Kingman.

Medicine Lodge Chamber of Commerce (620-886-3417), 215 S. Iliff, Medicine Lodge. Open 8–noon Mon.–Wed.

Pratt Area Chamber of Commerce (620-672-5501), 114 N. Main, Pratt. Open 9–5 weekdays.

Stafford Main Street (620-234-6025; stfdmainstreet@sbcglobal.net).

GETTING THERE AND GETTING AROUND *By car:* This is the best way to reach south-central Kansas and travel through the area. *By air:* See above. By train: **AMTRAK's Southwest Chief** train serves Hutchinson at North Walnut and East Third Streets. There is a waiting room but no ticket office hours. It also serves the Newton AMTRAK Station. Call 1-800-USA-RAIL for more information. *By bus:* Greyhound does not serve towns in this area.

MEDICAL EMERGENCY (arranged alphabetically by city name)

Anthony Medical Center (620-842-5111), 1101 E. Spring St., Anthony.

Ellinwood District Hospital (620-564-2548), 605 N. Main, Ellinwood.

Ellsworth County Medical Center (785-472-3111), 1604 Aylward Ave., Ellsworth.

St. Francis at Ellsworth (785-472-4453), 1655 Avenue K, Ellsworth.

Central Kansas Medical Center (620-792-2511), 3515 Broadway, Great Bend.

Great Bend Regional Hospital (620-792-8833), 514 Cleveland St., Great Bend.

Promise Regional Medical Center-Hutchinson (620-665-2000), 1701 E. 23rd Ave., Hutchinson.

Kingman Community Hospital (620-532-0167), 750 W. D Ave., Kingman.

Rice County Hospital District #1 (620-257-5173), 619 S. Clark, Lyons.

Medicine Lodge Memorial Hospital (620-886-3771), 710 N. Walnut St., Medicine Lodge.

Pratt Regional Medical Center (620-672-7451), 200 Commodore, Pratt.

Stafford District Hospital (620-234-5221), 502 S. Buckeye, Stafford.

✸ To See

HISTORIC PLACES, LANDMARKS, AND SITES

In Great Bend

⚴ **B29 Memorial Plaza** (620-793-5125), airport entrance, Great Bend. Always open. A miniature plane flies beneath a blue metal commemorative arch, surrounded by commemorative plaques that honor men and women of the Great Bend Army Airfield from World War II. They practiced with these planes around the clock, knowing that their mission is critical to the war effort. Free.

⚴ **Kansas Quilt Walk and Great Bend Mural Project** (620-792-2750), downtown Great Bend. You'll never look at a sidewalk the same way again. At each corner of the square there's a quilt pattern made of granite and marble, with names such as Rocky Road to Kansas, Windmill, and Kansas Troubles. Along the way, watch for murals painted by students, volunteers, professional artists, and youngsters, depicting Great Bend's history. Free.

Ellinwood's Underground World (620-564-2400), 1 N. Main, Ellinwood/west of Great Bend. Open daily; call for tour. The people who founded Ellinwood came from Munich, which had an underground city in its center, so they created one in their adopted town, too. Meet enthusiastic tour guide Bill Starr at Hotel Wolf, where he runs Starr Antiques and Elliott Antiques and Interiors, a place you'll want to spend some time, too. But underground is the real treasure. See a harness shop and a barbershop full of virtually untouched tools, cowboy bathtubs, and soiled dove quarters. Tours: ages 10 and up $5; children 9 and younger $2.

Elsewhere

& **Anthony 9/11 Memorial** (9-11memorialanthonyks.org), Anthony. Always open. Dedicated on September 11, 2004, this unusual memorial, with steel from the World Trade Center, commemorates brave individuals who assisted at the three crash sites. It also signifies the relationship that developed when the residents of Anthony adopted the family of fallen New York City firefighter Joe Spor, including his four young children. In March 2002, one of Spor's firefighter brothers visited and thanked the town, and Anthony soon received their steel. Learn more about this moving story at the memorial and/or through the website listed above. Free.

Pawnee Rock State Park (785-272-8681), 0.5 mile north of US 56 and the town of Pawnee Rock. Open dawn–dusk; ADA accessible. This handsome rock lies on an overlook marked by several historical signs and autographs etched there by passing travelers—both Indian and white. It was considered the midpoint on the Santa Fe Trail between Missouri and New Mexico. Some people speculate that its name came from a dark night in 1826 when young Kit Carson supposedly shot his own mule, thinking that it was a Pawnee Indian. Settlers and railroad builders eventually quarried the rock to about half of its original height, but the breathtaking view remains.

Santa Fe Depot and Cannonball Welcome Center (316-532-2142), 201 E. Sherman, Kingman. Open 8:30–11:30 Mon.–Fri., some afternoons, and some Sat. mornings. This old brick depot is on the National Register of Historic Places. It currently offers travel brochures about the state and is under restoration, including its railroad museum that already showcases HO gauge model trains.

In Larned

Fort Larned National Historic Site (620-285-6911, nps.gov/fols), KS 156, 6 miles west of Larned. Open 8:30–4:30 daily, except holidays; guided tours by reservation. Living history presentations take place almost daily in the summer, and it would be easy to spend a couple of hours here at any time. Built in 1859, this is the most complete fort surviving from the time period of Custer and Buffalo Bill Cody. At least 33 infantry companies operated from Fort Larned, including Company A of the buffalo soldiers, and the fort had its highest troop levels in 1867 and 1868. Step back in time as you visit barracks where 1866 Springfields line the walls. See where 340 loaves of bread were made each day and view the cook's quarters behind the kitchen and the blockhouse with approximately 100 gun portals. Free.

Santa Fe Trail Center (620-285-2054; santafetrailcenter.org), 1349 KS 156, Larned. Open 9–5 daily. This nonprofit regional museum informs visitors about the Santa Fe Trail and the blending of American, Indian, and Mexican cultures. There's a small canon with cannonballs outside, plus a historical one-room school, a sod house, a bright yellow train depot, and an antique limestone-post fence. Enter the museum beside a full-size diorama of a trader in a serape. See a stuffed buffalo honoring the millions of head that once roamed the plains, and vintage vehicles that range from a covered wagon to a sleek horse-drawn buggy and an early, motorized car. Adults $4; students 12–18 $2.50; children 6–11 $1.50; children under 6 free.

In Pratt

ら **B-29 All Veterans Memorial** (620-672-1944; prattairport.com), Pratt Industrial Airport, just off US 54. Pratt Army Air Field was the nation's first B-29 base and pioneer of the B-29 program. Visit the current airport for a look at this beautiful monument, which honors all veterans, prisoners of war, and MIA soldiers for their peace-time and war-time sacrifices. You'll see an F-4 from the Vietnam War, a T-38 trainer plane, and a military helicopter. Commemorative bricks pave the area. Plans are underway for an adjacent museum, with army training corps memorabilia. Free.

Hot and Cold Water Towers (620-672-5501), 114 N. Main, Pratt. For more than a century these side-by-side water towers have amused residents and visitors alike.

MUSEUMS Barton County Historical Village and Museum (620-793-5125, bartoncountymuseum.org), 85 S KS 281, Great Bend. Open year-round, 10–5 Tues.–Fri.; April–Oct., 1–5 Sat.–Sun. See the amazing Lustron—a prefabricated ranch-style home that was one of under three thousand produced with porcelain enameled steel walls, partially in response to the need for additional homes to house soldiers returning from World War II. Two barns display vehicles from the 1930s to '50s. There's a country church with a wood barrel ceiling, a tiny post office with a Bonnie and Clyde WANTED poster, and the Belpre Railroad depot. Clothed human mannequins provide startling realism. See an outdoor collection of farm machinery and a two-room 1873 stone cabin. Adults 16 and up, non-members $4.

Kansas Underground Salt Museum (620-662-1425; undergroundmuseum.org /index.php), 3504 E. Avenue G at Airport Rd., Hutchinson. Open 9–6 Tues.– Sat., 1–6 Sun.; advance reservations recommended. As visitors stand outside this museum it's hard to imagine an entire world full of salt walls located 650 feet below. But you'll arrive there only 90 seconds after the double-decked elevator door closes. The museum has a new visitors center with a remarkable display of the world's oldest living organism, a 250-million-year-old live bacteria that was found inside a salt crystal. A new outdoor exhibit showcases GE Engine No. 2, a 1919 train that served the Carey Salt Mine for more than four decades, completely fills a flatbed trailer, and weighs 60,000 pounds. Gallery tour: adults $13.25/with dark ride $15.75; seniors, children 4–12 $11.90/with dark ride $14.40; joint tickets available with the Kansas Cosmosphere and Space Center.

Kansas Cosmosphere and Space Center (316-662-2305; cosmo.org), 1100 N. Plum, Hutchinson. Open 9–5 Mon.–Thurs., 9–7 Fri.–Sat., noon–5 Sun.; closed on holidays. The nation's second-largest space display features the *Apollo 13* command module, newsreel of Kennedy talking about flights to the moon, and information about the U.S./USSR. Gemini 7 space capsule. See the Apollo-Soyuz Test Project, whose docked display is longer than several long-haul trucks. Visit the Cold War gallery, the planetarium, or the Carey IMAX Dome Theater. See live demonstrations that replicate those of Dr. Robert Goddard, who created modern rocketry in the 1930s. All-day, all-inclusive pass: adults $17; seniors 60 and up, children 4–12 $15. Single-venue tickets available.

Coronado Quivira Museum (620-257-3941), 105 W. Lyon, Lyons. Open 9–5 Tues.–Sat. A replica of a Quiviran Indian Grass Lodge from 1500 A.D. and a country general store with complete inventory are just a few sights at this impressive museum. You can also look at a Victorian home through open walls, a restored vintage fire engine, and even Spanish weapons from the time of Coronado. Adults $2; children 6–12 $10.

Stockade Museum (620-886-3553), 209 W. Fowler Ave., Medicine Lodge. Open daily 10:30–5, except holidays. Five American Indian tribes signed peace treaties here with the white man. See a pony express saddle, a Civil War cavalry uniform, mastodon bones, and a completely furnished 1877 log cabin on this site. The stockade walls that were initially built to protect whites from Indians were never needed for that purpose. Admission includes the Carrie A. Nation House, next door—see below. Adults $4; seniors 54 and up $3.50; children 14 and under $3.

Carrie A. Nation House (620-886-3908), 211 W. Fowler/US 160, Medicine Lodge. Open 10:30–5 daily, except holidays. After Carrie Nation's first husband died of alcoholism she became a temperance lady. Her second husband divorced her on grounds of desertion after he became seriously ill, but she would not halt her temperance-related travels and sold hatchet pins when she needed jail bail. There's a 6-foot-tall life-size portrait of Nation in the home, plus her own bed frame, dresser, and kitchen cupboard.

Pratt Fish Hatchery and Museum (620-672-0749), 2 miles east and 1 mile south of Pratt on KS 64, Pratt. The best visiting time is in the morning, late March–April, or in June; call for a tour. Learn about the development process of fish. The hatchery does all catfish spawning for the state, and for fish trades with other states that include New Mexico and Nebraska. A blue, 3-million-gallon tank is used to hatch walleye. Visit the holding room with up to 13 species based on biologist requests, and 87 ponds that hold individual species of various ages.

TOWNS Plains. This town has the widest Main Street in the United States and plenty of community pride. The thoroughfare received a major face-lift in 2009 with planters, a new median, new sidewalks, new streetlights, and elimination of all high wires, plus a new LED sign. Original brick streets and a new concrete median add a fresh look.

Ellinwood. Founded by German immigrants in 1872, Ellinwood lies just north of the Arkansas River in Barton County near US 56. Now owned and operated by the Kansas and Oklahoma Railroad Company, the original Santa Fe mainline passed through town. The Santa Fe Trail brought up to four hundred wagons through Ellinwood each week at its peak, and nearly a dozen saloons thrived until Prohibition, including many located in Ellinwood's parallel underground city. (To learn more, see *Historic Places, Landmarks, and Sites*.)

Kingman. This is the county seat of Kingman County and has approximately four thousand residents. This small city located near US 54, KS 42, KS 17, and KS 14 offers a bustling downtown of several blocks, yet it is surrounded by great hunting and fishing areas, with several professional outfitters available. Kingman County was established in 1874 in a prairie area where plains Indians hunted. It was also the beginning of the Cannonball Stageline Highway—US 54—through to Greensburg.

✳ To Do

BOATING AND FISHING Cowley State Fishing Lake (620-876-5730), 20467 US 166, Dexter. This pretty 197-acre lake nestles in a shallow valley just south of US 166 near Arkansas City. Extremely clear water offers plenty of channel catfish, bass, bluegill, walleye, and more. There are 113 acres available for hunting, particularly quail, rabbits, and squirrel, with some waterfowl.

DAY SPA Mainly For You Day Spa (620-653-2255), 167 S. Main, Hoisington. There are six treatment rooms at this full-service salon and spa in the center of town, where massages are a bargain at $60 for a one-hour hot-stone treatment or $30 for a mud mask facial. No credit cards.

Just for You Exclusively LLC, including The Homestead Inn (620-294-5421), 302 N. Broadway, Sharon. The spa offers massage, quantum pulse treatments, and detoxification treatments such as ionized footbaths. The inn is a little house that offers twin, full, and queen beds, plus a living room futon and lounge chairs. Enjoy a fully equipped kitchen with washer and dryer. There's also the two-bedroom Sunflower Cottage, The Haus, and The Castle, newly renovated with dormitory-style lodging. No credit cards. $50 lodging; call for individual treatment rates.

HUNTING Big Dog Outfitters (620-243-3263; bigdogoutfitter.com), 101 N. Main, Kingman. Bill Suenram loves to share his passion for hunting with other people, as do the five other guides in this eight-year-old company. His wife, Charlene, oversees lodging and meal services. Hunt for whitetail on 12,000 to 15,000 acres. Six-day deer bow hunts $375–450/day; five-day rifle hunts $3,000/day; three-day turkey hunt $750; waterfowl hunts also available.

GOLF Lake Barton Golf Club (620-653-4255), 673 N KS 281, Great Bend. The lake has been gone since the 1970s, but this club at the end of a serpentine road has survived nicely. Play a round and then grab a sandwich and a cold beer in the clubhouse. Par 70, 18 holes, 2,611 yards.

Carey Park Golf Course (620-694-2698), 9 Emerson Loop (take Main Street south until you reach the Emerson Loop), Hutchinson. This 1932 course is surrounded by hills full of lush vegetation. The clubhouse has a snack bar that serves sandwiches, daily specials, and beer, plus a large pro shop. Par 71, 18 holes, 6,410 yards.

OUTDOORS ✍ ❧ **Brit Spaugh Park and Zoo** (620-793-4160; visitgreatbend .com/parks), 24th and Main, Great Bend. Park open 6–midnight daily; zoo open 9–4:30 daily, but wait until 10 AM to arrive in summer because it takes that long for all animals to be on display for the day. This shady park is located a few minutes north of downtown and includes the city zoo. Visitors will occasionally see a live bird that is in rehabilitation at the educational raptor center. Though the cages are well maintained, the fineness of the mesh on some can make seeing the animals a challenge. There's a large pond surrounded by picnic tables and benches. Free.

Cheyenne Bottoms Refuge (620-793-7730), US 56 NE 40 Rd., off N US 281, out of Great Bend. Open daylight hours. This is the nation's largest inland wetland with water as far as the eye can see. Listen to bullfrogs, see sun-speckled water, and hear the gentle lap of waves. Watch a white pelican disappear into tall grass, a great blue heron standing silently, and a white egret with black-tipped wings glide across the water. The Nature Conservancy owns and manages 7,300 acres of this amazing area. There's also the Kansas Wetlands Education Center that offers guided tours. Free.

Byron Walker Wildlife Area (620-532-3242), 8685 W US 54, Cunningham. A gravel and dirt road leads south to the office of this prime wildlife viewing area located approximately 7 miles west of Kingman. Enjoy more than 4,600 acres of wooded areas, prairie, marshes, and wetlands—including Kingman State Fishing Lake. Boating, picnicking, and hunting for turkey, waterfowl, and deer are particularly popular here. Shelter houses, outhouses, grills, and primitive camping are also available.

Quivira National Wildlife Refuge (620-486-2393; fws.gov/quivira), 6 miles north and 6 miles east of Stafford. The visitor center is accessible 7:30–4 weekdays, with hands-on displays. As part of the central flyway, Quivira hosts more than four hundred bird species. Watch a pelican splash into the water or an egret land in the treetops. Special features include a disabled accessible observation tower, a photo blind, and the paved Birdhouse Boulevard. Free.

✍ ❧ **Dillon Nature Center** (620-663-7411; hutchrec.com), 3002 E. 30th Ave., Hutchinson. Grounds and trails open 8–sunset weekdays, 9–sunset weekends/ holidays. Visitors center open Oct.–March, 8–5 weekdays; April–Sept., 8–7 weekdays, 10–5 Sat. As part of the National Recreation Trail System, the nature center offers nearly 3 miles of concrete trails where visitors see prairie, woods, and gardens. Inside the visitors center learn about the wildlife that live in Kansas Woodlands, see the Kansas Children's Outdoor Bill of Rights, and watch prairie dogs scurry by. At the Underground Theater a recording begins as you walk in, with individual windows that light up as information is given about life under the prairies. View wildlife from the observation deck and visit the Davis Nature Library. Free.

QUIVIRA NATIONAL WILDLIFE REFUGE, NEAR STAFFORD, IS A WONDERFUL PLACE FOR BIRD-WATCHING AND HUNTING.

Avenue A Park, Hutchinson. This is a beautiful park with loads of benches and riverside brick walkways below street level that flank Cow Creek. There's a view of the wall-spanning mural painted on a nearby building.

✳ Green Space

In Pratt

Texas Lake Wildlife Area (620-895-6446), 10270 NW 130th Ave., Pratt. See a diverse combination of grasslands, extensive wetlands, and other habitats in this 1,200-acre wildlife area where you'll see plenty of migrating waterfowl and shorebirds. Camp in parking lots and obtain day-use permits for hunting.

Pratt Sandhill Wildlife Area (620-895-6446), 13 miles west and 6 miles north of Pratt. You'll find 640 acres of ADA-accessible area here, where hunting with guns is especially heavy during opening weekend of quail and pheasant season and during deer season; other hunted animals include rabbits, doves, and even coyotes. It's a good idea to drive a vehicle with high clearance because of sandy roads, and be prepared to walk 1 or 2 miles to some spots.

Lemon Park (620-672-5501), near Pratt, located just off Santa Fe Road, past the train depot, and east of downtown Pratt. Lemon Park is a lush, extremely well maintained, 117-acre park with loads of picnic tables and 80 varieties of trees.

Elsewhere

Tuttle Creek State Park and Tuttle Creek Reservoir (785-539-7941), 5800 A River Pond Rd., Manhattan. Most of this 12,500-acre reservoir lies in north-central Kansas, but there's access here, too. River Pond, Spillway, Fancy Creek, and Randolph (the horse campground) are four distinct park areas that collectively offer beach area, boat ramps, and docks. More than 150 campsites with water and electric or several with electric/water/sewer are available; choose from more than 500 primitive campsites, or rent a modern cabin with fully equipped kitchen, A/C, and even a fire ring. Hundreds of large trees also shield campers from summer heat. This is a great place to fish for bass, flathead, and channel catfish, and the adjacent 12,000-acre wildlife area offers viewing, traveling the trails, and hunting opportunities. You can also rent canoes, kayaks, and paddleboats from the park office.

Kanopolis State Park (785-546-2565), 200 Horsethief Rd., Marquette. See American Indian petroglyphs on Faris Cave walls in Kansas's first state park, established in 1955. Fish for crappie or channel catfish and rent one of the more than 300 campsites available. Hike or ride horseback amid the rolling, wooded Smoky Hills region. Boating and swimming are also available.

Riverside Park, Main and First Streets, Kingman. The river makes a slight horseshoe at the end of this park, where there's lots of shade, commemorative benches, and streetlights around the edges of the Hoover Pond built by the Works Progress Administration (WPA). Kids will enjoy the fenced playground equipment and ball diamonds.

✳ Lodging

BED & BREAKFASTS ✐ **Hedrick's Bed & Breakfast Inn and Exotic Animal Park** (888-489-8039; hedricks.com), 7910 N. Roy L. Smith Rd., Nickerson. Office open 8–noon and 1–5 Mon.–Fri. You'll never stay at another bed & breakfast like this. What looks like an Old West streetscape holds suites where hand-painted murals depict animals you'll see on site, including zebras, giraffes, ostriches, and more. Decor in the camel suite resembles The Arabian Nights, or sleep under mosquito netting in the kangaroo suite. Rates include evening tour and snack, breakfast, morning tour, and camel/pony rides. From $99; call for individual rates.

5th Ave. Suites Inn (620-200-2279; 5thavesuitesinn.besttimevacations .net), 201 W. 5th St., Hutchinson. Located in the heart of downtown Hutchinson, this pair of Victorian homes offers four suites including two with full, modern kitchens, and two with a shared kitchen. There are comfortable furnishings, off-street parking, and access to a brick patio or deck, depending on the suite. Nightly rate $60–110.

& (ᵞ) **The Bunkhouse Bed & Breakfast at Wildfire Ranch** (620-739-4788; bunkhouseatwildfireranch .com), 1374 Northeast Goldenrod, Medicine Lodge. People from 28 states, 9 foreign countries, and 97 Kansas cities have found their way to this rustic, relaxing retreat with every modern amenity. Watch gorgeous sunsets from the front porch of your log cabin. Full breakfast. $89.

LUXURIOUS MODERN ACCOMMODATIONS INSIDE LOG CABINS CHARACTERIZE THE BUNKHOUSE BED & BREAKFAST AT WILDFIRE RANCH.

Elsie Mae's Bed & Breakfast (620-845-2766; bbonline.com/ks/elsiemaes/index.html), 108 S. Market St., Caldwell. This lovely home with expansive front porch is a calm, welcoming place full of antiques and original woodwork. The Mona Lisa and other Renaissance women point you upstairs. Breakfast in bed comes with a flower vase on the tray. Rooms $90–125.

♿ ((ᵠ)) **Savannah House Bed & Breakfast** (620-532-3979; savannahousebb.com), 336 N. Main St., Kingman. Celebrating 10 years of operation in 2011, this lovely spot offers "Southern hospitality geared for businesspeople and efficiency." Antiques set the mood, with modern amenities that include some whirlpool tubs. There are 11 rooms (two without TVs); one is ADA accessible. Enjoy a lovely courtyard with hot tub, fountain, table and chairs, and grill. $79–149.

((ᵠ)) **Prairie Crossing** (620-459-6787; crossingkansas.com), 5408 NE 50 Ave., Kingman. Near the tiny town of Pretty Prairie. Diana and Leon McDaniel welcome you to their country home, where each room has a different vibe, from the log bed frame with Southwestern decor to jewel tone linens and matching stained glass. Guests from 35 states, a Hollywood movie crew, and visitors from Canada, Germany, and Vietnam have shared homemade breakfasts around the dining-room table. RVs are welcome and hunters appreciate available dog kennels. No credit cards. Rooms start at $69.

Henderson House Bed & Breakfast and Retreat/Conference Center (1-800-888-1417; hendersonbandb.com), 518 W. Stafford,

Stafford. Henderson House is a two-story 1905 home listed on the National Register of Historic Places. It's now part of a bed & breakfast and conference center with four historic homes and an antique church that house 18 bedrooms, private baths, and meeting facilities. Hand-carved stair railings, antique brass beds, broad porches, and luxurious robes are just a few features of this B&B neighborhood. Check the website for special events that range from organized bird-watching with renowned nature photographer Jerry Segraves to murder mystery weekends. $59–79.

HOTELS AND RESORTS & (ᵖ)
Highland Hotel and Convention Center (866-212-7122; highland hotel-gb.com), 3017 10th St., Great Bend. The main building is circa 1970s, and what was once an outdoor pool is now enclosed with rooms surrounding it. There's also a sauna, small exercise room, game room, restaurant, and a lounge. Enjoy Wi-Fi, and pets are welcome. $59–99.

& (ᵖ) **Grand Prairie Hotel and Convention Center** (620-669-9311; grandprairiehotel.com), 1400 N. Lorraine St., Hutchinson. Located near the Kansas Cosmosphere and Space Center, this enormous hotel offers plenty of amenities, from an expansive continental breakfast to an indoor pool area with a realistic space theme and a huge, sunlit atrium. There's a grand piano in the lobby and a sports bar with daily food and drink specials, plus more than 20 TVs. Double occupancy $79–89.

MOTELS, LODGES, CABINS, AND CAMPING
Travelers Budget Inn (316-793-5448; budgetinn.com), 4200 10th St., Great Bend. This little

HENDERSON HOUSE

motel offers clean comfortable rooms at a great price. There's a desk with data port, microwave, coffeemaker, and small refrigerator with relatively large freezer. $42–47.

Baltzell Motel (620-792-4395), 705 10th St., Great Bend. When was the last time you slept on a Tempur-Pedic mattress and enjoyed refrigerators and microwaves in your room for less than $35? By spring 2011 this decades-old property received a complete makeover, including those Tempur-Pedics. $29–33; one- and two-bedroom houses with full kitchen $40; weekly and monthly rates available.

The Lodge Micro Motel (620-791-7549/0098), 102 N. Walnut, Hoisington. This lodging is a revelation tucked in just a few blocks off Hoisington's main street. Four modern rooms offer one king, queen, or twin beds, plus microwave, refrigerator, coffeemaker, and flat-screen TV or full kitchens and more. Call for information about other rooms. $50–125 or $225 for the whole place.

(ᵖ) **Welcome Inn** (620-532-3144), 1101 E US 54, Kingman. There's a coffeepot in the lobby and a microwave and refrigerator in every room. Enjoy clean, comfortable rooms with AAA approval and easy access to restaurants. $50.

((¡¡)) **The Evergreen Inn Motel and RV Park** (620-672-6431; evergreeninn.biz), 20001 W US 54 (west end of town), Pratt. Sixteen rooms are spacious and clean with '50s-style furniture. The front building was built in 1949 and the second, several years later. For an unusual experience book the refurbished caboose suite. $59–68; $80 for the caboose. 25 RV slots $22–25.

& **Mi Grate Inn** (620-234-6005), 506 Martin Ave./KS 50, Stafford. The name of this recently renovated lodging is a play on words related to bird activity at the nearby Quivira National Wildlife Refuge. Singles, doubles, and one suite with a sitting room are available. There's a refrigerator in every room with microwaves available on request. Their busiest times are October to December and in the summer. $50; discounts available.

Mule Creek Hideaway (620-738-4331), Wilmore. What began as a spot for friends who came to the area for hunting has become a rural getaway for anyone. The owners live next door to this little house with queen and double beds, plus a futon. There's a new bathroom, DirectTV, and a fully equipped kitchen. $50 for two; $5–10 per extra person.

✳ Where to Eat

DINING OUT **Pretty Prairie Steakhouse** (620-459-7399; prettyprairiesteakhouse.com), 112 W. Main, Pretty Prairie (near Kingman). Open Tues.–Sat. 11:30–1, 5–9. Chris and Christine Seneff took over Main

Street Steakhouse in 2005 and receive rave reviews. There's a full bar and a delightful ambience full of wood and outdoor murals, trophy heads, and black-and-white photos of child movie stars. Great steaks and seafood—such as salmon with dill sauce—are only the beginning of this sophisticated menu. Inexpensive–moderate.

EATING OUT

In Great Bend

& **The Page** (620-792-8700), 2920 10th St., Great Bend. Open 11–10 Mon.–Thurs., 11–11 Fri.–Sat., 11–9 Sun. This place has a bar feel, with multiple TVs and sports memorabilia, where families are also welcome. There's a large menu that includes a wonderfully sweet and spicy house Italian dressing and warm, soft rolls with soft sweet butter. The blackened chicken pasta is delicious, decadent, and enough for two people. House specialties include chicken-fried chicken, the Santa Fe wrap, and the Tijuana burger. Inexpensive.

Granny's Kitchen (620-793-7441), 925 10th St., Great Bend. Open 7–2 Wed.–Sun. This is a very cute and homey place with terrific food made to order. Breakfast is available all day and biscuits and gravy combine soft biscuits with creamy gravy and huge sausage chunks. Other customer favorites include homemade banana cream pie and potato bacon soup.

4 Legs Up BBQ and Steakhouse (620-792-7892; 41egsupbbq.com), 2212 Main St., Great Bend. Open 11–2 and 4:30–8:30 Wed.–Sat. After five years spent as a rancher and farmer, Kelly Wertz attended and competed in his first BBQ contest in

2003. He is now on the professional BBQ circuit while his wife, Roni, runs the restaurant. Hundreds of ribbons line the walls and several 4-foot trophies are on the counter. They make sauces once a week, from a sweet, zingy, award-winning American royal sauce to a smoky-sweet chipotle raspberry and butter maple. The tender pulled-pork sandwich arrives with a caddy of sauces and a large helping of coleslaw. Buy meat by the pound and try decadent fried Oreos for dessert.

The Rack Billiard Café (620-792-5851), 3322A Railroad Ave., Great Bend. Open 11–midnight Tues.–Sat., 11–9 Sun. This café near the railroad tracks offers at least six pool tables and is known for its food. Try Mexican cheez steak, third-of-a-pound burgers, or the walleye dinner, cooked Louisiana-style and served with potato and salad. Or sample the armadillo eggs, fresh jalapeños stuffed with cheese, wrapped in bacon, and fried crisp.

Delgados (620-793-3786), 2210 10th St., Great Bend. Open 11–2 and 5–8:30 Mon.–Fri. Sit amid turquoise booths, ceramic chiles, and Mexican wall murals. They're well known for chips fried upon order and pork chili made with pork butt, tomatoes, and seasonings. Try their new dessert, too—fried ice cream in a flour tortilla bowl with cinnamon/sugar, caramel or chocolate, whipped cream, and a cherry. No credit cards.

In Hutchinson

& ϒ **Playa Azul** (620-663-7004), 701 E. 30th St., Hutchinson. Open 11–9:30 Mon.–Fri., 11–10:30 Sat., 11–8:30 Sun. Dine in a brightly painted Mexican village where pico de gallo is spicy and full of cilantro and the chicken burrito is moist and fla-

vorful. Try the Jalisco special, with grilled steak, chicken, and shrimp cooked with onions, bell peppers, and tomatoes, served over rice with cheese sauce, and a cool margarita. Ask about daily food and drink specials. Inexpensive.

Anchor Inn (620-669-0311), 128 S. Main. St., Hutchinson. Open 11–2 and 5–5 Mon.–Thurs., 11–2 and 5–9 Fri., 11–9 Sat. This legendary spot has served Mexican food for decades, including chorizo and eggs or fajitas with your choice of meat or seafood. They're known for their enormous buffet, with rice, refried beans, potatoes, and onions, plus pork ribs, corn on the cob, green beans, desserts, multiple fruits, and an extensive salad bar. Inexpensive.

& ϒ **Carl's Bar and Delicatessen** (620-662-9875; carlsbar.biz), 103 N. Main St., Hutchinson. Open 11–11 Mon.–Thurs., 11–2 Fri.–Sat. When a business has operated for more than 65 years, they must be doing something right. Three large Southwest eggrolls are a terrific appetizer, and Carl's famous Reuben is a knockout on marble rye with Thousand Island dressing. Build your own sandwich or burger or order a specialty hot dog. Check for daily specials. Inexpensive.

Fraese Drug Co. (620-662-4477), 100 N. Main St., Hutchinson. Store open 8–6 Mon.–Fri., 8:30–1:30 Sat.; soda fountain open 8–4 Mon.–Fri., 8:30–10:30 Sat. (limited menu); hot lunch served 11–1:30. The vintage soda fountain offers a dynamite chocolate malt. Breakfast choices include French toast and breakfast sandwiches; try their burgers or grilled chicken at lunch. Homemade pies, cobbler, and cake are legendary. Inexpensive.

& Y **Metropolitan Coffee** (620-662-8401; metrocoffeehutch.com), 1329 17th Ave., Hutchinson. Open 6:30–10 Mon.–Fri., 7–10 Sat., 8–10 Sun. Enjoy premium espresso, Celtic grog, tiramisu coffee drinks, or a plain cup of coffee in this warm and cozy spot. They also serve teas, pastries, and wintertime soups. Jewel-tone walls surround high-top tables and upholstered furnishings. Hit the book/magazine/game shelves or view rotating displays by local artists. Enjoy live music on weekends, too. Inexpensive.

In Larned
& **El Dos De Oros** (620-285-6238), 421 W. 14th St., Larned. Open 11–9:30 Tues.–Sat., 11–9 Sun.–Mon. Bright folkloric painting decorates this family-run business that also has seven other locations. There's a full bar and a Wednesday margarita special, plus lunch specialties. Try the burrito real—a flour tortilla filled with seasoned ground beef or chicken chunks and topped with Mexican rice and beans—or the *molcagete,* which combines beef, chorizo, shrimp, and chicken topped with cheese, sour cream, guacamole, pico de gallo, and flour tortillas. Mostly inexpensive.

& **Scraps-The Coffee Shop and Scrapbook Store** (620-285-8977; scrapslarned.com), 612 Broadway, Larned. Open 7–5:30 Tues./Thurs.–Sat., 7–9 Wed. This is clearly a local hangout. It's also an unusual hybrid that offers its own line of scrapbook papers, stickers, and other scrapbooking equipment. Check out the jewelry and purse case, a line of health and beauty products, and food. Enjoy a latte, a waffle with hot apples and homemade syrup, or the daily lunch special, from chicken gorgonzola pasta salad with cantaloupe and corn-bread crackers to the brisket sandwich.

In Pratt
Y **Uptown Café/Club D'Est** (620-672-6116), 202 S. Main St., Pratt. Open 11–10 Mon.–Sat., 11–2 Sun. buffet. This is a cozy place with large movie posters on the walls. Try the two-thirds-of-a-pound burger topped with smoked ham, bacon, and melted cheese; the beef chimichanga; french-fried vegetables; or choose from a dozen steaks. Inexpensive–moderate.

Y **Woody's Bar and Grill** (620-672-7744), 418 Main, Pratt. Open 11–12 Mon.–Thurs., 11–2 AM Fri.–Sat. Spacious, with high original tin ceilings, corrugated metal, red walls, and full of university flags and jerseys and televisions. Shandra and Jimmy Woody pride themselves on Woody burgers, jalapeño poppers, and breaded mushrooms, plus grillers and sandwiches. There's a full bar and even a few desserts. You'll find drink specials on most nights, from $1.25 for a small draw, and customers of all ages.

Elsewhere
& Y **C. J.'s Overtime Sports Bar and Grill** (620-532-2377), 130 W. A Ave., Kingman. Open 3–close Tues.–Thurs., 3–2 AM Fri.–Sat. Find one of the largest gumball machines ever, near the entrance to this beautiful place, holding $770 worth of candy. You'll also find great steaks, a full bar, a friendly on-site owner, and karaoke on some Friday nights. Inexpensive–moderate.

& **Anthony Motel and Café** (620-842-5185; anthonymotel.us), 423 Main St., Anthony. This 1960s building is completely updated and inviting; themed rooms feature horse racing and Harley Davidson. The eight-table café serves breakfast all day and there are two daily specials. Café is inexpensive.

Carolyn's Essenhaus (620-538-4711), 104 E. Main, Arlington. Open Mon.–Sat.; call for hours. Located in a 1912 building, the Mennonite owners create delicious homemade breakfast pastries, from huge cinnamon rolls with caramel icing to twist donuts. There's a full breakfast and lunch menu. On Friday evenings they offer *vernike,* a traditional pastry filled with cottage cheese that is boiled and fried, served with gravy and sausage or ham, with a salad bar.

&. **Lone Wolf Restaurant and Catering** (620-564-2829), 106 N. Main, Ellinwood. Open 11–2 and 5–8 Tues.–Sun. with pizza and subs all day. Enjoy a full-service bar and dozen-item salad bar, plus a full menu of favorites such as Reubens, burgers, and green chile fries. Order a 16-ounce rib eye on weekends after 6, with potato or fries and salad bar for only $22. Inexpensive–moderate.

&. **Country Creamery Ice Cream** (620-896-2761), 123 E. 14th St., Harper. Open 11–8 Tues.–Sat., 11–2 Sun. This family-operated restaurant has developed a loyal following during its 25 years of operation. In addition to premium ice cream and homemade desserts like strawberry shortcake, there's a page of Southwest-inspired menu offerings. Other favorites include the jumbo hickory bacon burger, San Jose chicken with sautéed vegetables, and homemade chicken and noodles (on Fridays). Inexpensive.

Kristy's Kafé (620-842-3722), 110 W. Main, Anthony. Open 11–8 Tues.–Sat. This cute country-style café offers lunch buffets on weekdays and delivery after 5. Most items are homemade, from the super club sandwich with beef, turkey, ham, bacon, provolone, Swiss, and cheddar cheeses to baked potato pizza, featuring sour cream, mozzarella, provolone, and cheddar, plus sliced potatoes, bacon, onions, peppers, and a side of ranch dressing. Kid pricing is available, too. Inexpensive.

&. **D'Mario's Pizza** (620-896-2414), 720 W. 14th St., Harper. Winter hours, Sun.–Thurs. 1–8, Fri.–Sat. 11–9; longer summer hours. With a homemade crust and sauce, D'Mario's is a pizza-lover's destination. Inexpensive.

R J's Café (620-862-7110), 108 Main, Haviland. Open 7–2 Mon.–Fri. Known for pies, including large slices of coconut cream, and hot beef sandwiches, R J's offers good home cook'n, such as a breakfast omelet with onion, peppers, tomato, cheese, sausage, or bacon, hash browns and toast, or a homemade cinnamon roll. Or try chicken-fried steak served with gravy, mashed potatoes, green beans, and a roll. No credit cards. Inexpensive.

Rancher's Café (620-594-2206), 201 S. Main St., Isabel (near Pratt). Open 6–1:30 Tues.–Sat., 5:30–8:30 Fri., 7–1:30 Sun. This popular café has operated at the base of a bright blue water tower since 2005 after restaurant stints in three larger towns. Chicken-fried steaks feature the owner's father's special recipe, and he makes a mean three-egg omelet. Enjoy smoked BBQ ribs, and fried chicken on Sun. Inexpensive.

✳ Entertainment

In Great Bend
Santas around the World (620-792-1614), 24th St. and Kansas Ave.,

Great Bend. Open Nov. 26–Dec. 30, 4–8 Thurs.–Fri., 10–6 Sat., 1–5 Sun., and by appointment for groups of 10 or more. This is a truly remarkable collection of more than 20 handmade Santas. Italy's La Befana carries a bell and a tiny tree and a snowflake-covered coat; France's Père Nöel dresses in maroon velvet; and China's Christmas Old Man fills stockings from the wicker basket that he carries. Admission $1; children under six free with adult admission; $2 by appointment.

& **Great Bend Community Theater/Crest Theatre** (620-792-4228), 1905 Lakin, Great Bend. The Crest was a movie theater until at least the 1970s. The balcony is original, as are draped stage curtains. Of the nearly four hundred seats, all are new except in the upper balcony. The group has offered three shows per year, mostly for adults, in the last 20 years, such as *The Long Weekend*. Extremely cheap beverages and snacks are available in the lobby. Tickets are $10. No credit cards.

✿ **Walnut Bowl and Mini Golf** (620-793-9400), 3101 N. Washington, Great Bend. Bowling and golf open 11–11 Mon.–Thurs., 11–12 Fri.–Sat., noon–8 Sun. This 1961 bowling alley still offers 24 lanes, used primarily on evenings and weekends; the golf course opened in 2002 and has 18 holes. Also enjoy video games, foosball, and vending machines inside. Bowling: 11–6 Mon.–Fri. about $3; about $4 after 6; 11–midnight Sat. $4; noon–8 Sun. $2. Shoe rental $2. Minigolf: $4 evenings or weekends; $3 Mon.–Fri. afternoons. Check for cosmic and moonlight rates.

✿ **The Wetlands at Great Bend** (620-793-4111; wetlandsatgb.com), 2303 Main St., Great Bend. Open Memorial Day–Labor Day, 12:30–5:30 daily; family nights 7–9 Tues./Thurs. This is a bright, colorful, and busy place throughout the open season. What more could a kid want

GREAT BEND COMMUNITY THEATER OFFERS SEVERAL SHOWS EACH YEAR IN THE RENOVATED CREST THEATRE.

than huge slides, an enormous tipping water bucket, and plenty of places to catch some rays? Adults 18 and up $4; youth 3–17 $3; children under 3 free.

☙ **Heartland Farm** (620-923-4585), 1049 CR 390, Pawnee Rock/near Great Bend. Tours by appointment. Nine people live in this experiential ecumenical community, including three Dominican sisters and two couples who attempt to be as self-sustaining as possible. See a solar oven and composting toilet, the oat bale solarium that houses starter plants, and the greenhouse that is heated using gallon milk jugs and steel drums. Visit the alpaca herd, soap-making facilities, and massive garden with everything from rhubarb and carrots to cabbage and beet potatoes. There are also pear, apricot, and peach trees. Limited lodging is available, and Sister Mary offers massages for an additional charge. Free.

& **L. E. "Gus" and Eva Shafer Memorial Gallery** (316-792-9342), 245 NE 30th Rd., Barton County Community College/Great Bend. Open mid-Aug.–mid-May, 10–5 Mon.–Fri., 1–4 Sun., or by appointment. Gus began to create figures in bronze at age 59 while working as a commercial artist. Twenty-three bronzes include a bust of artist Thomas Hart Benton and one of a cowboy on horseback with gun drawn, titled Prayer and a Winchester II. The gallery also houses art by Great Bend native Charles B. Rogers and artists such as Audubon and Picasso.

In Hutchinson

☙ **Salt City Splash Aquatic Center** (620-663-6179), 1601 S. Plum, Carey Park/Hutchinson. Open 12:30–6:30 in season. Enjoy a traditional pool with diving board and a second one with massive water slides at this bright, colorful, and inviting aquatic center. Adults 18 and up $4.75; youth 8–17 $3.50; children 3–7 $1.75 with paying adult; children under 3 free with paying adult.

Hutchinson Zoo (620-694-2693), 6 Emerson Loop E, Hutchinson. Call for hours. This 9-acre zoo has held up to 120 animals and is currently undergoing a massive renovation. Free.

☙ **The Family Children's Theatre /The Flag Theater** (620-662-SHOW; familychildrenstheater.com), 310 N. Main, Hutchinson. Now in its 22nd season, the Family Children's Theatre offers kid-friendly theater productions performed in the restored Flag Theater that involve dozens of Hutchinson residents. Individual shows include musical versions of You're a Good Man, Charlie Brown and Alice in Wonderland, plus drama such as To Kill a Mockingbird and Christmas Carol. Adults $10; seniors $8; children $5.

Fox Theater (620-663-5861; hutchin sonfox.com), 18 E. First Ave., Hutchinson. Gorgeous original workmanship on the exterior of this restored 1931 art deco movie palace only hints at the restoration work done inside. Listed on the National Register of Historic Places and the state register, its marquee was the first in Kansas to feature flashing neon, and in 1994 the state legislature named the Fox the State Movie Palace of Kansas. It currently seats about 1,200 people with complete, unobstructed views, and offers a wide range of entertainment. Call for schedule and ticket prices.

Elsewhere

Gypsum Hills Trail Ride (620-886-5390), 3212 NW Forest City Rd., Medicine Lodge. Call to schedule guided rides and for special events; camping also available. Explore the red sandstone bluffs and white, gypsum ledges of the Gypsum Hills at the Gant-Larson Ranch. Access more than 10,000 acres of land on organized or private rides with your own horse. Join an all-women ride with potluck or other May weekend trail rides that include several meals, and special overnight pack trip rides. Ride on your own for $10; ask about other rates.

Nuss Equestrian Center LLC (620-653-2700), 158 E. State Rd. 4, Hoisington. Call for appointment. Candace Nuss spared no expense when building this facility that overlooks Cheyenne Bottoms. Two horses are available on the property; guest horses must be current on all vaccinations. Nuss offers boarding for six horses or on 160 acres of pasture; $30/night; $60 for 45–60 minute riding lessons.

Anthony Downs (620-842-3796), 521 E. Sherman, Anthony. Opened in 1909 but with minimal recent use, this longtime racing facility is in the sights of locals, who hope to get it running regularly again in the near future. Call for an update.

✳ Selective Shopping

In Great Bend
My Town (mytown-greatbend.com), 1919 Lakin, Great Bend. A phenomenon designed to transform the downtown area, this entrepreneurial collective includes **Perks Coffee Shoppe, Mali Jewelry and Accessories, and Heart of Kansas Mercantile,** with sunflowers everywhere, plus Kansas food, photos, and more. **R. B. Teller's,** named after the Great Bend pioneer and Fuller Brush sales-

man, offers Fuller Brush products, deeply discounted backpacks, and luggage, plus name-brand T-shirts and hats. **Renue Salon and Spa** is known for massages, facials, pedicures, and hair coloring amid earth-tone walls, a pergola, and rustic wood doors, low lighting, and a large fountain reminiscent of Tuscany. Stay tuned for a new infrared sauna, steam shower, tanning services, and a rentable party room.

&. **J&L Coins and Jewelry LLC** (620-793-6732), 1203 Main, Great Bend. Open 9:30–5:30 Mon.–Fri., 9–1 Sat. Browse eight jewelry and coin cases or purchase guns for self-protection, hunting, and big game. Sixty-five percent are new, there are hundreds in inventory, and all purchases require a background check.

In Haviland
Antique Junction (620-862-7232), 308 S. Lawrence, Haviland. Open 10–5 Tues.–Sat. This store offers vintage furniture, Depression glass, military items, fishing lures, and a book nook with unusual educational, history, and Little House books. Handcraft enthusiasts will appreciate the quilts and afghans. No credit cards.

&. (ᵗ) **Haviland Hardware** (620-862-5202), 114 N. Main, Haviland. Open 6:30–5:30 weekdays, 6:30–noon Sat. In this circa 1911 building, Vic Hannan has maintained the original tin ceiling and plank floor while offering milk, bread, and canned and packaged foods, as well as paint and loads of small hardware items, since 2006. Sip coffee or cappuccino while you shop.

In Hutchinson
Hutchinson offers multiple antiques stores in its downtown district. However, it's important to note that many are not open on Sunday or Monday. Other popular stores include:

&. **Apron Strings** (620-259-7339; apronstringsstore.com), 201 S. Main, Hutchinson. Open 10–6 Mon.–Fri., 10–5 Sat. Enjoy free Saturday demonstrations and fee-based cooking classes, and a huge array of tastefully arranged kitchen essentials and gadgets. The building owners were from California, live upstairs, and started the very popular Third Thursdays downtown, featuring musicians and artists throughout the neighborhood.

&. **Smith's Market** (620-662-6761; smithsmarketks.com), 211 S. Main, Hutchinson. Open 7–6 Mon.–Sat. This grocery store has operated for more than 75 years and offers fine fruits and vegetables with a lot of specialty, local, and Kansas-made items. There's a pastoral mural on the back wall, and the store is beautifully arranged.

Becker's Bunkhouse (620-543-2297), 4 miles north of Hutchinson on KS 61, Medora. Thurs.–Sat. 10–4 or by appointment. Browse a massive collection of Old West collectibles and cowboy antiques, from skulls and saddles to spurs and furniture. There are also reenactment items and Western decor.

In Pratt
&. **K Lane's** (620-933-2159), 301 S. Main, Pratt. Open 10–6 weekdays, 10–5 Sat. K Lane's offers some hard-to-find items such as SPANX, Brighton watches, and jewelry, as well as Not Your Daughter's Jeans, Niki Biki layering pieces, and Yummie Tummies. There are also scarves and tights, and you'll always find a sale.

Maurice's (620-672-3348), 324 S. Main, Pratt. Open 10–8 Mon.–Sat., 1–5 Sun. Once a men's clothing store, Maurice's now offers young, hip women's fashion, from jeans to hippy skirts, shoes, and even faux alligator purses. There's a section for sizes 14–24, too. They strive to be the best small-town specialty store offering work and weekend clothing.

&. **Simply Southwest** (620-672-7722), 213 S. Main, Pratt. Open 10–6 weekdays, 10–5 Sat. This enormous store has gone far beyond its Southwestern roots. Browse metal and terra-cotta wall suns, plus KU and K-State items, a baby section, and a gourmet foods section. And stop by the beverage cantina for cappuccino with homemade fudge or cinnamon rolls.

Elsewhere
Prairie House Flowers and Gifts (620-587-3755), 307 W. Hamilton, Hoisington. Open 9–5 Mon.–Fri., 9–2 Sat. Visit a gorgeous home decor store that also offers gourmet foods, silk and fresh flowers, scent chips, and Department 56 miniature houses. There's a year-round Halloween and Christmas display, including decorator black holiday trees and a coffee of the day to sample before purchasing a pound of your favorite.

Highway 56 Antiques and Market (620-659-2334/3153), 213 Sixth St., Kinsley. Open 9–5 daily or later by appointment. Admire the antique green and cream stove, barber chair, or pinball machine and find the perfect vintage quilt in this block-deep store. Other nearby antique shops include Painted Pony and Midway Consignment.

Gun Room at the Grand (620-930-3006), 124 S. Main St., Medicine Lodge. Open 10–5 Tues.–Fri., 9–5 Sat. Robert Stutler was senior vice president of Ruger firearms for more than 20 years and his father was a gun major, so selling fine firearms—from antique to modern—is second nature to him. It's a gorgeous room in this renovated hotel, which also includes a tea room, available by reservation. There are banquet facilities downstairs.

State Bank Treasures and Antiques (620-478-2268), 207 S. Main St., Norwich. Open 1–6 Tues.–Fri., 6–6 Sat. This lovely vintage building on the corner is full of small antiques, welcoming staff, and even fresh donuts on Saturdays. Have some coffee and a treat and then find the perfect home decor item.

The Stafford Mall (620-234-6845), 111 S. Main, Stafford. Open 10–5:30 daily. This antique and collectibles mall, with a smattering of handcrafts, showcases 36 vendors from as far away as Wichita, Larned, and Hoisington. Purchase a sterling tea service, small antique furniture, or vintage Fiestaware, plus hunting and fishing equipment. No credit cards.

The Lodge (620-653-4288), 120 N. Main, Hoisington. Open 8–6 Mon.–Fri., 8–2 Sat. This compact store located at the back of Cheyenne Hardware sells hunting and fishing licenses, ammunition, boat parts, hunting/camouflage clothes, fishing poles, and other equipment.

✳ Special Events

June: **Juneteenth** (316-227-2227), alternates between Larned and Great Bend. This is a celebration of African American heritage and freedom, with traditional food, arts and crafts, music, and dancers.

September: **Kansas State Fair** (1-800-362-3247; kansasstatefair.com), Kansas State Fairgrounds, Hutchin-

son. Kansas agricultural heritage is on display throughout this 10-day event, which began in 1913. See livestock including goats, cows, poultry of every color and size, and even alpacas, plus educational crop displays. Cowboys perform and there are contests, games, and plenty to eat. **Medicine Lodge Peace Treaty Pageant** (peacetreaty.org) and **Kansas Championship Ranch Rodeo** (620-886-9815), Medicine Lodge. Witness historical reenactments surrounding the peace treaty established in 1867 with Kiowa, Comanche, Plains Apache, Southern Cheyenne, and Southern Arapaho Indians and world-class rodeo events held at Pageant Arena.

October: **Oktoberfest** (620-234-6951; call to confirm event), Stafford. Enjoy crafts and ethnic/American food, free entertainment, a street dance, and a Mr. Oktoberfest pageant.

November: **Lemon Park Lights,** Pratt. Thousands of holiday lights and displays line the city's most beloved park from dusk to 11 PM through January 1.

THE KANSAS STATE FAIR HELD IN HUTCHINSON IS THE STATE'S BIGGEST ANNUAL PARTY.

Northwest Kansas: Wide-Open Spaces

HAYS

L ocated at the eastern edge of northwest Kansas, and with more than twenty thousand residents, Hays is the largest city in this part of the state. It's known as the German Capital of Kansas and the seat of Ellis County. The median household income is approximately $37,000.

Few trees grew in the Hays area during the early years because of how much limestone was in the ground, resulting in many sod or stone buildings. The county was named after Civil War lieutenant George Ellis, who served with the 12th Kansas Infantry. After Fort Hays was established in 1865, it protected railroad operations from Indians and sent supplies to other forts that lacked railroad access. The Union Pacific Railway arrived in fall 1867, around the time that Volga-German settlers began to move here.

Hays was known as a wild town with dozens of places to drink alcohol and plenty of "dance hall ladies" during the 1860s and 1870s, and the nation's first Boot Hill Cemetery became the resting place of many rowdy revelers. General Custer visited the area several times, and Wild Bill Hickok was sheriff for a while. Catch a glimpse of more city history at the Merci Boxcar donated by France after World War II, the Volga German Haus and Ellis County Historical Museum located in downtown Hays, and the Sternberg Museum at Fort Hays State University.

German heritage still influences the town, from the handmade sausage available at various meat markets to *bierocks* served at local restaurants. You'll find several antiques stores downtown near the county museum, including one dedicated to Scottish items and culture.

Visitors can stay in a 1909 home turned bed & breakfast, a privately owned motel, or chain lodging. Plenty of dining options include a family owned bakery, a coffee shop housed in the original Semolino Flour Mill, several popular Mexican restaurants, and, of course, fried chicken. There are four to five gallery walks throughout the year sponsored by the Hays Arts Council, and a self-guided historical walking tour includes nearly 30 sites. And Hays is easy to reach, with its location at I-70 and US 183.

GUIDANCE Hays Convention and Visitors Bureau (785-628-8202; haysusa .net; includes Ellis), 2700 Vine St., Hays. Open 8–5 Mon.–Thurs., 8–7 Fri., 9–5 Sat., 1–5 Sun.

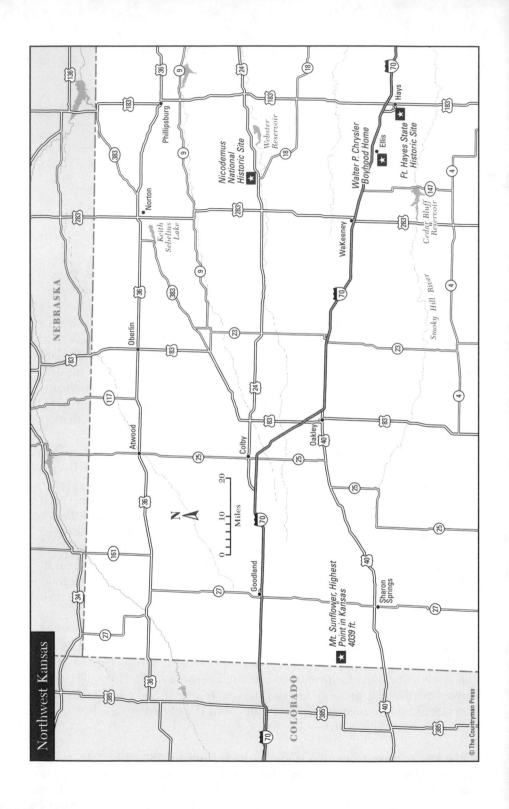

Northwest Kansas

MEDICAL EMERGENCY Hays Medical Center (785-623-5000), 2200 Canterbury, Hays.

GETTING THERE *By car:* Major highways include I-70 and US 183. *By air:* The closest large airport to northwest Kansas is **Denver International Airport** (303-342-2000), 8500 Pe a Blvd., Denver, CO. **Hays Regional Airport** (785-628-7370), 3950 E. Eighth St. also serves this area via Great Lakes Airlines (785-623-4820). *By bus:* **Greyhound** comes to 3610 Vine St./Golden Ox Truck Stop in Hays. Call 785-628-8321 for information and reservations.

GETTING AROUND Northwest Kansas is definitely a place for car travel, or you can walk through much of downtown Hays.

✳ To See

HISTORIC PLACES, LANDMARKS, AND SITES & **Fort Hays** (785-625-6812), 1472 US 183 Alt., Hays. Open 9–5 Tues.–Sat. There were no walls around this fort that housed up to 565 soldiers. Established in 1867, it initially protected railway workers from Indian tribes. Fort Hays later became a supply depot to southern forts without railroad access. The fort closed in 1889 and most buildings were torn down, but visitors can tour a guardhouse, a blockhouse, and two fully furnished buildings where the families of two junior officers shared quarters, including parlors and joint kitchens. Interpretive signs indicate the location of other buildings and their functions. The visitors center offers informational brochures, tours, and a gift shop. Adults $3; students $1; KSHS Inc. members/children under five free.

Boot Hill Cemetery (785-628-8202), 18th and Fort Streets, Hays. Open sunrise–sunset. Outlaw and horse thief graves from Hays's wildest Western days are at this site, named because so many buried here died with their boots on. This Boot Hill Cemetery actually began seven years before Dodge City's Boot Hill Cemetery and operated from 1867 to 1874. Look for Louisa Sherwood's grave. This "dance hall girl" supposedly committed suicide over a man and was one of only two women buried here. There's also the grave of a Mexican bull-train driver who was stabbed by another driver.

MUSEUMS & **Sternberg Museum** (785-628-4286; sternberg.fhsu.edu), 3000 Sternberg Dr., Fort Hays State University/Hays. Open 9–6 Tues.–Sat., 1–6 Sun.; also open Mon. in summer. This educational museum was named after the Sternberg family. A complete mastodon skeleton greets visitors. See fossilized fish within fish from Kansas's ancient inland sea and enter a massive room where dinosaurs fly overhead and a T. Rex turns his head and roars. There are small displays of minerals, meteorites, and igneous and metamorphic rocks, plus other dinosaur and mammoth bones found in Kansas. See a portrait biography of Charles Darwin and rotating displays such as SUPERCROC. Adults 13 and up $8; seniors 60 and up $6; children 4–12 $5.

Ellis County Historical Museum and Volga German Haus (785-628-2624), 100 W. Seventh St., Hays. Open Tues.–Fri 10–5; longer hours in summer. Museum visitors learn about Hays's rowdy early days, marked by violence; 57 whiskey/beer emporiums; and five dance halls. There's information about General Custer's visits from the 1860s to early 1870s, such as a buffalo hunt with Grand Duke Alexis of Russia and early immigrants. Learn about tragedies that struck the town, including a massive 1895 fire, the 1919 gas explosion, and 1930s dust storms. See an antique harness shop and the children's learning center, which features period hats and clothing. The Volga German House is a reproduction of an early immigrant house with simple wood bed, armoire, dining table, and period linens and tableware. Admission for both: adults $4; children 3–12 $1.

✳ To Do

BOATING AND FISHING Cedar Bluff Reservoir (785-726-3212), 32001 KS 147, Ellis. This 6,000-acre reservoir is known for great crappie, bluegill, and catfish populations. Cedar Bluff State Park includes two distinct sections—the Bluffton area features boat ramps, utility and other campsites, shelters, shower houses, five cabins, and picnic spots. Other activities include a BMX track or swimming from the beach, plus basketball and volleyball or horseshoes. The Page Creek area offers utility and other campsites and is a favorite area for boaters and skiers.

A COMPLETE MASTODON SKELETON IS ONLY THE BEGINNING OF ANCIENT CREATURES AT STERNBERG MUSEUM.

GOLF Fort Hays Municipal Golf Course (785-625-9949), 1450 Golf Course Rd., Hays. This course is largely flat, with one hole that is located only yards from the fort blockhouse. Par 72, 18 holes, 6,280 yards.

Smoky Hill Country Club (785-625-8297), 3303 Hall St., Hays. Non-Ellis-County residents may play here at any time. In addition to the course, there's a putting green, chipping green, and driving range available. Water figures into six holes on this tree-dotted, well-maintained course. Par 71/72, 18 holes, 6,291 yards.

✳ Green Space

Frontier Park (785-628-7375), 1546 E US 40 Bypass, Hays. Hike beside the winding creek and through wooded areas in this 89-acre park and recreational area with limestone shelters and restrooms. Kids will love the playground equipment, and three shelter houses are great for picnics. You may see buffalo nearby, or play disc golf.

* Lodging

BED & BREAKFASTS  **Tea Rose Inn B&B** (785-623-4060; tea rose.net), 117 W. 13th St., Hays. Built in 1909, this B&B merges historical features, comfort, and privacy, plus wonderful food, such as cinnamon swirl French toast served with black-berries, blueberries, strawberries, and banana slices. Sleep comfortably on an iron bed in the Homestead room, sip complementary tea in the rocking chair, and wake to morning light. $89–129.

CABINS AND CAMPING El Charro RV Park (785-625-3423), 2020 E. Eighth St., Hays. This unusu-al RV park with 14 pull-throughs sits beside apartments and a convenience store with gas pumps that are owned by the same couple. Campers may access Wi-Fi and cable TV ($1), and use the apartment pool and laundry facilities. $18 for 20–50 amp hookups; water and sewer hookups available.

* Where to Eat

EATING OUT & **Augustine's Bak-ery** (785-621-2253; augustinesbakery .com), 1305 Main St., Hays. Open 7–3 weekdays, 7–noon Sat.; 11–2 for full sandwich menu. Chad Augustine worked at a previous bakery owned by family members before he and his wife, Holly, opened their own bakery. Known for wedding cakes, they also offer a display case full of homemade cupcakes, cookies, brownie chunk and New York–style cheesecake, and even *bierocks*—a four-pack for $10. Inex-pensive.

& **Café Semolino** (785-621-2520; semolina.com), 110 W. 11th St., Hays. Open 7–10 weekdays, 7–11 Fri., 8–11 Sat. This was the original office build-ing for Semolino Flour Mill, and the antique ceiling and hardwood floors remain. Whole bean coffee is ground fresh for every cup. Most baked goods are made from scratch, including bagels, and there are specials such as half a panini with choice of side. In wintertime cozy up to the fireplace on a leather couch with a Red Eye—brewed coffee with an espresso shot. On weekends music performances include touring bands. The monthly Science Café (usually held the third Tuesday of every month) offers edu-cational programs such as information about wind farms. Inexpensive.

HAYS'S POPULAR CAFÉ SEMOLINO OCCU-PIES THE ORIGINAL OFFICE BUILDING FOR SEMOLINO FLOUR MILL.

& **Gella's Diner and Lb. Brewing Co.** (785-621-BREW; lbbrewing .com), 117 E. 11th St., Hays. Open 11–10 Sun.–Wed., 11–midnight Thurs.–Sat. See the spotless brewing room where Lb. Brewing Co. crafted beer that was a silver medalist in the Great American Beer Festival. Then chow down on a *bierock* bursting with ground meat, plus cheese sauce, paired with a frosty pale ale. Or try chicken pesto pasta with chopped grape tomatoes and freshly grated Parmesan. Big burgers, fish and chips, and beerwurst are other choices. Inexpensive.

& **Guiterrez Mexican Restaurant** (785-625-4402; thelocalsfavorite.com), 1106 E. 27th St., Hays. Open 11–9 Sun.–Thurs., 11–10 Fri.–Sat. A local favorite, Guiterrez offers the owner's recipes, taught to all cooks at the restaurant. Guacamole goes easy on spice, sour cream sauce is a delicious enchilada topper, and shredded burrito chicken is perfectly cooked. Enjoy cocktails, from mango martinis to black raspberry margaritas, plus beer and wine. Their adjacent Bravo Coffee Bar is Starbucks licensed and certified, with Wi-Fi and a patio. Open 7 AM to restaurant close. Both are inexpensive.

Al's Chickenette (785-625-7414), 700 Vine St., Hays. Open 11–9:30 Tues.–Sat., 11–8:30 Sun. Go for the legend and stay for the fresh, never frozen fried chicken. This Hays landmark has operated for more than 60 years in its current location—a place with the feel of an old-fashioned diner. The three-piece chicken dinner comes with choice of potato, salad, and dinner roll. Chicken-fried steak is another crowd favorite. Additional sides include green or baked beans,

coleslaw, potato salad, and even chicken toes. Inexpensive.

✳ Entertainment

Hays art galleries sprinkled throughout the downtown area include **The Art Gallery at Commerce Bank** (718 Main), with two- and three-dimensional works by artists from across the state; **Bruce Burkholder Studio and Gallery** (116 E. 11th); **The Artists at Work Studio** (717 Main), which features work and workspace by women; and **711 Studio** (711 Main), featuring the work of local artist Michael Jilg.

🐎 **Blue Sky Miniature Horse Farm** (785-625-6725; blueskyhorses.com), 10 miles outside of Hays; call at least one day in advance for specific address and appointment. The tiny equines raised here are no bigger than a large dog. They were historically bred as pets for children of European royalty and are intelligent and affectionate. Today, they represent a distinct recognized breed called American Miniature Horse, and all the Schmidts's horses are registered show horses. The family offers education about the breed and their care, plus rides on small carts. Groups of at least three people preferred; call for current rates.

🐎 **Fairview Farms Alpacas** (785-628-6352; fairviewfarmsalpacas.com), 1811 E. 26th St., Hays. By appointment only or during special tours/events. Get up close and personal with these gentle animals at a working alpaca ranch. Pat the alpacas, learn what it takes to raise and compete with these animals, and, if you like, participate in some daily farm chores. A gift store is in the works. Adults $3; children 2–12 $2.

Heartland Community Theatre

(785-625-6577; heartlandcommunity theatre.org), various locations. Offering several shows per year. Community volunteers lend their musical, acting, and behind-the-scenes talents to create productions that the whole family will enjoy. They include a Christmas show and a summer show. The troupe also offers dinner theater events. Contact for rates.

Mid-America Rodeo Co. LLC

(785-628-6272), various locations/Hays office; call for upcoming event information. This company produces between 3 and 13 Kansas rodeo events per year, which may include roping, riding, barrel racing, bronc riding, and more. Events free–$8.

✷ Selective Shopping

&. **C. S. Post and Co./Regeena's Flowers and Events** (785-628-3000; cspost.com), 117 W. 11th St., Hays. Open 9:30–5:30 weekdays, 9:30–5 Sat. This lovely shop serves customers from throughout the United States and overseas, and *Elle* magazine has called it "a hip, updated version of a general store." C. S. Post carries name-brand clothing such as Lacoste, Joan Vass, and ISDA & CO, and a collection of tabletop Santas. There's also a 4-foot-tall sock monkey near some vintage-style kid aprons. Buy metal polishing cloths, clear plastic dining chairs, ceramic vases, and basil olive oil. Or order a gift basket for a special occasion.

&. **Northglen Antiques** (785-623-4005; northglenantiques.com/info .html), 801 Main St., Hays. Open 10–5 Mon.–Wed., 10–6 Thurs.–Sat., 1–5 Sun.; longer summer hours. Molly, the Scottish terrier, greets visitors to this store with plenty of clan colors and Scottish antiques, including dressing tables, chamber pots, and rocking chairs. There's also Celtic music and jewelry, with iced tea in summer or hot tea in the winter, just as authentic Scottish shops offer their customers.

&. **Quilt Cottage Co.** (785-625-0080), 2520 Vine St., Hays. Open 10–5:30 weekdays, 10–3 Sat. Browse more than 3,500 bolts of quilting fabrics and the state's largest stock of flannels. You'll also find cross-stitch fabrics, knitting yarn, plus related books, patterns, and supplies, and DMC floss.

Simply Charmed (785-625-7476; shopsimplycharmed.com), 1011 Main St., Hays. Open 10–6 weekdays, 10–5 Sat. The bead design studio at the back of this store offers a mind-boggling array of beads to make custom creations—on your own or with assistance. In front, you'll find women's clothing and accessories, including jewelry.

&. **Warren's Meat Market** (785-625-4902), 1010 E. 29th St., Hays. Open 9–6 Mon.–Sat. Warren Wittman has worked in the meat and sausage business for more than 40 years. He makes German bologna, slab bacon, ham steak slices for sandwiches, and more in his own little shop now. The store also carries steaks, chicken, cheeses, and some prepared foods.

&. **Hays City Quality Meats** (785-621-2233), 2306 Vine St., Hays. Open 9–6 weekdays, 8–6 Sat. Beef is the number one seller at this popular butcher shop. They cut and grind everything in-house, and the homemade sausage is created from area recipes.

SCOTTISH ANTIQUES RULE IN THIS ANTIQUES AND COLLECTIBLES STORE ON HAYS'S MAIN STREET.

✳ Special Events

April: **Fort Hays State University NIRA Rodeo** (785-628-4196; fjsu .edu/rodeo), Hays. More than six hundred entrants compete from universities throughout Kansas, Missouri, and Oklahoma. **Wild West Festival** (785-623-4476; wildwestfestival.com), Hays. This multiday extravaganza is filled with country music, art exhibits, and soccer and baseball tournaments. Check out the water games and gigantic parade. **Midwest Deutsche Oktoberfest** (785-625-5395; midwest deutschefest.com), Hays. Polka rules at this annual event. Visitors also enjoy historical and wheat-threshing demonstrations, plus plenty of good food and beer.

December: **FrostFest** (chestnutstreet district.com/leisure/frostfest.html), Hays. From a horse-drawn hayride and holiday music to Father Christmas at Fort Hays, this event gives participants a taste of Christmas in the 1860s.

OAKLEY, COLBY, AND GOODLAND

The town of Oakley has approximately two thousand people and lies at the intersection of I-70 and US 83. US 40 also passes through the town. One of the most impressive remnants of Kansas's inland sea lies approximately 25 miles south of town. Monument Rocks is a series of hauntingly beautiful rock outcroppings surrounded by relatively flat land and well worth a 7-mile trip on gravel roads.

Visitors see more fossils and learn more about their presence in Kansas at Oakley's Fick Fossil and History Museum, which includes dinosaur bones found in the state. The privately owned Keystone Gallery, located near Monument Rocks, offers another look at Kansas fossils and geological finds from other areas. Hunters in this area have more than 10,000 acres of walk-in hunting land at their disposal, too.

One fun piece of history is demonstrated in a massive bronze statue at the edge of town that commemorates an 1868 competition between two buffalo hunters regarding who could keep the nickname of Buffalo Bill. Wild Bill Hickok brought down the most buffalo and gained the title that day.

Kansas's first RV park operates in Oakley, plus chain and independent lodging. Dine at one of the most beautiful truck stop restaurants around and sample steak, fried chicken, or fresh baked goods in multiple spots. There's also a small airport in town.

Nicknamed the Oasis of the Plains, the town of Colby was formed in 1882 and named for J. R. Colby, a Civil War veteran who homesteaded and then secured a patent for town. The town moved slightly north to its current location in 1885. Agriculture is big business here, with major crops of wheat, sunflowers, corn, and milo.

This was an area full of sod houses until lumber became readily accessible. Multiple historical structures include the 1906 Thomas County Courthouse, the 1886 First Presbyterian Church, and Colby city hall, a sand-colored, art-deco building from the 1920s. The Union Pacific Railroad came through in 1887 and the Rock Island line followed in 1888.

Colby's wide streets feature 1920 brick paving and well-kept neighborhoods. Recent construction has included a new fire station and a state-of-the-art wastewater treatment plant. More than five thousand people call the city home. I-70 reached the Colby area in 1965, and KS 25 and US 24 also intersect here. You'll find a terrific RV park near the edge of town, with chain and locally owned restaurants to choose from, and a handful of motels/hotels.

Goodland is a city of approximately five thousand people, located within 17 miles of the Colorado State line and part of the mountain standard time (MST) zone. I-70 and KS 27 intersect here, but Denver offers the closest major airline service. The city is known for its hot, dry summers, strong winds, and relatively high snowfalls. It's also known for growing sunflowers, commemorated by the giant reproduction of a Van Gogh sunflower painting outside the central business district.

Goodland is the seat of Sherman County, which was named after Union general William Tecumseh Sherman. The small city lies near the Republican River and is considered part of the High Plains.

The 1867 Kidder Massacre and Battle of Beaver Creek took place near here, in which Sioux and Cheyenne Indians killed Lt. Lyman Kidder and his patrol of 11 men. Through the years, notable residents have included two federal judges, football player Brook Berringer, and Charles Sparks, a U.S. representative from the state.

Early settlers were considered hardy, thrifty, and tenacious, which were important qualities in order to live successfully in this challenging environment. Goodland also saw its share of massive dust storms during the 1930s, including black blizzards, which rose as high as 8,000 feet before turbulent winds, and were sometimes accompanied by thunder and lightning. The High Plains Museum offers visitors a look at these pieces of Goodland's past, plus a view of the nation's first helicopter. The area is known for good hunting, particularly for turkey, deer, and pheasant.

Goodland families make a decent living—near $40,000 for the median household—particularly given the low cost of living. Local restaurants offer everything from quality Chinese food to chicken-fried bacon, Mexican *horchata* and *taquitos*, and upscale coffee shop fare.

GUIDANCE Colby Convention and Visitors Bureau (785-460-7643; colby chamber.com), 350 S. Range Ave., #10, Colby. Open 8–5 weekdays; closed 12–1.

Oakley Tourism and Convention Board (785-671-1000; discoveroakley.com).

Sherman County Convention and Visitors Bureau (785-890-3515; goodland net.com/cvb, includes Goodland), 925 Main, Goodland. Open 9–5.

GETTING THERE AND GETTING AROUND *By car:* Colby is located at the intersection of KS 25 and US 24. Reach Goodland at I-70 and KS 27, or Oakley at US 40 and US 83. This is definitely a place for car travel and, in good weather, a fun place to drive. You may travel for an hour or longer between chosen stops. *By air, train, or bus:* There is no commercial air, AMTRAK, or Greyhound service in this area. The closest full-service airport to northwestern Kansas is **Denver International Airport** (303-342-2000), 8500 Pena Blvd., Denver, CO.

MEDICAL EMERGENCY Citizens Medical Center (785-462-7511), 100 E. College Dr., Colby.

Goodland Regional Medical Center (785-890-6002), 220 W. Second St., Goodland.

Logan County Hospital (785-672-3211), 211 Cherry St., Oakley.

✷ To See

HISTORIC PLACES, LANDMARKS, AND SITES

In Goodland

The Ennis-Handy House (call Sherman County Convention and Visitors Bureau, 785-890-3515; goodlandnet.com/history), 202 W. 13th St., Goodland. Open 1–5 Wed.–Mon. Built in 1907 for $5,000, this Queen Anne Victorian home was one of the earliest in Sherman County to have electricity, indoor plumbing, a phone, and walk-in closets. Occupied until 2001 (it was even used as a funeral home), it was later given to the Sherman County Historical Society. Loaned and donated furnishings complement 1930s carpeting, an original fireplace, and woodwork that includes pocket doors. Adults $5; seniors 60 and up $4; children 2–11 $3.

♿ **World's Largest Easel/Giant Van Gogh Painting** (call Sherman County Convention and Visitors Bureau, 785-890-3515; bigeasel.com), Cherry St., Goodland. Always open. A 40,000-pound replica of Vincent Van Gogh's *3 Sunflowers in a Vase,* this 24' x 32' painting stands on an eight-story easel near the downtown area. Artist Cameron Cross decided to create replicas of the painting in countries that have a close connection to sunflower agriculture, while trying to break a Guinness Book record. Other sites chosen, because of their connection with sunflowers or Van Gogh, included Australia, the Netherlands, Japan, South Africa, and Argentina. The artist used 10 layers of acrylic urethane enamel paint, known for its long-lasting qualities and ultraviolet protection. Free.

In Oakley

Twice-Life-Size Buffalo Bill Bronze Sculpture (785-671-1000; discoveroakley.com), US 83 at Oakley. Always open. Created by Charlie and Pat Norton, this magnificent sculpture commemorates a competition

ENNIS HOUSE

that was held for the name of Buffalo Bill between William F. Cody and Bill Comstock, chief of scouts at Fort Wallace. Their challenge was to see who could bring down the most buffalo in an eight-hour day. Cody won the competition, $500, and the title. The sculpture features breathtaking detail, while a nearby log cabin provides printed information, stuffed animal buffalo, and other trinkets. Free.

& **Dough Boy Statue,** located on Second St., one block east of downtown Oakley. Open daily. This statue with outstretched arm and lowered gun honors and lists the names of eight soldiers who served among Dough Boy troops during World War I. It's one of only three such monuments in the state. Free.

& **Palace Community Theatre** (785-672-3115), 101 Center Ave., Oakley. Shows at 7:30 Fri.–Sat., 7 Sun. In 1949 the Center Theatre held its first open house, including the movie *Take Me Out to the Ballgame.* In 1977 a new owner undertook a $60,000 renovation and changed the name to Palace Theater. But there was enormous competition from other local theaters, so it closed again until 2003. The theater, featured on ABC in December 2009, is now sponsored by local businesses, while seniors in the high school's entrepreneurship class receive firsthand experience in running a business. General admission $6; 3-D movies $8.

MUSEUMS Prairie Museum of Art and History (785-460-4590; prairiei museum.org), 1905 S. Franklin (0.25 mile north of I-70, between exits 53 and 54), Colby. Open Nov. 1–March 31, 9–5 Tues.–Friday, 1–5 Sat.–Sun.; also open

GOODLAND STREETSCAPE

9–5 Mon. during regular season. Constructed within an earth berm, this museum property showcases Cooper Barn, Kansas's largest barn, measuring 114' x 66' x 48'. A sod house, one-room school and country church, and 1930s farmstead are also part of the 24-acre complex. The Kuska Galleries/The Little Smithsonian of the West has an appraised value of $1 million and was shipped from California to Kansas in 1975. It features decades of treasures, from antique buttons to lady's hatpins, and a roomful of dolls from the 1800s through 1980s. See stuffed animals through the years and wedding dresses through the years. Adults $5; children 6–16 $2; senior discount available.

The High Plains Museum (785-890-4595; kansastravel.org/highplainsmuseum .htm), 1717 Cherry, Goodland. Open 9–5 Mon.–Fri., 9–4 Sat., 1–4 Sun. (MST). This small museum is big in its depiction of prairie life, from a full-size replica of the country's first helicopter—with two sets of wings and no cabin—to a complete sod house that was common on the Great Plains, and depictions of storefronts such as a dressmaker's shop and a barbershop. See amazing photos of black blizzards, too, when drought caused massive dust storms. Free; donation suggested.

✍ ♿ **Fick Fossil and History Museum** (785-672-4839; discoveroakley.com), 700 W. Third St., Oakley. Open Labor Day–Memorial Day, 9–noon, 1–5 Mon.–Sat.; longer summer hours, including Sun. From a 25-cent shark-tooth piece to a full-size stuffed buffalo and fossils from Oakley to Washington State, this is a rock-lover's paradise. See barite roses from Oklahoma, glistening pyrite, rocks with fern impressions, and the oldest-known mosasaur fossil, discovered by fossil hunter George Sternberg. There's also a full-size farm wagon, printing press, sod house with a cast-iron stove, antique glassware, and stuffed waterfowl. Free.

✳ To Do

GOLF Sugar Hills Golf Club (785-899-2785; sugarhillsgolf.com/html), 6450 CR 16 off KS 27, Goodland. The only 18-hole course between Hays and Denver was established in 1921. The club bar is lovely and offers lunch and dinner Tues.–Sat. Par 71, 18 holes, 6,351 yards.

HUNTING Shap's Beaver Creek Ranch (785-899-5942; shapsranch.com/ contact/contact.htm), 6404 CR 23, Goodland. This husband and wife outfitting team offers multiple hunting packages, with or without lodging, in a cabin that has a fully equipped kitchenette. Three-day turkey hunts $500; three-day deer hunts $1,500; one-day pheasant hunt without lodging $125; lodging only $100.

North Fork Hunting and Lodge (785-672-4729), 425 US 83, Oakley. Call for rates. Hunt or fish and then enjoy a campfire near your waterside A-frame log cabin with private bedroom and king bed (bring your own bedding). Additional amenities include a fully equipped kitchen with microwave. $100; $25 per additional person; 50 amp camper hookups for additional fee; kennel available. Gun hunts from Sept.–March, starting at $125 plus cost of individual birds; dog service if needed; must have current license.

✳ Green Space

Fike Park (785-460-4400), Franklin Ave. and Eighth St., Colby. The city's most popular park is 9.9 acres. A mini Statue of Liberty anchors the corner, where families enjoy a picnic shelter, playground, tennis courts, and adjacent community building.

Steever Park, Arcade Avenue (beside Prairie Museum of Art and History), Goodland. Pool open in season, 1–7 Mon.–Sat., 1–5 Sun. A skateboard area joins typical park picnic shelter and playground area in this pretty park. Play tennis on one of four courts or enjoy Steever Water Park.

Memorial Garden, near the Fick Fossil and History Museum, 700 W. Third St., Oakley. Open daily. Native grasses and beautiful flowers enhance this spot where cement and metal monuments and multiple flags honor area soldiers. Enjoy walking trails when visiting this serene area. Free.

✳ Lodging

CABINS AND CAMPING

Bourquin's RV Park and Event Hall (785-462-3800; colbycamp.com), 155 E. Willow/I-70 Frontage Rd., Colby. This park tucked behind Wal-Mart offers more than 50 sites, plus a shower and laundry building and 10 acres of riding area. An office, event hall/restaurant, and Bourquin's Farm Market and Trading Company Inc. operate in a 120-year-old Union Pacific Railroad depot on site. The owner specializes in baked goods made from scratch, including 100 percent whole-wheat bread and large, delicious cinnamon rolls. The events menu may include steaks, pecan chicken, or BBQ pulled pork. There's also a tea-room for groups of up to 20 people. Campsites $26–28, or rent a Bourquin Rustic Wilderness Cabin.

High Plains Camping (786-672-3538; highplainscampking.com), 462 US 83, Oakley. This just may be the ultimate campsite, and Kansas's first RV park affiliated with Best Parks in America. Climate-controlled restrooms with double-head showers and a large laundry are only the beginning. There are hot tubs behind a privacy fence, a library, and a seasonal U-pick organic garden. Relax at the 18-hole minigolf course, play volleyball or horseshoes, and take the kids to the spray zone. The office/store sells souvenirs, gifts, and travel guides in addition to RV supplies. $22–38.

MOTELS ⅞ **Annie Oakley Motel** (785-672-3223), 428 Center Ave., Oakley. Recently renovated, this pleasant and comfortable 12-unit motel offers a microwave, refrigerator, and coffeepot in every room. There's also a public computer in the lobby and a public laundry. $36–46.

✳ Where to Eat

EATING OUT

In Colby

&. **Bamboo Garden** (785-462-7722), 1715 W. Fourth, Colby. Open 11–9:30 Tues.–Sun. Wall fans and Chinese lanterns decorate this popular restaurant with 34 lunch specials, 13 chef specials, and 5 daily specials. Customer favorites include sweet and sour chicken, beef and broccoli, or vegetable fried rice with peas, carrots,

ANNIE OAKLEY MOTEL OFFERS CLEAN, COMFORTABLE ROOMS FOR A GREAT PRICE.

toast or an omelet. OTB also makes its own potato chips and pies. Other favorites include pork tenderloin, raspberry chipotle chicken salad, and steaks. They're swamped at lunch, with a dinner line beginning at around 4:30. Inexpensive.

China Gardens (785-890-3345), 1108 Main St., Goodland. Open 11–9 Mon.–Sat. Customers love the crab rangoon and cashew chicken served in this small, dark, cozy restaurant that only uses 100 percent vegetable oil. Inexpensive.

& **The Vault Creamery** (785-890-7001), 921 Main St., Goodland. Open 2–10 Mon.–Sat. Despite the fact that this 1902 building was only a bank for five months, the original vault door remains behind the counter of this spot that's perfect for a summer night. Original tin ceilings and meticulously decorated woodwork give the feel of another time. Their creamy, chocolate

and chicken bits. Lunchtime is quite busy. Inexpensive.

& ☿ **City Limits Grill** (785-460-0131), 2227 S. Range, Colby. Open 5–10 Mon.–Sat.; bar open until midnight. Attached to the convention center, this restaurant full of wood and animal trophies offers a salad bar with more than a dozen items, wine by the glass or bottle, and dozens of beers. Try spicy fried pickles, flat iron steak that can be cut with a table knife, and sides such as beer-battered fries or garlic sautéed mushrooms. Inexpensive.

In Goodland

& **On the Bricks** (785-890-6630), 1530 Main St., Goodland. Open 7–3 Mon.–Sat., 5–9 Fri.–Sat. This is a spectacularly restored spot with tin ceiling and Tiffany-style lights. Try the almond pecan crunch French

LOCATED IN THIS RENOVATED 1902 BUILDING, THE VAULT CREAMERY IS A GREAT PLACE FOR ICY SUMMER TREATS.

12-ounce malt is a steal for under $3. The Vault also creates large sundaes, old-fashioned ice-cream sodas, and coffee drinks. Inexpensive.

&. **El Reynaldo's** (785-899-7077), 2320 Commerce Rd., Goodland. Open 7–10 daily. This Mexican destination, near several chain hotels, offers decent homemade fast food. Try refreshing *horchata* or crunchy *taquitos* with shredded beef, fresh guacamole, lettuce, creamy refried beans, and fluffy rice. Inexpensive.

The Crazy R's (785-890-3430), 1618 Main St., Goodland. Open 11–9 Mon.–Sat. MST. This huge place has served such specialties as the Ragin' Cajun burger, Papa's chicken-fried bacon, and wing zings (breaded wings that are hotter than buffalo wings) for more than 20 years. Steaks and pork tenderloins are other favorites, and there is a full bar. No credit cards. Inexpensive.

In Oakley
&. **Buckhorn Restaurant** (785-672-3565), at Mitten truck stop, US 40, Oakley. Open 24 hours. This must be one of the prettiest truck stop restaurants ever, with tile floors and a copper wall fountain. Try a Big Rig Reuben with melted Swiss and oozing Thousand Island dressing on grilled deli rye, plus thick and light onion rings, or the country-fried steak dinner. Inexpensive.

* Selective Shopping
J&B Meat Market (785-460-0414), 365 Franklin, Colby. Open 10–8 Mon.–Sat. Try their delicious homemade summer sausage, plus bratwurst and German, Italian, and country sausage with all-natural casings. All of the meat comes from Ellinwood Packing Plant, from Kansas and Nebraska animals.

A Moment in Time (785-672-4833), I-70 and US 83 interchange, Oakley. Open 9:30–5:30 Mon.–Sat., 11–5:30 Sun.; shorter winter hours. Antiques and collectibles lovers should allow an hour or two to browse this place, crammed full with everything from prints of original Oz and Elvis movie posters to antique Avon bottles, fossils, and baby Indian moccasins. No credit cards.

* Special Events
July: **Northwest Kansas Free Fair** (785-899-4886), Sherman County Fairgrounds, Goodland. Sample western Kansas culture, see art exhibits, and learn about farming/ranching in the area. **Pickin' on the Plains Bluegrass and Folk Festival** (1-800-611-8825; colbybluegrass.org), Bourquin's Farm Market, Colby. Enjoy three days of hot bluegrass music and activities.

September: **Northwest Kansas Motorcycle Show and Parade** (888-824-4222), Goodland. Everything in this event is motorcycle-related, including an after-dark parade and show with bikes from around the world. **Flatlander Fall Festival** (785-899-9290; flatlanderfestival .com), Goodland. This all-around three-day event includes motorcycle and car shows, dance, golf, classic stock-car races, and more.

December: **Story of Christmas** (888-824-4222), Goodland. This is an outdoor community art exhibit that illustrates scenes of Christmas.

COUNTRY QUIET

Along western I-70 the wind blows most of the time and small tumbleweeds career across the road. During wintertime the highway may close because of snowstorms. Wide-open spaces here offer spectacular views of incoming weather fronts, and residents learn to recognize rain showers as gray fuzziness that hides the horizon. In the springtime, new grass throughout rural northwest Kansas is as brilliant-hued as Astroturf and ripples like a wind-disturbed pond.

For some unexpected views of Kansas landscape, drive through the rock formations known as Arikaree Breaks, which resemble a mini Grand Canyon, view distinctive yellow-orange rock outcroppings located between Leoti and Russell Springs, or travel gravel roads to visit Mt. Weskan, the state's highest point of elevation. From WaKeeney to Hill City along US 283 you'll see massive threshers in the wheat fields and oil wells pumping on both sides of highway.

Northwest Kansas is famous for wonderful pheasant hunting, and Atwood offers a small airport with a 5,000-foot runway favored by visiting hunters. The season runs from early November into January. Dove, quail, waterfowl, and wild turkey, plus deer and antelope, are also ripe for hunting. You may see the jerking strut of a pheasant crossing US 283 near Norton or a wild turkey resting beside the road outside of Atwood. Deer often cross the highway in this area, particularly near dusk.

Agriculture also plays an important role in northwestern Kansas, where roadside signs say ONE KANSAS FARMER FEEDS 128 PEOPLE AND YOU. The existence of the Ogalla Aquifer is part of the reason for successful farming here and throughout the state.

Learn everything there is to know about the state in Kanorado, at the Kansas-Colorado border. Located along I-70, this wonderful visitors center offers free coffee and tourist guides with information about bed & breakfasts, hunting and fishing, entertainment, and individual Kansas regions.

Other small towns throughout northwest Kansas each have claims to fame. With something of a 1950s atmosphere, golden wheat fields nearby, and picturesque sunsets, WaKeeney lies halfway between Kansas City and Denver. The town is known to create one of the largest holiday displays available between these two large cities. In Russell Springs, the Butterfield Trail Museum commemorates the Butterfield Despatch Stage that traveled through this area.

Ellis was the boyhood home of Chrysler Corporation founder, Walter Chrysler, and offers an expansive museum dedicated to railroad history. Oberlin has a charming downtown area with an antique brick street and its Decatur County Last Indian Raid Museum depicts life at the time of the state's last Indian raid, with 14 period buildings available for tours. There are natural and man-made gems in small towns all over northwest Kansas.

Items in this section are listed alphabetically, by city.

GUIDANCE These organizations serve small communities in northwestern Kansas:

Rawlins County Economic Development (785-626-3640; atwoodkansas .com), serves Atwood.

Bird City Century II Development Foundation (785-734-2556; birdcity .com), Bird City.

Decatur Area Chamber of Commerce (785-475-3441; oberlinkansas.com), 104 S. Penn, #8, Decatur County/Oberlin. Open 10–3:30 weekdays.

OBERLIN

Nicodemus National Historic Site (785-839-4233; nps.gov/nico), serves Nicodemus.

Norton Chamber of Commerce (785-877-2501; discovernorton.com), 104 S. State, Norton.

St. Francis Chamber of Commerce (St. Francis/Wheeler) (785-332-2961; stfranciskansas.com), 212 W. Washington, St. Francis.

GETTING THERE AND GETTING AROUND Please see *Getting There and Getting Around* in the previous section. *By bus:* **Greyhound** comes to 3610 Vine St./Golden Ox Truck Stop in Hays. Call 785-628-8321 for information and reservations.

MEDICAL EMERGENCY (arranged alphabetically by city name)

Rawlins County Health Center (785-626-3211), 707 Grant St., Atwood.

Graham County Hospital (785-421-2121), 304 Prout St., Hill City.

Clara Barton Hospital (620-653-2114), 250 W. Ninth St., Hoisington.

Sheridan County Health Complex (785-675-3281), 826 18th St., Hoxie.

Edwards County Hospital (620-659-3621), 620 W. Eighth St., Kinsley.

Minneola District Hospital (620-885-4264), 212 Main, Minneola.

Ness County Hospital (785-798-2291), 312 Custer, Ness City.

Norton County Hospital (785-877-3351), 102 E. Holme, Norton.

Phillips County Hospital (785-543-5226), 1150 State St., Phillipsburg.

Rooks County Health Center (785-434-4553), 304 S. Colorado, Plainville.

Grisell Memorial Hospital (785-731-2440), 210 S. Vermont, Ransom.

Cheyenne County Hospital (785-332-2104), 210 W. First St., St. Francis.

Trego County-Lemke Memorial Hospital (785-743-2182), 320 13th St., WaKeeney.

✳ To See

HISTORIC PLACES, LANDMARKS, AND SITES Waller-Coolbaugh 20th Century House (785-425-7227), 421 N. Walnut, Stockton. Call for tours on weekends, June–Aug. This stately three-story home in high Classical Revival style has graceful columns and a broad front porch. Local businessman Waller Coolbaugh, founder of the State Bank of Stockton, had the home built in 1904. The current owners have maintained the original solid oak trim, ornate fireplaces, and period furnishings. Call about admission.

Cottonwood Ranch State Historic Site (785-627-5866; kshs.org/places/cottonwood/index.htm), RR 1, Studley. John Fenton Pratt was a middle-class Englishman who built a sheep ranch with 3,500 animals in the late 1800s. The ranch design followed the Yorkshire, England, pattern of building placement.

NICODEMUS

This town and Nicodemus National Historic Site (785-839-4233; nps.gov/nico) are completely intertwined, and the current community includes descendants of the original emigrants. Established in 1877, with three hundred settlers from Kentucky, this was the first western town built by and for black settlers after the Civil War. It remains the oldest surviving town west of the Mississippi established by African Americans during the postwar period and located along the western frontier. The original town became a National Historic Landmark District in 1976. Self-guided tours take visitors to sites for the local school, two churches, a hotel, and the old township hall (although most property is now privately owned); prearranged ranger-led walking tours are also available. Special events include an annual emancipation celebration on the last weekend of July and a jazz blues festival during the second weekend in June. The visitors center is open 8:30–5, except on Christmas, Thanksgiving, and New Year's Day. Free.

The home was a mansion by most housing standards, including running water. See the fully furnished house with a sky-blue porch ceiling to ward off flies, a bunkhouse, a shearing shed, an icehouse, and a washhouse. Twenty-three acres of the original ranch, part of the National Register of Historic Places, were purchased by the state in 1982. J. F. Pratt was also a photographer, and 450 photos of the ranch and the surrounding area were reproduced from his glass negatives. Drive-through interpretive tours are available. Call about guided building tours. Adults $2; students/seniors $1.

Natoma Presbyterian Church sits in tiny Natoma, where it was built in 1899. Considered the finest Carpenter Gothic structure in the state, it is also the second building anywhere in the world with the no-sag roof invented by Natoma native Louis Beisner. Free.

Stagecoach Station 15 (785-877-2501; Norton chamber of commerce), US 36, near the edge of Norton. Always open. Billy the Kid was only one notable character who passed through Norton's Stagecoach Station 15 during operation of the Leavenworth and Pikes Peak stagecoach line. This small replica of the original station features mannequins in period dress, from traveling captains of commerce to an American Indian mother and child, with recorded information available. Free.

Heym-Oliver House (785-483-3637), 503 Kansas St., Russell. Open Memorial Day weekend– Labor Day weekend, 11–4 Sat., 1–4 Sun., or by appointment. Located on a corner lot, this home housed a family of seven children in two stories no bigger than about two car lengths per side. There's a narrow porch along two sides. Free.

COTTONWOOD RANCH STATE HISTORIC SITE OFFERS VISITORS A TASTE OF LIFE ON A SHEEP RANCH IN THE LATE 1800S.

Rawlins County Museum (785-626-3885), 308 State St., Atwood.
Open 9–12 and 1–4 Mon.–Fri., 1–4 Sat., during summer. Two long rooms house
artifacts from life on the Great Plains, including a mural by Rudolph Wendelin,
who created Smokey Bear. See dinosaur skulls and Indian garb, stuffed game
birds, and antique kachinas. There's a parlor with piano, country kitchen, and a
millinery shop with period coats and wedding dresses. Quite a change from
when this building was a parking garage with a tire shop and tractor/car dealer-
ship next door. Free.

✍ **Ellis Railroad Museum and Doll Display** (785-726-4493), 911 Washington, Ellis. Open limited hours Tues.–Sun.; call ahead. A massive case nearly fills
one large room with model train displays that include dozens of tiny city
vignettes along each route, but it's only part of the 5,000 square feet of model
train layouts spread across four rooms. Upstairs, little girls will particularly enjoy
a display that features more than a thousand antique dolls. There's also a brightly
painted vintage caboose located beside the building. Ages 12 and up $2; children
5–12 $1.

Walter P. Chrysler Boyhood Home and Museum (785-726-3636), 102 W.
10th St., Ellis. Open 11–3 Tues.–Sat., 1–4 Sun; longer summer hours. At age
three Chrysler moved to Ellis, where he milked cows and sold milk, worked in
the grocery store, shot marbles, played softball, and developed an enormous fas-
cination for machines. See a 1924 Chrysler and many personal items in the
museum behind his home. Adults $3; youth 8–15 $1; seniors 62 and up $2.50.

♿ **Hill City Chamber of Commerce Oil Museum** (call Graham County Economic Development Inc., 785-421-2211), KS 24, Hill City. Open 8–5 Mon.–Fri.
Look for the 1940s oil derrick in front of this museum. This facility tells the story
of Kansas oil, particularly in this county, which has one of the state's richest oil
supplies. In fact, Halliburton had a presence here from the 1960s to '80s. See
geology facts about how oil is created, drilling equipment that includes a wrist
pin wrench from a pumping unit, and antique oilcans. Free.

Decatur County Last Indian Raid Museum (785-475-2712; rootsweb.com
/~ksdclirm), 258 Penn, Oberlin. Open April–Nov., 9:30–noon, 1–4 Tues.–Sat.
Fourteen fully restored buildings depict prairie life at the time the last Indian
raid in the state of Kansas took place, including Duke's Grocery, an original sod
house, a general merchandise barn, Pauls' Oil Company, and an old school.
Adult $5; children 6–12 $3.

Butterfield Trail Museum (785-751-4242; windyplains.com/butterfield), Russell Springs. Open first Tues. of May– Labor Day Weekend, 9–noon Tues.–Sat.,
1–5 Sun. Housed in the Logan County courthouse, this multistory Renaissance-
style building was built from brick and native stone. It commemorates the Butterfield Overland Despatch, which passed through this area in the 1860s during
trips from Atchison to Denver. Items from the despatch trail include fossils,
horseshoes, firearms, and photos. See an antique Russell Springs post office window and a lady's full steamer trunk. Free.

The Rhea Reed Organ Museum (785-852-4951), 117 Main St., Sharon
Springs. Call for a tour. Richard Rhea decided he would restore an old pump

organ rather than take it to the dump, and the rest is history. Today his private museum houses dozens of pristine working organs originally built between 1848 and 1918. Rhea has traveled 35,000 miles to retrieve them. He also restores organs for individual clients. Free.

Fort Wallace Museum (785-891-3564; ftwallace.com), KS 40, Wallace/near Sharon Springs. Open 9–5 Mon.–Sat., 1–5 Sun. The fort offered protection for the Butterfield Overland Stage Route and area settlers. See an 1883 safe and an 1898 organ. Learn about the 1874 German family massacre; Custer, Hickok, Cody, and other Western notables; and the private Floris and Viola Weiser collection of arrowheads, bullets, buttons, and spurs from General Custer's 7th Cavalry, plus a scale model of the fort. The west building houses a cowboy chuck wagon, a 1750 Conestoga wagon replica, and a 1928 fire engine. Free.

✳ To Do

DAY SPA Mainly For You Day Spa (620-653-2255), 167 S. Main, Hoisington. There are six treatment rooms at this full-service salon and spa in the center of town where massages are a bargain at $60 for a one-hour hot-stone treatment or $30 for a mud mask facial. No credit cards.

GOLF Atwood Country Club (785-626-9542), N. Lake Rd., Atwood. This is a challenging course with many trees and several creeks to play around. Built in 1930, it's semiprivate and offers a chipping green but no driving range or practice bunker. Par 36, 9 holes, 3,000 yards.

HUNTING Walk-In Hunting Access (WIHA). This is an Atwood program in which hunters park and walk onto property for hunting. Individual Atwood residents lease their ground to the Kansas Department of Wildlife and Parks for turkey, pheasant, turtle dove, mule, and whitetail deer. By 2004 there were already more than 1 million acres in the program. Although most acreage is for hunting game birds, some does accommodate deer or waterfowl hunts. Payments are made to landowners based on the amount of acres enrolled and the length of contract, and they have immunity from damages/injuries related to negligence. The property is regularly patrolled with marked safety zones.

✳ Green Space

Lake Atwood, near the north end of Atwood. Old cottonwood trees surround this pretty 43-acre lake with plenty of picnic areas and campsites offering shade, hookups, and bath/shower facilities. Fish or canoe or feed waterfowl. Follow Hayden Nature Trail to see more of the West Lake area or cross the road for a game at Atwood Country Club and Golf Course.

Cedar Bluff State Park and Reservoir (785-726-3212), 32001 KS 147, Ellis. At nearly 10 miles long from east to west, Cedar Bluff Reservoir began in April 1949 for the purposes of flood control, agricultural irrigation, and also recreation. By 1962 the Park was developed, and it draws more than two hundred and fifty thousand visitors per year. Lake views extend almost to the horizon of this

IRRIGATION

park with sporadic trees in some areas, and there are two visitor sections located along the shorelines. The Bluffton area features boat ramps, utility and primitive campsites, large shower houses, modern cabins for rent, and activities from horseshoes or basketball to the BMX tack or the beach. Boaters and skiers especially enjoy the smaller Page Creek area.

Prairie Dog State Park, Keith Sebelius Reservoir, and Norton Wildlife Area (785-877-2953), 13037 KS 261, Norton. At more than 1,100 acres, this park beside the massive reservoir offers loads of outdoor options, beginning with a small area where wild prairie dogs scurry about. But you'll have to watch from a distance, because their habitat often draws poisonous snakes and large spiders. You can also see the state's last remaining and fully furnished adobe house, built on site in the 1890s, and can step back in time at the one-room schoolhouse. Primitive and RV campsites are available, as well as two cabins with shower and restroom facilities. Fish for bass, walleye, and several other species, or hunt deer, pheasant, waterfowl, and rabbits.

Castle Rock (785-754-3538; the Quinter chamber of commerce), from exit 107 on I-70, outside Quinter. Cross a cattle guard to enter this area of Smoky Hill chalk, where reptiles and other sea life have been found from the Cretaceous Sea that once covered much of Central North America. It's not a landscape that most people would expect in Kansas. See a gorgeous overview of the Badlands of Kansas from Table Rock bluff and the eroded chalk pinnacle christened Castle Rock in June 1865. A rock house and cistern that once occupied this area have eroded over time.

Arikaree Breaks (785-332-2961; stfranciskansas.com), Parks Rd., CR BB, CR 15, and CR 117, north of St. Francis. Known by some as the mini Grand Canyon of the High Plains, this geological wonder is 36 miles long and more than 2 miles wide. Few trees grow in this rough terrain full of yucca, two sage species found

THE ROUGH CANYONS OF ARIKAREE BREAKS EXTEND FROM KANSAS TO NEBRASKA AND COLORADO.

nowhere else in the state, and 16 rare native plants. The Three Corners extends into Nebraska's Rawlins County and several miles into Colorado. Self-guided tours are available but signage can be poor and travel is discouraged during wet weather. Free.

South Fork and St. Francis Wildlife Areas (913-877-2953), South Fork is 12.5 miles northeast of St. Francis. St. Francis Wildlife Area is 3 miles west and 2 miles south of St. Francis. The Republican River bisects both of these areas, where you'll see rippling grasslands and crops of corn, milo, sunflowers, and alfalfa. There are plenty of whitetail, mule dear, and Rio Grande turkeys, with some ducks in the spring and fall.

Webster State Park (785-425-6775), 1210 Nine Rd., Stockton. With its location in the central flyway, this is a great spot to see and photograph or hunt for birds of all kinds, especially because of how unbusy the water is. Camp beside the peaceful lake in one of more than 60 campsites that offer electric and water hookups. Fishermen and boating enthusiasts appreciate multiple boat ramps and docks, too.

Mt. Sunflower (kansastravel.org/mountsunflower.htm), 15 miles northwest of Weskan. There's a great view of the surrounding countryside from this spot on the Harold Family Ranch in rural Wallace County. At 4,039 feet above sea level, this is the highest point of elevation in the entire state. But be prepared—gravel roads will mark much of your trip to this simple metal sunflower monument accompanied by sunflowers that thrive from late July to early August. From US 40 take CR WA S-3 north for 13 miles and turn west at the Mt. Sunflower sign. About 1 mile after that, turn right/north onto the ranch where the Mt. Sunflower entrance is clearly marked.

Springs. This church building has been transformed into a luxury bed & breakfast, with luscious linens, hardwood cupboards and furnishings, and plush carpet. Choose from rooms, suites, and even an apartment. Full breakfast. $78–164.

HOTELS LandMark Inn at the Historic Bank of Oberlin Bed & Breakfast (888-639-0003; landmark inn.com), 189 S. Penn, Oberlin. As seen in *Midwest Living* magazine, this lovely country inn operates in a restored bank building, seamlessly merging antique and modern decor elements. There's also an exercise room and guest parlor. Enjoy breakfast in the adjacent Teller room amid linen and antiques. Full breakfast. $79–119.

LODGES AND CABINS Beaver Creek Ranch (785-538-2363; beavercreekranch.org), 11503 Beaver Creek Rd., Atwood. You can see the lodge for this hunting outfitting operation down a short gravel drive. This outfitter offers hunts for multiple varieties of game birds and deer, but ring-neck pheasant hunts are their biggest draw. Hunting packages are also available for quail, turkey, fall rifle deer hunts, and fall dove hunts, with dogs available and certified hunting guides on hand. Stay in a comfortable, restored 1920s lodge built with native stone. Full-service hunting packages feature all meals, plus snacks, bird cleaning and freezing, and transportation to local airports. Call for rates.

The Resort Lodge at Kuhrt Ranch (785-899-5306; kuhrtranch.com), 2735 CR 75, Edson. Leave your cell phone and computer behind, but

MT. SUNFLOWER

✴ Lodging

BED & BREAKFASTS Spring Hill Guest House (785-421-5478; davis charolais.com/springcreek), 3127 W Rd., Hill City. Rent this one-party farmhouse set amid a working family farm and cattle ranch, 10 miles out in the country. You'll have a fully equipped kitchen stocked with continental breakfast items and even a waffle iron; an outdoor grill and quilted-covered beds for seven people. Enjoy a whirlpool bathtub, Wi-Fi, and laundry facilities, plus 6,000 acres for hunting. Double occupancy $60; additional charge for extra people.

♿ ⟨⟨ᴪ⟩⟩ **Mt. Sunflower Bed & Breakfast** (785-852-4004; mtsunflowerband b.com), 229 N. Gardner, Sharon brush up on your Ping-Pong game or choose a book from the library. Native limestone and natural beauty surround groups who rent the lodge, which offers a fully equipped kitchen, outdoor gas grills, and bath and bedroom linens. $100 for three people; extra for additional people. Two small groups may share the lodge.

Covert Creek Lodge (888-942-3245, covertlodge.com), 1982 CR 671 Ave., Waldo (west of Luray). Controlled hunts available Sept. 1–March 31. Check out the huge mural that depicts this small town in its heyday. This is the quintessential spot for hunting wild pheasant, prairie chickens, turkey, and deer. The Schneiders offer hunting licenses, guided hunts, and firearms and archery packages beginning at $3,250 for five days. Not a hunting enthusiast? Hike or bike across acres of open country. $50 bed & breakfast only; full breakfast.

MOTELS ((¹₁)) **It'll Do Motel** (785-626-9615), 205 Grant St./KS 36, Atwood. The owner is very pleasant, and this recently renovated spot backs up to Lake Atwood Park with rooms that offer microwaves and refrigerators. There's also a small convention center with several apartments per night). Hunters will appreciate their location near a gun shop. $60-140, rooms/suites.

((¹₁)) **Western Hills Motel** (785-421-2141), W KS 24, Hill City. Buy your hunting and/or fishing licenses here and then stay in a basic but nicely maintained motel. $34–50; five RV slots with full hookups $15.

The Boarding House (785-421-8872; theboardinghouseks.com), 613 W. Walnut, Hill City. Stay in a 1905

house with three bedrooms, a fully equipped kitchen, and access to hunting acreage. There's also a welcoming treat and a VHS/movie library. $50–150.

The Rose of Sharon Inn (785-877-3010), 603 E. Main St., Norton. Rose decor abounds on the main floor of this Victorian home turned guest lodge. Lace and antiques also hark back to the early days. Watch television in the common room and enjoy a private bath or a shared bath with adjoining rooms available for traveling companions. Call for rates.

((¹₁)) **Heyl Traveler Motel** (785-852-4293; heylmotels.com), 702 N KS 27 and KS 40, Sharon Springs. Built in 1963, this 12-unit motel offers comfortable surroundings, plus a coffeemaker, cable television, refrigerator, and microwave in each room. Major property updating was begun in spring 2010. $48.

✳ Where to Eat

DINING OUT Aberdeen Steakhouse and Pub (785-626-3740; westks.com/Aberdeen), 503 Main, Atwood. Open 6 PM Fri.–Sat., or by appointment. Check the live music schedule online, including "perform for your supper" contests. Serving choice Angus steaks on weekends with homegrown vegetables in-season and homemade desserts, this family-owned restaurant located in the 1907 Shirley Opera House has a Western vibe and a loyal following. There's an original tin ceiling, an antique wood bar, and plenty of wildlife trophies on the walls. In the pub, order steak or burger dinners, or try a catfish hoagie with your cocktail. Moderate entrée pricing.

THIS ONE-TIME TRADITIONAL CHURCH HAS BECOME THE LUXURIOUS MT. SUNFLOWER BED & BREAKFAST.

EATING OUT

In Bird City

Bird City Diner (785-734-2780) 2845 KS 36, Bird City. Open 7–2 Tues.–Sat., 8–2 Sun. Enjoy breakfast all day. At lunch you'll join many regulars savoring favorites like the chef salad, club salad, or Italian sausage sub. Pepper jack burgers come on thick, fresh buns, and Bird City's known for its twister fries. No credit cards. Inexpensive.

Big Ed's Steakhouse and Lounge (785-734-2475), 104 W. Bressler, Bird City. Open 5–10 Mon.–Sat. People in this area say there isn't a better place to get a steak anywhere, and the restaurant treats customers like they're always right. Try one of the filets with choice of potato, salad, or roll for $22. No credit cards. Inexpensive–moderate.

Elsewhere

My Place (785-626-9677), 305 Grant, Atwood. Open 7–8. Linda Anderson's well-known morning fare includes the country breakfast, with biscuits and gravy, two eggs, hash browns, and your choice of ham, bacon, or sausage. Burgers, made with meat from the owner's farm, are a big favorite, too. No credit cards. Inexpensive.

&. Y **Boondocks Bar and Grill** (785-394-2264), 306 N. Main (17 miles west of US 183), McCracken. Open 11–midnight (grill closes at 9) Wed.–Thurs., 11–2 AM Fri.–Sat., and 11–2 Sun. Within only six short months Eric and Melissa Davis's restaurant became a favorite of locals, and surgeons traveling from as far away as Hays. It's bright and spacious, with old license plates and beer signs on the walls. They're known for steaks, burgers such as a habanero cream cheese, and Sunday specials like fried chicken. On Saturday nights enjoy drink specials and the smoked prime rib special. Inexpensive– moderate.

Y **Corner Bar and Grill** (785-781-4940), Cawker City. Open 11:30–1:30, 5–close Mon.–Sat. People drive from miles around for KC strip or rib eye steak dinners that include salad, potato, and Texas toast for $15.95 at this world-famous bar. But you'll also get a terrific beef enchilada plate or char-grilled burger for under $6 and a large supreme pizza for only $10. No credit cards. Mostly inexpensive.

Stephen's Restaurant (785-852-4182), US 40 and KS 27, Sharon Springs. Open 6–8:30 Mon.–Sat., 7–1:30 Sun., closed every second Sunday. Darrin and Debbie Summers have a great location, which locals fill up by 10 AM on Sunday. Try the trucker's special with 12 ounces of ground beef, two eggs, and two biscuits with gravy or cinnamon rolls, plus steaks, appetizers, soups, and more. Sunday buffets and daily specials are also available. Inexpensive.

& Y **Diamond R Bar and Grill** (785-332-8936), 118 W. Washington St., St. Francis. Open 6 daily; close time depends on the day. Breakfast plates include three eggs, sausage and bacon, potatoes, and toast, cakes, or biscuits and gravy. Or try a juicy quarter-pound burger—another favorite at this friendly, comfortable bar with cowboys riding horseback on a mural. Enjoy a beer, too. Inexpensive.

✳ Entertainment

WaKeeney Speedway (785-769-6045/president Mike McCurdy; wakeeneyspeedway.com), 116 N. 13th St., WaKeeney. Open April–Sept. on select weekend evenings; most races begin at 6 PM. A 10-member association of local residents, most of whom are racers or former car owners, runs this IMCA-sanctioned track with a 0.375-mile semibanked dirt oval. See up to 85 cars in 4 classes on each race evening. Adults $10; children 6–12 $5; children 1–5 free.

✳ Selective Shopping

The Great Outdoors Gun Shop (785-626-9100; greatoutdoorsgun shop.com), 102 Grant St., Atwood. Open 8–6 Mon.–Fri., 9–4 Sat. Since opening in May 2008 this gun shop has served customers from Hawaii to New York and internationally. They handle all firearm types, with approximately eight hundred in stock at all times, plus clothing, reloading supplies, gun safes, and ammunition.

Mahanna Pharmacy (785-675-3461), 833 Main, Hoxie. Open 9–6 Mon.–Fri., 9–noon Sat. This is a third-generation, family-owned pharmacy once operated by one of the state's earliest female pharmacists, who was also an RN. Order a fresh-made limeade or thick malt at the antique soda fountain, where locals often socialize. No credit cards. Inexpensive.

Rocking R (785-475-3113), 163 S. Penn, Oberlin. Open 9:30–5:30 Mon.–Sat. This shop in the heart of Oberlin offers the largest selection of

FIND EVERYTHING NEEDED TO OUTFIT A HORSE—AND YOURSELF—AT ROCKING R IN OBER-LIN.

tack and saddles in the tristate corner of Kansas, Nebraska, and Colorado. Choose from dozens of pint-size cowboy boots, cowboy hats, and horse blankets, plus Western clothing and gift items.

Prairie House Herbs and Treasures (785-332-3997; highplainsfood.org), 1676 US 36, St. Francis. Open 9–5 daily. Purchase dried and fresh herbs at this delightful little shop set back from the highway, including aloe, bergamot, lemon balm, and tarragon, plus cactus jelly made with cactus from the property. There's an on-site greenhouse and fresh dairy and eggs for sale. No credit cards.

✳ Special Events

June: **Butterfield Trail Ride and Butterfield Trail Museum** (785-751-4242), Russell Springs. Listed as a ghost town, Butterfield's population swells to about two thousand on this weekend, marked by a 10–12-mile ride on the Butterfield Trail along the Smoky Hill River.

November: **Kansas's Largest Christmas Display** (785-743-2077), downtown WaKeeney. See the largest Christmas tree and lighting display between Kansas City and Denver as WaKeeney becomes The Christmas City of the High Plains.

Southwest Kansas: The Old West

INTRODUCTION

Y ou'll still see plenty of cowboy hats and boots in southwest Kansas and meet plenty of ranchers. Landscape near the western border has a desert quality, and rock outcroppings seem to resemble classic rock structures in states lying farther south. Many locals think of themselves as westerners, in relation to the nation as a whole, and often vacation in Colorado or further west.

Long before settlers arrived here from the east, Francisco Vázquez de Coronado explored the area during the 1500s, and Indians from Taos briefly lived in what is now Lake Scott State Park as they fled Spanish conquerors. During the 1800s cowboys and cattle drives were a major part of the culture in southwest Kansas. With them came continuous raucous behavior and sometimes a serious lack of law enforcement. Bat Masterson and Wyatt Earp became legends here at this time.

Massive buffalo herds once roamed these wide-open spaces that are occasionally marked with areas of rugged terrain, and the last Kansas battle fought with American Indians took place just south of Lake Scott State Park. Battle Canyon, a national historic site, provides visitors views of where the Northern Cheyenne ambushed U.S. Cavalry members before fleeing.

When the Santa Fe Trail opened in 1821 Dodge City offered a stopping point between Missouri and Santa Fe. Today Santa Fe Trail wagon ruts remain clearly visible where thousands of wagons crossed the area. The trail, plus the arrival and growth of the Atchison, Topeka, and Santa Fe Railroad, was critical to the growth of southwest Kansas. So was the U.S. Land Office in Garden City.

Water was a precious commodity here for many years until the advent of irrigation, but it wasn't the only precious natural resource found in the area. Natural gas was discovered west of Liberal around 1920, resulting in development of the Panhandle-Hugoton gas field. In 1951 oil wells sprung up nearby, and the world's largest helium plant opened there during the early 1960s.

Many hunting enthusiasts come to southwest Kansas, and qualified outfitters operate everywhere. The Jetmore area is known for terrific hunting amid native grasslands, creek bottoms, and lake areas, and favorite targets include ring-neck pheasant, deer, or turkey.

Particularly closer to the central part of the state, the open country that is characteristic of southwest Kansas can spawn ferocious tornados. One of the

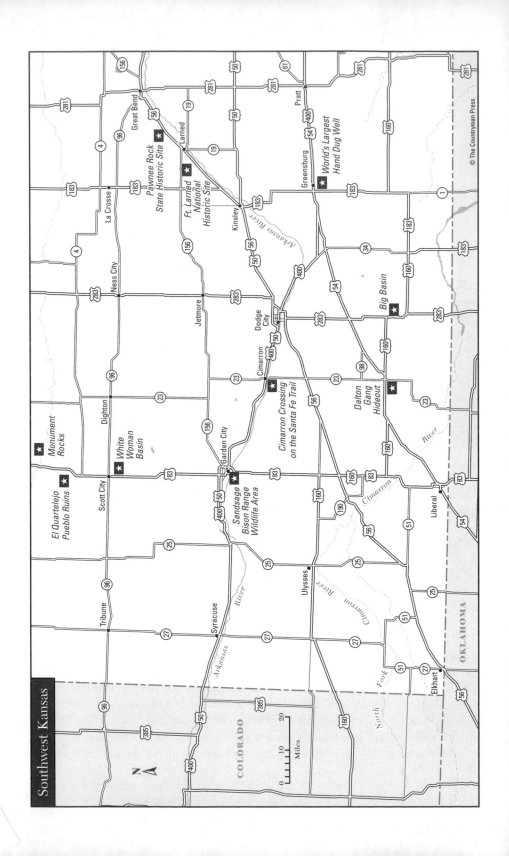

Southwest Kansas

most notorious occurred in May 2007 when a giant, 2-mile-wide twister ripped through Greensburg, leaving only one building intact on the main street and leveling most of the town. Rather than accept defeat, Greensburg is recasting itself as a green, ecologically friendly town. Southwest Kansans are a hearty and resilient lot who know how to merge urban amenities with a deep appreciation for their natural surroundings.

DODGE CITY, GARDEN CITY, AND LIBERAL

Dodge City, with approximately twenty-six thousand inhabitants, is one of the largest cities in southwestern Kansas. Spanish, French, Mexican, and U.S. flags all flew over some of this area, and a large cross commemorates Coronado's presence near what later became Fort Dodge. Established in 1865, the fort helped to protect wagon trains and outfit soldiers with supplies. But it was abandoned by 1882 and unused until it became a soldier's home seven years later. Today, Fort Dodge still serves this purpose, amid restored buildings and beautiful landscaping.

Dodge City marked the end of the United States in the 1860s. By the early 1870s the Atchison, Topeka and Santa Fe Railroad came through the town, which grew by leaps and bounds. From the 1870s to 1880s the atmosphere was like a continuous carnival, with half as many cowboys as citizens, all of which contributed to Dodge's reputation as a wild and lawless town. Soiled doves and saloons were a big part of the landscape and the town was known for poor law enforcement.

The reconstructed Boot Hill streetscape offers a taste of what this Western outpost looked like during its heyday. Dodge City celebrates its Western heritage for two weeks each year, including one of the nation's largest rodeos. The city also has 11 miles of brick streets that are listed on the National Register of Historic Places.

Railroads still play a major role in the city; in fact, you can get a ticket if you block the train tracks with your car. Buffalo were a big source of commerce in the 1870s, but their population quickly dwindled. Today cattle production is a primary industry. Three feedlots hold forty thousand head of cattle, and two of the nation's largest meat-processing plants operate in this area.

Modern Dodge also offers museums and an arts center housed in a Carnegie Library building. There's memorabilia from the 9/11 attacks in Wright Park, a state-of-the-art baseball facility, a raceway park, a new casino, and an 18-hole golf course. A Western vibe remains, and hunters appreciate game bird and deer hunting throughout the area.

It has been said that Garden City got its name after a visitor complemented the garden tended by the wife of town founder William Fulton. With its proximity to the Arkansas River and then the addition of irrigation, the area became an oasis in the Great American Desert.

The presence of the Atchison, Topeka, and Santa Fe Railroad and a U.S. Land Office spurred growth of the early Garden City, and, as people moved westward, its population reached six thousand residents between 1885 and 1888. Horses, oxen, and the vehicles that they pulled always crowded the streets, and raising cattle and agriculture became major factors in the area's development. Sugar beets were one of the largest early crops grown here. Today, several feedlots and grain elevators continue the agricultural tradition.

Garden City's population includes approximately twenty-nine thousand people. The city offers the enormous multiuse park that includes Finnup County Museum with a fully furnished 1884 home; The Big Pool, which is one of the nation's largest municipal pools; and Lee Richardson Zoo—the biggest zoological park in western Kansas. You'll see buffalo along US 83 in Finney Game Refuge and will enjoy hunting in the surrounding area.

Visitors can choose from many chain hotels, an RV park, locally owned motels, or a hilltop bed & breakfast. You'll also find just about every type of cuisine here, from Mexican family recipes to BBQ, Chinese, and classic American dishes.

With a current population of around twenty thousand, Liberal lies near the Oklahoma border at the intersection of US 83 and US 54. US 270 runs south from Liberal, with US 83. The closest major airports are in Amarillo, Texas, and Denver.

The town of Liberal began when S. S. Rogers built the area's first house here in 1872. The railroad came through Liberal by the late 1880s and its population grew. For a taste of Liberal's old railroad culture dine at Ruffino's, located in the renovated Rock Island Depot and Grier Eating House.

Water was scarce in this part of the country, so the well that Rogers built and offered to travelers became the source of the town's name. He said the water was always free, and they called his attitude "mighty liberal." Rogers subsequently built a general store and the U.S. Postal Service arrived soon afterward. Since their discoveries in this area, natural gas, oil, and helium industries have remained a large source of income for Liberal's surrounding towns.

You won't find much humidity or precipitation in this western city. Liberal rarely sees rain and less than 20 inches of snow fall annually. But you will find a thriving agricultural environment where growing winter wheat and broom corn, or raising cattle, top the list. Other popular crops include sugar beets, milo, and alfalfa. National Beef Packing is a major employer, as are two commercial feedlots.

This town has become famous for its yellow brick road and Land of Oz attraction located near the Seward County Museum. Additional museum exhibits include items from Coronado's exploration here and from American Indians who live in this area. Liberal has also gained fame because of the annual Pancake Day festivities that it shares with a small British town, and the Mid-America Air Museum. The fifth-largest of its kind in the nation, the museum displays more than a hundred planes under one roof.

The Liberal area is well known for terrific pheasant hunting opportunities on private lands or at numerous public hunting grounds that include Cimarron National Grasslands, Clark State Lake and Wildlife Area, and others. There are also multiple spots for some great fishing. Southwest Kansas's largest cities offer urban amenities combined with western flair and outdoor adventures.

GUIDANCE These organizations serve the cities of Dodge City, Garden City, and Liberal:

Dodge City Visitors Center (620-225-8186), 400 W. Wyatt Earp Blvd., Dodge City. Open Labor Day–Memorial Day, 8:30–5; Memorial Day–Labor Day, 8:30–6:30.

Finney County Convention and Tourism Bureau (620-276-3264; garden citychamber.net/ctb), 1511 E. Fulton Terr., Garden City. Open 9–5 weekdays.

Liberal Convention and Visitors Bureau (620-626-0170; cityofliberal.com), 1 Yellow Brick Rd., Liberal. Open 8–5 weekdays, 10–4 Sat.

GETTING THERE *By car:* Plan to drive through southwest Kansas, primarily on US 50, US 400, US 56, or US 283. Garden City is located at the junctures of US 50, US 400, and US 83, and the US 50 business route passes through town. *By air:* The nearest full-service airports are in Wichita and Denver. Flights do come in to Dodge City from Denver and Kansas City. Limited flights also depart from **Dodge City Regional Airport** (620-225-5065), **Liberal Mid-America Regional Airport** (620-626-0101), and **Garden City Regional Airport** (620-276-1190). *By bus:* **Greyhound** does not serve southwest Kansas. *By train:* **AMTRAK's Southwest Chief** route serves Dodge City from the former 1898 Santa Fe Railway depot at Central Avenue and Wyatt Earp Street, and from Garden City's vintage Santa Fe station at 100 North Seventh Street. But there are no ticket office hours in Dodge.

GETTING AROUND Your best bet is a personal car with good ground clearance, which will allow you to easily navigate some rugged roads that lead the way to select natural wonders.

MEDICAL EMERGENCY (arranged alphabetically by city name)

St. Catherine Hospital (620-272-2561), 401 E. Spruce, Garden City.

Kearny County Hospital (620-355-7111), 500 Thorpe St., Lakin—serving the Dodge City and Greensburg areas.

Southwest Medical Center (620-624-1651), 15th at Pershing, Liberal.

✳ To See

HISTORIC PLACES, LANDMARKS, AND SITES ♿ **Monument Rocks National Natural Landmark/Chalk Pyramids** (785-671-1000; discoveroakley .com), 25 miles south of Oakley, off US 83 to turnoff, followed by 7 miles of dirt and gravel roads. This was the first national natural landmark chosen by the U.S. Department of the Interior (now on private property). As the rocks come into

MONUMENT ROCKS NATIONAL NATURAL LANDMARK WAS THE FIRST CHOSEN BY THE U.S.
DEPARTMENT OF THE INTERIOR.

view they almost resemble a natural version of Stonehenge. Two million years
ago western Kansas and eastern Colorado were covered by a large inland sea.
After it receded and the area dried up, Monument Rocks were revealed—some
soaring up to 100 feet. Many visitors have found fossils of ancient sea animals in
the local sediment and taken hundreds of photographs. Return to Oakley or continue south on gravel, ending at the highway and Keystone Gallery.

MUSEUMS

In Liberal

Dorothy's House-Land of Oz and Coronado Historical Museum (620-624-
7624; dorothyshouse.com), 567 Cedar St., Liberal. Open 9–5 Tues.–Sat., 1–5
Sun.in winter; longer hours in summer. Here you'll find items that date back to
1541 and Coronado's visit, an antique train station's ticket booth, and a room full
of Plains Indian clothing, moccasins, blankets, and headdresses. Tour Dorothy
Gale's world, from her simple bedroom in Auntie Em's house to the cornfield
where she meets Scarecrow and the gates of Emerald City; you'll feel like you're
in the middle of the movie. A huge, two-day Oz fest takes place the second
weekend in October. Adults $7; youth 6–18 $4.50; seniors 60 and up $5.50.

& **Mid-America Air Museum** (620-624-5263, kansastravel.org/airmuseum.htm),
2000 W. Second St., Liberal. Open 8–5 weekdays, 10–5 Sat., 1–5 Sun. One third
of all aircraft in the world are produced in Kansas. In fact, during World War II
sixty thousand people in Wichita built airplanes, and Kansas has trained more
pilots than most other states combined. With more than a hundred planes, this is
the fifth-largest such collection in the nation. One man, Col. Tom Thomas,
donated 56 of the planes. A 15-minute film describes the state's impressive air
history, which includes such luminaries as Amelia Earhart, Lear, Boeing, and
Cessna. Admission $7.

MULTIPURPOSE PARK

& **Frederick Finnup Park,** Garden City. This 111-acre park honors Finnup, who purchased the first two deeds issued by the Garden City Town Company. In addition to the zoo and county museum, visitors can enjoy basketball and tennis courts or swim in **The Big Pool** (620-276-1255), 403 S. Fourth St., Garden City. Open 1–6 Mon.– Thurs., 1–7 Fri.–Sun. The world's largest outdoor municipal swimming pool was built in 1922. It's bigger than a football field and holds 2.5 million gallons of water, which makes it big enough for water skiing. There's a two-story slide, and the place is absolutely packed on steamy summer days.

& **Lee Richardson Zoo** (620-276-1250; garden-city.org/zoo), 312 E. Finnup Dr., Garden City. Open April 1–Labor Day, 8–6:30; Labor Day–March 31, 8–4:30. This is a pleasant diversion amid the shady Finnup Park, with a giraffe barn, a black rhino display, and opportunities to watch elephant training. Walk near storks, herons, and kookaburra, among others, in the aviary. Drive through for $3 per vehicle, except before 10 AM or from Dec.–Feb. Free.

& **Finney County Museum** (620-272-3664), 403 S. Fourth St., Garden City. Open daily 1–5 in winter and 10–5 in summer. Winner of a 1994 Kansas Museums Association Award for Excellence, the museum features multiple permanent displays that include the fully furnished two-story 1884 home of William and Luticia Fulton, as well as information about C. J. "Buffalo" Jones, who helped to preserve American bison, became Garden City's first mayor, and was featured in Zane Gray's book *The Last of the Plainsmen*. Free.

Elsewhere

Mueller Schmidt House Museum (1-800-653-9378), Dodge City. Open June–Aug., 9–5 Mon.–Sat., 2–4 Sun., or by appointment. This 1881 stone house listed on the National Register of Historic Places is the county's oldest, and only, limestone house. German immigrant John Mueller was a boot maker who also invested in a saloon, cattle, and 3 ranches, and this large family home took 18 months to build. See period furnishings, documents from Bat Masterson and Wyatt Earp, and antique dolls and toys. Donations welcome.

✳ To Do

GOLF Yucca Ridge Golf Club 620-624-4653), 404 N. Kansas Ave., Liberal. Opened in 2006, this regulation course located near a fly-in golf community also offers a driving range. Par 35, 9 holes, 3,287 yards.

Willow Tree Golf Course (620-626-0175), 1800 W. 15th St., Liberal. Open since the 1960s, this course offers beautiful greens, a great pro shop, and a fellow who's terrific at fitting clubs. Par 72, 18 holes, 6,329 yards.

Mariah Hills Golf Course (620-225-8182), 1800 Matt Down Ln., Dodge City. Blue grass fairways and manicured greens lie within site of the high plains. Enjoy a dedicated driving range, plus a pro shop that carries golf clothing, balls, hats, and more. Par 71, 18 holes, 6,920 yards.

HUNTING Cecil's Trail End Hunting (620-227-7809; hunttrailsend.com), 1010 E. Beeson, Dodge City. The new pheasant hunting lodge sleeps 4–6. It is clean, comfortable, and full of trophy heads, fish, and other animals, plus leather couches and a big-screen TV. Packages include home-cooked meals. Hunters also may sign on for dove, deer, and goose hunting, plus elk and antelope hunts in northeast New Mexico.

✳ Green Space

Clark State Fishing Lake (620-227-8609), 8.5 miles south and 1 mile west of Kingsdown on KS 94, Dodge City area. Travel tall rolling hills to this pretty lake with a depth of 42 feet. Enjoy fishing and boating, with four ramps, or camp near the water.

Wright Park (620-225-8100), 806 N. Second St., Dodge City. Open daily. This city-operated park has a small zoo with an aviary, a band shell, and the Liberty Garden—with remnants of 9/11 from the World Trade Center, the Pentagon, and the Pittsburgh crash site.

Arkalon Park (620-626-0531), off US 54, 10 miles northeast of Liberal. Open April 1–Oct. 15, 7–10 daily; shelter open 7–9:30, fishing 7–9. This is a great place to spend time with nature—fishing, camping, picnicking, birding, and hiking. You'll also find a nature trail, volleyball, and horseshoes, and even geocaching. Camping fees are $10; $5 for electricity due in advance.

THE ROAD TO CLARK STATE FISHING LAKE

WRIGHT PARK

Finney Game Refuge (316-276-9400; gardencitykansas.com/gamerefuge.htm), 785 S US 83, Garden City. The oldest publicly owned bison herd (1924) grazes here amid native grasses and wildflowers. Look carefully to see them, plus several varieties of game birds.

✳ Lodging

BED & BREAKFASTS ((ᵖ)) **Boot Hill B&B** (620-225-0111; boothill dodgecity.com), 603 W. Spruce, Dodge City. High atop one of the city's highest hills lies a gracious old home that offers casually luxurious and spacious rooms. Each one has its own small refrigerator and includes complementary beverages, a coffeepot, and homemade cookies. You'll find a huge library of movies in a hallway alcove, and an owner who is locally famous for her baked goods. Full breakfast. $99–175.

((ᵖ)) **Sunnyland Bed & Breakfast** (620-276-0500, sunnylandbandb .com), 501 N. Fifth, Garden City. It took Fred and Kathryn Askren a year

BOOT HILL B & B

to renovate and restore this mansion to its Victorian splendor, with five guest rooms that display antique-looking wall photos and have Bible verses on the doors. The sunny suite with sleeping alcove full of windows is a delight in blues and white. The third floor ballroom offers billiards amid a black-and-white color scheme. $85–110.

CAMPING AND RVS ⅃ (ᵗᵖ) **Gunsmoke RV Park** (620-227-8247), 11070 108 Rd., Dodge City. Ninety-four RV sites feature full hookups, and cable. Voted the state's number one RV park for 12 years, this place is very busy during summertime. While you're there, visit the ice-cream parlor, a game room with electric games, and an in-ground pool. Fifty tent sites from $20 (double occupancy), bunkhouse cabin (bring your own bedding) $32, RV sites $31–33.

HOTELS AND RESORTS ⅃ (ᵗᵖ) **Dodge House Hotel** (316-225-9900), 2408 W. Wyatt Earp Blvd., Dodge City. Recently renovated, this hotel offers 130 rooms. Extensive renovations include several two-story suites with loft sleeping area and whirlpool tub where cleaning staff leave origami towel "animals." Call for current rates.

MOTELS (ᵗᵖ) **Garden City Inn** (620-276-7608; gardencityinnkansas .com), 1202 W. Kansas Ave., Garden City. There's some beautiful landscaping outside of this AAA-rated motel near the edge of town. All rooms face interior corridors and have microwaves, refrigerators, and Internet access. Enjoy an indoor heated swimming pool with spa and 24/7 coffee. Expanded continental breakfast. $80.

VICTORIAN DETAILS ABOUND THROUGHOUT SUNNYLAND BED & BREAKFAST.

✳ Where to Eat

DINING OUT ♿ **Ruffino's Restaurant in the Historic Rock Island Depot and Grier Eating House** (620-624-3855), 4 Rock Island Rd., Liberal. Ruffino's offers homemade Italian food amid antique surroundings with dark wood and leather that create a classy, clubby atmosphere. They're especially busy during Sunday lunch. The pasta sampler is a good way to try several items simultaneously—lasagna, manicotti, and one large ravioli arrive beneath shared sauce and melted cheese. Inexpensive.

EATING OUT

In Dodge City

((ᵀ)) **A Cup of Jo-Nes** (620-789-5282), 909 W. Wyatt Earp Blvd., Dodge City. Open 6–6 Mon.–Sat., 8–4 Sun. Enjoy coffee and lunch in a renovated bungalow with a small dining room and a living room full of leather couches. A 20-ounce cappuccino will only set you back $4, cinnamon rolls and cookies are homemade, and lunch salads are full of fresh greens and vegetables. Try a Venetian sandwich with Italian flavors or a Kansas wrap with turkey, ham, bacon, romaine, Swiss cheese, tomato, red onion, and ranch dressing. Inexpensive.

♿ **Casa Alvarez** (316-225-7164), 1701 W. Wyatt Earp Blvd., Dodge City. Open 10:30–2, 5–9 Mon.–Thurs.; 11–9:30 Fri.–Sat.; 10–8 Sun. Known as Dodge City's best Mexican restaurant, Casa Alvarez offers dozens of items, from steak ranchero and savory pork green burritos and extremely popular fajitas to the sopaipilla delight, a Mexican pastry filled with ice cream and topped with strawberries or cherries. You can also visit them in Liberal, or Boulder, Colorado. Inexpensive.

Casey's Cowtown Club (620-227-5225), 503 E. Trail St., Dodge City. Open 11 AM weekdays, 4–10:30 Sat., 8–2 Sun. Located 10 minutes from the main drag, this vintage building is full of pre-1900s decorative stained glass and faux-hide tablecloths. The small original building was a rib house that burned out in 1986 and reopened in 1996. There's also an outdoor shelter and beer garden. Ninety percent of customers order steak, and the cooks get compliments for fish, including salmon steak and catfish fillet. Burgers, salads, and chicken and pork dishes are available, too. Inexpensive–moderate.

♿ **Dodge House Restaurant** (620-225-9100; dodgehousehotel.com/dining.html), 2408 W. Wyatt Earp Blvd., Dodge City. Open 6–10 Mon.–Sat., 7–10 Sun. This legendary restaurant has served meals since 1873. Full of sepia photos and white tablecloths, this is a spot to order certified Angus beef, Dodge strip steaks, or delicious deep-fried chicken tenders. You'll also find burgers, sandwiches, and salads here, plus full breakfast and lunch menus. Check out the bullet hole in one drawer of the historical bar. Inexpensive–moderate.

In Garden City

♿ **El Zarape** (620-275-5401; elzarapesalsa.com), 606 W. Fulton, Garden City. Open 11–2, 6–9 Mon.–Thurs, 11–2, 5–9 Fri., 11–9 Sat.–Sun. Dine in a bright and colorful spot. Mexican food lovers have enjoyed this restaurant since 1967, and the family makes their own salsa from grandmother's recipe. Try a combination plate or create your own from the à la carte menu, or enjoy the deep-fried gordita—a corn patty filled with your choice of meat and served with plenty of fixings. Inexpensive.

♿ **Plank's Barbecue** (620-276-2943), 912 E. Fulton, Garden City. Open 11–8 daily, 10 on Sat. This is a cheerful restaurant known for good food. Their meat comes from the adjacent Ehresman Packing Company, and their Mexican dishes from grandma's recipes. Inexpensive.

Benny's Grill (620-272-0737), 1408 Buffalo Jones Ave., Garden City. Open 6–9 Sun.–Thurs., 6–10 Fri.–Sat. There's a huge crowd here at lunchtime that particularly appreciates the premium quality burgers. Its big menu offers plenty of choices, but be sure to save room for homemade pie. Inexpensive.

In Liberal

♿ **Congo's Mexican and American Cuisine** (620-624-6555), 748 Pancake Blvd., Liberal. Open Mon.–Thurs. 11–10, Fri.–Sun. 11–11 (plus bar/music until 2 AM Fri./Sat.). Here you'll find delicious quesadillas—four quarters filled with large chunks of fajita chicken (or steak) and melted cheese, accompanied by creamy, unsalted refried beans; shredded lettuce; mild, creamy guacamole; and tomato bits, all topped with a large dollop of sour cream. Inexpensive.

♿ **The Pancake House** (620-624-8585), 640 Pancake Blvd., Liberal. Open 6–1 Tues.–Sun. In a town that hosts the annual International Pancake Race simultaneously with Olney, England, you've just got to eat pancakes. A pair of ex-Liberal residents always stops here on the way to their winter home and order coconut pancakes plus tropical syrup. You can also try apple pancakes with cinnamon glaze; Hawaiian, Swedish, or Dutch pancakes; and crepes or waffles. Try fruity or butter pecan syrup, too.

Lunch and dinner items and sandwiches are also available. Inexpensive.

SNACKS

In Garden City
Sinfully Sweet Bakery (620-276-3198), 105 W. Chestnut, Garden City. Open 7–5 Tues.–Fri., 8–2 Sat. Since January 2010 this little bakery has delighted customers with huge cinnamon rolls, scones made with a Swedish grandmother's recipe, and cookies that come from a Greek grandfather's recipe. Their cupcakes are a big hit and they make gorgeous wedding cakes. Inexpensive.

Patrick Dugan's Coffee House (620-271-9131), 301 N. Main, Garden City. Open 7–6 weekdays, 8–6 Sat. High-top tables and Sweet Granada chocolates from Emporia are just a few features of this small coffee shop. This delightful spot serves P. T.'s Coffee from Topeka and fruit smoothies full of vitamins and minerals from Dr. Smoothie. Get $1 off mochas on Monday or off frozen blended drinks on Friday. Inexpensive.

THE PANCAKE HOUSE IS A FAVORITE SPOT FOR BREAKFAST IN LIBERAL.

✳ Entertainment

In Dodge City

Dodge City Historic Trolley Tours (1-800-653-9378), 40 W. Wyatt Earp Blvd., Dodge City. Available Memorial Day–Labor Day. These popular trolleys are air-conditioned during Dodge's hot summers and offer a one-hour narration that gives visitors a comprehensive tour of local historic sites. Adults $7; children $5.

Boot Hill Casino and Resort (877-906-0777; boothillcasino), 4000 W. Comanche St., Dodge City. Open 24/7. Opened in 2009, with a spectacular view to the southeast, this is the first casino in Kansas whose profits help to support state programs. The 20,000-square-foot casino offers roulette wheels and slot machines; blackjack, poker, and craps tables; and a bar, restaurant, and snack bar. By 2012 a 124-room hotel should open, too. An event center built nearby will host ice shows, concerts, etc., and offer breakout rooms.

Dodge City Raceway Park (620-225-3277; dodgecityraceway.com), US 56 and 14th Ave., Dodge City. Open April–Oct.; call for schedule. This is one of the nation's finest dirt-racing facilities, with a 0.375-mile track. But there's more going on than dirt racing. See tractor and school bus races and even concerts at this popular facility. Featured events include the National Sprint Tour, World of Outlaws, Late Model Shootout, and Midgets and Winged Sprints. Call for ticket prices.

Elsewhere

Baker Arts Center (620-624-2810), 624 N. Pershing Ave., Liberal. Open 9–noon, 1–5 Tues.–Fri.; 2–5 Sat. The nonprofit arts center offered its first exhibit in 1986 and features two floors of two- and three-dimensional art pieces. In addition to rotating displays, there's a gift shop with consignment art, from wooden bowls to blown glass globes, and desktop metalwork. The center also holds a national juried show each year, typically opening in January. Free.

BOOT HILL CASINO BEGAN TO TAKE SHAPE IN FALL 2009.

✳ Selective Shopping

In Dodge City

& **Out West Inc.** (620-225-9025), 309 N. 14th, Dodge City. Open 9–7 Mon.–Sat., 1–5 Sun. From cowboy boots and hats to large-size jeans and shirts and American Indian handcrafts, you'll find plenty to look at— and buy—in this Western-inspired store.

& **Long's Inc.** (620-227-2805), 2207 Central Ave., Dodge City. Open 9–8:30 weekdays, 9–6 Sat., 1–6 Sun. This expansive store includes a big and tall department and jeans of all sizes, plus cowboy boots and casual shoes. It's a Western lover's paradise.

Dodge City Antique Mall (620-225-5656), 1701 N. 14th St., Dodge City. Open 10–5:30 Mon.–Sat., 12–4 Sun. This is a very manageable little mall, with about 15 nicely laid-out booths full of antiques and collectibles.

In Liberal

Bears and Hares Mercantile (620-626-4273), 13 E. Second St., Liberal. Open 10:30–5 Tues.–Sat. This long, narrow store stocks loads of household and gift items, including fine china and glassware, gourmet foods, a plethora of kitchen gadgets, and much more. It's dark and cozy with exposed ceiling beams, metal pheasants, cattle paintings, and items that fill every nook and cranny.

& **La Princesa Bakery** (620-624-9448), 10 S. Kansas Ave., Liberal. Open 7:30–9. Sample cinnamon and sugar–dusted churros with smooth caramel filling or yo-yos—pink and coconut-covered sweet balls of dough with chocolate filling—or gingerbread-flavored pigs, which are a local favorite. Local customers come here up to three times a week! No credit cards.

& **Carlson's Yippee Yi Yea!** (620-624-6382), 210 N. Kansas Ave., Liberal. Open 10–5:30 Tues.–Sat. This is a pleasant place to shop with a Southwestern vibe. You'll find *chimeneas* and drums here. Or buy handcrafted silver and turquoise belt buckles, a large tin wall star, or a Mexican rug.

Fashion Tree Boutique (620-626-7550), 202 N. Kansas Ave., Liberal. Open 10–5:30 Mon.–Sat. This very welcoming shop bills itself as a boutique with a new attitude. It offers women's clothing, jewelry, and accessories. There are petite sizes, jeans to size 18, robes/loungers, and plenty of purses with loads of sparkle.

✳ Special Events

February: **International Pancake Day** (620-624-6423; pancakeday.net), downtown Liberal. Four days include a pancake race in competition against residents of Olney, England, who began their annual pancake race in 1445. Try the pancake eating and flipping contests, an authentic English high tea, and more.

July: **Dodge City's Old Fashioned Fourth of July** (1-800-OLD-WEST), Dodge City. Enjoy one of the largest Independence Day celebrations between Wichita and Denver, drawing up to twenty-five thousand people. **Dodge City Days** (620-227-3119), Dodge City. Operating for 50 years, this 10-day event offers the Dodge City Roundup Rodeo, a professional BBQ contest, top musical performances, and a Western parade.

EAST OF GARDEN CITY

GUIDANCE **Lane County Area Chamber of Commerce** (620-397-2211), 147 E. Long, Dighton. Open 8–noon, 1–5.

Greensburg Chamber of Commerce (620-723-2131; ask for Chamber), 315 S. Sycamore, Greensburg.

Hodgeman County Economic Development (620-357-8831), 308 Main St., Jetmore. Call ahead.

Meade County Economic Development (620-873-8795; meadecountye codevo.com), 200 N. Fowler/Court House, Meade. Open 8–5 weekdays.

Ness County Chamber of Commerce (785-798-2413), 102 W. Main, Ness City. Open 8–11 Tues.–Thurs.

GETTING THERE AND GETTING AROUND Please see *Getting There and Getting Around* in the previous section.

MEDICAL EMERGENCY (arranged alphabetically by city name)

Lane County Hospital (620-397-5321), Dighton.

Kiowa County Memorial Hospital (620-723-3341), 701 W. Kansas Ave., Greensburg. **Edwards County Hospital and Healthcare** (620-659-3621), 620 W. Eighth St., Kinsley.

Rush County Memorial Hospital (785-222-3707), 801 Locust St., La Crosse.

Meade District Hospital (620-873-2141), 501 E. Carthage, Meade.

Minneola District Hospital (620–885-4238), 222 Main St., Minneola.

Montezuma Clinic (620-846-2251), 304 N. Aztec, Montezuma.

✳ To See

HISTORIC PLACES, LANDMARKS, AND SITES **Dalton Gang Hideout** (620-873-2731), 502 S. Pearlette St., Meade. Open 9–5 Mon.–Sat., 1–5 Sun. The Dalton gang used the home of Eva Dalton Whipple as a hideout in 1887. The house and barn, connected by an escape tunnel, are now a museum. Upstairs from the tunnel/ground level is the kitchen and a small room with historical artifacts; the second floor has a fully furnished period bedroom and parlor. The museum shop offers coin purses, 25-cent candy sticks, and a pencil sharpener shaped like an iron stove. No credit cards. Admission $4.

Fromme-Birney Barn (620-723-3263; skyways.lib.ks.us/orgs/barns/roundbarn), southwest of Mullinville. Open daily. This 16-sided round barn built in 1912 is 50 feet tall and 70 feet in diameter. Inside, see pictures and stories of other round barns, farm machinery, life in 1912, and information on the builders.

World's Largest Hand-Dug Well (620-723-4102; bigwell.org/bigwell.html), 315 S. Sycamore, Greensburg. Open 9–5 Mon.–Sat., 1–5 Sun. During the 1990s divers found $1,200 in this well, built in the late 1800s to support a growing population and trains that passed through the area. Marvel that this well, built with shovels, picks, and pulleys, is 109 feet deep and 32 feet in diameter. In 2007 the viewing canopy was damaged during an F-5 tornado and required repair. Plans are in the works to complete repairs so visitors can travel 105-steps down into this cool stone passageway. Free.

Ness County Bank Building (620-798-2237), Main St. and Pennsylvania Ave., Ness County Bank Building/Ness City. Open 1–4:30 weekdays; call for a tour. An antique bank vault door features an original oil painting with 22-karat gold, and tall arched windows provide a broad view of the town. Largely used for special events, the onetime Skyscraper of the Plains also houses Prairie Mercantile.

LEGEND HAS IT THAT THE NOTORIOUS DALTON GANG USED THIS ESCAPE TUNNEL IN MEADE.

You'll see Kansas-made foods and other products, including a quilt room and a holiday decor room. Free.

Edwards County Historical Society Museum (877-464-3929), Midway Park at US 50 and US 56 intersection, Kinsley. Open 10–5 Mon.–Sat., 2–5 Sun.; call for tour. This surprising little museum offers a glimpse of life along the Santa Fe Trail. See an authentic sod house, room vignettes fully furnished with antiques, a John Deere wagon and saddles, and a gun collection. You can also visit a 1910 parlor and a 1920s kitchen. Historical photos enhance the visit. Donations.

MUSEUMS Pioneer-Krier Museum (620-635-2227), 430 W. Fourth St./KS 160, Ashland (south of Dodge City). Open 10–12, 1–5 Tues.–Fri., or by appointment. At this blend of two museums you'll find antique pump organs from the middle 1800s through early 1900s, the Krier collection of small aircraft, an antique harness shop, a 1778 clock, and items from a prehistoric dig in the north part of the county. Free.

& **Meade County Museum** (620-873-2359; oldmeadecounty.com/museum .htm), US 54, midtown Meade. Open 9–5 Mon.–Sat., 1–5 Sun. This impressive little museum features a full boardwalk with a general store, barbershop, harness shop, blacksmith, children's bedroom, and train depot office. See an antique photo studio, a doctor's office, and a full livery barn created in 2000, plus vintage women's dresses and evening coats and military uniforms. Admission $3.

Haun Museum (620-357-8794/Mary Ford or -8473/Charles Guthrie), 421 Main St., Jetmore. Open Memorial Day–Labor Day, 9–noon, 1–5 Sat., 1–5 Sun., or by appointment. An 1854 sword, a framed collection of arrowheads, and an 1885 public school are just a few attractions at this museum housed in six of the town's earliest limestone buildings. Mannequins in period dress occupy a law office with library, a vintage bedroom, and military displays from the Revolutionary War through Vietnam. Free.

Rush County Historical Museum, Barbed Wire Museum, and Post Rock Museum (785-222-2719/785-222-9900/785-222-2719), W. First St., La Crosse. Open 10–4:30 Mon.–Sat., 1–4:30 Sun. See period furnishings, antique tools, and vintage children's clothing in the county museum, which occupies an old railroad depot from the town of Timken. More than five hundred varieties of barbed wire, plus old photographs and liniment for barbed-wire injuries, are in the Barbed Wire Museum, while the Post Rock Museum features a miniature post rock quarry as well as stone artifacts, including grinding stones used by American Indians and early settlers to the area. Free.

TOWNS Cimarron. Nearly two thousand people live in the seat of Gray County. It lies along the Arkansas River, which is often dry, and US 50, which follows the original Santa Fe Trail at this location. Learn more at Cimarron Crossing Park. The soda fountain at Clark Pharmacy on Main Street still serves ice-cream treats from a 1900s soda fountain with original counter and Coke memorabilia on the walls. Beautiful old homes are visible throughout town.

Dighton. The county seat of Lane County has about a thousand residents with a median household income of approximately $45,000. Dighton lies at the intersection of KS 96 and KS 23, about 180 miles from Wichita, and the majority of residents commute to work. Restored historical buildings include the opera house and bank and the Lane County courthouse. The town promotes itself as a place where children can safely walk to school.

Jetmore. When this town of approximately a thousand people was founded in 1879 it carried the name of Buckner. After Abraham Buckles Jetmore facilitated creation of a railroad line through town, it was rechristened Jetmore. This county seat of Hodgeman County lies in a valley surrounded by rolling hills, and natural limestone characterizes several downtown buildings. Located at the intersection of KS 156 and US 283, Jetmore and the surrounding area are well known for wonderful hunting opportunities.

Greensburg. Kiowa County was organized in 1886 and named after Indians who lived in the area. Greensburg was named after Donald R. "Cannonball" Green, who helped to organize the town. For a time, his stage line was integral to the town's success, until the railroad came through the prairie. With approximately 1,200 residents, Greensburg will likely be forever remembered because of the enormous tornado that struck on the night of May 4, 2007, and destroyed 95 percent of the town. In its wake, Greensburg has picked itself up and is recreating itself as a green town. Green buildings include the LEED-certified 5.4.7 Arts Center and Greensburg business incubator, where new small businesses receive a jump-start with minimal overhead costs. The can-do spirit of Greensburg since the tornado was the subject of a PBS documentary in 2008.

Meade. Coronado crossed the current Meade County in 1541. During the 1800s the area was under French, Spanish, and finally, U.S. control. The state of Kansas was organized in 1854, and Meade County was established in 1885 with its present borders. The first settlement in the county had occurred in 1878. Located near US 54, US 160, and KS 23, this small town has approximately 1,600 residents.

MIDWAY USA

Kinsley. The seat of Edwards County, Kansas, has more than 1,500 residents. It's also known as the Midway City, reputedly because it lies 1,561 miles from both New York and San Francisco. It's also near the intersection of the narrow Arkansas River and Coon Creek, and small sand dunes seem to surround this area where a battle took place between Comanches and Osages and 140 soldiers. Bandits also tried to rob a safe at the train depot in 1878.

La Crosse. Around 1,300 residents live in this small town, which is the seat of Rush County and located at KS 4 and US 183. Know for its Barbed Wire Museum, La Crosse also offers the Post Rock Museum and a small county historical museum in the same parklike setting.

Ness City. The seat of Ness County operates at the intersection of KS 96 and US 283, with service provided by the Central Kansas Railway. This town of about 1,500 residents lies in the heart of farming, ranching, and oil country. Four stories tall, made of native limestone, and with a massive tower at the street corner, the beautiful Ness County courthouse was known as the Skyscraper of the Plains when townspeople completed it in 1890 and was one of the state's most impressive structures west of Topeka.

Sublette. This town of approximately 1,500 residents was named for French Huguenot William Lewis Sublette, who worked with the Rocky Mountain Fur Company. Today the median income is near $40,000. Jack Christiansen, hall of fame football player for the Detroit Lions, is a Sublette native.

✸ To Do

BOATING AND FISHING Lake Coldwater (620-582-2702), 1 mile south and 1 mile west of Coldwater. This 250-acre man-made lake lies in a beautiful 930-acre park with large flat areas, rolling hills, and sun-dappled shade. The Kansas Wildlife and Parks Commission stocks fish annually, and there are loads of picnic and campsites available. Tent camping $10; camper w/o hookups $12.50, with electric/water $18, with electric/water/sewer $20. Long-term site rentals available.

HorseThief Reservoir (620-357-6420; horsethiefres.com), 514 W KS 156, Jetmore. Closed 11 PM–6 AM. Jetmore residents can enjoy water sports in their own backyard with the June 2010 opening of this sparkling new reservoir. It's the result of a 7,200-foot-long, 86-foot-tall Hodgeman County Dam, offering swimming, boating, hunting, and fishing and trail riding/hiking opportunities. Daily vehicle pass $5 ($4 area residents); daily camping $9/$7; daily utility fees $9.

Meade State Lake and Park (630-873-2572), 13051 V Rd. off KS 23, Meade. Kansas's first state lake has been called the top spot for bird watching in the central U.S. See more than three hundred species as you fish, hunt, camp, or swim in the lake with plenty of trees along some shoreline areas. Purchase fishing and hunting licenses and park permits at the park office.

Goodman State Fishing Lake and Wildlife Area (620-276-8886), 5 miles south and 2.5 miles east of Ness City. A 40-acre lake and 225-acre wildlife area offer loads of fishing and hunting opportunities, plus hiking and picnicking. Bring your boat and tent and stay for the weekend.

GOLF Cimarron Golf Course (620-855-7003), 812 Golf Course Rd., Cimarron. A gravel driveway leads from KS 23 to the club where picnic tables occupy a deck that wraps around the clubhouse. Par 36, 9 holes, 3,408 yards.

LAKE COLDWATER IS A SOUTHWEST KANSAS LAKE THAT ALLOWS WATER SPORTS.

HUNTING RuffHouse Outfitters (1-800-487-1981; ruffoutfitter.com/lowres/theruffs.html), Hanston. Farming and hunting have been family passions for five generations. Guided hunts in a controlled shooting area take place Oct. 1–March 31. RuffHouse offers wild- and released-bird hunts across 4,000 acres, catering to families and small groups. Made-from-scratch meals (built around beef), dogs provided or boarded, loaned guns, and lodging are other features. There's an 8-person cabin and a 2-year-old, 12-person lodge in an old farmhouse just south of Hanston. $40 per person in cabin when not involved in hunt; pheasant hunt packages $425–850.

J. W. VANDERPOOL OPENS HIS CROOKED CREEK HUNTING RANCH, OUTSIDE OF MEADE, TO HUNTERS.

Vanderpool Exotics and Crooked Creek Hunting Ranch/Vanderpool Exotics Incorporated (620-873-5200/7189), 25048 CR 15, Meade. Call a day ahead for 2–3 hour hunts. Hunters are welcome in season for meat and/or trophy hunts of two to three hours. J. W. Vanderpool has also opened his ranch to visitors for 15 years to see the exotic animals he raises, from bobcats and coyotes to raccoons and ostriches. Prairie dogs pop up all over the property, and you can visit 54 head of buffalo. A lodge with two bedrooms, kitchen, TV, and computer and decorated with buffalo head and bearskin is available for hunters.

✷ Green Space

Big Basin Prairie Preserve, 15 miles south of Minneola off US 283. The highway bisects the Big Basin, a natural sinkhole thought to have been created by dissolving salts a few thousands years ago, dropping the surface 100 feet. The highway traverses 1.04 miles through the basin before climbing to the rim, which has nearly vertical walls. The entrance to the Big Basin Prairie Preserve lies in the bottom of the basin, home to a free-roaming buffalo herd. Follow a very rugged rock road to St. Jacob's Well, but use caution when exiting your vehicle, as the buffalo can be unpredictable.

Meade City Park (620-873-2461), located on US 54, east of Meade. Cottonwood trees shade this pretty little park beside the creek on the east side of town with a merry-go-round, swings, seesaws, a jungle gym, and picnic tables. Free overnight camping also is permitted.

✷ Lodging

BED & BREAKFASTS Wild Horse Canyon Bed & Breakfast (620-397-5914; wildhorsecanyonbnb.com), 255 N. Longhorn Rd., Dighton. This rural bed & breakfast lies on gorgeous property with deep canyons, wide vistas, and abundant wildlife, from owls to deer. Hike to historic Wild West Canyon and Corral or hunt for deer, pheasant, quail, or antelope nearby. The small house features several bedrooms that share a bath, a living room with reclining chairs and couch, computer access, and embroidered robes. Ask for a guided ranch tour and get a great history lesson, too. Full breakfast. $50–75.

((ᵧ)) **Cimarron Crossing Bed & Breakfast** (620-855-3030; cimarron crossing.com), 307 W Ave. A/US 50, Cimarron. Aunt Sally's 1907 home near the Santa Fe Trail has become a lovely bed & breakfast inside bright yellow walls. Drink coffee on the front porch with white latticework. View the historic trail through leaded glass windows, eat breakfast in the

garden room, and enjoy the hot tub on a sun-drenched deck. No credit cards. $50–80.

((ᵧ)) **Cimarron Bed & Breakfast** (580-696-4672; cimarronbedandbreak fast.com), State Line Rd., 3.5 miles west of Elkhart. Located near the Kansas, Oklahoma, and Colorado borders, this rural bed & breakfast with enormous windmill offers complementary evening snacks in addition to breakfast. Play a game of pool, watch a movie, enjoy the therapeutic spa, or check your e-mail. $85.

CABINS, CAMPING, AND RANCHES Moore Ranch (620-826-343; moorelonghornranch.com), 2933 CR E, 40 miles southeast of Dodge City, Bucklin. Stay overnight from April to October and help with daily ranch activities. Ranch vacations of 7–10 days, 3-day cattle drives with chuck wagon, or special events such as girls' weekends are several options, typically with one to five guests. The Moores have averaged about 250 head

THERE IS GORGEOUS TERRAIN AND VISTAS AT WILD HORSE CANYON BED & BREAKFAST.

of Texas longhorns for 35 years and raise approximately 200 chickens, from which they sell meat and eggs. Guests share meals with the family

NANCY MOORE VISITS ONE OF HER TEXAS LONGHORNS AT MOORE RANCH.

and bunk in 1950s cabins with shower, sink, beds, and camp blankets, but no TV. Check for availability and rates.

MOTELS AND LODGES & **The Elite Suites** (785-798-2160; theelite suites.com), 121 S. Topeka Ave., Ness City. This lodging company offers three suites and three houses. Suites have reclining couches and Internet AirCards available for checkout. The Colorado suite features two bedrooms with a fully equipped kitchen, a snack basket on arrival, plus a washer and dryer. $70–80; $85 for the house.

((ᵖ)) **Dalton's Bedpost Motel** (620 873-2131), E US 54 at the east edge of town, Meade. Each room in this motel, operating 21 years and AAA approved, offers a recliner and a refrigerator; microwaves are in some. It's clean and neat with morning coffee in the lobby. November is her busiest time due to hunters and snowbirds traveling to Arizona. $58.

✳ Where to Eat

EATING OUT

In Coldwater

((♦)) **The Timberwolf Café and Inn** (620-582-2033; timberwolfcafe.com), 502 N. Central St., Coldwater. This 12-room 1960s motel was nicely renovated a few years ago with the addition of a Laundromat, lobby, coffee, microwave, movie rentals, and an ATM. The café has a Southwest vibe and specials change weekly. Order biscuits and gravy, a homemade cinnamon roll, or pork and eggs for breakfast, and rib eye or sirloin at dinner. $55 rooms; inexpensive café.

♿ **Dave's Pizza Oven** (620-582-2775), 100 N. Central St., Coldwater. Open 11–9:30 Sun.–Thurs., 11–11 Fri.–Sat. Urbanspoon.com has named this enormous restaurant the state's number two pizza place. Everything is made from scratch, including taco or luau pizza, breadsticks, and create-your-own pies. There are even fruit dessert pizzas. Check out the weekday lunch pizza buffet or try some spaghetti with meatballs, too. Inexpensive.

Kremee (620-582-2831), 400 N. Central St., Coldwater. Open 10–8 Mon.–Sat. Homemade fries, meal-size tacos and chef salads, thick malts and Philly cheesesteak sandwiches are a few highlights of this diner menu. Get a large sundae for under $2 or steak fingers for about $3. No credit cards. Inexpensive.

In Jetmore

✎ **Agustino's Restaurante** (620-357-3575), 509 Main, Jetmore. Open 11–2, 4–9, Tues.–Sat.; 11–3 Sun. Dine in a cheerful, spacious spot while enjoying delicious chicken tequila fettuccine or pasta *caronera*, with bacon,

peas, and cream sauce. Pizzas are a big seller here, too, with several specialty pies that include supreme or meat lover's; otherwise, choose your own toppings. You'll also find big burgers and hefty sandwiches, plus special pricing for kids. Inexpensive.

Judy's Café (620-357-8537), 303 N. Main, Jetmore. Open 7–8 daily. Locals have enjoyed Judy's home cooking for years, whether ordering steak and eggs for breakfast, a double cheeseburger, or a slice of freshly baked peach cobbler. It's nothing fancy, but the food is good. No credit cards. Inexpensive.

Elsewhere

Bob's Drive-In (620-873-2862), E US 54, Meade. When you find the original owners eating lunch in a place, the current owners must be doing something right. Bob and Elsie retired, but they still think the burgers at Bob's are the best. "When you make hamburgers at home, are they ever as good as this? Never," they said. Enter a tiny hallway, place your order at the window, and head for the dining room with your paper-wrapped sandwich. Bus your table and then check out the pool table or electronic games in the back. Inexpensive.

Clark Pharmacy (620-855-2242; clarkpharmacy.com), 101 S. Main St., Cimarron. Open 8:30–6 Mon.–Fri., 9–5 Sat. Long before Oprah created a smoothie sensation here, residents and visitors knew where to find the ultimate handmade chocolate shake. Sit beside the antique bar and chat with your friendly soda jerk while admiring the original tin ceiling, tiled counter, and vintage Coca Cola items for sale in this full-service pharmacy. Inexpensive.

Romano's Pizza (620-659-2249), 1000 E. Tenth/US 50, Kinsley. Open 11–9 Sun./Tues./Thurs., 11–10 Fri.–Sat. No credit cards. Pizza is king here. Choose pan or thin crust and your own toppings, including shrimp, anchovies, bacon, pineapple, jalapeños, and more traditional items such as pepperoni or mushrooms. Try a large veggie or all-meat pizza, with Canadian bacon, beef, pork, Italian sausage, and pepperoni for about $16, or try the super sancho and sub sandwiches. Mostly inexpensive.

Y **Antlers Sports Bar and Grill** (620-598-2078), E US 56, Moscow (near Hugoton). Open 11–2, 5–10 daily; longer bar hours. Folks who live nearby recommend this eatery located in a large, warehouse-style building. Order all kinds of steak cuts: a third-of-a-pound or half-pound burger and the prime rib special on Saturday evenings. Inexpensive–moderate.

& **Neon 57** (620-646-5775; neon57 .com), 500 Main St., Fowler (near Meade). Open 9–4:30 weekdays, 10–2 Sat. Decor in this popular diner emulates 1957 diners, and the spot has such a great reputation that NBC's *Today Show* talked about it in 2003. It all starts with 50 desserts that range from decadent black raspberry sour cream pie to rich peanut butter cream pie. Add sandwiches, and a gift store with loads of Coke and Elvis memorabilia, for a memorable stop.

& **Kook's Meats** (620-723-2121), 100 S. Sycamore, Greensburg. Open 7–7 Mon.–Fri., 7–1 Sat. Coffee for 25 cents, Friday lunch specials that include *bierocks,* and 100 percent Kansas Angus beef are just a few things this two-year-old restaurant is known for. They also serve cinnamon rolls or biscuits and gravy at breakfast and make their own sausage and pie. Inexpensive.

Mama Fina's (620-563-9222), US 54, east of Plains town center. Open 8:30–10 Mon.–Sat., 8:30–3 Sun. This open, inviting place with red and white walls has served authentic Mexican food for more than seven years. Try the beef fajita dinner served with rice, beans, lettuce, tomato, bell pepper, onions, tortillas and guacamole, or, at breakfast, a Spanish omelet or huevos rancheros. Inexpensive.

& **Cattleman's Café** (620-675-8454), 110 S. Inman St., Sublette. Open 10:30–10 daily. This is a local hangout, particularly on Sundays, offering lunch and dinner specials. On Saturdays check out their prime rib dinner with potato, salad, vegetable, and rolls. Inexpensive–moderate.

& Y **Cactus Club** (785-798-3639), 124 S. Pennsylvania, Ness City. Open 5:30–2 and 5–9. There's a huge lunch buffet available in this spacious local hangout with friendly staff. Order chicken-fried chicken with potato, toast, and salad bar, or chicken salad. The Reubens are huge, and mushroom Swiss burgers are another favorite. Inexpensive.

& **Pizza Plus** (785-798-3939), 108 S. Pennsylvania, Ness City. Open daily 11–8. Since 1985, Pizza Plus has become a Ness City favorite, largely because of the family sauce recipe. Half of all orders in this spacious, no-frills spot are for pizza, but customers also enjoy the salad bar and sandwiches. It's become a favorite gathering place for local groups, too. Inexpensive.

✳ Entertainment

In Dighton

Dighton Bowl and Diner (620-397-5518), 530 E. Long, Dighton. Open 7–8 Mon.–Fri., 7–2 weekends. Stop in for a bite and then request a turn at bowling next door. Small vintage posters and signs decorate this inviting little diner where locals requested liver and onions on the menu and got it. Try the diner breakfast with hash browns, ham, onions, green peppers, American cheese, two eggs, and toast. The crispy chicken salad is another winner, with mixed greens, crispy breast strips, cheddar, egg, and fresh vegetables. There are also burgers and sandwiches. No credit cards. Inexpensive café; bowl 1–5 games for $2.50 and 75-cent shoe rental.

The Old Bank Gallery (620-397-2273; oldbankgallery.com/restoration.html), 146 E. Long St., Dighton. Call for hours. Artist Patrycia Ann Herndon has turned this 1800s bank building into a lovely gallery and studio. Using funding from the Kansas Heritage Trust Fund, she maintained some of the site's original character, including a wall of original hand-carved teller windows, with leaded and etched glass. Her standing easel and loads of framed art fill her historical workspace.

Elsewhere

The Great American Dirt Track at Jetmore Motorplex (620-385-0551; greatamericandirttrack.com), 100 Motorplex Dr., Jetmore. Check web site for race schedule; events generally begin at 7 PM or later. In 2001, seven area residents pooled their money to build a dirt-racing track at this old air base. After a new investor bought the property in 2009, racing

became a family-friendly staple in beautiful facilities every other Saturday, mid-May–Aug. 28. The bleachers hold more than three thousand spectators, and 30 sprint cars race on an average evening. Adults $12; children 12 and under free.

& **Stan Herd Gallery** (620-622-4886), 404 N. Broadway, inside Protection Township Library/Protection. Open noon–6 weekdays. This Kansas native shares his love of the state through his oil paintings, and murals painted on buildings in multiple cities. See photos of his crop pictures, completed across the country, including portraits of Saginaw, Grant, and Amelia Earhart. Free.

The Palace Theatre (620-659-2225), 223 E. Sixth St., Kinsley. Step back in time to the old-style lobby with a small crystal chandelier overhead. Run by volunteers, this vintage theater offers first-run movies that cost $5 for customers ages 12 and up. Saturday date night includes admission for two, two pops, and popcorn for only $12.

✳ Selective Shopping

Studio 54 Glass Art Studio and Gallery (620-723-2511), 101 S. Main St., Ste. 113, Greensburg. Open 10–6 Mon.–Fri., 10–4 Sat. This store—one of the town's early success stories from its post-tornado business incubator—exemplifies the can-do spirit of Greensburg residents. Here you'll find a multitude of gift and household decor, including unusual paperweights in which debris from the tornado and recycled glass are suspended.

Highway 56 Antiques and Market (620-659-2334; 657-3153), 213 Sixth

STUDIO 54 GLASS ART STUDIO AND GALLERY HAS CREATED ART THAT INCLUDES DEBRIS FROM THE MAY 4, 2007, TORNADO THAT DEVASTATED GREENSBURG.

St., Kinsley. Open 9–5 daily. This shop in an old building is a full block in depth. Find such items as an antique green and cream stove or antique barber's chair, a pinball machine, quilts, or a vintage Singer sewing machine.

✳ Special Events

June: **Dalton Days Wild West Fest** (620-873-2731), The Dalton Gang Hideout, Meade, final weekend. Enjoy historical reenactments as well as Western skits, gunfights, and quick draw and other competitions throughout this popular event.

WEST OF GARDEN CITY

GUIDANCE Scott City City Hall (620-872-5612), 221 W. Fifth St., Scott City. Open 8–5 weekdays.

Syracuse-Hamilton County Chamber of Commerce (620-384-5459), Syracuse.

Grant County Chamber of Commerce (620-356-4700), 113B S. Main, Ulysses. Open 8–5 weekdays.

GETTING THERE AND GETTING AROUND Please see *Getting There and Getting Around* in the previous section.

MEDICAL EMERGENCY (arranged alphabetically by city name)

Stevens County Hospital (620-544-8511), 1006 S. Jackson St., Hugoton.

Satanta District Hospital (620-649-2761) 401 Cheyenne, Satanta.

Scott County Hospital (620-872-5811), 310 E. Third, Scott City.

Bob Wilson Memorial Grant County Hospital **(620-356-1266), 415 N. Main, Ulysses.**

✳ To See

HISTORIC PLACES, LANDMARKS, AND SITES El Quartelejo. See *Lake Scott State Park*.

Mighty Samson of the Cimarron (skyways.lib.ks.us/history/Samson.html), off US 54 and 13 miles northeast of Liberal. Always open. One of the largest railroad bridges in the world, the massive 1,269-foot-long structure was considered an engineering marvel when it was built in 1939. Free.

Wagon Bed Springs, located approximately 7.5 miles south of Ulysses off KS 25. Also known as Lower Cimarron Spring, this rural site was a critical spot to find water along the shortest route to Santa Fe, after settlers crossed the Arkansas River and headed south. The current site has a small memorial and wide prairie vistas. It is generally accessible, except after heavy rains, when a truck or SUV is preferable. The final mile of your drive goes through cow pasture, with a rough cow grate and a narrow two-track route. Free.

MUSEUMS ⅛ **Morton County Historical Society Museum** (620-697-2833; mtcoks.com/museum), E US 56, Elkhart. Open 1–5 Tues.–Fri. during the winter, or by appointment. This museum serves as an official interpretive facility for the Santa Fe National Historical Trail. Inside, see a barbed-wire display and a fully equipped doctor's buggy. Outside, visit a Santa Fe Railroad car; a country school, barn, and chapel; and a Vietnam veterans memorial. Free.

Stevens County Gas and Historical Museum (620-544-8751; skyways.lib.ks .us/towns/Hugoton/museum.html), 905 S. Adams, Hugoton. Open 1–5 Mon.– Fri., 2–4 Sat. in winter, or by appointment; longer summer hours. Tour 11 buildings full of early 1900 furnishings, including Little House, the first house built in Hugoton, plus an 1886 jail house and a country store, a professional building, an 1886 church building, a train depot, and a 1945 gas well that is still producing. Inside the museum, check out dentist and doctor equipment, a beauty and barbershop, a Western shop and Indian arrowheads, Indian artifacts, and vintage farming tools.

⅛ **El Quartelejo Museum and Jerry D. Thomas Gallery** (620-872-5912), 902 W. Fifth St., Scott City. Weekdays 1–5 or by appointment. One-third of the exhibits in this adobe building provide information about Monument Rocks and area fossils, with a replica of El Quartelejo Pueblo—a Taos Indian settlement in what is now Lake Scott State Park. See a prehistoric American Indian village, a sod house, and a blacksmith shop, and learn about Maria DeGeer, who founded Scott City as a temperance community. Thomas's gallery offers realistic paintings with largely Western themes. Free.

⅛ **Grant County Museum** (620-356-3009), 300 E KS 160, Ulysses. Open 10–5 weekdays, 1–5 Sat.–Sun. Housed in an adobe building listed on the National Register of Historic Places, this is a terrific museum that displays a fully stocked covered wagon, a furnished sod house, and a tiny streetscape with period furnishings in a '50s-era diner, bank, newspaper office, and more. See a piece of the Victorian-era Hotel Edwards and a one-room schoolhouse on the grounds, too. Free.

TOWNS Elkhart. Set on the Oklahoma border and located 8 miles from Colorado, this town has less than 2,500 residents. A railroad engineer laid out the town in an attempt to discourage other rail companies from competition. There are five city parks and a nine-hole golf course. The main thoroughfare recently received new sidewalks and streetscape. Cimarron National Grasslands lies north of town, providing terrific bird-watching, scenic drives, fishing, hunting, and camping. At 108,175 acres, it's the state's largest public landmass. You'll also find a tristate marker, decorated with a windmill, 8 miles west of town.

Hugoton. Pronounced "Hyou-gu-tun," this town is the seat of Stevens County. Prosperous largely due to natural gas and agriculture, Hugoton has a current population of approximately 3,700. Settlers from McPherson established a settlement here in 1885, but the economy soon declined and with it, the town. After

GRANT COUNTY MUSEUM FEATURES WONDERFUL DISPLAYS THAT ILLUSTRATE THE HISTORY OF THE ULYSSES AREA.

the Santa Fe Railway arrived and the discovery of natural gas in 1927, the town gradually grew again, becoming a major location for natural gas. Today, this gas field is the largest in the nation and second largest in the world. Hugoton lies at the intersection of US 56, KS 25, and KS 51, and it's approximately 220 miles from Wichita.

Lakin. More than two thousand people live in Lakin, located at US 50 and KS 25, and near the Arkansas River. The town emerged after John O'Loughlin created a trading post to serve rail passengers and pioneers on the Santa Fe Trail. You can still see wagon ruts from the Santa Fe Trail outside of town, and a historical marker tells about Chouteau's Island, where an 1800s battle occurred with Pawnee Indians. Multiple city parks offer ball fields, picnic facilities, and playgrounds.

Leoti. The question of the source of the town's name, pronounced "Lee-oh-tee," remains unanswered. Possible origins include an Indian word that means "prairie flower" to the name of a founding father's daughter. Men from Garden City arrived here by 1885, and a bloody county seat fight followed two years later. The seat of Wichita County is at the intersection of KS 96 and KS 25, with a population hovering around 1,700 residents, whose median household income is approximately $32,000.

Satanta. Named for Chief Satanta of the Kiowa Indian tribe, Satanta was established in 1912 after the Santa Fe Railroad arrived. The area produces large wheat, corn, soybean, milo, sunflower, and other crops, and benefits from the production of oil and natural gas. The town is currently promoting the availability of free land as a way to increase the county's population. Satanta lies in Haskell County, on US 56.

Scott City. This small city lies approximately 48 miles south of I-70 at the intersection of US 83 and KS 96 and just 62 miles from the Colorado border. You may not think you're in Kansas anymore when you see the red rock formations nearby. The area has 17 soil types and served as the site for scenes in the movie *Dances with Wolves.*

Commanding Officer Lt. Col. William H. Lewis and his men were the last military casualties in Kansas, resulting from altercations with Indians at what is now called Battle Canyon; near today's Scott City. Scott County was created in 1873 and named for Gen. Winfield Stock. The Temperance crusader Maria DeGeer created the first permanent settlement here, in the 1880s.

Scott City is the seat of Scott County. Its four thousand residents have a median household income above $40,000, and you'll find several locally owned motels, bed & breakfasts, and restaurants, plus a sprinkling of chains. But the Scott City area also offers plenty of outdoor opportunities for nature lovers of all kinds, from bird-watcher to hunter or fisherman. Without the influence of big-city lights, and with largely wide-open spaces here, you'll also see clear blankets of stars at night.

Syracuse. Approximately 1,700 people call Syracuse home. Located in Hamilton County, the town is easy to reach from I-70, only 16 miles from the Colorado border, and flanked by the Arkansas River. Unusual sand hills, south of the river, create a highly popular entertainment venue for all terrain vehicles, while the renovated Northrup Theater offers current movies amid antique movie-house splendor.

Tribune. This city has wide streets with big intersection dips, nicely maintained homes, and community buildings and an increased community focus on antiques.

Ulysses. Along US 160, don't be surprised to see signs marked CAUTION. WIND CURRENT. The natural environment is always a strong presence in Ulysses. This vibrant city of approximately six thousand residents has a busy downtown area with many full storefronts. Named for Ulysses S. Grant, Ulysses celebrated its centennial in 2009. The town lies at the intersection of US 160 and KS 25, 40 miles from both the Oklahoma and Colorado borders, and near the north fork of the Cimarron River. It also hosts a wonderful county museum located in a historic adobe building.

✳ To Do

DAY SPAS Renaissance on Fourth Day Spa and Boutique (620-872-2209), 110 W. Fourth St., Scott City. Open 9–5 weekdays or by appointment on Saturday. Known for their spa services, Renaissance also offers Ethel, PB&J, and Multiples clothing, plus OPI nail polish and designer purses. Three massage rooms, a steam room, a pedicure room, and a steam room are several features, and an enclosed deck provides private outdoor relaxation for clients. Call about rates for services.

GOLF **Point Rock Golf Club** (620-697-9801; mtcoks.com/golf/golf.html), 619 Airport Rd., Elkhart. This beautiful county-run course has operated behind the museum since 1998; the terrific clubhouse opened a year later. Plenty of trees provide shade without crowding. Par 36, 9 holes, 3,200 yards.

Stanton County Prairie Pines Golf Course (620-492-6818), 50 N. Airport Rd., Johnson City. This nicely maintained course with gentle rolling hills operates about 15 miles from the center of Ulysses. Par 35, 9 holes, 3,207 yards.

Tamarisk Golf Course (620-384-7832), CR 21 and KS 27, Syracuse. There's a pay-before-you-play box and a trail fee if you bring your own cart at this course with fair maintenance. Enjoy a clubhouse overlooking a lake, a snack shop, and a driving range. Par 36, 9 holes, 3,251 yards.

Point Rock Golf Club (620-697-9801), 619 Airport Rd., Elkhart. Clubhouse open 8–8 in summer and 10–6 in spring/fall. Play on this course features bentgrass greens and bluegrass fairways; the clubhouse offers snacks and limited clothing or equipment. You may even hit your ball into Oklahoma from the fourth hole. No credit cards. Par 35, 9 holes, 2,908 yards.

HUNTING **Wild Wings Hunting** (620-874-1547; wildwingshunting.com), Scott City. Pheasant hunters will appreciate the expertise of this southwest Kansas out-

STONE FOUNDATIONS REMAIN FROM EL QUARTELEJO RUINS BUILT BY TAOS INDIANS IN MODERN-DAY LAKE SCOTT STATE PARK.

fitter, which offers multiple hunting packages that include lodging at Lady Di's Court, a comfortable bed & breakfast in a residential neighborhood serving homemade meals around a large, cozy dining table. Hire a guide and borrow dogs, or bring your own. Wild pheasant hunts take place from the first weekend in November to January. Chukar hunts, in controlled shooting areas, are also available. Wild and controlled shooting area pheasant hunts $220–440.

((𝕪)) **Barrel Springs** (620-376-2701; barrelspringshuntclub.com), 416 Railroad Ave., Tribune. Twenty-four renovated rooms offer private showers/baths and a comfortable commons area. Use the paved runway in nearby Tribune or arrange special pickup service from commercial flights via Denver, Colorado Springs, Amarillo, Wichita, Garden City, or Goodland. This outfitter offers more than 6,000 acres of bird habitat for ring-neck pheasant from Sept. 1–March 31. Bring your own dog or use one of theirs. Packages include lodging, three daily meals, field transportation, dogs, and guides. $445 per day.

✳ Green Space

Cimarron National Grasslands (620-697-4621), 242 E US 56 (also accessible from KS 95/27/51), Elkhart. Stop by the park office on US 56 before visiting this grassland area of more than 108,000 acres to get a map and other information. At the shared borders of Colorado and Oklahoma you'll find Eightmile Historical Monument, a commemorative plate in the road. Another special feature is Point of Rocks; at 3,540 feet, it is the state's third-highest elevation point and has functioned as an important landmark since the first pioneers headed west. Enthusiasts of the outdoors also camp, fish, hike, and travel scenic drives throughout the grasslands. The Kansas Department of Wildlife manages fishing and hunting, particularly for deer and game birds, throughout the area.

Lake Scott State Park (620-872-2061; kansastravel.org/scottstatepark.htm), 520 W. Scott Lake Dr., Scott City. Enjoy the 100-acre lake set in this park that was once part of the Steele Homestead from the late 1800s. A museum displays period furnishings and tools. There are 55 utility campsites, two shower buildings, and multiple docks. The beach house and bait and tackle shop offer boat rentals and groceries in season. Horse-lovers can use a camp area with a watering facility and hitching post. Marvel at stone ruins left behind at El Quartelejo—this country's northernmost pueblo—created when Taos Indians migrated in the 1660s to escape Spanish rule. After they left, 20 years later, Picurie Indians occupied the area from 1701 to 1703. Vehicle permits Oct.–March $3.70 daily; April–Sept. $4.20.

Whistle Stop Park, located along US 56, Elkhart. This pretty 23.5-acre park creates a green space between the railroad tracks and the highway, with plenty of park benches, a gazebo, and decorative streetlights that line paved walking paths.

Hugoton City Park (620-544-4305), 630 S. Main, Hugoton. This is a truly lovely spot, with a shelter, picnic tables, and a pool with water slides. There are open and adult swims daily, plus playground equipment.

✳ Lodging

BED & BREAKFASTS Cottage Inn Bed & Breakfast (620-697-1010; cottageinnelkhart.com), 129 Baca Ave., Elkhart. Innkeepers Susie and Becki operate this remodeled 1928 Tudor brick home, offering four suites (two with private baths). Enjoy the den fireplace in cold weather, an in-house exercise room, and continental breakfast in the tropical sunroom. Check out the country-inspired treasures in the Cottage Inn Gift Shop, too. Full breakfast. $70–75.

Creek Side Farm (620-646-5586), 26131 A. Rd., Fowler (near Elkhart). Located near the Kansas-Oklahoma-Colorado border, this bed & breakfast operates in a 1920s house on a working farm. Choose from three rooms and a suite (with two private and one shared bath). You'll find fresh cookies and soft drinks in each room, with a spacious gazebo and beautiful landscaping outside. $40–65.

The Guest House (620-872-3559; guesthousebandb.com), 311 E. Fifth, Scott City. Serene is a good way to describe your first view of this lovely guesthouse. Stay in the private cottage with a 1900 claw-foot tub, spacious living room, or bedroom breakfast nook for two. Individual rooms in the main house are full of rich colors and fabrics, and all accommodations overlook the courtyard with brick walkways. From $60.

(ᵠ) **Lady Di's Court Bed & Breakfast** (620-872-3348; ladydiscourt.com), 1520 S. Court St., Scott City. This comfortable B&B offers three guest rooms with safari, regatta, and rose-themed decor, plus a king-size or two twin beds. There are two shared baths, a screened patio, and a large television room. Deb Gruver serves big breakfasts around a six-person dining table. $60–70.

(ᵠ) **Shady Lane Bed & Breakfast** (620-544-7747; user.pld.com/ngilles), 110 N. Main, Hugoton. This gregarious owner has completed massive property renovations and offers four rooms including a suite, plus a guesthouse with four bedrooms and two baths. Enjoy a cozy TV room beneath the eaves, a bedroom, separate shower, and whirlpool tub in the suite. There's also an aboveground pool surrounded by decking, a hot tub, and a large, spacious dining room. You may be in competition with hunters starting the second weekend of November—the start of pheasant season. Reservations recommended. Continental breakfast. $55–75.

Fort's Cedar View (620-356-2570; fortscedarview.com), 1675 Patterson Ave., Ulysses. Each room in this native stone home has a distinct character. Stay in the Wildflower room with its brick fireplace, trundle bed,

SHADY LANE BED & BREAKFAST OFFERS SPACIOUS, MODERN ACCOMMODATIONS IN HUGOTON.

private bath, and seating area; the Maiden Fair; the dark and cozy Bachelor Bay; or the Frontier room, with wood paneling and cowboy hat decor. Evening snacks and a heated outdoor pool (available by request) are part of the package, too. Full breakfast. $85.

HOTELS & (ᵞⱼ) **Corporate East** (620-356-5010; corporateeasthotel .com), 1110 W. Oklahoma Ave., Ulysses. Enjoy spacious new rooms and suites with luxurious bedding, plush recliners, small desks with ergonomic seating, and a gorgeous lobby. Continental breakfast. $77–119.

MOTELS AND LODGES

In Ulysses
(ᵞⱼ) **Single Tree Inn/Ulysses Inn** (620-356-1500; discoverourtown .com), 2033 W. Oklahoma Ave., Ulysses. This property underwent complete renovation in 2008. Forty-three rooms include suites with Jacuzzis and several ADA-accessible rooms. Each suite has a table and chairs, a pullout love seat, and a double vanity with refrigerator, microwave, and coffeemaker. $85105.

(ᵞⱼ) **Peddler's Inn Motel** (620-356-4021), 2093 W. Oklahoma Ave., Ulysses. Rooms appear clean and comfortable with refrigerators, coffeemakers, and flat-screen TVs. There's a little peeling paint. $51.

Sands Motor Inn (620-356-1404), 622 W. Oklahoma Ave., Ulysses. The wood paneling is a bit dated, but it's a clean, neat place with a white picket fence out front, plus a refrigerator, microwave, and coffeemaker in each room. $50.

Elsewhere
& (ᵞⱼ) **El Rancho Motel** (620-697-2117), 604 E US 56, Elkhart. The lobby feels like a sunroom with wicker furniture, a full-size fountain, and plants. The co-owner managed this property for 12 years before ownership. All rooms have a refrigerator, there's a microwave in the vending room, and coffee is available in the morning. One suite offers two bedrooms and a living area. $58–80.

& (ᵞⱼ) **Pawnee Valley Lodge LLC** (620-357-6330; jetmoremotel.com), 209 Main St., Jetmore. This new 12-unit motel offers flat-screen TVs, wooden blinds, and quilts inside, plus a welcome mat and outdoor grills. There are two ADA-accessible rooms and a bunkhouse basement. Continental breakfast. $59–69; $10 more during pheasant season.

✳ **Where to Eat**
EATING OUT

In Hugoton
& (ᵞⱼ) **Common Grounds** (620-544-8333), 531 S. Main St., Hugoton. Open 6:30–4 weekdays; 6:30–3 Sat. Housed in a one-hundred-year-old building that was once the town drug store, this is an inviting coffee house with turquoise and deep red walls. Enjoy gourmet sandwiches and desserts made in-house. The coffee is Solar Roast—a 100 percent organic and carbon neutral brand from Pueblo, Colorado. Inexpensive.

& **Ranchito Tex-Mex Café** (620-544-2396), 611 S. Main St., Hugoton. Open 11–3, 5–8:30 weekdays; 11–2 Sun. The original Ranchito was started by the owner's grandmother 37 years ago. The bright, airy café is known for its Tex-Mex cheeseburger steak served with jalapeños, onion, tomato, rice, beans, and tortillas, as well as the *ranchito* special, with beans, beef, cheese, lettuce, tomato, avocado slices, and sour cream, but you'll have plenty of other choices, too. Inexpensive.

In Scott City
♿ **Peking Garden Restaurant** (620-872-7221), 324 Main St., Scott City. Open 11–2:30, 5–9 daily. A Scott City favorite for 15 years, Peking Garden offers a large buffet, which includes lo mein, pepper steak, chop suey, and crunchy egg rolls, and you'll dine amid Chinese lanterns and wall hangings. There's also a full menu. Inexpensive.

Majestic (620-872-3840), 420 S. Main at KS 96 and US 83, Scott City. Open 11:30–1:30 Tues.–Fri., 5:30–8:30 Thurs.–Sat. Step back in time at this renovated 1922 theater turned upscale dining room. Great steaks are only the beginning of the menu at this swank spot, with a tiered dining room and a full stage draped in holiday lights. Try Fleming's fettuccine with chicken, blackened red snapper, or marinated beef salad. Moderate.

In Ulysses
Down-Town Restaurant (620-356-2232), 100 N. Main, Ulysses. Open 10–9 daily. There may be duct tape on the booth seats, but it's a cheerful place with the feel of a seaside Mexican joint. Chilaquiles Mexicanos features refried beans, corn-studded rice, tender shredded chicken, and mild tomato sauce. Most lunch specials are Mexican, but there are also steaks, burgers, and roasted chicken. Buy a purse or perfume in the front retail area before you leave. Inexpensive–moderate.

♿ **The Fuel Barn** (620-353-1751), 1845 W. Oklahoma Ave., Ulysses. Open 4:30 AM–10 PM daily. There are two kinds of fuel here. Grab a homemade breakfast burrito or a freshly prepared burger for about $3 and sit in a handful of booths in this spacious convenience store with something more. Inexpensive.

♿ **M&Vs Popsicles** (620-353-1554), 204 N. Main, Ulysses. Open 5 AM–1 PM and 4 PM–8 PM for iced treats. On a steamy summer day there's nothing better than a cucumber and chile *paleteria*—a Mexican version of the popsicle made with fresh fruit by a family member two hours away. Eat it quickly before it completely melts. Or enjoy a breakfast chile relleno stuffed with cheese and eggs at one of the bright yellow tables for only $3. Inexpensive.

♿ **Wagon Wheel Café and Bakery LLC** (620-424-1368), 8551 E US 160, Ulysses. Open 8–3 Mon.–Fri.; lunch served 11–2; also open 5:30–8:30 Fri. This spot is worth the 9-mile drive east of town. Come for a deluxe garden salad, third-of-a-pound burger, or club wrap. But save room for warm, oozing chocolate peanut butter pie with an inch of meringue and buy a pan of cinnamon rolls, *bierocks*, or pumpkin bread from the freezer. Inexpensive.

Elsewhere
♿ **Jim-n-I's Restaurant** (620-697-9886), 634 E US 54, Elkhart. Open 6–9 Mon.–Sat., 8–2 Sun. Located across the parking lot from El Rancho Motel, this family-owned restaurant has operated for more than 20 years. Each fall the owner purchases fresh

chiles, roasted in Clovis, New Mexico, to use at the restaurant. They take pride in their prime rib, aged on site and pierced with garlic cloves. They're also known for Mexican food, such as the Southwest scramble, and noon buffets. Inexpensive.

& **KC's Mexican American Restaurant** (620-384-5519), 401 W US 50, Syracuse. Open 6–8:30 Mon.–Sat. Tile floors, adobe archways, Mexican framed artwork, and a garden scene mural decorate this bright and cheerful restaurant. Try their beef chimichangas or fajitas with beef, shrimp, chicken, or a mix. Breakfast favorites include huevos con chorizo and freshly made breakfast burritos. They also serve American and Mexican 3.2 percent beer. Inexpensive.

& **The Chatterbox** (620-376-4221), 516 Third St./KS 96, Tribune. Open 7–2 Tues.–Sun., 5–8 Wed. This is a

BUFFALO GRAZE AT DUFF'S BUFFALO RANCH NEAR SCOTT CITY.

spacious, open place with a terrific chef salad featuring mixed lettuce and grated cabbage, plus tons of ham chunks and cheese gratings. Try the skillet special—two eggs, your choice of meat, hash browns, onion, green pepper, and cheese, a third-of-a-pound burger, or chicken-fried steak. No credit cards. Inexpensive.

✳ Entertainment

In Syracuse
Syracuse Sand Dunes Family Recreation Park (620-384-2480; syracusesanddunes.com), S KS 27 and River Rd., Syracuse. Open 24/7. On a cloudy day this park may seem extremely quiet until a random pair of off-road drivers zoom out from behind grass-covered hills at the park perimeter. Dune buggies, jeeps, trucks, and sport-utility vehicles all take advantage of this unusual sand dune area located just outside town. Roll bars, seat belts, red or orange flags, and helmets for riders under 17 are required, and signs warn riders about shifting dunes. A drop box allows visitors to pay fees even when there's nobody in the office. Camping is available, with bathrooms and showers, and fishing is allowed with KDWP license. Daily dunes pass $5 per driver.

Northrup Theatre (620-384-7688), 116 Main St., Syracuse. Box office opens 6:40 MST Fri.–Sun. for evening movies. Step back in time where a curved glass wall surrounds the outside ticket window and the lobby features a neon-encircled clock and studded leather counter face. Call for ticket prices.

Elsewhere
Morton County Community Theater Group (620-593-4743), multiple

locations, Doric Theater, Elkhart. Since 1997, this nonprofit group has offered the only live civic theater within 100 miles. The group is currently restoring brick and plaster at the 1918 Doric Theater, which once offered silent movies. Admission by donation.

Duff's Buffalo Ranch (620-872-5762; duffmeats.com), Scott City. For an unforgettable experience call Richard Duff and find out if he'll take you to see his four hundred head of buffalo, an animal that his family has raised in this area since 1974. Hear a buffalo growling like a lion and see them grazing against a red rock backdrop that appeared in the movie *Dances with Wolves*.

✳ Selective Shopping

In Scott City

Keystone Gallery (620-872-2762), 401 US 83, Scott City. Usually open 9–sunset; winter hours vary. Ask about guided fossil tours. Listed in *1,000 Places to See before You Die*, this fossil museum and gift store in a renovated 1916 church has hosted a hundred thousand visitors since opening 20 years ago. Co-owner Chuck Bonner's dad started fossil hunting in 1935. Now Chuck and his wife, Barbara Shelton, collect and prepare fossils, and items in their permanent collection come from Kansas. They also sell amethysts, geodes, and stone-based jewelry, plus Barbara's photos. Chuck's wall-spanning mural depicts the massive inland sea that once covered this area.

Gifts, Etc. (620-872-2222), 424 S. Main St., Scott City. Open 9–5:30 weekdays, 9–3 Sat. Packed from floor to ceiling, this nicely decorated corner store offers loads of variety, from Culinary Institute of America items and Wind Willow foods to Vera Bradley purses, Yankee Candles, and Thymes body care products.

In Tribune

Colleen's Antiques (620-376-6249), 314 Third St., Tribune. Open 1–5 Thurs.–Sat. Colleen knows a story behind most items that she sells in this two-room shop nicely arranged to display everything from doll furniture to chandeliers and vintage tablecloths. No credit cards.

M&M's Antiques and Collectibles (620-376-2006), 402 Broadway, Tribune. Open 9–4 Mon.–Fri., 9–noon Sat. This is a tidy corner building with iron benches and massive flower planters outside and several rooms of antiques/collectibles. There's also complementary flavored coffee for customers.

In Ulysses

&. **Main ARTery** (620-424-3828), 103 S. Main St., Ulysses. Open 10–5:30 Mon.–Fri., 10–4 Sat. Don't miss this open, airy, and inspiring art space, full of framed photos, batiks, acrylic and oil paintings, decorated turkey feathers, gorgeous ceramics, handmade jewelry, and wood inlay vases. Displays change every six to eight weeks and always represent a specific theme such as red hot or tight rope.

&. **Trendsetters Coop** (620-356-3244), 101 S. Main St., Ulysses. Open 10–5:30 weekdays, 10–4 Sat. Ulysses residents purchased $1,000 shares to raise funds toward acquiring the initial inventory for this unusual clothing coop. Brands include Woolrich, Nomadic Traders, Tribal, Cactus Bay, and Libra. Shoppers can also purchase baby items, a little jewelry, and some small antique items. It's a delightful shopping spot.

Elsewhere

Heritage Meats Inc. (620-375-5151), 406 E. Broadway, Leoti. Open 7:30–5:30 weekdays. Most of the meat used in this longtime family-owned butcher shop is locally sourced. They're well known for homemade jerky, bologna, and sausage.

✳ Special Events

May: **Satanta Day** (620-649-3602), Satanta. The one-day event honors Kiowa Indian Chief Satanta, with a parade, BBQ, golf tournament, carnival, and other activities. It began in October 1941 to culminate a citywide beautification program

July: **Grant County Fair/Annual Ulysses Bit and Spur Rodeo**, Ulysses. Rodeos begin and end this annual county fair with plenty of food, livestock shows, free BBQ, and more. **Beefiesta** (620-872-5612), Scott County Fairgrounds, Scott City. This BBQ event is part of the Scott County Free Fair, offering several hours of free tastings.

September: **Whimmydiddle Arts and Crafts Fair** (whimmydiddle .org), Scott City. This is one of the largest craft shows in western Kansas, drawing exhibitors from across the United States. See original art, jewelry, pottery, woodcrafts, and more, and enjoy multiple food concessions.

INDEX